01/24
STRAND PRICE
$5.00

01/24
STRAND PRICE
$5.00

Advancing Executive Coaching

Advancing Executive Coaching

Setting the Course for Successful Leadership Coaching

Gina Hernez-Broome and Lisa A. Boyce, Editors

Foreword by
Allen I. Kraut

JOSSEY-BASS
A Wiley Imprint
www.josseybass.com

Published by Jossey-Bass
A Wiley Imprint
989 Market Street, San Francisco, CA 94103-1741—www.josseybass.com

Jossey-Bass books and products are available through most bookstores. To contact Jossey-Bass directly
call our Customer Care Department within the U.S. at 800-956-7739, outside the U.S. at 317-572-3986,
or fax 317-572-4002.

Jossey-Bass also publishes its books in a variety of electronic formats. Some content that appears in
print may not be available in electronic books.

Library of Congress Cataloging-in-Publication Data

Hernez-Broome, Gina.
    Advancing executive coaching : setting the course for successful leadership coaching /
Gina Hernez-Broome, Lisa A. Boyce. — 1st ed.
      p. cm. — (J-B SIOP professional practice series ; 29)
    Includes index.
    ISBN 978-0-470-55332-9 (cloth); 978-0-470-90226-4 (ebk); 978-0-470-90236-3 (ebk);
978-0-470-90238-7 (ebk)
      1. Executive coaching. I. Boyce, Lisa A. II. Title.
  HD30.4.H46 2010
  658.4'07124—dc22

                                                  2010028697

Printed in the United States of America
FIRST EDITION
HB Printing 10 9 8 7 6 5 4 3 2 1

The Professional Practice Series

The Professional Practice Series is sponsored by The Society for Industrial and Organizational Psychology, Inc. (SIOP). The series was launched in 1988 to provide industrial and organizational psychologists, organizational scientists and practitioners, human resources professionals, managers, executives and those interested in organizational behavior and performance with volumes that are insightful, current, informative and relevant to *organizational practice*. The volumes in the Professional Practice Series are guided by five tenets designed to enhance future organizational practice:

1. Focus on practice, but grounded in science.
2. Translate organizational science into practice by generating guidelines, principles and lessons learned that can shape and guide practice.
3. Showcase the application of industrial and organizational psychology to solve problems.
4. Document and demonstrate best industrial and organizational-based practices.
5. Stimulate research needed to guide future organizational practice.

The volumes seek to inform those interested in practice with guidance, insights and advice on how to apply the concepts, findings, methods, and tools derived from industrial and organizational psychology to solve human-related organizational problems.

Previous Professional Practice Series volumes include:

Published by Jossey-Bass

Handbook of Workplace Assessment: Evidence-Based Practices for Selecting and Developing Organizational Talent
John C. Scott and Douglas H. Reynolds, Editors

Going Global: Practical Applications and Recommendations for HR and OD Professionals in the Global Workplace
Kyle Lundby, Editor

Strategy-Driven Talent Management: A Leadership Imperative
Rob Silzer and Ben E. Dowell, Editors

Performance Management
James W. Smither and Manuel London, Editors

Customer Service Delivery
Lawrence Fogli, Editor

Employment Discrimination Litigation
Frank J. Landy, Editor

The Brave New World of eHR
Hal G. Gueutal, Dianna L. Stone, Editors

Improving Learning Transfer in Organizations
Elwood F. Holton III, Timothy T. Baldwin, Editors

Resizing the Organization
Kenneth P. De Meuse, Mitchell Lee Marks, Editors

Implementing Organizational Interventions
Jerry W. Hedge, Elaine D. Pulakos, Editors

Organization Development
Janine Waclawski, Allan H. Church, Editors

Creating, Implementing, and Managing Effective Training and Development
Kurt Kraiger, Editor

The 21st Century Executive
Rob Silzer, Editor

Managing Selection in Changing Organizations
Jerard F. Kehoe, Editor

Evolving Practices in Human Resource Management
Allen I. Kraut, Abraham K. Korman, Editors

Individual Psychological Assessment
Richard Jeanneret, Rob Silzer, Editors

Performance Appraisal
James W. Smither, Editor

Organizational Surveys
Allen I. Kraut, Editor

Employees, Careers, and Job Creating
Manuel London, Editor

Published by Guilford Press

Diagnosis for Organizational Change
Ann Howard and Associates

Human Dilemmas in Work Organizations
Abraham K. Korman and Associates

Diversity in the Workplace
Susan E. Jackson and Associates

Working with Organizations and Their People
Douglas W. Bray and Associates

The Professional Practice Series

Advancing Executive Coaching

Contents

Foreword

A recent cover story in *Business Week* (Brady, 2010) makes a telling comment about the current state of coaching. It reports that CEO Jeffrey Immelt of GE, a company with an outstanding reputation for developing leaders, has just recently "launched a pilot program to bring in personal coaches for high potential talent, a practice that GE once reserved mainly for those in need of remedial work."

It is clear to most people in modern organizations that coaching has become a mainstream human resource management practice. It was not always so. In a recent conversation with the well-known coaching consultant Marshall Goldsmith, he noted that only twenty-five years ago, the need for coaching was a sign of trouble (personal communication, April 2010). In one large and well-regarded organization he worked with on management development, the very top performance rating for executives was labeled "Does the job in an outstanding fashion without any need for coaching."

The field of leadership coaching has matured and grown greatly during the last two decades. As befits any maturing and growing field, today there are many debates on crucial issues about coaching. These controversies, along with "established truths," are the subject matter of this book. For anyone interested in coaching, this book brings great wisdom, experience, and suggestions for superior coaching.

My own sense is that coaching is a relatively new phenomenon within the practice of industrial/organizational (I/O) psychology. A brief if unsystematic look at some popular textbooks confirms this impression. One well-used text, published in 1992, does not even have an index reference to coaching (Miner, 1992).

A more popular concept at that time was the notion of mentoring. As noted by Noe (1988), mentoring had two major dimensions. The first was job-related and involved sponsorship, exposure to visibility, and providing challenging assignments. These were functions often expected of an individual's manager. The second dimension was psychosocial in nature and involved personal acceptance, counseling, and interpersonal coaching. Though some managers may have been good at this, it often created a split in their responsibilities that was difficult for many managers to bridge.

Less than a decade ago, another popular text in I/O psychology (Muchinsky, 2003) also had no index reference to coaching, although it did include one on mentoring. However a more recent and well-used text in the field does have index references to coaching as well as to mentoring. In fact, it notes that "coaching has become an important part of leadership development" (Landy & Conte, 2007). Moreover, this current text includes a table on the old and new assumptions about coaching as it has moved from being a remedial practice to one of positive and proactive leadership development.

Over the last two decades, many people outside of I/O psychology became involved in coaching. Entry into the field was relatively easy. The opportunities for more income and more apparent glamour drew people from clinical and counseling psychology as well as from social work and from human resource management. To bolster this trend, many organizations emerged to train and certify coaches, and professional associations such as the International Coach Federation were formed.

Meanwhile, a subset of I/O psychologists were also actively involved in coaching. Many of them were thoughtful and literate practitioners who wrote about the issues and controversies they felt needed attention. For example, the pieces by Hollenbeck (2002) and by Peterson (2002) discuss many of the same issues described in the current volume. A lively recent discussion on the similarities and differences that executive coaching shares with psychotherapy, along with the implications for who are suitable practitioners, is one of the contemporary concerns among I/O psychologists (see McKenna & Davis, 2009, and related commentaries).

This volume, edited by Lisa Boyce and Gina Hernez-Broome, is based on a 2008 Leading Edge Conference sponsored by the

Society for Industrial and Organizational Psychology. This conference brought together several dozen of the leading practitioners in executive coaching for a two-day session of presentations and discussion on issues in coaching.

This volume is not a "proceedings" of those presentations. Indeed the conference serves merely as the framework on which this book is based. The contributions in the book may be rooted in the earlier 2008 sessions, but the authors have added the thoughtful reflections that came out of the discussions and commentaries on those sessions. This book's editors have put together a wonderfully useful book. They and their invited contributors share with us the best thinking and practices of expert professionals in this field.

A signal contribution from the editors is the framework under which they have organized the contributions in this book. As shown in Figure I.1 in the Introduction, the framework helps us to appreciate all of the many complex elements that go into a successful coaching engagement. They point out that this includes the characteristics of both coach and client on several dimensions. More than that, they also note that several elements of the coaching process, including the mechanics of the relationship, as well as the content, techniques, and the coaching relationship itself, must all be considered. And we are led to realize that there are several ways to judge the outcomes of the coaching process.

All in all, this book is a "must read" for anyone who needs to use or engage in the coaching of executives. Practitioners, administrators, and researchers will all find the contributions in this book very helpful. The work of the editors and the chapter contributors are very much appreciated.

References

Brady, D. (2010). "Can GE still manage?" *Business Week*, April 15.

Hollenbeck, G. P. (2002). Coaching executives: Individual leader development. In R. Silzer, (Ed.), *The 21st century executive: Innovative practices for building leadership at the top* (pp. 77–113). San Francisco: Jossey-Bass.

Landy, F. J., & Conte, J. A. (2007). *Work in the 21st century: An introduction to industrial and organizational psychology* (2nd ed.). Malden, MA: Blackwell.

McKenna, D. D., & Davis, S. L. (2009). Hidden in plain sight: the active ingredients of executive coaching. *Industrial and Organizational Psychology: Perspectives on Science and Practice, 2*(3).

Miner, J. B. (1992). *Industrial-organizational psychology*. New York: McGraw-Hill.

Muchinsky, P. M. (2003). *Psychology applied to work* (7th ed.). Belmont, CA: Wadsworth/Thomson.

Noe, R. A. (1988). An investigation of the determinants of successful assigned mentoring relationships. *Personnel Psychology, 41*, 457–480.

Peterson, D. B. (2002). Management development: Coaching and mentoring programs. In K. Kraiger, (Eds.), *Creating, implementing, and managing effective training and development: State of the art lessons for practice* (pp. 160–191). San Francisco: Jossey-Bass.

Rye, New York
October 2010

ALLEN I. KRAUT
Series Editor

Preface

Leadership coaching is a journey. A journey in terms of the progress a leader makes towards achieving success. A journey in terms of the distance coaching has traveled to evolve into an evidence-based practice. A journey in terms of the adventure on which we embark as we explore leading-edge thinking to advance our understanding of executive coaching. Though these journeys began decades ago when coaching emerged as an accepted mode of leadership development, we, as practitioners and researcher professionals, have a responsibility for setting the course to enrich our own and our organizations' coaching programs and contributions to the knowledge of the coaching field.

Executive coaching is a relatively new discipline evolving from an outgrowth of developmental, educational, psychological, and organizational practices in the mid-1980s and gaining prominence as a profession by the late-1990s. During this period, we witnessed a growth in practice and publications with the emergence of successful coaching companies, coach training schools, certification and graduate programs, professional coaching organizations, peer-review articles, popular press publications, and dedicated coaching journals. Today, an estimated 70 percent of organizations with formal leadership development initiatives use coaching in their development strategy. For coaching to continue to grow and maintain momentum as a viable and significant means for leadership development, we must establish a strong link between research and practice.

Clearly, industrial/organizational (I/O) psychology offers such a science-practitioner perspective and is obliged to take a leading role in advancing executive coaching. This book presents an evidenced-based perspective by leading-edge practitioners and scientists in the field of coaching. A natural outgrowth of the Society for Industrial and Organizational Psychology's

4th Annual Leading Edge Consortium on *Executive Coaching for Effective Performance*, our international colleagues joined forces with the consortium's contributors to address the most critical issues affecting the future of leadership coaching and guide coaching programs and practices into the future.

Audience

Advancing Executive Coaching provides a resource for managers, executives, and HR professionals who are increasingly called on to coach as well as implement coaching initiatives as part of their roles. It identifies important issues to consider for those who have direct responsibility for making strategic choices about how and when to implement coaching both formally and informally.

Professional coaches who contract with individual executives or organizations will also find this book invaluable in providing insights to coaching from both the individual and organizational levels. In addition, the book's central themes and comprehensive reference lists make it an invaluable tool for graduate and business students studying coaching and leadership development. Finally, all audiences will benefit from the global perspective provided on a variety of topics and issues.

This book presents progressive perspectives and practices for a variety of areas and contexts, thus it is not a rudimentary step-by-step handbook to coaching but an advanced guide to coaching for those interested in thinking about leadership coaching beyond the traditional perspective. The contents and the discussion consider the broader issues critical to effective coaching and the field as a whole.

Overview of the Contents

This book examines leadership coaching by organizing the issues within a Leadership Coaching Framework, which employs a systems approach to frame the myriad issues associated with executive coaching (discussed in detail in the Introduction). The framework examines coaching in terms of the inputs, processes, and outcomes and therefore the book is structured into three sections representing each aspect of the framework. If you will humor us, the variety of topics is organized around your traveling companions, the journey itself, and "recalculating" directions.

The first section provides insights on the key players in a coaching engagement: the coach, the client or coachee, and the organization. Chapter One provides a foundation by exploring the influence of coaches' theoretical orientation on individual change in terms of the "active ingredients" that have an impact on leadership coaching outcomes, including the client, the relationship, and the process of coaching. Chapters Two, Three, and Four focus on the coach's including guidance on sourcing, screening, training, and developing great leadership coaches. The focus then turns to the client in Chapter Five by examining the relevant client characteristics and the associated challenges and implications for coaching. Chapter Six transitions to the role of the organization in creating successful partnerships to align, support, and evaluate coaching at both the strategic and individual levels. Combined, these six chapters provide a greater understanding of what the participants, including the coach, the client, and the organization, bring to the coaching engagement, with insights on how to increase coaching effectiveness.

The second section of the book examines processes and practices of leadership coaching. The coaching relationship is considered by many to be the cornerstone of coaching and Chapter Seven applies a series of lenses to understand and build the coach-client alliance. Chapter Eight moves the discussion beyond the one-on-one relationships by highlighting the value of strategically focused coaching programs in promoting a coaching culture across organizations. Core to both individual and enterprise-wide practices is understanding the nature of ethics in coaching, which is presented in Chapter Nine. Chapter Ten amasses nearly a hundred tools, techniques, and frameworks and discusses their use in the practice of leadership coaching. Chapter Eleven then focuses on the use of technology in coaching. Combined, these five chapters provide insight into the complex processes of coaching at both the individual relationship and the organizational context, while emphasizing fundamental issues critical to maximizing the impact of coaching practices.

The third and final section examines the research, models, and applications for evaluating the impact of leadership coaching.

Chapter Twelve provides a conceptual perspective of coaching evaluation informed by research and executive coaching experience, whereas Chapters Thirteen and Fourteen offer insights on how to calculate Return on Investment (ROI) and systematically perform evaluation, showcasing successful evaluation programs. Chapter Fifteen provides an organizing schema to understand and identify future coaching needs of organizations. Finally, our closing chapter reviews the major themes in the book, highlighting common threads and conflicting ideas, with recommendations to practice and science for advancing leadership coaching.

Advancing Executive Coaching provides three unique contributions to the field of coaching: the science-practitioner framework provided by I/O psychologists, an integration of a global perspective within each chapter, and the originality of chapter content, including a strategic-level perspective. The unique perspective provided by I/O psychologists grounds each chapter in systematic thinking, often integrating models to frame the topic, related recommendations, and future directions. Further, coaching is inherently global and therefore our authors made a conscious decision to incorporate a global discussion into each chapter, as we agreed that it was inappropriate to relegate global issues to a single chapter at the conclusion of the book. Finally, a majority of coaching books available focus on tactical-level issues from a clinical perspective for practicing coaches. Our goal was to provide a more comprehensive and strategic view from a science-practitioner perspective for a broader audience, including human resource professionals.

Acknowledgments

We are honored to have been instrumental in the preparation of this volume. Much of our professional identity and work has been focused in the coaching arena and has resulted in our being coeditors for this volume. There are many people in both of our professional lives who have contributed to our interest and excitement for the field of coaching.

Gina's professional influences include the talented cadre of coaches she had the pleasure to work with and learn from in her twelve years at the Center for Creative Leadership (CCL). Her time at CCL also afforded her the opportunity to meet and get to know some of the most talented professionals in the coaching industry, many of them authors in the book. The University of the Rockies and, in particular, Steve Kirkpatrick, have been very generous with their support and provided the time and space this project required. It is a pleasure to work with an organization and colleagues who understand the value of this book and have supported it with such great enthusiasm. On a more personal note, I want to thank my husband, Jim, and my daughters, Rachel Lee and Hannah Jane. Their patience and constant encouragement throughout this endeavor made all the difference. Finally, I would like to give a special thanks to my coeditor, Lisa. She gently twisted my arm to continue this project at a time when it seemed a very daunting task. She is a friend as well as a colleague and epitomizes the meaning of both.

Lisa's professional influences include both the United States Air Force (USAF) as an organization and their commanders (Gen. McCarthy, Col. Enger, and Col. McCrae) who provided her opportunities and supported her interest in coaching practice and research as well as her colleagues at the USAF Academy, who not only introduced her to coaching but encouraged her to understand and build an evidence-based program. Reaching back nearly twenty years, I must acknowledge three particular colleagues who embody the essence of USAF leadership coaching: Laura Neal, Jeff Jackson, and Joe Sanders. Without their initial and continued vision and friendship, I would not have begun or continued my leadership coaching journey. In addition, I am fortunate to be able to continue to learn from my former adviser, Steve Zaccaro, as he continues to challenge and expand my thinking and guide my professional growth. On a personal note, my husband, Scott Dudley, and children, Colton and Trigg, sacrificed many personal moments and provided both moral support and the gift of time which allowed me to complete this project. Finally, my warmest appreciation is extended to my coeditor, Gina. She is the ideal complement to my natural tendencies and, as a professional partner and personal friend, a role model in life's journey.

We want to acknowledge the Professional Practice Series editorial board for their enthusiastic support and comments. They include Seymour Adler, Larry Fogli, Elizabeth Kolmstetter, Kyle Lundby, Bill Macey, and Lise Saari. Of course, Allen Kraut, the series editor, was particularly encouraging, especially in the beginning of this endeavor.

Without doubt, the lion's share of our appreciation goes to the authors of the chapters in this book. They are among the most successful and expert in the field of executive coaching with schedules that reflect such. Their generosity in sharing their knowledge and time is estimable and an invaluable contribution to the field. We know you will find this book to be a valuable resource regardless of where you are in your coaching journey.

Colorado Springs, Colorado   GINA HERNEZ-BROOME

London, England   LISA A. BOYCE
October 2010

The Editors

Gina Hernez-Broome is a core faculty member for the Organizational Leadership Program at the University of the Rockies. Prior to joining the University, Gina spent twelve years at the Center for Creative Leadership, where she designed and delivered leadership development and coaching programs and was lead researcher for the Center's coaching research and evaluation efforts. Gina's research interests include leadership coaching and leadership development on which she has published and presented extensively in a variety of professional and scholarly venues such as the Society for Industrial and Organizational Psychology, the Academy of Management, the International Coach Federation, the International Leadership Association, *Human Resource Planning*, and *Leadership Quarterly*. Gina also spent several years as an associate for a Denver-based consulting firm and worked closely with a diverse mix of client organizations, designing and facilitating customized training. She gained extensive experience designing and implementing various assessment processes including certification processes, assessment center technology, and 360-degree feedback processes. She earned both her doctoral and master's degrees in industrial/organizational psychology from Colorado State University and her bachelor's degree in psychology from the University of Colorado at Colorado Springs. Gina is a member of the Academy of Management, the American Psychological Association, and the Society for Industrial and Organizational Psychology.

Colonel Lisa A. Boyce is the Reserve Scientist and Deputy Site Commander at the European Office of Aerospace Research and Development in London for the United States Air Force (USAF). Previously, she was the Director of Behavioral Science

Information Technology Applications Research at the USAF Academy. Lisa's research interests include leadership and character development, military leadership with a focus towards application of technology, advancing leadership coaching, and applied social network including technology-supported decision making. She has over sixty publications and presentations on related topics and is currently on the editorial board of the *Journal of Business and Psychology*. In addition to over twenty years applying and teaching industrial/organizational psychology with the United States and Australian militaries, Lisa has consulted with numerous private and nonprofit organizations, including Hallmark, HELP Line Service, and Lonestar Brewery Company. The recipient of the Center for Creative Leadership's Kenneth Clark Award and SIOP's Rains Wallace Award, Lisa earned her PhD in industrial/organizational psychology from George Mason University, MS in industrial/organizational psychology from St. Mary's University, and BS in behavioral science from the USAF Academy. Lisa is a member of the Academy of Management, the American Psychological Association, the Society for Industrial and Organizational Psychology, and Society of Military Psychology.

The Contributors

Allen I. Kraut is professor emeritus of management at Baruch College, City University of New York, which he joined in 1989. For much of his professional career, he worked at the IBM Corporation, where he held managerial posts in personnel research and management development, until leaving in 1989. In 1995, he received the Society for Industrial and Organizational Psychology's Distinguished Professional Contributions Award, recognizing his work in advancing the usefulness of organizational surveys. In 1996, Jossey-Bass published *Organizational Surveys: Tools for Assessment and Change*, by Allen Kraut and Associates. His latest book, *Getting Action from Organizational Surveys: New Concepts, Technologies, and Applications*, is a 2006 publication by Jossey-Bass (a John Wiley imprint).

Merrill C. Anderson is a business consulting executive, author, and educator with over twenty years' experience improving the performance of people and organizations. He is currently a principal and chief business architect of Cylient, a professional services firm that offers coaching-based leadership development, culture change, and MetrixGlobal® evaluation services. Merrill has held senior executive positions with Fortune 500 companies, including chief learning executive and vice president of organization development. He has consulted with over one hundred companies throughout the world to effectively manage and measure strategic organization change. He has over one hundred professional publications and speeches to his credit, including his latest book, *Coaching That Counts*. Merrill was recognized as the 2003 ASTD ROI Practitioner of the Year. His work with Caterpillar University to align training to the business was recognized by ASTD with an Excellence in Practice award. Merrill's work has also been recognized by many other professional industry groups. Merrill has served as adjunct professor for graduate learning and organization development programs at Drake, Pepperdine, and Benedictine universities. He earned his PhD at New York University, MA at the University of Toronto, and his BA at the University of Colorado.

Mariangela Battista is vice president of organization capability at Pfizer, Inc., where she is responsible for the research center of excellence, including all engagement research, manager development and capability, including assessments and organization-wide change management practices. Prior to Pfizer, Mariangela spent eight years at Starwood Hotels & Resorts Worldwide, Inc., as vice president, Organizational Culture and Effectiveness. During her career at Starwood, Mariangela had strategic design and oversight for Internal Communication, Organizational Measurement, Community Affairs and People Programs, including mentoring, recognition, and ethics and compliance. She was also responsible for the design and implementation of broad talent management and leadership development processes and systems, including competency modeling, performance management, executive and leadership development programs, 360-degree feedback programs, executive coaching, succession planning, engagement surveys, change management, and the Starwood Associate Relief Fund. In her twenty-year career, Mariangela has also been part of the Human Resources function of the Pepsi Bottling Group (PBG), American Express, IBM, and the Interpublic Group of Companies (IPG). Mariangela earned a PhD in industrial/organizational psychology from the City University of New York. She is a member of the American Psychological Association, the Society for Industrial and Organizational Psychology and the Academy of Management.

David Clutterbuck is visiting professor of coaching and mentoring at both Sheffield Hallam and Oxford Brookes Universities and special ambassador for the European Mentoring and Coaching Council. His extensive research and publication, as author or coauthor of fifty books and hundreds of articles, is in the quality of dialogue and, in particular, learning dialogue. His interests in this area have taken him into the fields of employee communication, corporate governance, work-life balance, diversity management, the psychological contract, and team dynamics. His books in coaching and mentoring include: *Everyone Needs a Mentor, Mentoring in Action, Mentoring Executives and Directors, Implementing Mentoring Schemes, The Situational Mentor, Techniques in Coaching and Mentoring* (two volumes), *Mentoring and Diversity, Coaching the Team at Work*, and *Virtual Coach, Virtual Mentor*. His international consultancy, Clutterbuck Associates, specializes in helping organizations develop internal capability in coaching and mentoring and strategies for achieving coaching and mentoring cultures. His doctoral dissertation was a longitudinal study of the dynamics of developmental mentoring dyads. David was listed as one of the top twenty-five most influential thinkers in the field of human resources by *HR Magazine* and was described by *The Sunday Independent* as second in the list of top business coaches in the United Kingdom. He is a fellow of the Chartered Institute of Personnel Development and of the Royal Society of Arts.

Sandra L. Davis is CEO and cofounder (in 1981) of MDA Leadership Consulting in Minneapolis, a leadership development, talent assessment, and organizational performance firm. Davis specializes in senior executive talent evaluation, CEO selection, and succession planning and is widely known as an executive coach and thought leader in the industry, counting numerous Fortune 500 firms among her clients. She earned her BS from Iowa State University and her PhD in counseling psychology with an emphasis in industrial/organizational psychology from the University of Minnesota. She served on the Strong Interest Inventory Advisory panel for Consulting Psychologists Press, was selected as a "Women Change Maker" by *The Business Journal*, is the author of the book, *Reinventing Yourself: Life Planning After 50*, and has contributed numerous chapters and articles in professional books and journals on topics related to assessment, leadership development, coaching, and succession. She is a member of the American Psychological Association and the Society for Industrial and Organizational Psychology.

Jennifer J. Deal is a senior research scientist at the Center for
Creative Leadership (CCL) in San Diego, California. Her work
focuses on global leadership and generational differences.
She is the manager of CCL's World Leadership Survey and the
Emerging Leaders research project. In 2002 Jennifer coauthored *Success for the New Global Manager* (Jossey-Bass/Wiley),
and has published articles on generational issues, executive
selection, cultural adaptability, global management, and women
in management. Her second book, *Retiring the Generation Gap*
(Jossey-Bass/Wiley), was published in 2007. An internationally
recognized expert on generational differences, she has spoken on the topic on six continents (North and South America,
Europe, Asia, Africa, and Australia), and she looks forward to
speaking to Antarctic penguins about their generational issues
in the near future. She holds a BA from Haverford College and
a PhD in industrial/organizational psychology from The Ohio
State University.

Erica Desrosiers is currently director, Organization and
Management Development, for PepsiCo. Prior to joining
PepsiCo in 2004, she ran the Organization Development function for a software company in Chicago and spent several years
working as an external consultant for Saville and Holdsworth
Ltd. (SHL), designing competency models, selection systems,
assessment, and development centers and conducting individual executive assessments. Erica's primary focus at PepsiCo is
executive talent development and coaching, and she leads the
organization's global 360-degree feedback and upward feedback processes. Erica received her BA in psychology and crimi-
nal justice from the State University of New York at Albany and
her master's and PhD in industrial and organizational psychology from Purdue University. She is a member of the Society for
Industrial and Organizational Psychology and has published and
presented in the areas of leadership development, performance
management, 360 feedback, and executive coaching. Erica is on
the board of the Mayflower Group and also serves on the executive committee of the Conference Board Council on Executive
Coaching.

Katherine Ely earned her PhD and MA in industrial and organizational psychology from George Mason University and BA in
psychology from the College of William & Mary. Her research
interests include organizational training and development, specifically the use of technology in training, the evaluation of the
effectiveness of training interventions, and training designs that
enhance adaptive performance. Katherine was the 2007 Society
for Industrial and Organizational Psychology John C. Flanagan
Award recipient. Her research has been published in the *Journal of
Applied Psychology, Leadership Quarterly, Military Psychology, Academy
of Management Learning and Education,* and *Learning and Individual
Differences.* She is a member of the Society for Industrial and
Organizational Psychology and the Academy of Management.

Michael H. Frisch has been delivering executive coaching services for over twenty years with clients in a wide range of organizations and roles. He also serves as a supervising coach and
coaching instructor for both internal and external coaches
through his affiliation with iCoachNewYork, a coach training
and consulting firm, and is on the adjunct faculty at New School
University and the Zicklin School of Business, Baruch College,
CUNY. Previously, Michael held the position of senior consultant and director of Coaching Services for Personnel Decisions
International's (PDI) New York operating office, and earlier roles
included a position as manager of Management Development for
PepsiCo. Michael's publications include a chapter in *Individual
Psychological Assessment,* published by Jossey-Bass, and an article,
The Emerging Role of the Internal Coach, in the *Consulting Psychology
Journal.* Michael received his PhD in industrial/organizational
psychology from Rice University and his MS from Georgia
Institute of Technology. He is a member of the Society for
Industrial and Organizational Psychology and the Consulting
Psychology Division of the American Psychological Association.
Michael is a licensed psychologist in New York State.

Ann M. Herd is assistant professor of leadership and human
resource education at the University of Louisville. She has served

as an executive coach and leadership development special-
ist for over twenty years for organizations including Lockheed
Martin Corporation, the Springfield Massachusetts Chamber of
Commerce Leadership Institute, Tennessee Valley Authority,
Tennessee Assessment Center, and The University of Maryland's
Robert H. Smith School of Business. She has also designed and
conducted leadership training for executives on such topics as
coaching through change, conflict management, communication skills, leadership, team building, and effective hiring. In
addition to her work in coaching and leadership development,
Ann has served as a training consultant for Aluminum Company
of America and as the principal investigator on contracts for
the United States Army Special Operations Command, John F.
Kennedy Special Warfare Center and School, United States Army
Accessions Command, and United States Army Cadet Command.
Ann has served in full-time faculty positions at a variety of universities, including Marymount University, Gettysburg College, The
United States Air Force Academy, and University of Maryland
University College. She received her PhD in industrial/organiza-
tional psychology from The University of Tennessee and her BA
in psychology from the University of Kentucky.

Travis Kemp is the managing director and chief psychologist of
The Teleran Group Pty. Ltd, working with clients spanning fed-
eral and sate governments, national and international publicly
listed companies, professional service firms, and nonprofit organizations. He holds post-graduate degrees in education, social
science, and psychology and is a registered secondary teacher,
registered psychologist, and accredited HR professional. Travis
holds adjunct academic appointments as senior lecturer in
the University of Sydney's Coaching Psychology Unit, senior
research fellow in the University of South Australia's School of
Management, and affiliate senior lecturer in the Discipline of
Psychiatry at the University of Adelaide. Travis has published
widely in the professional and research-based literature in leadership and executive development. He coedited the first evidence-based coaching psychology text, *Evidence-Based Coaching
Volume One: Theory, Research and Practice from the Behavioural*

Sciences and is co-editor of the *International Coaching Psychology Review.* In 2008 he was made an honorary vice president of the International Society for Coaching Psychology and was a foundation national committee member of the Australian Psychological Society (APS) Interest Group in Coaching Psychology and is a member of its College of Organisational Psychologists. Travis is a fellow of the Australian Human Resources Institute, the Australian Institute of Management, and the Australian Institute of Company Directors.

Jeffrey Kudisch is a Distinguished Tyser Teaching Fellow and associate department chair at the University of Maryland's Robert H. Smith School of Business. Jeff teaches MBA seminars on human capital management, leadership, teams, and negotiations and is an active guest lecturer at Smith partner universities around the world. Consistently honored for being an outstanding (top 15 percent) teacher, Jeff received the 2006 and 2009 Krowe/Legg Mason Teaching Excellence Award, as well as the Best MBA Team Teaching Award in 2006, 2007, and 2008 in Zurich. As cofounder and principal partner of Personnel Assessment Systems, Inc., a firm specializing in management and executive assessment and leadership development, he has served as a consultant for organizations including Black & Decker, Home Depot, Lockheed Martin, McCormick and Company, NIH, and Anne Arundel Health Systems. Jeff earned his PhD in industrial/organizational (I/O) psychology from the University of Tennessee, Knoxville, his MS in I/O psychology from the University of Central Florida, and his BS in psychology from the University of Florida. He has published articles and presented research on assessment centers, personnel selection, multisource feedback, executive coaching, and leadership development. He is a member of the Academy of Management and the Society for Industrial and Organizational Psychology.

Robert J. Lee is in private practice in New York City as a coach to senior executives regarding leadership, transition, and development issues. Previously, he was CEO of the Center for Creative

Leadership and was founder and president of Lee Hecht Harrison, a worldwide career services firm. Bob is the managing director of iCoachNewYork, which provides training for internal and external executive coaches. He is on the adjunct faculty at New School University and is a senior fellow with the Zicklin School of Business, Baruch College, CUNY. Bob is coauthor of *Discovering the Leader in You* and of *Executive Coaching: A Guide for the HR Professional.* He is a fellow of the Society for Industrial and Organizational Psychology, and he received the Distinguished Psychologist in Management award in 2008 from the Society of Psychologists in Management. His PhD is in industrial/organizational psychology from Case Western Reserve University.

D. Douglas McKenna is CEO and cofounder of the Oceanside Institute. He earned his PhD in differential psychology at the University of Minnesota. After fifteen years as a professor of psychology and management, Doug became the original architect of the executive and management development function at Microsoft. Since leaving Microsoft in 2001, he has focused on the challenge of helping leaders develop the emotional composure and maturity necessary to be successful in complex jobs under high pressure. Based on Whidbey Island in Washington State, Doug continues his research, writing, and teaching on emotional reactivity and leadership. His leadership course, "Lead Where You Stand" has been delivered to thousands of executives and managers around the world.

Lance Mortimer is a director and cofounder of A Mind to Perform Ltd, a business and sport psychology coaching and consultancy firm that works with organizations, athletes, and individuals to coach them to realize their true potential. Combining over twenty-five years' experience of working in finance and telecoms with large companies such as Barclays Bank, ABB, and Cadbury, Lance also has a BSc in psychology from the University of Greenwich and an MSc in occupational and organisational psychology from the University of East London (UEL). His past research interests have led him to look at the effects of burnout within the workplace as well as the key factors preventing sales people from achieving their true potential. Lance has trained numerous U.K. public sector groups in coaching and effective leadership and continues to develop training programs and development tools for business people. Lance maintains a close working relationship with UEL within their Human Capital Performance Group, assisting on a number of exciting projects, including research into the positive effects of delivering coaching to a number of different occupations, and is also developing an innovative coaching tool for the sporting arena.

David H. Oliver is vice president, Talent Sustainability, for PepsiCo's foods business in the Americas. His responsibilities include talent management, leadership development, assessment, organizational surveys, 360 feedback and performance management. He has been actively involved in supporting executive coaching across PepsiCo's international business for the last five years. He has worked in various divisions of PepsiCo, including Frito-Lay and PepsiCo International. Prior to PepsiCo, he worked at GTE (now Verizon), where he led test development and validation efforts for selection. He is a member of the Society for Industrial and Organizational Psychology and has published and presented articles in the areas of leadership development, executive coaching, organizational surveys, and employee selection. David also serves on the board of the Mayflower Group, where he is currently chair. David received a BA in psychology from the University of Texas and a PhD in industrial/organizational psychology from the University of Southern Mississippi.

Jonathan Passmore is programme director for coaching psychology at the University of East London, United Kingdom. Prior to joining UEL he has worked in both the public and private sectors at board level as a local government director, charity chief executive, and also as a non-executive chairman in the leisure sector. After his time in management, he worked in consulting for PricewaterhouseCoopers, IBM Business Consulting, and the Office of Personnel Management. Jonathan is a chartered psychologist, a fellow of the CIPD, and accredited coach and coaching supervisor and holds five degrees. He has published widely, with books on social networking, appreciative inquiry, and coaching, and is the series editor for the Kogan Page coaching series, which includes *Excellence in Coaching, Psychometrics in Coaching,* and *Leadership Coaching.* He also contributes to numerous journals including the *Annual Review of Industrial & Organizational Psychology, Consulting Psychology,* and the *International Coaching Psychology Review* and is a regular speaker at conferences across the world. Jonathan was awarded the Association for Coaching *Impact* award for his contribution to the profession in 2010–2011.

David B. Peterson is senior vice president at PDI Ninth House, where he leads executive coaching services with responsibility for two hundred coaches around the world. Based in San Francisco, his consulting work specializes in coaching for CEOs and other senior executives in Global 100 companies, as well as helping organizations design their own coaching programs. David is the author of two best-selling books that provide practical advice to help people develop themselves and coach others: *Development FIRST: Strategies for Self-Development* (1995) and *Leader as Coach: Strategies for Coaching and Developing Others* (1996). An expert on coaching, executive development, and leadership effectiveness, he has been quoted in *Wall Street Journal, Fortune, Business Week, Time,* and *Harvard Business Review.* He serves as a senior fellow on the Research Advisory Board for the Institute of Coaching at Harvard and on the editorial boards of *Consulting Psychology Journal* and *Coaching: An International Journal of Theory, Research, and Practice.* He received his PhD from the University of Minnesota, specializing in both industrial/organizational and counseling psychology. His BA in linguistics and anthropology is from Bethel College in St. Paul, Minnesota. He is a fellow of the Society for Industrial and Organizational Psychology, the Society of Consulting Psychology, and the American Psychological Association.

Natalie Pothier is leading the executive coaching practice at the Center for Creative Leadership (CCL) in Europe, Middle East, and

Africa. In this capacity, she coaches executives from across all
industry sectors, facilitates executive coaching workshops and
programs. A qualified coach and certified in Strengths Performance Coaching, Natalie is responsible for creating, designing,
and deploying customized leadership coaching solutions for
a wide range of blue-chip clients across many different cultures. Natalie holds an MSc in occupational psychology from
Goldsmiths College, University of London. Accredited by the
British Psychological Society in psychometric assessments, Natalie
conducted an evaluation which led to the launch of an innovative psychometric instrument for the British employment service. Prior to joining CCL, Natalie was head of Talent at Yahoo!
Europe, where she led the talent development strategy across
Europe and initiated a "positive psychology" and leadership
coaching culture. Her career also included similar roles at multinational technology companies such as Dell and SITA. Natalie
has worked and lived in London, Rome, Brussels, and Nairobi,
where she worked on human development issues at the United
Nations. In particular, she conducted outreach education work
for HIV/AIDS–vulnerable groups in Eastern Africa.

Douglas Riddle is global director of Coaching Services and
Assessment Portfolio at the Center for Creative Leadership. He
drives the portfolio of coaching services and guides the assessment
strategy for the benefit of the clients of the Center. He supports
the management of coaching talent, including nearly four hundred professional coaches located in almost thirty countries. Doug
coaches senior leaders and their teams and continues to provide
thought leadership in the field, speaking and presenting papers
at major scientific and professional conferences around the world
on leadership, coaching, and organizational change. Doug earned
doctorates in psychology and theology, is a licensed psychologist
in California, and has served on the adjunct faculty of the graduate school of Human Behavior at Alliant University and helped
establish the Community Mediation Centers in San Diego. He
currently serves as an advisor on several nonprofit boards, including Project Rising Sun of the Fund for Theological Education and
the Foundation for International Leadership Coaching. Doug's

articles, blogs, and media interviews have appeared in numerous general circulation and specialty publications.

Joyce E. A. Russell is a Ralph J. Tyser Distinguished Teaching Fellow at The University of Maryland, Robert H. Smith School of Business. She also serves as the director of the Executive Coaching and Leadership Development Program and has developed and directed executive coaching programs for several universities and corporations and coached executives for the past twenty-five years. Her expertise is primarily in the areas of leadership and management development, executive coaching, negotiation tactics, and training and career development. Some of her clients have included Lockheed Martin, Marriott, Oak Ridge National Laboratory, Frito-Lay, Quaker Oats, M&M Mars, ALCOA, Boeing Corporation, Tennessee Valley Authority, State of Tennessee, Bell-South, Hughes Network Systems, Black & Decker, National Institute of Health, National Security Agency, and McCormick. She has received numerous teaching and research awards at The University of Maryland and at The University of Tennessee, where she previously worked as a professor. She has published over fifty articles, books, or book chapters and has presented her research at national conferences. She served as the associate editor for the *Journal of Vocational Behavior* and has served on the editorial boards of the *Journal of Applied Psychology, Human Resource Management Review,* and *Performance Improvement Quarterly.* She received her PhD and MA in industrial/organizational psychology from The University of Akron and her BA in psychology from Loyola University in Maryland.

Barry Schlosser is co-president of Strategic Executive Advisors, LLC, a professional services firm based in Madison, Connecticut, and Wayland, Massachusetts, that provides executive advisory and leadership services. Barry is a seasoned advisor whose work spans the range from C-level to new executives to national and global professionals responsible for technology, financial, operational, and organization-wide transformational initiatives. His professional experiences include leadership development for teams, advisory consultations with senior management, executive coaching, coaching program design, impact research, selection, and assessment of groups and individuals for a variety of purposes. He has frequently presented at workshops and professional meetings, authored or coauthored many national publications and presentations, and served in editorial capacities. He is one of the founding members of the Coaching Coalition, a network forum for knowledge sharing comprised of executive coaches and senior HR representatives/coaching practice managers. Before retiring as a licensed clinical psychologist to devote his full attention to organizational consulting, Barry was an individual and group therapist. He holds a doctorate in clinical/community psychology and an MA in experimental psychology, both from the University of South Florida in Tampa. Important to note, he has been a drummer for many years (providing an invaluable skill set for pacing, listening, and connecting).

Derek Steinbrenner is a principal consultant at Cambria Consulting, Inc., a leading human resource management consulting firm recognized for its focus on selecting, managing, and developing talent. Derek's consulting spans the talent lifecycle and has included competency framework development, performance management and talent development process design, organizational survey design and data analysis, 360-degree assessment and feedback delivery, training program design and delivery, and program evaluation architecture. Derek also manages the operation of Cambria's executive coaching practice, and he has developed a specialization in the design and implementation of strategic coaching programs, including executive and internal coaching practices, targeted coaching initiatives, and accelerated high-potential development programs for such clients as NASA, John Deere, Wachovia, and Credit Suisse. He has also led the development of Coaching Director™, Cambria's online coaching management system. Prior to Cambria, Derek worked as a consulting psychologist for the Institute for Psychological Research and Application, where he consulted with clients on such projects as organizational needs assessments, staffing models, recruitment pool analysis, performance appraisal system redesign, and job analysis. Derek holds a BA in clinical psychology from Tufts University, an MA in industrial and organizational psychology from Bowling Green State University, and an MBA from Columbus State University.

Lorraine Stomski is a senior vice president and Practice Leader for Leadership Development and Coaching in Aon Consulting's Human Capital Organization. Lorraine is responsible for the design and delivery of global leadership and executive on-boarding programs for top talent in a wide variety of organizations such as IBM, Hewlett-Packard, Toyota, Konami, Bank of New York, Discovery Communications, Texas Instruments, Sun Microsystems, Nestle Purina, Kimberly-Clark, BAE Systems, UTi, Ahold, U.S. Department of Interior–Bureau of Indian Affairs, BNY Mellon, and Agilent Technologies. Her areas of expertise include leadership development and retention of top talent, executive coaching and on-boarding, action learning, cross-cultural psychology, performance management, selection, and assessment processes. She has twenty years of experience in the field. Lorraine travels the globe throughout much of the year, fulfilling her passion to help leaders in organizations maximize their effectiveness and reach their full potential. Lorraine received her PhD in industrial/organizational psychology from Stevens Institute of Technology. She is a member of the Society for Industrial/ Organizational Psychology (SIOP) and the American Psychological Association (APA) and is a frequent speaker on the topic of best-in-class practices within the field of leadership development and executive coaching.

Paul Tesluk is the Tyser Professor of Organizational Behavior and Human Resource Management in the Department of Management and Organization at the Robert H. Smith School of Business at The University of Maryland, College Park. He currently is chair of the Department of Management and Organization, rated within the top five management departments in the world on research productivity and scholarly impact. He earned his PhD and MS in industrial/organizational psychology from Penn State University and BS from Cornell University. Paul is also the codirector of the Center for Human Capital, Innovation, and Technology. An experienced executive and leadership development coach, his recent clients include Marriott International, Sabre, Anne Arundel Medical Center, Choice Hotels, Black & Decker, and the U.S. Department of Energy. His research focuses on strategies to enhance team effectiveness and innovation, the development of management and leadership talent, and organizational culture and climate. He has published dozens of articles and book chapters on these topics and has received awards from the Society for Industrial and Organizational Psychology for his research on work team effectiveness and work experience and leadership development. He is currently on the editorial boards of *Journal of Applied Psychology, Personnel Psychology*, and *Organization Science.*

Brian O. Underhill is an industry-recognized expert in the design and management of worldwide executive coaching implementations. Brian holds a PhD and MS in organizational psychology from the Alliant International University and a BA in psychology from the University of Southern California. Brian is the coauthor of *Executive Coaching for Results: The Definitive Guide to Developing Organizational Leaders.* He is the founder of CoachSource and the Alexcel Group, and previously spent ten years managing executive coaching operations for Marshall Goldsmith. Brian's executive coaching work has successfully focused on helping clients achieve positive, measurable, long-term change in leadership behavior. He has also helped pioneer the use of "mini- surveys"—a unique measurement tool to help impact behavioral change over time. His clients have included Agilent Technologies, AT&T, California Public Employees' Retirement System, California State Automobile Association, Dell, Johnson & Johnson, MGM/Mirage, Microsoft, and Unum. His pro bono work has benefited various nonprofit and faith-based organizations. He is an internationally sought-after speaker, addressing The Conference Board, Linkage, and regional American Society for Training and Development, Society for Human Resource Management, and Human Resource Planning Society events.

Anna Marie Valerio, president of Executive Leadership Strategies, LLC, is a consultant specializing in executive coaching and leadership development. Her areas of expertise include one-on-one coaching, organization and individual assessment, women's leadership, and performance management. Both of her books have been practical guides written for the client population: *Developing Women Leaders: A Guide for Men and Women in Organizations*, published by Wiley/Blackwell in 2009, and *Executive Coaching: A Guide for the HR Professional* (coauthored with Robert J. Lee), published by Wiley/Pfeiffer in 2005. Her background includes more than twenty years of management and consulting experience in a variety of organizations and with Fortune 500 clients. She has consulted in executive coaching in a number of organizations including IBM, PepsiCo, MetLife, Wolters Kluwer, Starwood Hotels & Resorts, Bank of New York Mellon, and Yale University. Her corporate experience includes working in IBM with the CEO's direct reports to build worldwide leadership capability. Prior to joining IBM, she had responsibility for various strategic HR functions in Sony and Verizon. Her PhD is in psychology from The City University of New York.

Janis Ward has a PhD in industrial/organizational psychology from Stevens Institute of Technology, an MA from New York University in personnel psychology, and a BA in psychology from the State University of New York at Stony Brook. Janis has been a management consultant for over twenty years, with areas of expertise including executive, management, and leadership development, performance management and improvement, employee empowerment and motivation, organizational analysis of human resource systems, employee satisfaction and organizational culture, team building, self-managed team development, and action learning teams. For the last seventeen years, Janis has focused on executive coaching and managerial talent development, working with organizations ranging from Fortune 100 corporations, national and regional government agencies, U.S. and foreign based institutions of higher education, and nonprofit institutions. She has worked in a variety of industries including airlines, automotive, banking and financial services, chain restaurant management, consumer goods, food and beverage manufacture and distribution, health insurance, high-tech, manufacturing, marketing, news media, pharmaceuticals, risk management, retail, telecommunications, and utilities. She served in all officer positions of the Metropolitan New York Association for Applied Psychology (METRO) and as the director of professional development. She has also presented at several meetings of the Society for Industrial and Organizational Psychology.

Stephen J. Zaccaro is a professor of psychology at George Mason University, Fairfax, Virginia. He is also an experienced leadership development consultant and executive coach. He has written over one hundred journal articles, book chapters, and technical reports on group dynamics, team performance, leadership, and work attitudes. He is the author of *The Nature of Executive Leadership: A Conceptual and Empirical Analysis of Success* (2001) and coeditor of three other books, *Occupational Stress and Organizational Effectiveness* (1987), *The Nature of Organizational Leadership: Understanding the Performance Imperatives Confronting Today's Leaders* (2001), and *Leader Development for Transforming Organizations* (2004). He has also coedited special issues of *Leadership Quarterly* (1991–1992) on individual differences and leadership, and a special issue for *Group and Organization Management* (2002) on the interface between leadership and team dynamics. He has directed funded research projects in the areas of team performance, shared mental models, leader-team interfaces, leadership training and development, leader adaptability, and executive coaching. He serves on the editorial board of *The Leadership Quarterly*, and he is an associate editor for *Journal of Business and Psychology* and *Military Psychology*. He is a fellow of the American Psychological Association, Divisions 14 (Society for Industrial and Organizational Psychology) and 19 (Military Psychology).

Introduction: State of Executive Coaching

Framing Leadership Coaching Issues

Lisa A. Boyce and Gina Hernez-Broome

Executive coaching, as a method for developing leaders, has increased exponentially in both practice and research over the past decade. The popularity, use, and availability of coaching and coaching organizations, as well as the increasing number of publications and research focused on coaching, are commonly accepted by those in the field. Although putting concrete numbers on the coaching industry is difficult, we know that between 70 to 80 percent of companies report using coaching, with between 60 and 80 percent of the organizations reporting an increase in utilization (American Management Association, 2008; Anderson, Frankovelgia, & Hernez-Broome, 2009; Auerbach, 2005). Over 80 percent of nonprofit organizations focused on promoting coaching as a profession were established post-2000 with the largest boasting over 16,000 members representing over ninety countries worldwide (Nelson, Boyce, Hernez-Broome, Ely, & DiRosa, in press). APA Psycnet identifies eleven books, thirty-eight journals, thirty-one empirical studies, and thirteen dissertations published prior to 2000 with executive or leadership coaching content. These coaching publications escalated to 149 books, 169 journals, 107 empirical studies, and forty-eight dissertations in the decade between 2000 and 2010.

Anyone exploring the executive coaching field will discover two clear and consistent messages. The first is that the practice of executive coaching is flourishing and the second is that the research on executive coaching falls short in terms of providing needed empirical studies to support the growing practice. The research-practice gap is not unique to leadership coaching (Rynes, Giluk, & Brown 2007), with science lagging practice in fourteen of twenty-six industrial/organizational psychology fields (Cober, Silzer, & Erickson, 2009). Though executive coaching was among the most recognized differential, we need to understand why the gap exists. We contend, based on the relative infancy of the field and the recent rapid growth of related research, that the gap is a normal evolution in our field's maturation and that the coaching profession is thriving and striving to be an evidence-based practice.

Therefore, we reflect on the state of executive coaching from an optimistic but inquiring perspective in order to understand and frame current and future issues. We first consider the state of leadership coaching practice, including presenting the environmental drivers that may account for the increasing interest as well as the changes within coaching practice. We then focus on the state of research and present our Leadership Coaching Framework as a means to identify, organize, and integrate the myriad factors. Whereas we have primarily used the framework in our research efforts, we recognized the model's value as an organizing structure and therefore also employ it to assemble and position the contents of the book. Finally, we discuss the state of the art in the context of leadership coaching today.

State of Leadership Coaching Practice

Executive coaching practices are evolving to address the needs of the changing nature of leadership and organizations. We highlight these environmental changes and their resulting challenges before discussing the impact on coaching practices.

Changing Work Environment

Broader social, economic, and political changes have an impact on the work environment, particularly the composition of the workforce, performance requirements, and organizational structures. Demographic and societal shifts include an aging, more heterogeneous, and disparately educated workforce as well as a generation of tech-savvy employees (Howard, 1995). Leaders are expected not only to manage a diverse workforce but also to embrace individuals unlike themselves as colleagues, collaborators, and teammates. Leaders are also required to perform in more cognitively and socially complex, uncertain, dynamic, political, technological, and global environments (Zaccaro & Klimoski, 2001). Further, organizations are becoming less hierarchical, empowering their junior leaders with decision-making responsibility (Boyce, LaVoie, Streeter, Lochbaum, & Psotka, 2008), while at the same time restructuring and downsizing have shortened their career cycle (Hall & Mirvis, 1995).

A survey of nearly 250 senior executives by the Center for Creative Leadership (CCL) reinforced and expanded on these themes by identifying organizational trends, the obstacles they create, and their impact on leaders (Criswell & Martin, 2007). The results identified patterns that focused on the complex challenges that organizations currently face (for example, market dynamics, shortage of talent, globalization) and their reliance on innovation, leadership development, and virtual leadership and collaboration to overcome such challenges. As a result of these changes and challenges, there is a demand for leaders to lead a diverse workforce, develop cross-cultural and technological competencies, respond swiftly and effectively to ambiguous situations, be continuous learners, and produce results.

This is a tall order for today's leaders, and organizations are recognizing the value of executive coaching to support and develop individual leaders as well as contribute to the organization's competitive advantage and overall effectiveness. Thus, it is not surprising that the popularity of leadership coaching is exploding and, more important, that we are experiencing an evolution in how we think about and practice leadership coaching. We focus the following discussion on the expanded interest and use of leadership coaching across populations, purposes, mediums, and geography.

Changing Nature of the Coaching Population

Leadership coaching has evolved from executive coaching, exclusive to senior leaders at the top of organizations, to an integral component of leadership development programs that support the expanding needs of leaders at all levels. This evolution is reflected in our use of the terms *executive* versus *leadership* coaching. Executives are commonly defined as corporate officers, general managers, and heads of major organizational functions and business units (Silzer, 2002), which tends to be limiting in the coaching context. The more generic term "leadership" reflects the current state of thought and practice in coaching and is inclusive of executive coaching. Whereas some make a deliberate distinction, we have chosen to use the terms interchangeably, particularly in deference to our field's historical pedigree.

Changing Nature of Coaching Purposes

In addition to assisting junior and midlevel managers seeking coaching, the purpose has been extended from avoiding derailment to developing high-potential leaders (Boyce & Ritter, 2002; Corbett, Corbett, & Colemon, 2008). In a recent benchmarking study (Anderson et al., 2009), responding organizations indicated that less than a third of their coaching is for derailing leaders, with instead nearly 60 percent targeted at high potentials.

More organizations are also recognizing that the systematic implementation of coaching across organizational levels promotes a coaching culture, which is considered a critical contributor to their competitive advantage. Based on data from the Human Capital Institute's Center for Talent Retention (*HR Focus*, 2008), employees engage and stay with their organizations because they feel appreciated and valued, and are provided opportunities to develop new skills. Conversely, people leave their organization because they did not receive any coaching or management support. Given the importance and emphasis currently placed on employee engagement and talent management, coaching is evolving to contribute to both by developing the skills and abilities that employees need to be successful and advance as well as signaling to employees that the organization values them and is willing to invest in their development.

Further, coaching approaches and behaviors are increasingly being integrated with the appropriate people processes so that coaching tactics become a natural way of doing business.

This includes the integration of coaching programs into talent-management processes, learning and development initiatives, and job-competency models. Integrating coaching with talent-management processes such as selection, staffing, and succession ensures that people who are hired and promoted will be role models for the coaching culture. Integrating coaching with leadership development provides leaders with the required developmental experiences to incorporate coaching approaches into their leadership styles. The integration of coaching with job competency models ensures that coaching skills and behaviors are explicitly recognized as a critical component of effective leadership performance.

Changing Nature of the Coaching Delivery

Also notable is that coaching delivery is changing in two fundamental ways. First, leadership coaching has moved beyond just the one-on-one engagement with the focus on the individual's development. In-the-moment team coaching, group coaching, coach mentoring, coaching-skills workshops, and other coaching-based approaches are being used in comprehensive change initiatives and these initiatives are becoming increasingly strategic in nature (Anderson et al., 2009). Secondly, in terms of logistics, face-to-face coaching is increasingly being combined with and sometimes even replaced with coaching performed virtually (Boyce & Hernez-Broome, in press). Obviously, the integration of technology and distance has implications for a relationship-based practice that emphasizes the importance of rapport, trust, collaboration, and commitment.

Changing Nature of Global Coaching

The global future for coaching is promising and its use internationally on the rise. The American Management Association (2008) reported that coaching programs in Europe and the Middle East are relatively new compared to practices in North America, but indicators predict similar trends in increased coaches, clients, and support organizations. As a reflection of this global movement, most of the chapters in this volume address implications of leadership coaching occurring in international locations but also in terms of multinational organizations requiring global coaching abilities. For example, Riddle and Pothier (see Chapter Fifteen) discuss the upsurge in coaching in countries that would not immediately come to mind as consumers of coaching (such as India and western Africa). The geographic spread of coaching, along with the rapidly changing global business environment within which today's leaders operate, underscore the need to focus on coaching within a global context, taking into account cross-cultural differences and diversity issues.

State of Leadership Coaching Research

Just as the practice of coaching is changing, so too is the nature of the scientific research. The summary by Nelson et al. (in press) of the current state of leadership coaching research suggests several themes within the coaching literature. These include the fact that, although limited, the empirical research that does exist confirms the effectiveness and value of executive coaching (Dagley, 2006; Passmore & Gibbes, 2007) augmenting the abundance of anecdotal evidence to the same effect. Also worthy of note is the quality of research being conducted with more rigorous design strategies including systematic summative evaluation criteria employed (Ely et al., 2010). For example, recent research includes the utilization of experimental designs that measure client changes from pre- to post-coaching and control groups for comparison (for example, see Evers, Brouwers, & Tomic, 2006; Smither, London, Flautt, Vargas, & Kucine, 2003). In addition, there are valuable though discrete instances of empirical research that provide insight on the inputs, the processes, and the outcomes associated with leadership coaching (Joo, 2005; Nelson et al., in press; Passmore & Gibbes, 2007; Ting & Hart, 2004). We also recognize the contributions of several theoretical discussions, accompanied by a great deal of focus on the formulation and application of a variety of coaching models and methods (Cavanagh, Grant, & Kemp, 2005; Kilburg & Diedrich, 2007; Stober & Grant, 2006) that will likely generate future research streams. Combined, these encouraging trends address major criticisms of research in the field, particularly the lack of strong research methodology.

Despite these gains, we acknowledge the lack of a comprehensive agenda to guide and focus leadership coaching research. The result is that there remains an ad hoc approach to coaching research with no clear consensus regarding the most critical variables and combination of variables requiring investigation, a shortage of practitioner-academic collaborators, and a reactive versus proactive stance towards research needs. A solid research agenda would also provide a common foundation by addressing fundamental issues, such as a shared definition, accepted standards and requirements, as well as methods and models to elevate coaching as a profession.

That said, we appreciate the difficulties associated with performing coaching research given the unique nature of coaching as a leadership development initiative. Unlike other leadership development or traditional training programs, coaching focuses on a dynamic one-on-one relationship between a coach and client. Thus, the coaching process itself can vary greatly across coaches, between clients, and over time. In addition, coaching encircles distinctive confidentiality requirements. As a result, traditional methods for investigating and evaluating training interventions are not necessarily appropriate. Therefore, we have the additional challenge of needing to be clever and creative in conducting this undefined research agenda.

Though we cannot help with the clever or creative component, we would like to share our leadership coaching research framework to provide a mechanism to guide thinking and research on the variables and issues critical to leadership coaching. We do not propose the framework as *the* defined research agenda but perhaps as a tool to help navigate us towards more cohesive thinking about the field's research needs. In addition, we feel the model has value from a practitioner perspective and employed it as an organizing framework for the book. In the next section, we discuss the framework and its components. But first we are compelled to share our underlying definition of coaching.

The Leadership Coaching Framework

Leadership coaching can be broadly defined in terms of a relationship in which a client engages with a coach in order to facilitate his or her becoming a more effective leader (for example, see Douglas & Morley, 2000; Kilburg, 1996; Peterson & Hicks, 1999; Witherspoon & White, 1997). In developing the Leadership Coaching Framework we referred to the definition of coaching as a formal one-on-one relationship between a coach and client, in which the client and coach collaborate to assess and understand the client and his or her leadership developmental needs, to challenge current constraints while exploring new possibilities, and to ensure accountability and support for reaching goals and sustaining development (Ting & Hart, 2004, 116).

This definition highlights key aspects of a coaching engagement that are reflected in the Leadership Coaching Framework, including the coaching relationship, process, and outcomes, as well as its most unique characteristic: a focus upon a dynamic one-on-one relationship between a coach and client. The unique nature of coaching yields a multitude of variables that seemingly affect coaching effectiveness, from the coach's ability to self-reflect, to the medium that is used, to the organization's support. Coaching is a complex system in which many factors interact to have an impact on the success of a coaching program.

Systems theory (Katz & Kahn, 1978) provides a means to examine such a complex system by allowing us to frame the key variables that work together to produce effective results. Systems theory poses a three-part model, Input-Process-Output (I-P-O). The three central components are the Input or the external factors that enter the system, the Process or the actions taken upon the input materials, and Output or the results of the processing. The Leadership Coaching Framework (see Figure I.1) uses the I-P-O model to frame the key issues relevant to executive or leadership coaching, which includes the Coach and Client Characteristics (Input), Coaching Process, and Coaching Outcomes. Additionally, we include components that may moderate or impact the relationship between the input and process, that is, the Coach-Client Match and Organizational Support, and also the effectiveness of the process, or the Medium. These six components provide a framework to illuminate, organize, and understand the host of factors involved. In addition, the framework provides a mechanism for future research to systematically consider, investigate, and

Figure I.1. Leadership Coaching Framework

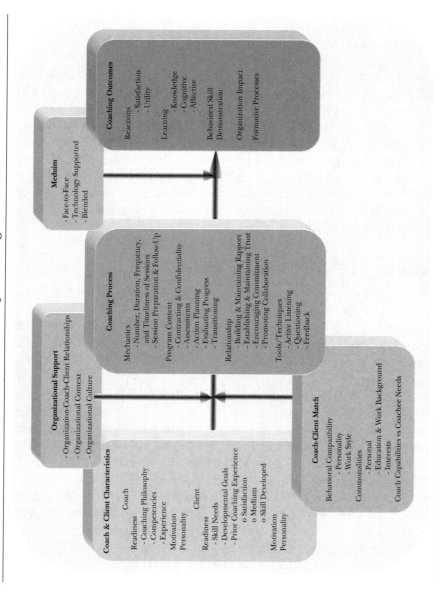

Source: Lisa Boyce and Gina Hernez-Broome, 2007.

promote evidence-based coaching, as well as a tool for practitioners to systematically examine and develop coaching practices.

We also introduce this model of leadership coaching to provide a general framework for the contents of *Advancing Executive Coaching*. The book is organized into three sections representing the three major components of the model, Inputs, Process, and Outputs. The first section provides insights on the key players in a coaching engagement: the coach, the client or coachee, and the organization. The second section covers topics on coaching processes and practices, and the third section includes research, models, and applications for assessing the impact of executive coaching. In addition to highlighting key variables within each of these sections, we offer issues to consider primarily targeted at practitioners, but also with the intent of guiding a future research agenda.

Coach and Client Characteristics

The two key input variables are, of course, the coach and the client and the unique combination of characteristics that each brings to the coaching engagement. The coach and client each bring a level of readiness, motivation, and personality to the coaching process. Level of readiness implies that coaches have varying degrees of experience, range and depth of competencies, and differing perspectives or philosophies about coaching itself. Every executive coach brings working theories about people, organizations, and change to the coaching engagement. Similarly, clients bring different levels of experience, skills, and needs to the coaching engagement. Particularly important is clients' motivation to actively participate in the coaching engagement as well as their unique personality styles and preferences. These factors influence not only the client's behaviors toward particular goals but also both the client's and coach's emotional and cognitive processing throughout the course of coaching.

In considering coach and client characteristics, several issues are particularly relevant to practitioners. Answers to questions that would provide evidence for good practice include: Who makes an effective coach? What are the requisite skills, knowledge, abilities, and attributes of a good coach and how does that differ for a great coach? Similarly, who is a good candidate to be coached? Can anyone be coached? In addition, there is organizational value in understanding the impact of motives and motivation of coaches as well as those of the client. For example, such insights may be useful in selecting cross-cultural coaches, targeting personnel for coaching opportunities, and identifying coaches who will operate as true partners with the organization.

Coach-Client Match

In addition to having insight as to who may make the best coaches as well as clients, a good match between coach and client is critical to the partnership and the success of the coaching engagement. A unique aspect of coaching as a developmental initiative is the one-on-one nature of the relationship between the coach and client. In order to increase the chances for a successful relationship, it is important to optimize the fit between a coach and client. A poor match between the client and the coach is often cited as a reason for unsuccessful coaching experiences and early termination.

Possible factors for practitioners to consider when aligning coaches with clients include personality preferences, areas of common interest or experience, and a coach's experience and capabilities relative to a client's developmental needs. Personality preferences refer to the compatibility between coach and client personality and work or learning styles that may affect coaching processes from establishing initial rapport to later stretch activities. It is important to note that compatibility does not necessarily imply similarity. In some instances differences in style may be advantageous. Commonalities in personal, education, and work backgrounds and areas of interest may also affect the development of the client-coach relationship, underlie credibility, and support communication. The importance of these factors and matching may be particularly pertinent when pairing clients to less experienced coaches or when coaching in a virtual environment.

Organizational Support

Leadership coaching does not occur in a vacuum; the organization in which both parties, client and coach, operate is a critical component of the coaching engagement. The relationships between key organization members, coach, and client, as well as the organizational context and culture, may affect the coaching process, such as program mechanics, contracting and confidentiality, and the effectiveness of the assessment tools and action strategies. Organizations also bring varying levels of readiness and commitment to their employee coaching initiatives with some organizations providing extensive support and participation, such as providing resources, assessment data, and performance opportunities. Also important to note is the support that organizations can provide to internal and external coaches, fostering partnerships that serve to maximize coaching effectiveness.

Organizational and contextual influences need to be considered in coaching practice and research. Of particular interest is the role of organizational support in effectively integrating client goals and action plans into their work environment, fostering learning transfer, and sustaining the developmental process. How is organizational readiness for coaching assessed? How is stakeholder buy-in achieved? What are the implications if support and buy-in are not present? Answers to questions such as these have huge implications for the degree to which successful coaching outcomes can be achieved and, more important, sustained.

Coaching Process

The coaching process is partitioned into four major subprocesses: mechanics, program content, relationship, and tools and techniques. The mechanics process focuses on the logistics of the coaching session (for example, number, duration, frequency, and timeliness or responsiveness of sessions, session prep, and closure, including preparing an agenda, completing homework, documenting the meeting, and so forth). Though individual coaches may identify with certain models of coaching, most coaching programs include similar content or elements, which include contracting, establishing confidentiality, assessments, action planning, evaluating progress, and transitioning. The four key processes associated with the client-coach relationship are building and maintaining rapport, establishing and maintaining trust, encouraging commitment, and promoting collaboration. These four social constructs involve a mutual responsibility between a coach and client. Finally, tools and techniques include the actual coaching behaviors (such as active listening, questioning, feedback, and so on).

In considering the coaching process, several issues are particularly relevant to practitioners and researchers. Fundamentally, the underlying questions are What coaching practices effectively lead to desired coaching outcomes? Why are these practices effective? Are there significant differences between coaching approaches with regard to coaching effectiveness? Within these broad questions are more specific issues, such as understanding which tools and techniques are most effective for particular clients, goals, or context. Answers to these questions have implications for the standardization of coaching methods and practices and the training of coaches.

Of particular note is the coaching relationship. Perhaps the most critical aspect of a coaching engagement is the unique relationship between the client and the coach. This relationship forms the context within which the coaching happens and is the cornerstone for successful coaching engagements. What are the key factors for developing effective client-coach relationships? How can the relationship be leveraged to maximize coaching effectiveness? Is the quality of a coaching relationship the single most important factor for creating successful coaching outcomes? If so, greater understanding is needed to guide best practices for developing and maintaining client-coach relationships.

Medium

Communication mediums have evolved translating our personal and professional interactions. With the majority of coaches coaching in a medium other than face-to-face, using tools ranging from e-mail to virtual simulations, the impact of the coaching medium is a growing interest (Boyce & Hernez-Broome, in press). Adding technology to the already unique nature of a one-on-one coaching interaction increases the complexity of the process. Therefore, the medium by which coaching is delivered (face-to-face coaching, technology supported, or blended delivery) is framed as moderating the relationship between the coaching process and coaching outcomes.

The impact of technology on coaching is a controversial topic. There are coaches who believe that the idea of virtual coaching is an oxymoron—that coaching by definition is about the personal nature of the relationship between a client and coach. Questions essential to the future of coaching and those interested in virtual or blended coaching include: Can quality relationships be developed with technology and, if so, what are the best methods? Are there particular goals or outcomes that are more or less suited for virtual coaching? Are there specific skills and abilities that are required for both clients and coaches involved in virtual coaching? The move toward the incorporation of technology into coaching is inevitable. Coaches and clients must decide whether to engage in virtual or blended coaching and the extent to which they want to use technology. Answers to questions such as these will provide the insights to help coaching professionals make that decision.

Coaching Outcomes

When all is said and done, the ultimate question is whether or not executive coaching is effective. Leadership coaching is qualitatively different from most approaches to leadership development and therefore holds particular challenges for evaluating coaching outcomes (Ely et al., 2010). Ely and her colleagues addressed the general difficulties of evaluating coaching by applying this systematic framework to the unique aspects of leadership coaching. Relevant coaching outcomes include traditional summative training criteria, including reactions, learning and behavioral skill demonstration, and organizational impact (Kirkpatrick, 1994) supplemented with cognitive (for example, self-awareness) and affective (for example, self-efficacy) learning outcomes, as well as formative or process criteria. Assessing coaching outcomes is critical to practitioners in determining the effectiveness of coaching programs and processes. The outcomes provide a means for understanding the impact of the coaching factors as they interact.

When thinking about coaching outcomes and evaluation, it is important to consider the stakeholders who may have a vested interest in the coaching initiative, including coaches, clients, clients' organizations, and coaching organizations. While there are overlapping needs, each stakeholder also has different interests. Therefore, broad issues to consider include not only what outcomes need to be assessed but at what phases of the coaching engagement, with what measurement tools and techniques, and from whom? What is the feasibility for collecting particular types of outcome data? What evaluation methodologies can be developed to be more acceptable and user friendly for clients and organizations? What can be realistically expected in term of the outcomes that leadership coaching can impact? Individual stakeholders need to understand how their individual needs merge with the needs of other stakeholders as well as how the feedback translates into practice, whether in the individual coaching engagement or organizational initiative.

Summary

The Leadership Coaching Framework provides a systematic structure to examine the multitude of variables that are important to increase our understanding of the state of the field, generate methodical research, and better inform and guide practice. As we have noted, a coaching intervention is guided by knowledge, skills, abilities, and perspective of the coach; the needs, characteristics, and experiences of the client; and the needs of the organization. As a result, there are no two identical coaching experiences. However, we believe that although the circumstances in any engagement will be unique, there is a common set of factors that should be considered in order to produce more effective coaching at both the individual client level and at a more systemic, organizational level. It is those factors that are represented in our framework and in this book.

State of the Art of Leadership Coaching

We understand there is no one best way to coach, and each coaching engagement, whether individually or organizationally focused, has unique content and varies in both the logistics and the practice of the process. We therefore appreciate the *art* of leadership coaching and consider it the intersection of science and practice. The art of coaching is the result of the coach's understanding the scientific research and converting that knowledge into sound practices to develop each individual client. The art is to understand the science and apply it.

There is good practice as well as good research to be found in the field of leadership coaching. As practice and research efforts continue to converge in the spirit of advancing the field, we can begin to articulate state-of-the-art leadership coaching. For coaching to reach a level that can be considered an "art" implies that we are able to take the practice and the study of coaching to a higher level, to a level of high quality and execution. There must be a synergy of thought, activity, and discussion among coaching practitioners, academics, and consumers that allows coaching to be more than the sum its parts; that is, more than a set of skills, principles, methods, or findings must be represented. The pieces must be transformed into a larger, cohesive picture as practice informs research and research informs practice.

We believe *Advancing Executive Coaching* illustrates this synergy and state-of-the-art leadership coaching. The book represents a scientist-practitioner, evidence-based means by which to approach coaching. We hope that coaches and those involved in developing and implementing coaching initiatives will actively engage with and apply this existing knowledge and literature while continuing to develop and evaluate their own unique approaches, methods, and orientations to coaching. As Stober and Grant (2006) articulately stated in their definition and use of evidence based coaching, "it's the use of best current knowledge integrated with practitioner expertise in making decisions about how to deliver coaching to individual clients and in designing and teaching coaching initiatives." This book represents the best current knowledge from practitioners and scholars with notable expertise in the coaching arena. Our intent is that the book serve as a model and a resource to advance leadership coaching, the practice, the science, and the art.

References

American Management Association. (2008). Coaching: A global study of successful practices. Current trends and future possibilities 2008–2018. www.amanet.org.

Anderson, M. C., Frankovelgia, C., & Hernez-Broome, G. (2009). Business leaders reflect on coaching cultures. *Leadership in Action, 28*(6), 20–22.

Auerbach, J. (2005). *Seeing the light: What organizations need to know about executive coaching.* Pismo Beach, CA: Executive College Press.

Boyce, L. A., & Hernez-Broome, G. (in press). E-Coaching: Consideration of leadership coaching in a virtual environment. In D. Clutterbuck & A. Hussain (Eds). *Virtual coach/virtual mentor* (pp. 139–174). Charlotte, NC: Information Age.

Boyce, L. A., & Ritter, A. (2002). *Executive coaching: The professional personal trainer.* Retrieved January 7, 2002, from Society for Industrial and Organizational Psychology Web site: www.siop.org/Media/News/NewsReleases.htm.

Boyce, L. A., LaVoie, N., Streeter, L. A., Lochbaum, K. E., & Psotka, J. (2008). Technology as a tool for leadership development: Effectiveness of automated web-based systems in facilitating tacit knowledge acquisition. *Military Psychology, 20*(4), 271–288.

Cavanagh, M., Grant, A. M., & Kemp, T. (Eds.), (2005). *Evidence-based coaching, Vol. 1: Theory, research and practice from the behavioural sciences.* Bowen Hills, QLD, Australia: Australian Academic Press.

Cober, R. T., Silzer, R., & Erickson, A. (2009). *Practice perspectives: Science–practice gaps in industrial-organizational psychology: Part I: Member data and perspectives.* Retrieved www.siop.org/tip/july09/16silzer.aspx.

Corbett, B., Corbett, K., & Colemon, J. (2008). *The 2008 Sherpa executive coaching survey.* West Chester, OH: Author.

Criswell, C., & Martin, A. (2007). 10 trends: A study of senior executives' views on the future. *A CCL research white paper.* Greensboro, NC: The Center for Creative Leadership.

Dagley, G. (2006). Human resources professionals' perceptions of executive coaching: Efficacy, benefits and return on investment. *International Coaching Psychology Review, 1,* 34–44.

Douglas, C. A., & Morley, W. H., (2000). *Executive coaching: An annotated bibliography.* North Carolina: Center for Creative Leadership.

Ely, K., Boyce, L. A., Nelson, J. K., Zaccaro, S. J., Hernez-Broome, G., & Whyman, W. (2010). Evaluating leadership coaching: A review and integrated framework. *Leadership Quarterly, 21*(4), 585–599.

Evers, W. J. G., Brouwers, A., & Tomic, W. (2006). A quasi-experimental study on management coaching effectiveness. *Consulting Psychology Journal: Practice and Research, 58,* 174–182.

Hall, D. T., & Mirvis, P. H. (1995). Careers as lifelong learning. In A. Howard (Ed.), *The changing nature of work* (pp. 323–364). San Francisco: Jossey-Bass.

Howard, A. (1995). A framework for work change. In A. Howard (Ed.), *The changing nature of work* (pp. 3–44). San Francisco: Jossey-Bass.

HR Focus. (2008). What is the "most important" metric? *85*(2), 13–15.

Joo, B. (2005). Executive coaching: A conceptual framework from an integrative review of practice and research. *Human Resource Development Review, 4,* 462–488.

Katz, D., & Kahn, R. L. (1978). *The social psychology of organizations.* New York: Wiley.

Kilburg, R. R. (1996). Toward a conceptual understanding and definition of executive coaching. *Consulting Psychology Journal: Practice and Research, 48,* 134–144.

Kilburg, R. R., & Diedrich, R. C. (2007). *The wisdom of coaching: Essential papers in consulting psychology for a world of change.* Washington, DC: American Psychological Association.

Kirkpatrick, D. L. (1994). *Evaluating training programs: The four levels.* San Francisco: Berrett-Koehler.

Nelson, J. K., Boyce, L. A., Hernez-Broome, G., Ely, K., & DiRosa, G. (in press). *Executive coaching: A sourcebook.* Greensboro, NC: Center for Creative Leadership.

Passmore, J., & Gibbes, C. (2007). The state of executive coaching research: What does the current literature tell us and what's next for coaching research? *International Coaching Psychology Review, 2,* 116–128.

Peterson, D. B., & Hicks, M. D. (1999, February). *The art and practice of executive coaching.* Paper presented at the annual conference of the Division of Consulting Psychology, Phoenix.

Rynes, S. L., Giluk, T. L., & Brown, K. G., (2007). The very separate worlds of academic and practitioner periodicals in Human Resource Management: Implications for evidence-based management. *Academy of Management Journal, 50*(5), 987–1008.

Silzer, R. (2002). Preface. In R. Silzer (Ed.), *The 21st century executive: Innovative practice for building leadership at the top.* San Francisco: Jossey-Bass.

Smither, J. W., London, M., Flautt, R., Vargas, Y., & Kucine, I. (2003). Can working with an executive coach improve multisource feedback ratings over time? A quasi-experimental study. *Personnel Psychology, 56,* 23–44.

Stober, D. R., & Grant, A. (2006). *Evidence based coaching handbook: Putting best practices to work for your clients.* Hoboken, NJ: Wiley.

Ting, S., & Hart, E. W. (2004). Formal coaching. In C. D. McCauley and E. Van Velsor (Eds.), *The Center for Creative Leadership handbook of leadership development* (pp. 116–150). San Francisco: Jossey-Bass.

Witherspoon, R., & White, R. P. (1997). *Four essential ways that coaching can help executives.* Greensboro, NC: Center for Creative Leadership.

Zaccaro, S. J., & Klimoski, R. J. (2001). The nature of organizational leadership: An introduction. In S. J. Zaccaro & R. J. Klimoski (Eds.), *The nature of organizational leadership* (pp. 3–41). San Francisco: Jossey-Bass.

Your Traveling Companions: Coach, Client, and Organizational Issues

Chapter One

ACTIVATING THE ACTIVE INGREDIENTS OF LEADERSHIP COACHING

Sandra L. Davis and D. Douglas McKenna

Peruse the business book selections online or in your local bookstore and you will encounter a sea of titles about coaching, executive coaching, or even life coaching. Connect with executives in organizations across the globe and ask them about their experience with executive coaching and you will undoubtedly hear positive, personal stories of how a coach helped to make a difference. Coaching has even become a status symbol: "Don't you have a coach?" Executive coaching is hot and it matters.

The field of executive coaching can benefit from the unique contributions of psychologists. Though some executive coaches or HR professionals may be wary of talking about psychology for fear of turning away hard-nosed or skeptical executives, it is psychology theory and even psychotherapy research that provide the magic and means for how individuals change through coaching. Those who do not understand the forces that sustain change may actually be harmful to clients, notes Dr. Steven Berglas of the Department of Psychiatry at Harvard Medical School. "In an alarming number of situations, executive coaches who lack rigorous psychological training do more harm than good" (Berglas, 2002, 87).

We use this chapter to provide food for thought, stories for learning, and practical principles for action to professionals who touch executive coaching in any way. Whether you coordinate coaching within your organization, train others to be coaches, or deliver coaching yourself, there are ideas here that you can begin to use immediately. Our conclusions come from our experiences as coaches, our education as psychologists, and our unending curiosity about how we help leaders change. We offer these ideas with the hope of advancing the effectiveness of all who are involved in executive coaching.

Consider the case of Keisha, a retail store president recently promoted into a group president role. She sought out and selected an executive coach with the encouragement of her manager and the blessing of her company's chief learning officer (CLO). Her stated goals for the engagement were to learn how to navigate the nuances of upper management and to lead a significant change effort through and with highly autonomous retail presidents. She anticipated resistance from many sides. In the first meeting with her coach, Keisha shared some of her worries and initial challenging experiences in her new role. She and her coach created goals, discovered they had some common interests, and collectively established a rhythm for their ongoing work together. Keisha's coach was tempted to jump in immediately with insights about the organization and its politics, which could help to explain others' behavior, but thought better of it. Instead, the two of them explored many possible reasons for others' behavior, including Keisha's collaborative style itself.

Over the course of the next several months, Keisha learned to trust her own judgment, to recognize others' motivations, and to experiment with multiple approaches to influencing. She made choices about what kind of role she would play with her peers. She forged ahead with confidence and began to provide leadership in areas outside her own retail group. In the end, Keisha, her manager, coach, and HR partner could all cite vivid examples of how she had changed and grown through coaching.

Did it matter that Keisha's coach had a deep understanding of psychology and the ingredients that influence coaching success? We think it did. In this chapter we delve into the theoretical underpinnings from psychology which have an impact on an individual client's ability to change and a coach's effectiveness in being a partner in the change process.

The Active Ingredients in Coaching

To understand the psychological variables at play in the coaching process, we turn to psychotherapy research. Although coaching is not therapy, and vice versa, there are lessons to be learned from what that research tells us. Early on, researchers (Bergin & Lambert, 1978) demonstrated overwhelmingly that psychotherapy works and then turned their attention to a more sophisticated question: If therapy works, what are its active ingredients? For executive coaches and for those who oversee coaching matches, that's where the treasure lies hidden.

Four factors account for almost all the systematic variance in psychotherapy outcomes (Asay & Lambert, 1999). These are the "active ingredients" that make therapy effective. They can also be called "common" factors because they are active in all effective therapeutic interventions, regardless of the theoretical orientation or techniques (for example, psychoanalytic, cognitive-behavioral) employed by the therapist. The relative importance of the four active ingredients based on variance accounted for in psychotherapy outcomes is shown in Figure 1.1 (based on Asay & Lambert, 1999). Here are the four factors in brief.

Figure 1.1. The Active Ingredients of Psychotherapy and the Percentage of Outcome Variance Accounted by Each Factor

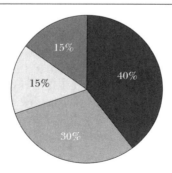

- ● Client/Extratherapeutic Factors
- ○ Expectancy, Hope, Placebo Effects
- ◐ Therapeutic Relationship
- ● Theory and Technique

Client/Extratherapeutic Factors (40%)

Wouldn't it be wonderful if we could take the majority of the credit for the behavioral change we see in our clients? It is exhilarating to know that we have made a difference and it is seductive to believe too much in our own power and magic. The fact is that some individuals are more predisposed to change than others.

Client/extratherapeutic factors are those capacities and conditions that a client brings with him or her to the engagement. The client brings herself, her work, and her social environment. Thus, we can begin to predict whether an individual will benefit from coaching by looking through the lens of individual differences. A client's motivations, skills, interests, defenses, thought patterns, experiences, relationships, and current environment all contribute to capacity for change or readiness to benefit from coaching. As coaches, we cannot control what our clients bring with them—either in terms of their current environment or who they perceive themselves to be. Ignoring individual differences or dismissing the power of a client's current organization or family system to shape behavior is misguided. Individual differences matter; context matters. Even in determining who should participate in coaching, we need to pay attention to these individual and environmental differences; almost half of the potential outcome depends on it.

What a favorable situation Keisha's coach encountered! There were multiple elements that she brought with her that worked toward a positive outcome. Keisha's own drive to succeed, her openness to learning, and her willingness to admit struggles led her to welcome coaching. Knowing the psychology of individual differences provided her coach with the data to move quickly into action. Additionally, Keisha's environment (the context) provided support as well. Her company had used coaching extensively in the past, her manager encouraged her, and the CLO provided the connection. All the external forces were aligned for success.

The Relationship (30%)

Once again, psychotherapeutic research points us in the right direction. The *quality* of the relationship between therapist and

client is the second most powerful active ingredient in psychotherapy (Lambert, 1992). The quality and durability of the
client-therapist relationship can make or break the outcome.
The applicability of this proven fact to coaching is obvious. Organizations that engage internal or external coaches worry about the
match between the coach and client. One chief learning officer
boasted, "I can tell in 10 minutes whether a coach can match our
culture." But the relationship ingredient goes far beyond the traditional chemistry check or beauty contest ("Which coach do *you*
want to work with?"). The *quality and reciprocity* of the relationship
is at play from the moment the coach and potential client meet.
It remains at play throughout the entire process.

It would be a mistake, however, to think that we are only talking about unconditional positive regard, à la Carl Rogers. There
are other compelling elements at play in the relationship, including client involvement and the therapeutic alliance. In coaching,
we are with a client a minimal amount of time; therefore, the
real work of behavior change takes place when the coach is not
around. The relationship has to help promote and sustain the
client's active involvement in the work.

Research on the therapeutic alliance teaches us a great deal
about the dynamic relationship between a coach and client that
leads to change. Bordin (1976) has written extensively about
(therapy) relationships, asserting that at their core they encompass
a *working alliance* based on collaboration and consensus. Bordin
notes that every effective alliance has three elements: goals, tasks,
and bonds. Together with our client, we need to create common and realistic goals, agree on how we will work together, and
we need to ensure that the partnership stays tight and intact. If
this is true, than any HR-initiated check-in with a coaching participant during the engagement should focus first and foremost on
the alliance and the quality of its goals, tasks, and bonds.

For Keisha, the relationship factor began working when her
coach listened, refrained from pontificating with advice, and collaborated with her so she could reach *her* goals. Empathy, respect,
and even common interests all helped craft a powerful relationship, but it was Keisha who did the work and was ultimately in
charge. Coaching was also a dynamic process for them. At every
stage of their work together, Keisha's coach continued to ask her

for feedback. They used the data to fine-tune their relationship, agree on new tasks, and refine their goals.

Expectancy, Hope, and Placebo Effects (15%)

Why do prospective clients on waiting lists for therapy improve *while they are waiting* for their first therapy appointment? They expect to get better. They have hope that tomorrow will be better than yesterday. Hope is a powerful variable in the medical world as well. Patients with confidence in their physicians experience more positive treatment outcomes than those who harbor doubt about their caregivers. Think too about the placebo effect: in classic research on the effects of a medicine, patients who receive an inert drug often show symptom improvement. The simple act of taking a medicine and expecting improvement creates some positive outcomes. We can use this expectation lever as coaches and as professionals who oversee coaching. In the case of Keisha, the company CLO and her manager's approval provided credibility for the coach and hope for Keisha. The solid connection that Keisha and her coach made in their first encounter strengthened Keisha's expectations for a positive outcome. Keisha's coach further activated this ingredient during their work by introducing Keisha to another executive who had successfully made the transition into the executive ranks and by pointing out each successful step she made along the way. We can too easily overlook the power of this ingredient; it's another hidden treasure.

Theory and Technique (15%)

In the therapy world, debate still rages about the power of the therapist's theoretical orientation. Does it matter which school of theory or technique the therapist embraces? Hundreds of studies and meta-analyses of psychotherapy outcomes have converged on a controversial and still not fully accepted conclusion: the power of psychotherapy to facilitate change comes primarily from factors that the various schools have in *common*, not from the differences between them. When we link this ingredient with hope and expectancy, we learn that the power of a particular technique or theory may well come from the fact that the therapist and the client *believe* it will be effective. Techniques and methodologies are important; through them we can give our clients tools for action.

Coaches and HR professionals alike come to the table with preferred theories. We have beliefs about organizations, psychology, individual development, and a point of view about how to approach our executive client. We all have our own theories of change, whether we have taken the time to bring them forward to our consciousness or not. Not only do we coaches have theories of change, but coaching clients have them too. Later in this chapter we will examine the intersection between our own and our client's "theory of change." When those theories have a significant disconnect, that negatively affects the ability of both the client and the coach to use the power of the active ingredients. If you and I disagree about the root causes of the situation in which I find myself, how can we possibly form a relationship alliance that will lead to aligned solutions?

Keisha's coach did have working theories about social systems, about life at the top of an organization for minority women, and about what it takes to succeed in a senior team. She used those when it made sense without making them the sole focus of coaching. Knowing the business world gave the coach sources of insight; but the focus of coaching was not about Keisha's status as the "only female."

These are the four key active ingredients that make our coaching powerful; they just happen to come to us via psychotherapy research. We are not encouraging coaches to stray over the line and practice therapy. Yet, we believe there is a functional similarity between the two processes that deserves exploration if we want to become better coaches. Our colleagues in psychotherapy have knowledge and understanding that can directly add value to our coaching; we would be remiss not to use it.

Theories and How They Apply to the Active Ingredients

As individuals interested in helping others change or become more effective, we all embrace certain techniques and theories of change. Whether we are aware of them or not, we hold them: there is no such thing as theory-free or technique-free coaching. We bring theories to issues a client presents to us, and each of us upon hearing the same issues will have a perspective and a way of thinking about the problem, its causes, its effects, and possible solutions.

Theory is important because it happens at the *intersection* of the coach's theory and the client's theory. If the coach can put these two theories into creative tension, they will strengthen the effects of the other three active ingredients. If the coach is too rigid to understand or flex with the client's theory, the other three active ingredients will be neutralized and coaching will not be successful. By the way in which we use theory, we can:

- Engage and motivate the client
- Activate his strengths, resources, and sense of personal agency
- Account for helping and hindering forces in his environment
- Strengthen and sustain the alliance
- Bolster her hopes for change

With the goal of shedding light on our own individual theories, we will draw on our psychology roots. Psychology encompasses many theories and schools of thought that help to answer the question, "What is the key to changing behavior?" In a recent publication, Davis and Barnett (2009, 353) summarized seven major theories within psychology that can be tapped by a practitioner (coach) interested in helping clients change their behavior. We have built on and modified their list, paring it down to five primary theories to help coaches and others recognize their own theories in action.

As you read through these five major theoretical groupings, reflect on which of these you use the most and how they influence your ideas about coaching. At a minimum we believe a coach must be clear about his own theory in order to see how it maps to the theory or perspective of the client. We have chosen to present those aspects of each theory that relate specifically to the client/environmental, relationship, and hope factors.

Psychodynamic Theories

Human beings, even billionaire executives, have limited awareness of the forces that drive their thoughts, feelings, and actions.

Psychodynamic theory takes this fact a step further by maintaining that the human mind protects itself automatically and unconsciously against the intrusion of unacceptable drives and motives into conscious awareness. Although they protect the individual from being swamped with anxiety, these defensive maneuvers can give rise to puzzling, ineffective behavior patterns.

A coach who subscribes to psychodynamic models is alert for characteristic ways the client defends herself psychologically, particularly those defenses that negatively affect performance. The path to helping involves bringing these dysfunctional patterns to the client's attention and probing for their unconscious roots. Naturally, such a coach expects the client to resist this probing and rebuff suggestions for change. After all, the individual's defenses serve a deep emotional purpose—ego protection. Change means giving up that protection and experiencing the anxiety that gave rise to the defense in the first place. It puts the client's sense of well-being directly at risk.

Transference and counter-transference are also critical concepts in psychodynamic theory. Your client may begin relating to you as she does to others who are close to her in her life, or you may relate to her as you do to other key figures in your life. When these forces come into play in coaching, they directly affect the quality of the relationship and your ability as a coach to create an alliance for change.

For example, a high-potential director who resisted being direct and candid in conflict situations had an "aha" moment when he realized that his accommodating approach had been learned in his family of origin. Expressions of candor were discouraged and punished. He was smart and had developed a convincing rationale (at least to him) for being "discreet" and "circumspect" in his communications. Because his intellectualized defense had kept his anxiety at bay, he had resisted seeing its roots and was reluctant to give it up. With the support of his coach, however, he was able to realize the source of his resistance and began to experiment with being more direct and honest in his communications with others. Even more important, he realized that this ingrained defense mechanism was also interfering with his ability to be honest with his coach about what he needed from the relationship.

Behaviorism and Work Motivation Theory

Coaches who subscribe to these theories don't spend their time worrying about the origins of behavior; they deal with the objective tasks of behavior change and step-by-step learning of new ways of operating. They focus on goals, situational cues, patterns of reinforcement and punishment, behavioral rehearsal, and successive approximations to the desired behavior. Behavior that is reinforced and rewarded will be repeated. Behavior that is ignored or coupled with negative outcomes will be extinguished.

Using this theory for coaching an executive who has difficulty in conflict entails trying out new behaviors, gaining success with them, and turning them into effective habits. For example, the executive who had received feedback about how he routinely avoided conflict stated that he needed a new skill set. He and his coach began by compiling an inventory of typical conflict situations, how he generally responded to each, and how he wanted to behave in the future. The situations ranged from differences of opinion to giving negative feedback to negotiating for resources. He and his coach began with the "easiest" circumstances first. In each meeting, they set goals for trying out new behaviors, role-played scenarios, and talked through what had worked or not worked from the previous meeting. They even built a flow chart of situational cues that the executive could use to take a new path and avoid old habits. After three months, the executive not only had a new skill set, but his manager told him he had noticed a dramatic change.

Cognitive Behavioral Theories

The coach who comes from the cognitive-behavioral or social learning perspective assumes that behaviors are a function of the individual's way of thinking about and making sense of the world around him. If we can discover the meaning someone makes of an event or understand how the client thinks, we can look for alternative ways of thinking about the same issue. Thinking also applies to experimentation with new behaviors: a client is willing to try new approaches if she thinks the odds are good that she can be successful. This perspective assumes that a new way of thinking will lead naturally to different behavioral choices.

For example, consider the executive who discovered that his reluctance to talk up the work of his staff came from his conviction that "boasting is wrong." He needed to change his thought patterns if he wanted to change his behavior. In the past, he had expected the good work of his team to speak for itself. But when he began to see how important it was for him to be his team's advocate in the company, his reluctance to spread the word about their accomplishments subsided and he began to act as their champion.

Adult Learning and Person-Centered Psychology

Adult learning theorists and person-centered psychologists believe that individuals have the capacity to learn and to heal themselves. Clients don't need an expert to tell them how to change; they need someone to listen and set the stage for them to solve their own problems and do their own learning.

One of the core tenets of adult learning theory is that adults want to direct their own learning. They do not want to be lectured or told what to do. They want information so they can make informed choices and learn on their own. A coach coming from this perspective is acutely aware of the importance of letting the client take the lead and be responsible for her own learning. Holding forth with "shoulds," giving advice, or touting one's own experience and expertise stands in direct contrast to being a catalyst to someone else's learning or work.

The adult learning and person-centered approaches are particularly useful with clients who have clear goals and a strong sense of how they want to work on them. Consider Karen, a senior finance executive, who wanted to work on having more patience and controlling her tendency to fly off the handle. She entered coaching having already decided what she wanted to work on, she had read more than one book on the topic, and simply wanted someone to guide her learning. Although she was open to having the coach do 360 interviews to get a clearer view of how she was perceived by others, Karen knew what she wanted to do from the start and took charge of her own development process. A coach who could not be her partner in learning would have been quickly dismissed.

Systems Theories

This theoretical perspective highlights the part-whole relationship between the individual and the social system in which he is embedded. Systems theories come in a variety of flavors (such as family systems, corporate culture, organizations as systems), but all systems-oriented coaches look for ways in which the individual affects and is affected by—directly or indirectly—the actions and expectations of others. The "others" could be as obvious and immediate as one's own team, or as subtle and distant as the board of directors, whose anxieties about the future may ripple down through the ranks of the company, affecting every employee in ways that are difficult to trace back to their source.

In any case, systems theory maintains that one cannot fully understand a client's perspective, feelings, and actions without knowing how the system works, what behaviors it expects, and how it reacts to unacceptable behavior. Some systems tolerate conflict and use it productively. Others avoid it at all costs. Clearly, a behavior labeled "aggressive" in one system or culture may be interpreted as "open and assertive" in another. Tension at the top of an organization can create serious rifts three or four layers down, and be attached to completely different issues at the different levels.

Here's an example. The coaching client, an executive who came from a highly competitive and sales-driven company, joined a health care organization that valued collaboration and "being nice." Understandably, he met considerable resistance trying to lead a change process in the health system's clinics. He found it difficult to work with others who had been socialized by the system. They were equally frustrated and came close to completely rejecting him. Until he could recognize how his behavior was perceived in the system and find ways to influence others to advocate changes *with* him, he was ineffective.

Recognizing Theories in Action

As executive coaches and professionals who manage coaches, we think it is important to understand how we make sense of the issues that coaching clients bring to us; that is, we need to be clear about theoretical perspectives that shape the way we understand and frame clients' challenges. The reason is that our clients have their own ways of understanding what they are up against (as in "my family taught me to operate this way" or "I would be able to handle this differently if the culture valued that approach") and their own theories about how to be more effective within that frame. When as coaches we understand our own theoretical assumptions and working hypotheses, it becomes much easier to discern where our perspective and the client's resonate and clash. There's an old saying among teachers: "Meet the student where she is, but don't leave her there."

Our task as coaches is to shine a new light on the client's situation, a light that allows her to see her own assumptions more clearly and expand her perspective in ways that open up new behavioral possibilities. Our task is not to force our theories or interpretation on the client. In fact, to do so is one of the most common ways in which the relationship is ruptured, thus neutralizing the active ingredient over which the coach has the most control. The alliance is damaged and progress stalls. Without an effective alliance for change, the coach and the client are potentially working in different directions or worse, at cross purposes.

Consider Keisha once again. She felt she was at a critical stage in her ascent as a leader. Though she was the first African American senior leader in a primarily white male executive team, she did not want to explore the social system dynamics of being the first or the only. She knew from others who had successfully navigated a promotion into the executive ranks that leadership and peer relations at that level were different from what she experienced at the director level. She wanted to understand her new leadership requirements. When her coach talked about the social dynamics of being the first or, the only, she bristled. "This is not about me as an African American woman; I refuse to hide behind that." She rejected systems theory as a perspective for understanding her leadership challenges.

She and her coach were able to find common ground through exploring the leadership pipeline and its explanation of how the focus of leadership changes as one moves up the ladder. They discussed the leadership behaviors needed at various stages of the pipeline. Keisha agreed that she needed to learn how to better influence her peers, not in terms of the system she was part of, but in terms of her new leadership requirements. Once they settled on a rationale for their work, she embraced her role as learner. Coaching could be effective because the coach and Keisha were able to build a working alliance grounded in a common perspective.

Imagine what might have happened had Keisha and her coach held rigidly to their divergent views of the situation. Had her coach persisted in forcing a social system view and had Keisha insisted on focusing on the demands of her new leadership role, they would have been speaking different languages. Their alliance would have been fragile at best and might never have gotten off the ground. By finding common ground and aligning their theories, they were able to forge a real alliance for change, and Keisha benefited greatly from coaching. In the same manner, if the chief learning officer had tried to define the issues for Keisha in terms of social systems, Keisha might have rejected the opportunity to participate in coaching altogether.

The Case for Conviction and Versatility

Every coaching session is a dance: a dance between the client and the coach in which their theories of the problem (and the path to a solution) are articulated and brought into lively contact. A great coach has a clear, convicted point of view, but holds space for the client to reveal her perspective as well. He welcomes the pushback that shows the client is thinking for herself. With each of their theories of the problem on the table, the coach will be able to see where he can join in support of the client's point of view. He will also be able to ask questions that challenge and potentially enrich the client's understanding of the situation.

For a coach to have this kind of flexibility and be able to dance with the client in this way, he needs more than one theoretical lens in his briefcase. We believe that the best coaches can find ways to use different theories and techniques to engage the client (and her theory of the problem) without sacrificing their core convictions about people, organizations, or change. In our work with clients, we are constantly looking for a way to hook into the client's way of thinking with a theoretical concept or angle that will stimulate a more robust framing of their challenge. During the coaching process, we find ourselves deliberately invoking concepts from different theories as it makes sense for the relationship and the stage of our work.

Linking Theory to the Active Ingredients

The theories we hold can help us better use the active ingredients because they are the lenses through which we view our client and our work together. The questions we raise and the areas to which we attend shift based on the theoretical perspective we use. We don't mean to imply that any particular theoretical perspective is better than another, but only that the more closely we can link our starting point with that of our client, the more impactful the coaching will be. Our starting point or theory in use affects how we ask questions, how we define the goals, how we build the relationship and of course, which tools or techniques we use. Use Table 1.1 as a starting point to explore how you raise questions or pose topics in the coaching you do.

We have pointed out that a disconnect between your client's theory and your own is problematic. But how do we identify that there is a disconnect? The first step is to recognize which theories most appeal to you and that you use most. The second step is to learn from your clients which theoretical orientation best fits them. Following are some questions you can pose to the client at the beginning of the coaching process to discern the coaching participant's theory in use and to decide where to begin.

- What does coaching mean to you? What do you expect your role and my role will be?
- What needs to change: yourself, the system, your role, others?
- Tell me about your most powerful developmental experience. What was the situation and what created development?
- What do you believe is hard-wired about leadership and what do you believe people can learn?
- What do you *not* want to change?
- When was the last time you decided to learn something or change your behavior? How did you go about doing so?

These questions are relevant as well for the coaching coordinator who is exploring whether coaching is appropriate for a given executive. The more we all can understand the circumstances *from the client's point of view*, the better we can set the stage for a successful outcome.

Table 1.1. Using Theory to Stimulate the Active Ingredients: What We Focus on and the Questions We Ask

Theories	Client and External Factors	The Relationship	Hope and Expectancy	Theories and Techniques
Psychodynamic and Developmental Stages	• What are the origins of the problem? • What do these behaviors have to do with your stage of development?	• How have you related to coaches or mentors in the past?	• What do you have in common with individuals who have shown great personal fortitude and persistence?	• Let's explore your personal values and how they play out in leadership.
Behaviorism and Work Motivation	• What happens positively when you behave in the old way?	• What are your goals and desired outcomes?	• What behavior changes have you successfully accomplished in the past?	• Let's use a system of successive approximation to get you closer to your ideal.
Cognitive	• How have you thought through the problem; what do you believe is happening?	• What role do you want me to play? • What information might I have that you are looking for?	• What tells you that our work together will be successful?	• What is it you tell yourself that keeps you from _____? • Let's figure out ways to think about this differently.

Adult Learning and Person-Centered	• What have you been most successful learning on your own in the past? • What are the issues and how motivated are you to change?	• What is the role of "teacher" in your learning process; what works best for you? • How are you responding to me; what will our relationship be like?	• How do you feel about getting started with coaching? • How hopeful do you feel and what can you envision for yourself in the future?	• What happened when you tried out the new behavior? • Critique yourself in terms of what you learned and what you need to do differently the next time.
Systems-Based	• How does the organizational culture support or resist your current approaches? • What is your manager expecting you to change?	• Who else in your current environment do you believe I need to know well? • What aspects of the culture will you and I have to navigate well?	• What positive things will happen in your world when you make changes? • How are your peers or your team engaged in your coaching?	• What can we do to activate help or support from your team?

How Theory Interacts with the Active Ingredients

Taking a deeper dive into the impact of theory matches or mismatches on the four active ingredients is our intention in this last section. We deal with each active ingredient separately, showing the effect that the coach's theory and the client's theory have on the ingredient. Using client stories, we show the impact of theory and then articulate some core lessons learned from each and provide some principles for practice. In this section, we also draw on our 2009 article "Hidden in Plain Sight: The Active Ingredients of Executive Coaching," published in *Industrial and Organizational Psychology, Perspectives on Science and Practice.*

Exploring the Client/Extratherapeutic Ingredient: A Client Story

In using this ingredient, we need to remember that it is the client's abilities, motivational readiness, and life circumstances that are the most powerful predictors of change. How the client makes use of what we have to offer sets the stage for outcomes. Though it is seductive to believe that we create great outcomes, it is true that some individuals embrace change more readily than others. Sometimes readiness can't be activated because the client and coach start from different perspectives.

Perhaps you have had the experience of being contacted by a client organization with a plea to "help one of our brilliant executives learn to play well with others." In Brian's case, the EVP of Human Resources sought out coaching for him because of significant complaints from his peers in the finance function. Known as an exceptionally skilled controller, Brian had the trust of the board and the respect of the CFO for his expertise. The notion that Brian needed help learning to play well with others was an understatement. His department was suffering from high turnover, his peers were avoiding him due to his outbursts, and the CFO was tired of dealing with the fallout. The coach asked the CFO what kind of feedback she had given Brian and whether she really believed that Brian could change. She said she envisioned coaching as the last possible strategy for saving Brian;

whenever she gave him feedback, he improved for a few weeks and then returned to his ineffective behaviors. Brian had accepted the notion of coaching, but seemed less than enthusiastic about the prospects.

When Brian and his coach first met they candidly discussed the context for coaching, what Brian had heard from his manager about the purpose for coaching, and Brian's motivation for change. Later, after reviewing several personality inventories with Brian and listening intently to his point of view, Brian's coach understood just how exceptionally low was his readiness to change. She confronted Brian with her observation that he seemed to be going through the motions to please his boss with little real commitment to change. He acknowledged she was right; he had concluded that the best strategy for dealing with the CFO's criticism was to find another job.

Brian believed that the problem he was experiencing was a systems issue. In his view, his behavior was fine and the company's culture was far too thin-skinned. His coach rejected a systems explanation; she expected Brian to accept responsibility for his behavior and take charge of his own learning. Given the clear disconnect between their concepts of the problem, the coach could not activate this ingredient with Brian and she terminated the coaching contract within two sessions.

Luckily, all coaches have numerous anecdotes of overcoming low readiness to change or moving quickly into action because of high client readiness to change. We activate this ingredient in many ways, from clarifying organizational mandates for behavior change to helping our clients see the real possibilities for change. By exploring our own and our client's theory about what is happening, we can directly affect commitment and motivation to change.

Here are some principles for *activating* the client/external ingredient:

- Immediately explore the client's concept of the issue; what he or she believes about what is happening can directly affect the outcome.
- Take the time to understand readiness and the individual difference variables that contribute to one's ability to learn and to change.

- Work with the executive's manager to jointly evaluate readiness and whether an investment in coaching is actually the right choice.
- When readiness is low or only moderate, work with the individual to increase readiness to change (for example, collect data to raise awareness of the challenges).
- Terminate the coaching relationship, or don't take it on in the first place, if there is no way to activate this ingredient.
- Tap into the individual's networks (social, business, friends, family) to forces that will promote change.
- Help the client identify specific strengths and resources that she can use to bolster efforts to change.

Exploring the Relationship Ingredient: A Client Story

Without a doubt, a good relationship is critical. Estimates of how much outcome variance is due to the therapeutic relationship vary from at least 30 percent (Lambert, 1992) to more than 50 percent (Wampold, 2001). Clients often single out the personableness, listening skills, and honesty of their coach as key to their progress and satisfaction with coaching. Yet, the relationship ingredient goes far beyond the openness and authenticity of the coach. To truly activate change, the coach and client create a collaborative alliance in which they work together to produce results. When coaching is effective, the client is engaged, committed, and responsible for doing the hard work of making changes *on her own*. As coaches, we need to tap into the power of this ingredient to be most effective; research even suggests that if we haven't solidified the alliance by the third or fourth session, that coaching will likely end early.

Sarah and her coach understood each other well. Both looked forward to their meetings and, almost from the first day, Sarah was actively engaged in learning. Their common goal was for Sarah to learn how to delegate, to quit "saving" her team members, and to focus on the strategic work most central to her role and level in the organization. The alliance between the two was strong; they had established common goals and outcomes. In each session Sarah would describe what she had done to change, report on progress (or lack thereof), and the two would agree on what Sarah might try next. Sarah's coach was pleased with the direction of their engagement and had also let Sarah's manager know they were on track with their coaching action plan.

Routinely, near the close of each coaching session, Sarah's coach asked for feedback: "What is working here; what do you want me to do differently; how satisfied are you with how we work together?" Sarah's feedback had always been enthusiastically positive. However, at the end of their fifth working session, Sarah expressed her disappointment that her coach had spoken with her manager, even though the communication was affirming. "If I am to take a stronger hold of my senior level role, then I don't need you to report about my progress as if I were your protégé. Also, you seem too quick to point out ways to improve on what I experimented with during any given session rather than celebrating with me or helping me discover lessons learned on my own." The conversation was a wake-up call for Sarah's coach.

Delving deeper into the feedback, Sarah's coach realized that operating out of a behaviorism framework helped them make progress, but Sarah's theoretical orientation was squarely centered in adult learning. They used the feedback to forge a new agreement about how they would proceed going forward. When the coaching engagement closed, Sarah took her coach with her to meet with her manager to review progress and how she planned to sustain what she had learned.

Imagine what might have happened had Sarah's coach not opened the door to feedback. The disconnect they had in terms of their working theories could have damaged their alliance and seriously blocked progress. Their feedback conversation shows how a relationship is established and strengthened over and over again, not just at a single point in time. As coaches, we need to constantly be attuned to the quality of the relationship through the eyes of our clients, which includes exploring the theories we are both using.

Here are some principles for activating the relationship factor:

- With new clients, make building the relationship a priority right from the start. Work toward establishing the three primary components of the alliance—goals, tasks, and bonds.

- Set an expectation that you will have regular conversations about how the coaching is going in order to fine-tune the work and the alliance. Include exploration of your own and your client's theories of change.
- Take stock of the quality of the alliance for each coaching engagement. Ask yourself how the alliance is affecting progress in the engagement and what you can to do improve it.
- Assess your own strengths and weaknesses in building client alliances. Where are your opportunities for improvement?
- Be vigilant in watching for disconnects between your client's theories about the situation and your own.

Exploring Hope/Expectation in Coaching: A Client Story

Hope and expectation account for 15 percent of the outcome of successful therapy. Although research shows that individuals improve slightly simply by making a commitment to work with a professional, hope is an active ingredient throughout a coaching engagement. A coach's confidence about her client's ability to change is contagious, even more so when there are significant challenges to confront or when setbacks occur. Research tells us that hope is a cognitive variable with two key elements (Snyder, Michael, & Cheavens, 1999). One element involves the individual's confidence that he can change and the second involves the individual's understanding of how to change. We want our clients to say, "I can imagine being able to change *and* I see what I can do to make it happen."

In his mind, Tom faced an enormous challenge. As an introvert, he relished closing his door, blocking out time on his calendar for careful planning, and exiting meetings once he was at his quota of "people" time. During his rise from systems analyst to IT operations director, this approach served him well. Now as the CIO of a large organization, he learned through his coach's multi-rater interviews that his peers and direct reports criticized him for being an introvert. By closing his door he telegraphed disengagement, by exiting meetings early he conveyed disrespect, and by blocking out so much "planning" time on his calendar he was seen as unavailable. The data startled and discouraged him. He was a private person; was being a senior leader in the organization incompatible with how he was hardwired?

Tom's coach thought they would focus on separating what was hardwired from overt behaviors that Tom could change or control. Tom resisted, saying that the last thing he wanted to be was inauthentic. His dejection was evident; the feedback cut to the heart of who he was. It was at that point that Tom's coach suggested they explore how their perceptions of the issue differed. A critical moment came when Tom realized that he had completely dismissed the notion that his introverted behaviors might be malleable. He fully assumed that introversion was a fixed trait that limited his behavioral flexibility. His coach had a developmental mindset and could point to examples of two other executives in the organization who, while both introverts, were able to express some extroverted behaviors in authentic ways. This activated Tom's hope that he could make the changes others seemed to be asking for without being artificial. By exploring the dynamic tension between their two different views on the issue, Tom's coach was able to activate hope and pave the way for new adaptability.

Here are some principles for activating hope and the expectation of a positive outcome:

- Explore your client's personal beliefs about change—what gives him confidence that he can change and what causes him doubt?
- Don't be shy about describing your capabilities or the changes you have seen individuals make in their lives through coaching. Enhance your credibility through storytelling and references.
- Build the credibility of coaches that your organization uses by describing their capabilities and how they have helped others change.
- Treat hope as a cognitive variable; what are you doing to build your client's confidence and belief in what he or she can do?
- Recognize that you are an agent of hope. Constantly ask yourself whether you believe in your client's ability to change and your own ability to assist. If you lose faith, figure out if you can regain it. If not, terminate the coaching engagement.

Exploring Tools and Techniques in Coaching: A Client Story

This is an ingredient that is central to our work as coaches; every coach has models, tools, and techniques she relies on. Before potential clients sign up for coaching, they also ask us for specifics about how we coach. Coaching is a mysterious process to many so they want to know what they will do, what will happen, and how the process will work. If the only answer a coach can give is, "Trust me, I have helped many senior executives change," there would be few participants in coaching. A coach's ability to describe techniques, processes and tools helps a potential client commit. The same thing is true when an amateur golfer seeks out a golf teacher. "How do you work; what do you believe in; what will we do?" We have to hang our hats somewhere. Review Table 1.1 once again. What do you believe in and how does that affect the tools, techniques, and processes that you use with your clients? As psychotherapy literature points out, a coach's belief in what he uses is more powerful in promoting change than the tools themselves.

Gordon had been an executive coach for ten years, working in the upper echelons of global corporations. His clients described him as highly effective, providing heartfelt testimonials about the impact he had made in their leadership and ultimately in the performance of the business. Through experience, he had adopted his own theory in use, which combined adult learning and behaviorism. He disliked anything that touched on psychodynamics and carefully steered his clients away from trying to figure out "Why am I the way I am?"

That is, until he started coaching Emily, who led the R&D function for a Fortune 100 medical products company. A gifted scientist, Emily had numerous patents to her name and loved encouraging younger scientists in their pursuit of innovative solutions or discoveries. She sought out coaching because she wanted to be a stronger risk taker and a more effective leader of her own team; she was sure she could do more to bring new products more quickly through the pipeline from idea to conclusion. In their initial coaching work, Gordon had Emily define what risk taking meant to her, and they crafted a few behavioral goals that would reflect true progress. To Gordon's surprise, Emily came into the fourth coaching session having read an article about the impact of growing up in highly strict, critical family systems. She insisted that they needed to explore these dynamics because she was convinced that her family history was preventing her from making progress. Gordon stated he was not a therapist and explained the differences between therapy and coaching. Emily persisted, saying that she did not need a therapist; she just needed to have someone listen while she talked through what was holding her back.

Emily was so insistent that Gordon reluctantly followed her lead and engaged in a conversation about Emily's family history. It was a telling conversation. The more Emily reflected on her parents' subtle demands for perfection, criticizing anything that stopped short of excellence, the more she recognized how she held herself back now. For Emily, understanding the origins of her fear of risk taking was key to taking control of the change she wanted to make. Eventually, she and Gordon returned to the behavioral focus they had started with. Gordon's openness and versatility to exploring his client's theory of change allowed real progress to happen; had he persisted with his own allegiance to a purely behavior-focused approach, the relationship would have been damaged.

Theories are critical for us to have, to believe in, and to follow. They inform how we approach coaching, but as we have learned from psychotherapy research, technique does not drive outcome by itself. Plus, rigid adherence to a single approach can damage any of the active ingredients. We need to have an approach and a starting point *yet* be willing to switch gears as needed. That is part of the dance of coaching.

Here are some principles for using theory and technique to promote change:

- Use theory, models, tools, and techniques that you believe in and can deliver with competence and confidence.
- Learn about those theories or models that you know the least about; don't get caught in adhering to a single perspective.
- Use your expertise on leadership and organizations to draw out and deepen the client's own theory of change. The client will ultimately take or not take action based on his own theory.

- Be confident and clear about how you see the coaching process unfolding and what your client can expect over the course of your work together.
- Explore how your and your client's views of the change process match; make sure you are working from the same base of assumptions about the situation and what it will take to change.

Conclusion

We have used this chapter to explore the active ingredients of executive coaching. Coaching, after all, is about individual change. Psychology offers powerful conclusions about how, why, and under what conditions individuals can change. Even though professionals who manage, deliver, or coordinate executive coaching do not need to be trained as psychologists, we believe they do need to embrace and understand the psychology of change that occurs through a one-on-one relationship. None of us is attempting to be a psychotherapist. Yet the field of psychotherapy holds evidence about change that is relevant to our work. The four ingredients contribute mightily to outcomes and it is our job to do all we can to activate them.

As we have shown, theories of change also affect the ability to activate these four ingredients. At every phase of the coaching process, we need to think about the resonance between our theory of the problem and the client's theory of the problem. Where there is resonance and creative tension, there's a good chance of igniting the factors. Without that resonance, the active ingredients will not come to life. The dynamics of coaching require our flexibility, energy, and intentional actions.

We would like to see more research conducted to validate how the active ingredients work in coaching. Further, though our list of theories in action is not exhaustive, it should stimulate more research and exploration of what happens when the coach and the client are either aligned or in conflict over their conclusions about the issues and the solutions.

We would also like to see HR professionals, executive coaches, and managers enlist the power of the active ingredients, as we all can be catalysts to exciting change in our clients. If you are further interested and inspired about the power of the active ingredients, we heartily recommend reading *The Heart and Soul of Change* by

Hubble, Duncan, and Miller (1999). There is treasure to be found in psychology. Let's hope none of us let it stay hidden. We hope that the ideas in this chapter—which have brought us to new levels in the coaching work we do—help you explore your own experiences, theories, and conclusions.

References

Asay, T. P., & Lambert, M. J. (1999). The empirical case for the common factors in therapy: quantitative findings. In M. A. Hubble, B. L. Duncan, & S. D. Miller (Eds.), *The heart & soul of change: What works in therapy* (pp. 33–56). Washington, DC: American Psychological Association.

Bergin, A. E., & Lambert, M. J. (1978). The evaluation of therapeutic outcomes. In S. L. Garfield & A. E. Bergin (Eds.), *Handbook of psychotherapy and behavior change* (2nd ed., pp. 139–189). New York: Wiley.

Berglas, S. (2002). The very real dangers of executive coaching. *Harvard Business Review,* June, 87–92.

Bordin, E. S. (1976). The generalizability of the psychoanalytical concept of the working alliance. *Psychotherapy: Theory, Research, and Practice, 16,* 252–260.

Davis, S. L., & Barnett, R. C. (2009). Changing behavior one leader at a time. In Silzer, R. F. & Dowell, B. E. (Eds.), *Strategy-driven talent management: A leadership imperative* (pp. 349–398). San Francisco: Jossey-Bass.

Hubble, M. A., Duncan, B. L., & Miller, S. D. (Eds.). (1999). *The heart & soul of change: What works in therapy.* Washington, DC: American Psychological Association.

Lambert, M. J. (1992). Implications of outcome research for psychotherapy integration. In J. C. Norcross & M. R. Goldfried (Eds.), *Handbook of psychotherapy integration* (pp. 93–129). New York: Basic Books.

McKenna, D. D., & Davis, S. L. (2009). Hidden in plain sight: The active ingredients of executive coaching. *Industrial and Organizational Psychology: Perspectives on Science and Practice, 2,* 244–260.

Snyder, C. R., Michael, S. T., & Cheavens, J. S. (1999). Hope as a psychotherapeutic foundation of common factors, placebos, and expectancies. In M. A. Hubble, B. L. Duncan, & S. D. Miller (Eds.), *The heart & soul of change: What works in therapy* (pp. 179–200). Washington, DC: American Psychological Association.

Wampold, B. E. (2001). *The great psychotherapy debate: Models, methods, and findings.* Hillsdale, NJ: Erlbaum.

Chapter Two

THE COACH

Ready, Steady, Go!

Brian O. Underhill

The largest corporate contract in executive coaching industry to date was on the line. In 2003, Dell Corporation was seeking to organize its disparate coaching activities into a coordinated effort under one vendor. Dell would offer coaching to its top six hundred executives around the world, with two hundred of them expected to engage a coach in the first year. Any firm lucky enough to earn this business would gain immediate credibility in the executive coaching industry.

Although our coaching firm already contained a decent pool of independent coaches (over five hundred), Dell required coaches in more locations (and some more exotic ones) than we had at the time (such as Panama City, Montpellier, or Porto Alegre). Dell wanted *EVERY* potential coach to complete a three-page application to submit *with our bid*. Coaches had to meet minimum criteria and would be telephone interviewed before a vendor was selected.

And the bid was due in two weeks.

We began a 24/7 flurry of activity to make this deadline. Coaches already in our network were invited to complete the Dell application and return it to us promptly, allowing us time to review, select those who would qualify, and edit the application if needed. Coaches also needed to redo their biographies into a consistent Dell format (which is a bigger project than it might seem—executive coaches are not generally known for their diligence in completing forms!).

Meanwhile, we had to rapidly mount a campaign to locate more coaches in various parts of the world. We put the word out to our more than five hundred coaches where we were looking for talent, knowing they would forward our request on to their networks. Within days, applications were flooding our offices. We had to screen these coaches in much greater detail (as we did not already know them previously). Because each was interviewed by telephone, we had to use everything we'd learned about screening coaches to quickly select only the right options for Dell. If we included them in our bid, we had to be absolutely comfortable in how they would represent us.

In the end, we were awarded the contract, which continues to this day. Though we already knew how to source and screen coaches, this experience brought that capability to an entirely new level of intensity.

Today we have a network of over 720 vetted coaches in thirty-nine countries. I have personally met with at least half of them face-to-face (which, jokingly, means I've seen the inside of more Starbucks than I can count). This, combined with our corporate research on coach sourcing and screening, enables us to be quite well versed on how to do this right.

This chapter will take a look at how coaches are sourced and screened. We will also talk about how organizations can build the capabilities of their coaching pools once established.

Sourcing Coaches

Recently (out of sheer curiosity) I spent several weeks searching for coaches on the Internet, particularly on YouTube. What I found was so humorous I felt compelled to compile a video of the findings to parade about in my public presentations. The audience is laughing heavily while watching "coaches" of all kinds (such as mortgage coaches, writing coaches, life coaches, even a divorce coach), some doing some incredible antics—presenting from the shower, while driving, or just trying to appear professional wearing a suit in their own kitchen. My recommendation is *not* to search for a coach this way!

Where (instead) do organizations go to find coaches in the first place? Do they search the Web, inquire with their current networks, or work with their existing vendors? How do they find coaches in those emerging markets, such as India, China, or Brazil?

Perhaps not surprisingly, the organizations we interviewed via our research told us finding coaches is generally not too difficult most of the time; there are plenty of coaches available—but always finding *good* coaches is another story. Those responsible for managing coaching inside large organizations report a regular influx of inquiries from potential coaches, especially in the United States and Western Europe.

We conducted a thorough research study into the executive coaching industry in 2005, examining it from a three-dimensional perspective: organizations, coaches, and executives themselves. Many name-brand Fortune 500 companies participated in the research, which included in depth interviews, Web surveys, and detailed case studies of four organization coaching practices. The full research is contained in *Executive Coaching for Results: The Definitive Guide to Developing Organizational Leaders* (Underhill, McAnally, & Koriath, 2007).

This research found most organizations rely on "warm recommendations" for new coaches from those they trust. Nearly 80 percent of organizations find coaches through their current vendors, and 55 percent rely on recommendations from other organizations (see Figure 2.1).

The "unsolicited" methods, such as the coach directly contacting executives or the organization coaching managers were less likely (between 35 percent and 27 percent of organizations selected this). Only 2 percent of organizations reported using the Web to find coaches.

As Figure 2.1 shows, coaches had differing views of how they were found, underrating the importance of the coaching vendors and overrating their success in contacting executives or coaching managers directly. Coaches also overrated the importance of being located via their Web sites.

We recommend that corporations look to vendors they know for sourcing coaches (not just coaching vendors but all types of

Figure 2.1. How Do Organizations Find Coaches?

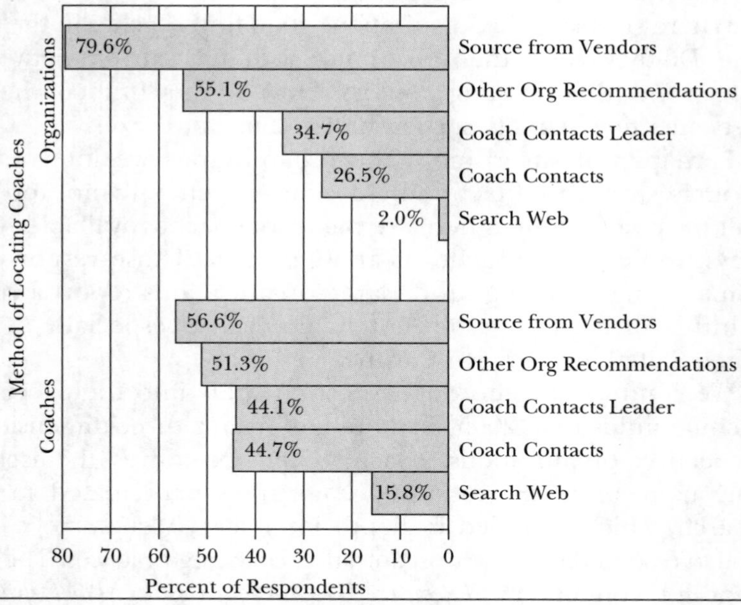

Source: *Executive Coaching for Results: The Definitive Guide to Developing Organizational Leaders* (Underhill, McAnally, & Koriath, 2007).

vendors, such as training, organization development, or leadership development firms). Those companies that are already trusted partners to the organization may be in the best position to make coach referrals. Querying the current coaching network will also yield additional talent, as coaches often know each other well. We've even seen organizations team up to share coach talent (they figure if a given coach is earning high marks at one firm, he'll probably do the same at another). Using networks to locate coaches is a good practice.

Global Sourcing

Sourcing quality coaches remains a particular difficulty, however, in some parts of the world. India and China remain the greatest challenges for most multinationals in locating coaches. The need is predicted to expand greatly in these countries, yet the number of coaches on the ground is still insufficient. Quality coaches in these countries are quite busy and can therefore command higher fees. It is anticipated that the industry will grow in these emerging markets as many local companies have not yet adopted coaching as the multinationals have done. Local coaches tell us it is only a matter of time before this happens, and the industry will grow yet again.

Brazil and Eastern Europe are other difficult locations to find coaches (though demand is not as strong). Quality executive coaches are virtually nonexistent in most parts of Africa (save South Africa), sections of Latin America, and much of the Middle East (save Turkey and Israel).

For years, Japan was a distinctly challenging place to find coaches. This is likely due to an underdeveloped mental health industry and a fear among Japanese executives that engaging a coach demonstrated managerial weakness. This perception is changing, especially among the multinationals, as coaching has gained credibility and the number of quality coaches is increasing.

Organizations are advised to tap into networks with vast international reach, such as for-profit coaching firms or nonprofit professional organizations (such as International Coach Federation) to locate coaches in locales where they are hard to find. We also suggest leaning more on virtual coaching (telephone or video-chat) and perhaps bringing a coach in from a more populous area on occasion. Again, peers in other organizations may have found good coaching resources in some of these distant locations as well.

Multiple Coaches Versus Single Vendor

As the Dell example highlighted, a trend in recent years is for corporations to consolidate coaching activities under a single vendor (or small number of vendors) in order to simplify management, restrain costs, and maintain one point of billing contact. Without this, some multinationals we know would have to establish individual contracts with each of their fifty to two hundred coaches, in all parts of the world, which can be a logistical nightmare. The single vendor solution can be preferable in locating coaches in far regions, screening those coaches, and then managing their activities as a coordinated whole.

The benefits can be substantial, in that there is now a known standard of coach quality, a relatively predictable coaching process, and aggregated activity reports from across the enterprise. The single vendor can gather coaches for company-wide calls and gatherings for mutual learning. The management activities of the single vendor save the corporation from hiring additional staff just to oversee all the coaching-related logistics.

Some organizations do not opt for the single-vendor solution. Those with fewer coaches in their pools may not need this management benefit, nor do those with limited operations outside a certain geographical region. In particular, decentralized organizations find it difficult to control which coaches are working with them anyway, such that moving to a single source could cause problems with some of their own business units. And locking in with one coaching provider may limit the pool of potential coaches only to those on the provider's payroll.

One organization we know purposely does not want any one vendor to overpower their coaching pool, thus they choose to establish individual contracts with each of their coaches and vendors separately. This serves to maintain some level of healthy competition, which may benefit the firm in enhanced services or contained costs. Yet another organization does not have the internal staffing to manage a large external network, thus finds great value in outsourcing management of coaching to a single-source provider.

Internal/External Coaches

A growing trend in recent years is to offer coaching via internal organizational resources (often HR, leadership development, or OD staff serving as coaches). In so doing, the organization can better utilize the talent it already has while containing costs. In our research, 57 percent of organizations planned to increase their use of internal coaches, another 40 percent planned to maintain their current use (although none of the organizations were using internals with C-level executives, rather for those at levels below, especially nonexecutive ranks). In our research 59 percent of the executives we met said they would prefer an external coach, 12 percent preferred an internal, and 29 percent did not have a preference, perhaps a reflection that internal coaching is not without its concerns.

The benefits are that internals know their organization's culture well. Internals are already in house: they can have better scheduling flexibility with leaders and observe them more regularly in action. And obviously, an internal can offer coaching at a much better rate than externals can. A few organizations we know will only use internal talent because they feel their culture is too unique for externals to navigate.

The drawbacks are that internals can be perceived as a less safe and confidential haven for conversation by leaders. Internals may not be seen with the same credibility as their external peers. And, surprisingly, our research found that internals' greatest challenge is they simply do not have enough time to both coach and maintain their day jobs at the same time.

Screening Coaches

Though organizations report it relatively easy to find coaches in many locations, screening these same coaches can be a particular challenge. What background should coaches have? How long should they have been coaching? Which instruments should they be versed in? Should they be certified? How does one know if they are good at coaching? These questions become more complicated because executive coaches often hail from varied backgrounds. One profile does not fit all for a strong executive coach.

As varied as coach backgrounds may be, many organizations are honing in on similar criteria for what they look for in their coaches. Our research has supported these criteria. These tend to be, in order of importance (from the organizational perspective, see Figure 2.2):

- Business experience (81 percent selected as important)
- Match with organization culture (79 percent)
- Industry experience (43 percent)
- Advanced degree (41 percent)
- Cost (41 percent)
- Certification (24 percent)

Figure 2.2. Selection Criteria for Choosing Coaches

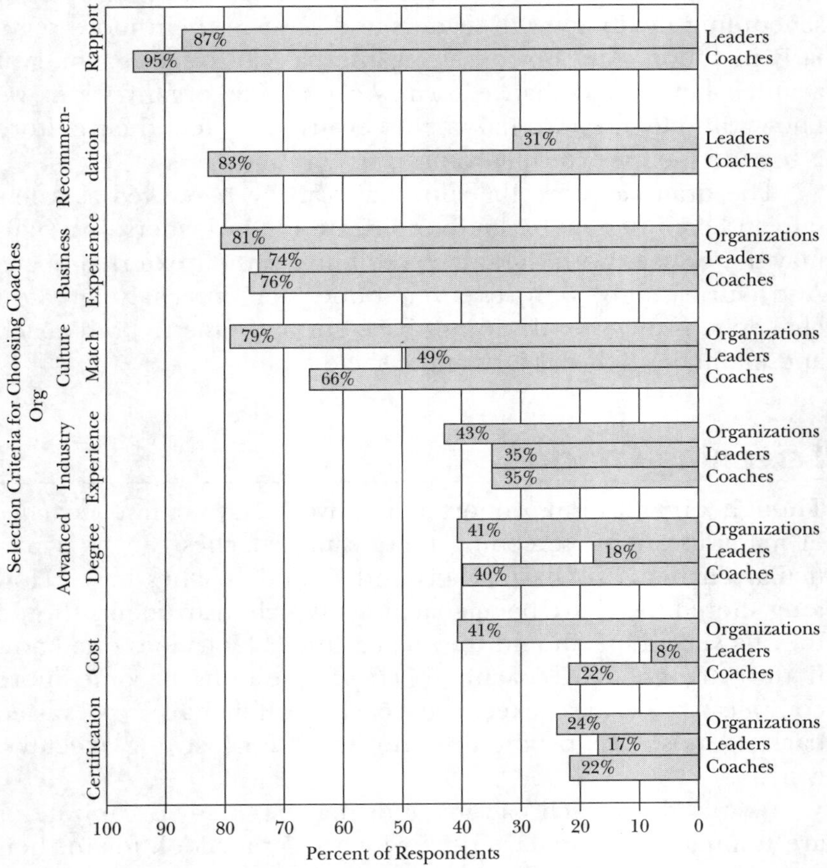

Interestingly, the executives we surveyed did not rate these factors with the same level of importance as did organizations. Executives selected business experience (81 percent) as most important. However, there is then a large dropoff before the next highest choice (match with organization culture—49 percent). Industry experience (35 percent), advanced degree (18 percent), and certification (17 percent) all received far fewer votes. Also of importance is the coach's ability to build rapport (87 percent) and recommendation from a colleague

(31 percent)—though organizations surveyed were not asked about these criteria.

Perhaps surprisingly, executives selected cost as *least important* at 6 percent (even though half of them were paying from their *own* budgets). Contrast this to the 41 percent of organizations that selected this option. One enterprising coach in a public presentation of these data pointed out that his new strategy would be to "smile more and charge twice as much"!

Coaches also answered these same questions as well. They concur that the most important criteria is ability to build rapport (95 percent selected this!). Beyond this, coaches believe being recommended from a colleague to be next most important (83 percent), followed by business experience (76 percent). Organization culture match (66 percent), industry experience (35 percent), advanced degree (40 percent), cost (22 percent), and certification (22 percent) rounded out the list.

In light of these findings, we now screen for *business experience* and *ability to build rapport* with greater intensity. Business experience is not necessarily a coach with C-level profit-and-loss responsibility (though that is a great plus), but that a coach has been in the business world such that he or she speaks the language of business. An executive needs to feel that the coach can relate to what he or she is facing in the business world. In evaluating this experience, we will often assign a score, with a "3" equating to line management P&L responsibility in a large organization, "2" for a staff role in these organizations, and "1" for those who have consulted to such organizations from the outside.

Ability to build rapport isn't as quantitatively easy to measure, but we gather plenty of intuitive data via our interactions with coaches. After years of screening, this can be sized up quite quickly: most coaches by their very nature are naturally skilled in building rapport, and it is easy to see. But if a coach has difficulty building rapport with us (for example, seems standoffish, conceited, or even nervous), we anticipate he will have much more difficulty with a senior executive of a major corporation. We would think twice before engaging the coach in a live assignment. (One coach made the poor decision of mistreating our administrative staff repeatedly, which was enough data to eliminate her from further consideration.)

Certification—Does It Matter?

An ongoing movement in the coaching industry is toward "certification" of executive coaches. Various organizations have tried to take the lead in being the official certifying body of the executive coaching field. At this point it still is not clear that there will be a definitive authority on this anytime soon. Nor is it clear that there will ever be a mandate or government requirement for certification in the future (fewer than a third of organizations predict mandatory certification in the future).

As the research depicts, certification was a relatively unimportant criteria from all rater groups (no group scored it above 24 percent). Six percent of organizations we met use only certified coaches and just 29 percent would be more likely to use a certified coach. Most leaders (63 percent) did not know whether their coaches held certification. Sixty-two percent of the coaches surveyed in our research were not certified.

The notion of certification is really about whether or not a coach is *qualified* to do the job, and not necessarily that she has accomplished certain certification requirements. Because so many people call themselves "coaches," buyers are looking for a guarantee that a coach is actually qualified to do the work. However, we have found screening for the other criteria aforementioned generally suitable enough to make this determination.

In my experience in screening hundreds of coaches, those with plentiful certifications (and lots of initials after their names) need additional screening: these coaches often don't have suitable business experience or an advanced degree (such as MBA, MA, MS, or PhD). Also of concern, certification programs often teach a "passive/no agenda" approach to coaching, where the coach is not encouraged to offer advice based on his or her experience. We've found this style to be less favored by corporate executives, who would like coaches to offer suggestions and advice as part of the coaching experience.

Methods of Coach Screening

As the criteria are clearer for selecting coaches, the process for screening coaches for these criteria has some variability, as we will see. This can range from no screening to a multistep, several-day process. Many organizations will use some of the following methods in screening potential coaches:

- *Vendor Screening.* Some organizations trust their vendors to screen coaches for them, knowing that only properly qualified coaches will be permitted to work at the organization site. These organizations don't really do any formal screening themselves, but do assume their vendors are amply experienced to make the selection decisions.
- *Application.* More developed coaching programs now require coaches to complete in-depth applications asking about the various criteria of interest. We no longer meet with a potential coach without an application in hand. This ensures that we have all the information we need up front. Coaches who do not meet minimum qualifications will generally not apply, thus saving us valuable time in not screening under-qualified coaches. For a sample application, many corporations may be willing to share their application form; we offer ours for free use at our Web site.
- *Interview.* Often conducted via telephone or in person. A recent American Management Association (AMA) study found an actual interview with potential coaches to be correlated with a successful coaching program. In screening coaches internationally, I cannot meet every coach in person, but I do require all virtual interviews to be done via videochat technology (such as Skype or iChat). This additional data point further assists the assessment of "ability to build rapport."
- *Reference Check.* Who are the executives the coach has worked with, and what do they have to say about the coach? Many organizations ask for references and check up on them. Organizations can also inquire with other local coaches near the applicant for any additional insights. Often coaches in emerging markets know and have worked with each other. We will usually call our local coaches "on the ground" to learn about applicant coaches.
- *Coaching Fishbowl.* At least one organization (Unilever) brings potential coaches in for a day-long assessment process, which includes coaching in a fishbowl type environment. In addition,

the assessors include Unilever line executives who are trained in assessing coach talent. Through this process, Unilever met sixty-nine coaches and invited only twenty-eight to remain in their pool. Departing coaches were provided feedback to assist them in their future growth.

- *Trial Assignment Period.* Some organizations will allow new coaches to begin working in lower-profile assignments and promote them after collecting satisfaction and effectiveness data. We routinely collect data on every coach working on our behalf, allowing us to determine if we could move the coach onwards to assignments of greater and greater visibility. American Express now uses "coach divorce" process, by which a leader can ask for a new coach within seven days of their first meeting.

What Coaches Look For

Organizations are not the only ones screening—coaches are screening the organizations as well! The busiest coaches, including those in emerging markets, can afford to be choosy in who they are going to work with. Perhaps not surprisingly, the fees that organizations pay are not necessarily the primary driver in whether or not coaches will want to work with those organizations.

We've seen over the years a complex milieu of criteria that coaches will use in determining whether or not they will take on a given assignment. Some of these factors will include:

- *Executive.* What level of leader is this? What is this leader's functional area? Is this leader a high performer or a performance problem? What is the chemistry like with the executive? Is she willing to engage in coaching?
- *Company.* Is this an organization that adds value to the résumé? For example, many of the coaches referenced in the Dell example agreed to work at below-market rates in exchange for the Dell name on their bios. What industry is the company in? How much travel is involved? What are the fees?
- *Coach.* How busy is the coach currently? Does he want to travel for this leader? Does he feel a "prior obligation" to this client due to their history together?

After watching premium CEO-level coaches accept non-profit coaching with no remuneration, and "middle of the road" coaches take underpaying work in exchange for coaching in exotic locales, we've learned cost is not a primary driver of coach decision making. Coaches will rate these other factors often more significantly than the pay.

Building Coaches

Creating a viable coaching pool does not end after screening for the right coaches. There is now an invaluable opportunity to grow this community, while learning from them at the same time. Most organizations miss this excellent, yet quite inexpensive, opportunity (we found that only 54 percent of organizations hosted any regular interaction with their coaches after their programs were under way).

Most external executive coaches work independently or in small networks, and thus greatly welcome the opportunity for meaningful interaction with other professionals. Many coaches, especially those who are former corporate staffers, find the external consulting world somewhat isolating. They long for collegial interaction, as evidenced by the preponderance of informal coaching networks springing up worldwide.

Building the coaching pool includes regular community conference calls, Webinars, and even hosting a several-day forum at company headquarters. During these gatherings, the organization can share quarterly financial updates as well as the latest news and any pertinent structural changes. Executives make guest appearances to describe the parts of the business they manage. Coaches can learn from each other via best-practice or case-study sessions. The organization can learn of the trends coaches are observing with their executives.

Organizations with vibrant coaching practices will generally host a community-building event on a regular basis, perhaps quarterly. Internal coaches, if applicable, can also be included in these sessions. Intel Corporation operates an extensive internal and external coaching pool and includes both in their network gatherings.

Microsoft recently hosted a two-and-a-half-day coaching forum at their headquarters in Redmond, Washington. The first full day included presentations by Microsoft executives. Coaches then engaged in roundtable discussions, followed by a unique evening at the Seattle Space Needle. In the second day, coaches and Microsoft HR spent time in dialogue and several executive coaching thought leaders presented. The day wrapped up with a memorable tour of the exclusive Home/Office of the Future demo, followed by a visit and (much-appreciated) discounts to the company store.

Although coaches were paid a small stipend, and their expenses were covered once they arrived, they were not compensated otherwise (not for travel or professional fees). Yet 70 percent of the pool attended, traveling from as far away as China, Ireland, England, Peru, and Australia. Feedback was incredibly positive, with coaches constantly inquiring as to when the next forum would be held. Despite the relatively significant cost of the event to the company, the mutual learning and goodwill it generated made it worthwhile.

Very few organizations invest in their pools to the extent as described above, and by not doing so, they miss a great opportunity to further a coaching practice in many ways.

Conclusion

With all this focus on "Who is the coach?" and "Is he any good?" we often lose sight of the real goal: to see long-term change in executive leadership behavior. A Marshall Goldsmith study of 86,000 respondents found that the leader following up with key stakeholders regularly was more important for leadership improvement than whether the executive had an external coach, internal coach, or no coach. In other words, *executive effort was more important than the qualifications of the coach.*

One company in our research said it well: "Let's measure the executives, not the coaches." If an executive is not willing to change, even a divine being himself would not succeed as a coach with the individual (and he'd probably be smart enough to walk away before wasting too much time!). Effective improvement lies with the leader, not with the coach. It is not possible to change the behavior of an adult who does not wish to change.

To this end, we advise organizations to put all the effort into sourcing and screening the best coaches that they can find and to build their community of coaches. At that point, allow the executives to make the selection: to choose a coach that he or she can not only relate to, but who will challenge him or her as well. This chemistry can't be prescribed, but we can do everything possible to set it up for success in the first place (we've found a great decrease in coach mismatches when the executive makes the choice).

But after that, make sure executives know they own their improvement; it is not upon the organization or the coach at that point to bring about the improvement—it is upon them and them alone.

Reference

Underhill, B. O., McAnally, K., & Koriath, J. J. (2007). *Executive coaching for results: The definitive guide to developing organizational leaders*. San Francisco: Berrett-Koehler.

Chapter Three

LEARNING TO COACH LEADERS

Robert J. Lee and Michael H. Frisch

Introduction

Executive coaching—the professional practice of coaching leaders—is one of the consulting world's significant success stories. Emerging in the 1980s, executive coaching channeled the prevailing Zeitgeist by melding individual growth initiatives, leadership theories, and the use of outside consultants into a rapidly expanding practice area. Initially performance problem driven, coaching has shed any perceived stigma, which has been largely replaced by an aura of perquisite and potential, further stoking its growth. Those of us with a significant track record of offering

Note: We would like to acknowledge that the content of this chapter relies on collaboration with our iCoachNewYork colleagues: Karen Metzger, Jeremy Robinson, and Judy Rosemarin. The double-loop process of delivery, discussion, and revision, aimed at improving our coach training programs since 2004, could not happen without them and is the source material for much if not all of this chapter. In addition, in the iCoachNewYork office, we benefited from the technical and editorial contributions of Barbara Christian. We would also like to acknowledge the continuing support of the Zicklin Business School of Baruch College, CUNY, and in particular the Management Department where our certificate course resides. Finally, we owe an enormous debt to the participants in our courses and our network of coaching case sponsors, all of whom encourage and challenge us to raise the bar on coach training.

coaching to our corporate and organizational clients have discovered that providing tailored, just-in-time development to busy leaders one by one is both possible and gratifying. These powerful drivers have pushed executive coaching to be the dynamic and pervasive practice that it is today.

This chapter captures our experiences in helping people learn to coach leaders. Those experiences are anchored in our reflections about the coaching services we provide but strongly influenced by our students' reactions to what we teach. Their questions, insights, frustrations, and successes have been folded back into the *how* and *what* of our courses. We believe that this feedback brings greater overlap between what we intend to teach and what they actually learn, but it will never be perfect. Just as in coaching, we are often surprised by what becomes most pivotal in others' learning. So this chapter is about both how we teach and what our students have told us has greatest impact on their emerging coaching skills.

It has been said that leadership cannot be taught, but it can be learned. Perhaps that same principle applies to learning how to coach leaders. In that spirit, this chapter will highlight key issues and important distinctions that coaches should consider, combined with teaching methods that engage the learner as an equal partner in the process. However, what we or others teach in the many courses on coaching is not the same as what coaches need to learn. We encourage active choice in what is useful for each coach because that resonance is a key principle of both our teaching and our coaching. By extension, a necessary challenge of learning to coach leaders is in shaping a personal approach to coaching. Both leadership and coaching require a tailored clarity about how one aspires to perform in those roles; thus, the learning needs to be similarly active.

Leading others is one of the most complex human endeavors. Coaches of leaders do not need to be great leaders themselves. Successfully entering the field of coaching does have certain prerequisite skills and characteristics, but leadership is not one of them. In fact, coaches have chosen to work one to one—a structure that does not draw upon traditional leadership competencies. Even so, coaches of leaders do need to understand the demands of being a leader in today's organizations. Though this is challenging, we have repeatedly witnessed coaches who do not possess leadership experience absorbing leadership vocabulary, appreciating organizational challenges, refining their grasp of leadership options, and most important, growing more confident about coaching leaders. Initially, they strive to assemble the external building blocks of leadership coaching, including principles, practices, and processes. At some point, however, if they are truly to stand on their own as leadership coaches, the learning challenge shifts internally, toward articulating an individualized approach that fits their values, beliefs, style, and motivation. We foster that transition and celebrate it as it happens, but it is not possible to describe it with certainty for every coach.

This chapter details our view of the essential elements enabling that transition, both pedagogical and personal. As such, the plan of the chapter is to describe *how* we teach coaching, highlight the core content of *what* we teach, and set expectations for what coaches need to ponder and resolve. Obviously, this chapter cannot fully replicate attending a course on coaching, but we aim to summarize the essential elements of that experience.

Toward a Definition of Leadership Coaching

There is no single definition of leadership coaching, nor should there be. However, clients and stakeholders often ask coaches to describe coaching, so defining it should be carefully considered. Coaches need to articulate their own definition of coaching, realizing it can evolve over time. Reviewing published definitions can be useful in considering how to describe coaching. These definitions often reflect particular *theoretical lenses* of practitioners and can be counterpoints to a coach's own ideas. Other variables may include the relative emphasis of personal versus professional growth, how much leadership *content* to include in the coaching, and clients' field or organizational level. The process of shaping one's own focal points in leadership coaching, whether similar to or different from well-known practitioners, has both profound and practical value in learning and delivering coaching.

The practical definition that guides both our own coaching and our teaching is that leadership coaching is an employer-sponsored, approximately six-month relationship between a coach and a leader in an organizational context aimed at enhancing or improving some combination of the leader's current performance, future development, or transition to a new role. It's not easy to set boundaries on the goals of leadership coaching, but broadly, those goals aim to strengthen a leader's self-management, interpersonal effectiveness, or leadership impact. When relevant, we do subsume under the leadership umbrella such traditional managerial skills as contracting for performance, delegating, and providing feedback. Case-specific coaching goals are always customized to the client; examples include being a stronger team leader, influencing in complex systems, clarifying vision and goals, taking on larger or global responsibilities, managing multilayer execution, or other aspirations tied to a leader's unique challenges.

In definitions of leadership coaching, the word *client* is particularly important. For some coaches, the *client* is the organization. For others, the *client* designation is shared between the organization and the person in the coaching relationship. In our practices and courses, we use the word *client* to refer to the person partnered with the coach. We view this as the primary relationship in leadership coaching rather than the relationship with the organization or its representatives (for example, the boss or the HR partner), whom we refer to as *sponsors* or *stakeholders*. Some might view this as merely a semantic distinction, but it is important for coaches to think through this issue for themselves. Where they stand on it shows in their coaching in important ways, such as in confidentiality, goal setting, and stakeholder involvement. In order to be clear and consistent in this chapter, we use the word *client* to refer to the person seeking growth through a relationship with a coach.

Some leadership coaches bridge their work into the "content" areas of executive roles, such as business strategy, integration of acquisitions, or talent management processes, for example. This is often the case with consultants, human resource professionals, and organizational psychologists who have added coaching to their practices. As organizational psychologists ourselves, we have found that though coaching and consulting can be synergistic, the activities are quite different. For us, coaching leverages the relationship with the client within a process that fosters self-discovery, whereas consulting brings particular content expertise to the foreground in making recommendations and solving problems. As such, our coaching is more aligned with organizational development values, emphasizing the process of discovering client-specific answers and empowering their application rather than prescribing solutions (O'Neill, 2007; Whitmore, 2002).

For those leadership coaches who also consult, our opinion is that these two activities need a bright-line separation if client confusion is to be avoided and coaches are to stretch and build their coaching skills. Said differently, coaches who also consult need to be clear with themselves and their clients about what *hat* they are wearing in every engagement, use different processes within those roles, and be willing to reaffirm roles and goals if within-engagement slippage occurs. Coaches need to actively choose their coaching-consulting balance; otherwise, clients will draw them into a consultative relationship by default.

Pedagogy: How We Teach What We Teach

It is possible to be a self-taught leadership coach (that's how some of us began doing it in the first place!), but that is not an efficient or comprehensive learning method. Like most coach training programs, ours uses a combination of methods, such as class instruction, textbook and journal reading, group discussions, role plays, case studies, and demonstrations. Various considerations go into instructional design decisions, such as: skill versus conceptual learning goals, broad versus deep topical treatments, behavioral models, class cohesion, and peer learning, as well as more mundane constraints of tolerance of sitting and time available for a topic. This chapter, however, is not about instructional design. Instead, we would like to highlight two key synergistic elements of our coach training: (1) each student's personal model of coaching and (2) case experience combined with supervision.

1. Personal Model of Coaching

A cornerstone of our coach training is each student's creation of a personal model, which links with a coach's definition of leadership coaching as well as other aspects of a coach's approach. The idea of creating a personal model of coaching rests on one of our core beliefs: *that there is no one best way to coach* and that learning to coach therefore must be an active process of creating, not just absorbing. A personal model attempts to describe what the coach is trying to do with clients, how the coach thinks coaching works, and what the coach brings as a human being and as a professional. Clients cannot be expected to know what coaching is, and they certainly cannot know what any particular coach has in mind as the engagement begins. It is the coach's responsibility to explain his or her approach and how it might fit into the client's experience in other helping and consulting relationships. Coaches are much more effective at doing this when they have previously articulated their own personal models of coaching. Personal models prompt coaches to consider various questions:

- What personal characteristics, education, and experience do I bring to coaching?
- How well do I navigate organizational dynamics and stakeholders?
- What is my range in terms of coaching methods and issues?
- Where do I want the focus of my practice to be? What are my strengths, preferences, and limitations as a coach?
- With what types of people and organizations can I be most effective?

As shown in Figure 3.1, we organize these important questions under three categories, which we call *inputs* to personal models. The first input category is *who the coach is as a person*. It is important to identify and acknowledge personal characteristics that may have an impact on one's coaching approach, such as life experiences, values, education, formative career events, interpersonal style, interests, skills, and gaps. Although this is potentially autobiographical, not everything about oneself will influence one's approach to coaching and it is worth the effort to identify those elements that are connected.

The second input category focuses on *thoughts and feelings about working within an organizational context*. Coaches need to consider their own experiences in organizations, including reactions to authority and structure, dealings with staff groups and stakeholders, connections between client development and organizational objectives, and responses to organizational culture variables. This

Figure 3.1. Personal Model of Coaching

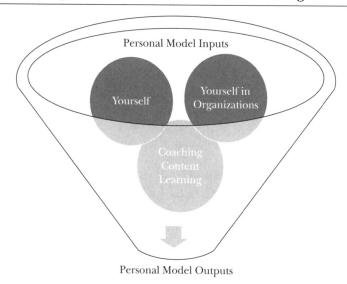

Coaching Approach	Practice Plan	Development Plan
• Signature presence • Boundaries • Stakeholder involvement • Coaching process • Assessment methods • Dialogue methods • Development planning • Evaluation	• Types of coaching services • Time available for coaching • Promotion of coaching services • Cross-selling	• Client challenges • Personal growth • Theories and concepts to explore • Models, approaches, and techniques of interest

also includes a coach's views on leaders and leadership. What is effective leadership? How should leaders exercise authority, form alliances, build teams, encourage diversity in thought as well as in staff, confront conflict, provide feedback and encouragement? The more a coach is a thoughtful student of organizational structure, dynamics, and leadership, the better he or she will be able to work with a real-life organizational leader who is now a client.

The third input category to personal models prompts coaches to consider their *preferences about coaching practices, theoretical underpinnings, emerging coaching topics, research questions, and other content areas*. In particular, this input asks coaches to reflect on approaches to adult learning and growth: What are the coach's leanings toward, and away from, various theories of adult change and their respective techniques? Some coaches are attracted to cognitive or behavioral approaches, others to motivational, life stage, humanistic, or systems approaches. Each of us has our theories of change, however formal or informal they may be, and they need to be brought to a conscious level by coaches.

Working through each of the three input categories to a personal model of coaching sets the stage for articulating three *outputs*. The first output is the broadest and taps insights and inclinations from the input categories, weaving them into a *description of a coach's approach to actually delivering coaching*. This empowers coaches to articulate a definition of coaching that suits them and to be able to answer the predictable question, "What's your approach to coaching?" More important, it asks coaches to describe their coaching processes, stakeholder inclusion, practice boundaries, presence, and other factors that define themselves in their coaching roles, which they can draw on as needed in discussions with clients and sponsors.

The second output asks coaches to plan the conduct of their coaching businesses and their efforts to secure more coaching work. We call this output a coaching *practice plan*. While some elements of this plan may be tactical, such as choosing a legal structure and marketing channels, other aspects tie conceptually to broader topics, such as one's identity in professional associations and collegial affiliations that may be beneficial.

The third output requires coaches to reflect on themselves, what they know about coaching, and their practice objectives to create a *development action plan* for their professional growth. This is practical, since there are always aspects of a complex field that we want to learn. It is also a leveling factor, to remind us that we are essentially no different from our clients in needing to address the constant challenge of growth.

The overall image of a personal model can be likened to an iceberg: some aspects are visible to clients, such as the outputs, but a lot of it is under the surface and out of sight. However, the visible parts cannot exist without the underpinnings, and together they make up a unified whole. Carrying the analogy further, the visible parts are likely to be more readily modified by external conditions and those changes need to be acknowledged so that the visible contours can be redrawn. Although the inputs to a personal model may not change much (although reflection does stimulate clearer self-observations and new insights), the outputs are intended to be works in progress that benefit from adjustment and updating. As you go through this chapter, you may wish to make notes about your own personal model, both inputs and outputs.

2. Case Experience and Supervision

Another core belief that guides both our coaching and our teaching is that *coaching is a whole-person activity*—it is cognitive, emotional, and behavioral, and it reflects who we are as individuals. In order to engage the whole person, one of the hallmarks of our teaching is that actually doing coaching and reflecting about it must be a significant part of the learning. This is not a deep insight, but in the world of workbooks, online tutorials, and Webinars, this hands-on requirement may present a distinct challenge. It certainly makes coach training more labor intensive for instructors and less conveniently packaged. More importantly, it requires students to open themselves up to close scrutiny: they will *walk the talk* about development. Just as clients do, coaches need to experience the struggle to leverage strengths and close gaps based on their actual coaching work.

We draw on the time-tested but simply structured apprenticeship model used for counseling and clinical skills training: case work done under the close supervision of an experienced practitioner. As faculty in our courses, we also serve in a case supervisor role so that we see students both in class and in individual meetings about their case experiences. In effect, we are coaching the student coaches about current cases that they are handling. We have no direct contact with their clients, although we secure pro bono cases from a network of sponsoring organizations so that students have no prior relationships with clients.

The coaching is designed to be as true to actual paid coaching as possible, although clients have volunteered to participate knowing that their coach is in a coaching course. Engaging the client and conducting the case toward a valuable outcome is the coach's responsibility, with the supervisor off-stage to support both case progress and coach learning.

The frequency and length of supervisory meetings that are needed to achieve necessary learning could be an interesting research question, but weekly meetings appear to work well to allow close observation of decisions about the unfolding case. Benefit to the client is obviously one objective, but there is an even greater focus on the coach's learning. Supervisors are therefore empowered to step off the immediate path of case progress to delve into the student's assumptions, struggles, anxieties, frustrations, and other reactions to the client and the coaching work. Just as in coaching, the supervisory relationship is aimed at important self-insight and integration of learning, which at times can be humbling and disconcerting, as well as freeing and uplifting. It channels the whole-person aspect of coaching into a *learn by doing* model, but it is personally challenging and requires a significant time commitment from both students and faculty. It is also an essential complement to the creation of each student's personal model of coaching.

Coaching Competencies

As mentioned earlier, people who become leadership coaches do not need to have experience as organizational leaders. Most have been in the helping, consulting, or human resource professions. Experience in formal leadership roles can be very useful, especially as a credibility boost when clients are interviewing prospective coaches, but it is not necessary in learning to become an effective coach to leaders. In fact, coaches who do have significant leadership experience risk over-relying on it in coaching and inadvertently shifting into consulting.

Although leadership experience is not required, there are many competencies and character traits that are legitimately important to assess before embarking on a journey to become a leadership coach and to continue to develop along the way. Most are well known and documented (de Haan & Burger, 2005; Valerio & Lee, 2005; White, 2006), including strong listening and communication skills, self-awareness and emotional intelligence, a helping orientation that balances empathy and challenge, and inner satisfaction from partnering with clients without needing much overt acknowledgment.

In our experience as instructors of coaches, we have observed additional dimensions that do not typically appear in lists of coaching competencies but that make noticeable differences in coaching effectiveness. Our view is that these can be honed and improved over time but that possessing more of them initially is an asset to both learning and delivering coaching. On the other hand, no one will have equally strong abilities in all of them. Insight about which ones come more naturally and which require more effort may have implications for personal model outputs in terms of coaching approach, practice model, and development planning as a coach.

The first of these additional coaching competencies is *optimism about human development.* Clients face many challenges, some of which are contextual and outside of their direct control. Effective coaches tend to see new options and ways to move that are actively hopeful, even with no guarantees of success. Clients may be overwhelmed and pessimistic, but coaches need to offer a genuine counterbalance, encouraging useful action while avoiding empty cheerleading. In extreme situations, there may be a temptation to join the client in a victim mind-set, but optimistic coaches empower clients even in the face of few degrees of freedom.

Second, many of our students come to us with a business or organizational background; others come from the helping professions and may not have had that experience. Both groups, however, need to possess *open interest about organizational life and how things are accomplished in complex systems.* This also ties into being a student of leadership and being able to grasp the importance of organizational objectives, whether financial or mission-driven. Leadership coaches do not need an MBA, but they do benefit from an enduring curiosity about both the organizational whole and its parts.

Third, during our years of teaching coaching we have increasingly emphasized the importance of *use of self* in coaching. This concept is actually broader than it may appear (Frisch, 2008), but it is always based on the coach reflecting on and selectively using his or her personal observations of and reactions to the client. While use of self can be consciously improved upon, those coaches who bring both attunement to others and the courage to use it appear to have a talent that serves them well in coaching.

Complementary with use of self is a fourth competency that we have observed, which is deceptive in its simplicity: *the willingness to ask for help.* Coaching, by its one-to-one nature, tends to isolate us from other practitioners. Only coaches themselves can sense their own need for collegial dialogue, new perspectives, or direct help in dealing with a challenging client or situation. In addition to sensing the need and being willing to ask for help, coaches also must be open and nondefensive in response to a helper's questions and observations. Part of why we include case reviews and supervision in our coach training is to model acceptance of the ongoing need for collegial help in being an effective, balanced coach.

Sometimes we are asked pointedly about what are the essential make-or-break prerequisites to consider before starting on a path to doing leadership coaching. With our coaching values in mind, it is difficult to isolate any factors not amenable to change, given enough time, energy, and support. However, the coaching competency that we have seen as most challenging to change involves *self-management.* Those who have difficulty maintaining a focus, both within and across coaching sessions, speak too much, and react to the client in an unreflective, spontaneous way appear to have the greatest challenges in becoming effective coaches. In some ways, this parallels our experience with clients who have these tendencies, as leader self-management issues can be very difficult to modify. Though such leaders may have other compensating assets, coaches must be able to manage themselves as a, and maybe *the*, primary lever in their work with clients.

Having addressed the core aspects about leadership coaching that guide our teaching, linked those to key components of our pedagogy, and examined key competencies for coaches, we turn our attention to the content of our coach training experience: *what we teach* as compared with *how we teach it.* In terms of personal model creation, what we teach informs the third input to personal models, after which personal model outputs are described in detail.

Coaching Topics and Processes

Teaching requires reductionist thinking. We break down complex subjects into discrete constituent topics that can be discussed, examined, and applied. This is useful in helping learners approach unfamiliar subjects in manageable pieces without feeling overwhelmed. Though all subjects can be broken down in this way, the resulting divisions are somewhat arbitrary, arranged to benefit teaching more than capturing an authentic picture of full performance. Most of us can appreciate that learning musical notes does not guarantee the delivery of an engaging song, yet learning the notes is a necessary step in eventually making music. In other words, coaching, when practiced well, will always appear more uniform and seamless than the sum of the parts that we divide it into, but our mission in teaching is to make those parts both useful to learners and true to the whole.

Consistent with what has already been described, our approach to coach training is not anchored in particular techniques or conceptual perspectives about change. Our emphasis has always been on *learning by doing*, reflecting on the experience, and pulling it all together into a personal model. At the same time, our students have expressed a strong need for practical, even concrete, guidance about ways to handle typical coaching processes and challenges. Though we want to meet their need, our response has been to provide guidance that gives students greater confidence without actually dictating a particular approach to coaching. Thus, our course content could be described as giving students a thorough preview of each step in coaching while at the same time inviting them to vary and experiment beyond that base. As such, we try to avoid labeling anything we teach as *best practice* both because such a claim is unproven and, more important, because it tends to narrow thinking (although the term is applied ubiquitously in the coaching field). Just as in our own coaching work, we walk a balance beam of providing alternative perspectives to stretch thinking about topics of interest that supports new skill application but at the same time avoiding strident recommendations or anything that might be interpreted as *this is how it should be done.*

Extending that value of providing support while also fostering independent thinking, there is much that we can say as teachers or coaches that can be interesting and useful without implying we have the answer. We have described this phenomenon as *constructive marginality*: we stand apart from students and clients so as to better support their efforts to grow and improve. Although teaching and coaching are aligned in some ways, teaching is not coaching, and there is much content about coaching practice that we must convey to our students. During our years of teaching coaching, we have *chunked* that coaching content into manageable pieces and tried to present them as creatively as possible. Furthermore, we have been able to modify our depictions based on student questions, reactions, and feedback. Our roster of modules and the way we present each reflect the results of real-world shaping. Obviously, we cannot recreate the full content of those modules here, but we provide our conceptual perspective about each, informed by what resonated for our students (see Exhibit 3.1). We hope that you will find ideas in this material that stimulate further exploration relevant to your own personal model of coaching.

(Note: This book contains complete chapters on client diversity/differences (Five), ethics (Eight), assessment tools (Ten), and evaluation of coaching (Thirteen) so we have not included those topics here although they are modules in our curriculum; readers are directed to those chapters for in-depth treatments of those coaching topics.)

1. Streams and Banks of Coaching

Coaches enjoy using analogies and metaphors. This carries over to our teaching as well. We use a water analogy to anchor coaching in the history of change interventions. The wide *river* that has become coaching is a relatively recent phenomenon; its headwaters go back only to the 1980s. It was created by the

Exhibit 3.1. Typical Coach Training Topics

1. Streams and Banks of Coaching
2. Theory Lenses About Adult Change and Growth
3. Engagement Management
4. Contracting the Coaching Process
5. Sponsor and Stakeholder Involvement
6. Building a Partnership with Clients
7. Coaching Session Preparation
8. Fostering Dialogue and Client Stories
9. Leadership Challenges
10. Responding to Client Resistance
11. Leveraging the Client Relationship and Coach's Use of Self
12. Facilitating Understanding of Feedback
13. Goal Evolution in Coaching
14. Development Plans and Action Ideas
15. Coaching Closure

As noted, although the following topics are covered in our course, they are addressed in depth elsewhere in this book, so we have not covered them as individual topics within this chapter:

16. Ethics
17. Assessment Tools and Techniques
18. Managing Client Diversity
19. Evaluating Effectiveness of Leadership Coaching

convergence of several key *streams* of professional practice. The first stream contributed the structure of coaching, springing from the *talking cure* of one-to-one therapy and counseling. The second stream shaped the context of coaching and bubbled up from consulting activities that brought external professionals to aid in organizational and HR problem solving. The third stream added content and flowed from organizational efforts to train leaders using feedback processes and experiential courses, both in-house and external. Though one could cite other streams that have contributed to coaching, these three provide a perspective about both the origins of the practice and sources of foundational thinking.

Banks, or boundaries, also are part of the analogy. In order for coaching to be recognized as a definable practice, it must have banks that separate it from other interventions. Clients are likely to have had experiences with consultants, therapists, and trainers and automatically associate coaching with those activities. Coaches need to be able to explain clearly both what coaching *is* and what it *is not*.

2. Theory Lenses About Adult Change and Growth

It is useful for coaches to be conversant in a repertoire of approaches to change that have become formalized in theory and practice. Although coaches need to make distinctions that inform their models of coaching, that does not imply that any one conception is closer to the truth than others. All provide useful ideas about how adults establish and change behavior, but at the same time, each extrapolates into somewhat different approaches to coaching. As they try on these theory lenses, coaches often find that one or more are especially engaging and increase their acuity about what they observe. As such, studying them helps coaches to be articulate about their own change philosophy and to expand the range of their thinking. We highlight six familiar approaches and illustrate how each could be part of shaping a personal model of coaching: psychodynamic thinking (see Kilburg, 2004, and Kets de Vries, Korotov, & Florent-Treacy, 2007); life stage conceptions (see Axelrod, 2005; Levinson, 1978); behaviorist approaches (see Goldsmith & Lyons, 2006); emotional intelligence and positive psychology perspectives (see Goleman, Boyatzis, & McKee, 2002; Seligman, 2002); existential and phenomenological thinking (see Flaherty, 2005; Spinelli, 2005); and cognitive behavioral approaches (see Peterson & Millier, 2005; White, 2006).

In addition, there are other useful conceptions of adult development that have been applied to coaching which come from *streams* other than individual change, such as learning models (de Haan & Burger, 2005) and systems approaches (O'Neill, 2007). Our goal is to increase awareness of and curiosity about the many ways that change can be understood to happen as a foil to arriving at a favored view. This helps coaches articulate their own beliefs about adult growth and consider how those beliefs extend to their actual coaching practice.

3. Engagement Management

Coaching is an engagement between a coach, a client, and the client's employer, with clear process elements that coaches need to manage. Some of these process elements produce tangible products, such as contracts for service and development plans. Most elements, however, are implicit and tied to the working relationship between client and coach, such as building trust and facilitating feedback to the client. Engagement management is the umbrella term we use to bracket all of them and to highlight the challenge of knitting them together into a seamless intervention.

A dynamic tension that runs through all coaching engagements is alignment: between coach and organization, between coach and client, and between client and organization. Engagement management frames a coach's judgment about these alignments in terms of coaching process and work products. The organization alignment about how the coaching will proceed is usually documented in the form of a written contract. Alignment with the client is determined by interpersonal chemistry and appropriateness of coaching to address likely needs. Later, alignments will be determined between coach, client, and the organization, focused on client development goals, progress in coaching, and finally, evaluation of its effectiveness in fostering client growth. The *art* of coaching is in making adjustments to these processes when misalignment on any of them becomes apparent to the coach. Other engagement management processes are topics in their own right, as described in the sections that follow.

4. Contracting the Coaching Process

Contracting is analogous to preparing a room before painting: a necessary delay in starting the needed work but one that pays off later in both efficiency and quality of results. Considerations include: What are the client's and organization's general objectives for coaching? Who are key sponsors supporting the client's development? What types of assessments might already be available or useful? Confidentiality often gets particular attention in contracting, particularly how sensitive information, such as interview and assessment results, will be handled. When organizations require the coach to provide reports or other coach-generated information, contracting should clarify what they should contain and who will have access to them. Contracting, both oral and written, helps to ensure consistent understanding of the circumstances and the mutual obligations required in supporting successful coaching.

Ideally, contracting reflects a melding of case-specific requirements and a coach's individual approach to coaching. Rarely, organizational practices may conflict with a coach's personal model, especially in terms of small but important details, such as telephone versus in-person sessions, brief timelines, boss involvement, shared assessment results, and teaching organizationally favored leadership models. When confronted with unusual requirements, a coach who has thought through his or her own preferred approach to coaching will be in a much better position to negotiate toward an acceptable compromise or decline the assignment. Contracting empowers coaches to bring their practice judgment to the foreground as other professionals do, even when that means choosing not to do work that is offered.

5. Sponsor and Stakeholder Involvement

Because of the role of sponsors in initiating coaching and supporting positive outcomes, managing their involvement is an important responsibility for coaches. To effectively channel sponsors' positive intentions to support coaching, coaches need to anticipate the legitimate needs that sponsors have for involvement and information. Specific contact points are often agreed to in the contracting phase, such as during initial meetings and development planning.

As with other points of inflection in coaching, choices about sponsor and stakeholder involvement reflect the coach's model of coaching. Some coaches prefer to have very little direct contact with sponsors during coaching to empower the client to build developmental relationships for the future. At the other extreme, coaches may prefer a high profile and to both observe the client in action and be available to the client's team for comments and suggestions about the client's progress. Professional coaches need to recognize that these choices reflect their beliefs about how best to foster change and be able to explain the basis of those choices and know how much they are willing to vary them in response to situational factors and sponsor requests.

6. Building a Partnership with Clients

Complementing the focus on sponsor management, coaches must pay close attention to how they manage themselves in relation to the client. Coaching diverges from other consultative activities essentially in facilitating a client's insight and development rather than in offering expertise and answers. For coaching to succeed, a productive partnership between coach and client must emerge early in the engagement. We believe that coaching shares with other helping professions the finding that the quality of the relationship between client and helper is a much more important determinant of positive outcomes than any other variable under the helper's control, including technique or theoretical orientation (McKenna & Davis, 2009). Coaches need to explore and refine their preferred ways of creating client relationships toward reducing distractions and fostering insight and change.

We have found that examining coach responses to nervousness and anxiety often reveals coach tendencies that can interfere with building a productive helping relationship. Bringing greater self-insight to these tendencies is a first step toward controlling them. Nervous reactions such as talking too much or too rapidly, being too quick to answer a client's questions or give advice, or being too casual or personal, often reflect a coach's maladaptive response to the insecurities of a new coaching relationship.

Successful coaches are able to define a coaching posture for themselves that channels anxiety into something productive. Mary Beth O'Neill (2007) calls this a "Signature Presence," and she lists several useful anchor points for it: stay focused on a goal for each session, accept ambiguity and quiet one's reactions to it, increase tolerance for client characteristics and disapproval, and be in the moment in making links between client behavior and potential issues. Focusing on her last point, as coaches gain more experience, they also gain confidence about leveraging their own observations in relationships with clients. Becoming an astute observer of client words, behavior, and nonverbal signals and eventually allowing those inputs to coalesce into an observation about a client are key skills in building working relationships. Personal models of coaching often describe unique sensibilities and insights that coaches discover they have and can use. Some may be attuned to career choices, others to leadership issues, and still others to emotional variables in a client's life. Coaches need self-insight about their presence and their preferred perspectives to build more productive relationships with clients.

7. Coaching Session Preparation

There are never any guarantees of what can be achieved in a single coaching session, but coach preparation increases the likelihood of great things happening. The first priority in session preparation is for the coach to orient him- or herself in the coaching process. The *true north* on that compass is the development plan: What is needed to get to a plan that engenders the client's commitment? A second important consideration is for the coach to find time to reflect about the client from several different angles: cognitive, career, behavioral, and emotional. Notes from previous sessions and a list of questions assist these reflections: What do I want to know about the client but haven't asked? What is the client's impact on me and how might that inform his or her impact more generally? These and other broad questions benefit from repeated reflection by the coach as part of session preparation.

Session preparation also taps into another parallel process in coaching—as the client's self-insight evolves, so should the coach's insight about his or her own effectiveness with this particular client and with clients in general. For example, reflection may reveal that a coach feels dominated by a very talkative client. The coach would have a development-driven agenda for a session, but also a goal for him- or herself, such as to be more in control of the session. Accompanying that goal would be tactics that the coach would use, such as interrupting in a more assertive way, making observations that compel the client to be more reflective, or sharing feelings about how difficult it is to get a word in. Conscious preparation about session structure, development progress, and coach choices provides a foundation for coaches to be in the moment and responsive.

8. Fostering Dialogue and Client Stories

Coaches use dialogue skills the way a chef uses ingredients to make a memorable dish or a skilled artist uses well-honed techniques to achieve a desired effect. Coaches need to evaluate their effectiveness in fostering dialogue and strive to improve these essential skills. Self-assessment and feedback from case supervisors is useful in that regard. We will not attempt to explore dialogue skills here (there are many lists available; see Whitmore, 2002, for examples applied to coaching), such as phrasing open questions, using nonverbal cues, phrasing thought-provoking probes, and summarizing facts and feelings that highlight what is emerging. All of these skills and others that support a deepening dialogue with clients are colors on the coach's palette to be mixed with ever-increasing finesse.

An extension of these skills, which has grown in popularity in recent years, is eliciting client stories. All clients have stories to tell about choices, transitions and setbacks, but coaches are in the unique position of helping clients make meaning from those stories. Really listening to stories about formative events in clients' lives cements trusting relationships. Furthermore, coaches can learn to listen for themes in client stories: success factors, coping mechanisms, interpersonal style, story authorship, and general tone. Coaches summarizing and highlighting what they hear in listening to stories can lead to significant insights for clients.

As a result, some coaches make storytelling a cornerstone of their coaching models. Stories take on even greater importance when coaching leaders, as described in the next section.

9. Leadership Challenges

Leaders have many challenges, both specific to their situations and general to their roles in their organizations. We have found that there are four issues that come up repeatedly in coaching leaders and yet do not appear in the usual leadership competency lists: choice to lead, leadership stories, organizational influencing and politics, and leadership polarities and choices. A coach's ability to work on these challenges with leaders, when appropriate, can lead to new ideas and progress.

Many people end up in leadership roles as a coincident effect of advancement in their careers or as a byproduct of seeking increased responsibility and compensation (Lee & King, 2001). For some leaders, not having consciously chosen to lead is a drag on their probability of leadership success. When faced with setbacks and challenges, these leaders may find their motivation, confidence, and effectiveness easily shaken. Coaches are in the unique position of being able to revisit the circumstances around, and reactions to, becoming a leader. Leaders who discover that they have not *chosen* to lead may be empowered to make that choice now. Alternatively, coaching provides a safe forum to consider options other than leadership when true preferences lie elsewhere.

Accessing a client's career story is a way to foster dialogue and build a relationship. For leaders, however, stories serve more compelling purposes. Leaders need stories. They need stories to tell themselves in order to make sense of their achievements and they need stories to tell followers to engage and inspire them. Coaches can help leaders explore the power in both types of stories. Eliciting the client's leadership stories, coaches can identify and articulate important insights into the leader's values, style, and motivation. Furthermore, in listening to the stories that leaders tell followers, coaches can provide both honest feedback and an opportunity to make the stories more compelling to followers.

Leadership is a process of influencing that leverages both positional and persuasive power. The persuasive part is often about the leader's vision and the stories that he or she tells about how the organization will progress. There are many insights and skills that coaches can use to help leaders improve persuasiveness in their storytelling. Often overlooked, however, are the informal processes of persuasion, which we call organizational politics. Unfortunately, politics has a negative connotation and can appear to be somehow unseemly to some leaders. As a result, leaders may reject the term entirely, not realizing that in doing so they are rejecting a natural influencing channel that will exist whether or not they acknowledge it. Coaches can help leaders understand political forces, both positive and negative, and choose to leverage those forces rather than rejecting them.

There have been many attempts to catalogue leadership competencies and define what is expected. Whereas those lists can be useful in identifying leadership strengths and development areas, we have found that polarities more realistically depict leadership challenges. That is because, in the flow of day-to-day leadership interactions, each choice a leader makes tends to eliminate an option at the opposite pole. For example, a leader who chooses to encourage harmony cannot at the same time foster debate. Under this perspective, leadership choices about stylistic elements need to acknowledge both what skill to apply and how much to apply it. In other words, leadership skills can be overapplied if used too frequently or too strongly (Kaplan & Kaiser, 2006). There are many polarities that relate to leaders that coaches can access, such as ambiguity versus structure, interpersonal closeness versus distance, pride versus humility, approachability versus toughness, or empowering versus directive. Coaches can help leaders identify poles that they overuse, which often link to development areas, and explore options for bringing greater choice and control to where they operate on those continua.

10. Responding to Client Resistance

Resistance is a widely used but unfortunate term in helping relationships. As with other terms originating in Freudian conceptions of psychological treatment, its original meaning has become obscured by casual usage and the easy appeal of blaming the client for lack of progress. That is why we encourage coaches to replace the word *resistance* with *reluctance*. For example, labeling a client as resistant when he or she is not implementing developmental action steps does not advance anyone's understanding. Reluctance, on the other hand, connects with the feeling that we all have when faced with the challenge of changing our behavior. We are appropriately cautious about deviating from patterns that are familiar and, at least from our perspective, effective. Accepting the legitimacy of these feelings, even as we support the need for change, prompts a dialogue about perceived risks, whereas labeling a client as resistant is judgmental and shuts down conversation.

With coaching moving into the mainstream of leadership development, motivation to embrace coaching may be higher than in the past. Still, there may be much initial hesitation from a client about the need for coaching in particular and development in general. A very useful guideline applicable in the early stages of coaching is provided in *Motivational Interviewing* (Miller & Rollnick, 2002). Helpers of all types need to be empathetic and understanding about the pros and cons of change being considered by clients. Motivational interviewing rightly empowers clients to freely decide whether the benefits of change have the potential to outweigh the effort and risk involved in making those changes. Coaches can support that due diligence effort by using the concepts and techniques of motivational interviewing.

Another reason to foster the client's openness when reluctance surfaces is that it conveys useful information to the coach about what matters most to the client. In fact, the stronger the reluctance is in terms of avoidance, excuses, and inactivity, for example, the more the client is working to protect a familiar situation or behavioral response. This awareness can suggest that the coach explore considerations weighing on the client about the real costs and benefits of behavior change. Clients need the safety of a coaching relationship and the coach's curiosity in order to explore these questions; doing so will reduce reluctance and increase motivation for change.

11. Leveraging the Client Relationship and Coach's Use of Self

Many of the earliest executive coaches were clinical psychologists who, by circumstance or choice, or both, were able to apply their training and skills to organizational assignments (Frisch & Lee, 2009). By contrast, organizational psychologists who are drawn to coaching have foundations in areas such as consulting, assessment, and training. The legacy of those traditions still appears in the personal models of individual coaches in their degree of emphasis on the coach-client relationship as being key to change. We are anomalies to some extent in having roots in organizational psychology yet emphasizing client relationships in our models and our teaching. This is all by way of saying that the extent to which a coach leverages the client relationship reflects an important choice he or she has made in shaping a personal model of coaching.

A recent article (McKenna & Davis, 2009) advocated that organizational psychologists who coach should pay much more attention to the quality of their relationships with clients because that variable has been shown in meta-research on psychotherapy to be a contributor to successful outcomes. For those coaches who agree or who would like to bring a greater emphasis on client relationships to their coaching, there are several key components to apply. These include the client feeling truly heard and understood, the coach being seen as authentic and caring, and goals that are shaped, not imposed, and tied to the reality of the client's context (Lee, 2008).

Though there are many coaching skills that are important in creating this experience for clients, a particularly important and challenging one is the coach's *use of self*. As mentioned earlier, by *use of self* we mean a coach's use of his or her insight, empathy, and intuition to tune into the experience of being with a client and then finding ways to use those perceptions as part of the coaching. Sometimes referred to as *in the moment feedback*, use of self is best explored in the context of case supervision that brings to consciousness reactions to a client and supports a willingness to take a few risks in reporting them out (Frisch, 2008).

Leveraging client relationships in general and use of self in particular can open exciting new windows for all coaches, but especially those who have come from more consultative disciplines.

12. Facilitating Understanding of Feedback

The task of gathering data and providing feedback varies greatly depending on the coach and his or her approach to the process. Almost all coaching, however, involves some amount of data gathering and therefore includes the challenge of facilitating the understanding of feedback. This is a challenge because there are many factors that can influence results independent of client behavior, such as myriad organizational context variables, client transient pressures and reactions, physical well-being, and error variance in specific measures. Interpreting results, therefore, always combines facility with the tool, awareness of what matters to the client, and the realities of the client's context. In other words, there are almost never clear, linear connections between measured client characteristics and conclusions about development planning.

This casts the term *feedback* as woefully simplistic in capturing what coaches need to do with client information that they collect and interpret. Feedback is meant to facilitate the client's self-insight and motivation toward growth, but that will not happen with an impersonal delivery. Feedback is better thought of as an exploration, a view through a different lens, or a new perspective worth discussing, rather than presented as *right* or *accurate*. This is somewhat more of a challenge with assessment tools yielding scored dimensions, as numbers can be confused with accuracy. Coaches need to translate scores into examples and illustrations, as well as deal with apparently inconsistent results and unusual score combinations. On the other hand, extracting a few interesting points and suggestions may be all that is necessary, because there are often too many scores to interpret them all, at least initially. In summary, feeding back qualitative and quantitative data to clients is best thought of as part of an ongoing conversation about development. It has the added challenge of requiring the coach to be facile with the measures or methods that are used, but the core questions are familiar: "How useful is that description of you and what, if anything, do you want to do about it?"

13. Goal Evolution in Coaching

A pivotal process in coaching is the evolution of development objectives as the coach-client working alliance forms and the client's challenges become clearer. This process deserves special attention because it is a way in which each coach's unique approaches and insights can clearly add value to client development. Some of the most exciting "aha" moments of coaching happen as clients realize, "That's what I should be working on!" These moments do not occur based on the need to fill in a box on the coaching authorization form. They occur in response to the power of a professional helping relationship and a shared problem-solving mind-set. On the other hand, the tyranny of administrative requirements cannot be denied, and there may in fact be usefulness in feeling pressure to define coaching goals as early in the process as possible.

The compromise is to celebrate goal evolution as a valuable process within coaching and identify the milestones of that evolution. This has led us to differentiate three notable phases in goal evolution: felt needs, negotiated goals, and designed objectives.

Felt needs are the initial goals articulated by organizational sponsors and sometimes by clients. They are often general or vague (executive presence, influence others, delegate better) or they focus on what *not* to do (control outbursts, be less pushy, stop micromanaging). Using the felt need as a point of departure, coach and client discuss and explore the client's history, prior feedback, and self-perceptions during the initial two or three sessions, arriving at what we label *negotiated goals.*

Negotiated goals are clearer and more engaging for the client but still may be somewhat tentative. (Empower my staff more and let go of some control; recognize challenging situations before I get into them and have strategies to control my reactions.) Their value is less in the particular phrasing but more in the client's participation with the coach in articulating them. Negotiated goals give the coach and client a way to target assessment choices and identify areas to explore within the collected data, while also allowing for unexpected themes to emerge.

After assessment results are summarized and discussed with the client, goal evolution occurs again, moving toward what we label *designed objectives*. These are the headlines on a development plan from which action ideas can emerge and be committed to. Designed objectives may be quite close to negotiated goals or diverge from what was previously identified, based on input from assessments of various types and informational interviewing of stakeholders, which is almost always included in a coaching process. The point is that the client feels both ownership in having helped to articulate the designed objectives and confidence that a rigorous process informs them. They are aspirational and optimistic, instilling a vision of the client's future leadership. Examples of designed objectives are: become a more empowering leader and stretch the skills of my team; expand my influencing style to be more positive and inspiring. Action ideas can then be generated that mobilize behavioral progress on these objectives by specifying when, where, and with whom to apply them, tied to the client's context. They almost always relate conceptually to the original felt needs but are obviously more specific and actionable. Designed objectives represent an important and tangible work product of coaching.

14. Development Plans and Action Ideas

Development plans are a focal point of coaching, helping to confirm what *is* confidential by opening up the development plans as *not* confidential. Development plans also represent an opportunity for direct collaboration between coach, client, and sponsors at a point in the coaching when sponsors can be very helpful in supporting change. In addition, development plans embody principles of adult learning by being anchored in a self-insight process and shaped to fit the individual client in his or her context and by articulating very specific behavioral action commitments that, if accomplished, will move the client closer to development goals. Though development plans need never be finished in any absolute sense and are amenable to adjustment, they provide both objectives and a means to achieve them.

As such, development plans frequently are discussed in a working meeting between client and sponsors, with the coach facilitating. This *three-way meeting* or *development planning meeting* is a real-time opportunity to strengthen the developmental partnership between client, sponsors, and coach. Though the meeting may occur in the first quarter or third of the coaching timeline, it actually anticipates the conclusion of coaching when sponsors will again be in the foreground of the client's development. Putting this into a meeting format, though not required, is useful on many levels: confirming for the coach that everyone will be on the same page developmentally, conveying to sponsors that they are integral to the development of the client, leveraging the power of the public commitment to change by the client, and observing the client-sponsor interaction for later discussion with the client. These meetings can be challenging but are truly gratifying to facilitate.

15. Coaching Closure

Coaches need to anticipate the end of coaching even at relatively early stages of the process. Coaching usually has an expected time frame that is part of the original contracting. Though that time frame does not need to be rigidly binding, it conveys that coaching is an intervention, a jump-start, and therefore time limited. Clients may forget that, but experienced coaches know that ideally they are working toward their own obsolescence in any individual case. That ending needs to be anticipated by the coach so that the client's closure experience is positive.

Done well, closure requires reflection by the client that begins several sessions before the end of coaching. Both coach and client can look back at the process and discuss what the client has taken away from coaching, what will need attention going forward, and what *watch outs* may exist that could undermine newly emerging behaviors. Other useful topics to reflect on include the client's future willingness to ask for feedback, how the client learns so that he or she approaches future development with more insight, and of course the client's feelings about ending coaching. Endings can be quite evocative and emotional for some clients, and it is important that coaches give them permission to share what is being experienced. Finally, ending coaching sometimes includes a planned event, such as a follow-up three-way meeting, to formally acknowledge progress and look toward the future.

Reaching back to the beginning of this chapter, we discussed the centrality of personal models to our teaching and coach learning. Inputs to personal models were summarized as who the coach is as a person, who the coach is as an organizational player, and coaching content areas that are useful to the coach. We now turn our attention to the very important challenge of shaping personal model outputs.

Personal Model Outputs

As explained earlier in this chapter, the three output areas of personal models are: describing one's approach to delivering coaching, presenting one's practice to the marketplace of coaching, and addressing the gap between current skills and aspirations as a coach. Just as with the input areas, the three outputs are interdependent, although each has a unique focus.

Describing One's Approach to Coaching

This personal model output carries substantial importance for coaches and can serve as a summary of your overall model. Much goes into thinking about a well-grounded description of one's approach to coaching, including all that we have presented, plus actual case work, supervision, classroom experiences, and colleague influences. This output operationalizes the three input areas into a description of how you actually show up as a coach. These include boundaries as a coach on the personal-organizational continuum, what topics and issues you are willing to address as a coach, and how you will handle confidentiality in the coaching work. Defining your coaching process in terms of structure, milestones, and timeline is important, as is how to involve stakeholders. Assessment preferences and feedback approaches can be articulated. Work products, such as progress reports and development plans, also should be considered and potentially designed. These and other concrete elements of your approach to coaching should be considered and described in this personal model output.

There are also broader aspects of oneself-as-coach that should be considered. Drawing on O'Neill's "Signature Presence" (2007) as a coach deserves attention: special insights about clients, interpersonal posture with clients, and use of self to tune into clients. Other aspects of that chemistry are coach skills for creating dialogue that facilitates reflection and insight. Coaches need excellent inquiry skills, but they also need to sense when to dig beyond the first level of client answers, even when the client may want to move on. Dealing with a wide range of client reactions and styles, such as compliant, resistant, friendly, angry, or critical, is also important. Coaches will have different affinities and challenges in response to these characteristics, but it is better to anticipate and plan for those rather than being reactive.

Finally, in considering how to describe their approach to coaching, coaches need to determine how they will get feedback for their own growth and improvement. Though this may include more formal, post-coaching evaluation processes, it also can occur during coaching engagements. Asking for feedback from clients and stakeholders is a usual part of the coaching process, but coaches vary in how they feel about it and how they actually do it. Coaches do need to model interest in and reflection about feedback they receive, but actually building it in is often overlooked. In summary, these conceptual and practical considerations are what determine coachs' descriptions of their approach to coaching.

Practice Planning in Coaching

It seems obvious, but learning to coach requires ongoing opportunities to deliver coaching services. That is why one of the outputs of a personal model of coaching needs to be a *coaching practice plan—a plan for securing more coaching work.* Coaches should formulate their coaching practice plan with the same seriousness and specificity that a business owner strategizes growth. For external coaches, this may be analogous to a marketing or business development plan. Internal coaches also need to plan for securing more coaching work. Although their marketing may be more contained, they need to promote themselves as coaches and gain support for their coaching work from internal sponsors and decision makers. Regardless of the breadth of a coach's practice, getting opportunities to do more coaching is a challenge that must be met actively.

Several questions are useful in creating a practice plan. These include:

- What time do you have available or can you make available both to do coaching and to market yourself as a coach?
- How will you get more coaching experience?
- What types of coaching services do you plan on offering?
- How will you promote your emerging ability to deliver coaching?
- How might you approach existing clients and offer coaching as a different service than you have traditionally delivered?

Continuing Professional Development

Most professions have a tradition of continuing professional development. In some, like medicine, continuing coursework and recertification are required. In psychology, depending on which state boards apply, refresher courses are sometimes required. The coaching field has not formalized any requirements along these lines, although there exist certifying bodies that do specify developmental milestones. Even without these formal requirements, a plan for continuing coach development is important enough to be included as an output component of every coach's personal model. Coaches should reflect on aspects of coaching they want to learn more about, as well as personal growth areas, to formulate plans for ongoing growth as a coach. This is partly because the practice itself is likely to touch on personal growth areas of the coach and partly to join with clients in the experience of professional growth. For the coach to *walk the talk* about development is invaluable in empathizing with clients struggling to change. For all these reasons, coach development planning is part of completing a personal model.

We strongly encourage the use of case supervision as a key component of coach development. A case supervisor can get to know individual coaches and help them learn from coaching experiences, with insight into their unique strengths and areas for growth; in effect, the case supervisor is coaching the coach using the dynamics of actual cases. Peer supervision and peer learning groups are also very useful sounding boards for coaches.

Whatever format is employed, discussing cases with trusted and knowledgeable colleagues should figure prominently into the ongoing development of coaches, both internal and external.

In Conclusion: A Paradox

I would not give a fig for the simplicity this side of complexity, but I would give my life for the simplicity on the other side of complexity.

—OLIVER WENDELL HOLMES

Leaders and coaches do share at least one common challenge. Both are faced with complexity that sometimes defies understanding. Yet for both, success is determined by finding a path through complexity to achieve an exciting and clarifying simplicity—not simplistic answers that ignore complexity but instead an honest and confident engagement of complex issues toward insight, hope, and action. This defines much of the challenge inherent in both leadership and coaching. In the most practical sense, simplicity is very much needed in coaching if the process is to be embraced by busy clients who expect rapid and direct benefit. Our challenge as teachers is to train coaches so they will achieve simplicity about their coaching work. In this chapter, we have moved through the complexity of coaching as we see it and suggested ways in which we have helped coaches get to the simplicity on the other side.

In summary, the robust growth of executive coaching has seen equally robust growth in programs aimed at training coaches. We have actively participated in both of those growth trends and have evolved an approach to coach training that our students have described as engaging and effective. Our approach is based on several principles:

1. There is no one best definition of coaching, let alone one best way to do it. There are no universal conceptions of leadership development or techniques of coaching that supersede considerations of coach and client style, preferences, context, and need.
2. Each coach needs to engage in a self-exploration process that is rigorous enough to yield a personal model of how he or she will operate as a coach.

3. There is a body of practices in coaching that coaches need to be familiar with to inform their practice choices.
4. Coaching is best learned in a multifaceted experience that includes content, actual case experience, and case supervision, as is done with other helping professionals, such as counselors and therapists.
5. Even after a comprehensive course of study is completed, coach development never actually ends but does become more individual and case-driven.

We encourage coaches, both new and experienced, to consider these principles as they embark on their professional growth and we hope that this chapter has provided a foundation to that experience.

References

Axelrod, S. D. (2005). Executive growth along the adult development curve. *Consulting Psychology Journal: Practice and Research, 57,* 118–125.

de Haan, E., & Burger, Y. (2005). *Coaching with colleagues: An action guide for one-to-one learning.* New York: Palgrave Macmillan.

Flaherty, J. (2005). *Coaching: Evoking excellence in others* (2nd ed.). Boston: Butterworth-Heinmann.

Frisch, M. H. (2008). *Use of self in executive coaching.* iCoachNewYork Monograph Series, #1.

Frisch, M. H., & Lee, R. J. (2009). More hidden but more useful than we realize; commentary on McKenna and Davis. *Industrial and Organizational Psychology: Perspectives on Science and Practice, 2*(3), 261–265.

Goldsmith, M., & Lyons, L. (2006). *Coaching for leadership* (2nd ed.). San Francisco: Pfeiffer.

Goleman, D., Boyatzis, R., & McKee, A. (2002). *Primal leadership: Realizing the importance of emotional intelligence.* Boston: Harvard University Press.

Kaplan, B., & Kaiser, R. (2006). *The versatile leader.* San Francisco: Pfeiffer.

Kets de Vries, M. R. R., Korotov, K., & Florent-Treacy, E. (2007). *Coach and couch: The psychology of making better leaders.* New York: Palgrove Macmillan.

Kilburg, R. R. (2004). When shadows fall: Using psychodynamic approaches in executive coaching. *Consulting Psychology Journal: Practice and Research, 56,* 246–268.

Lee, R. J. (2008). Learning to coach leaders. iCoachNewYork Monograph Series, #2.

Lee, R. J., & King, S. N. (2001). *Discovering the leader in you: A guide to realizing your personal leadership potential.* San Francisco: Jossey-Bass.

Levinson, D. (1978). *The seasons of a man's life.* New York: Knopf.

McKenna, D. D., & Davis, S. L. (2009). Hidden in plain sight: The active ingredients of executive coaching; focal article. *Industrial and Organizational Psychology: Perspectives on Science and Practice, 2*(3), 244–260.

Miller, W. R., & Rollnick, S. (2002). *Motivational interviewing; Preparing people for change* (2nd ed.). New York: Guilford

O'Neill, M. B. (2007). *Executive coaching with backbone and heart: A systems approach to engaging leaders with their challenges* (2nd ed.). San Francisco: Jossey-Bass.

Peterson, D. B., & Millier, J. (2005). The alchemy of coaching: "You're good, Jennifer, but you could be really good." *Consulting Psychology Journal: Practice and Research, 57,* 14–40.

Seligman, M. E. P. (2002). *Authentic happiness: Using the new positive psychology to realize your potential for lasting fulfillment.* New York: The Free Press.

Spinelli, E. (2005). *The interpreted world* (2nd ed.). London: Sage.

Valerio, A. M., & Lee, R. J. (2005). *Executive coaching: A guide for the HR professional.* San Francisco: Pfeiffer.

White, D. (2006). *Coaching leaders: Guiding people who guide others.* San Francisco: Jossey-Bass.

Whitmore, J. (2002). *Coaching for performance* (3rd ed.). Yarmouth, ME: Nicholas Brealey.

Chapter Four

GOOD TO GREAT COACHING

Accelerating the Journey

David B. Peterson

For the past fifteen years, I have asked participants in my coaching workshops to list the characteristics of a good coach. Virtually every group, whether consisting of managers, HR professionals, new coaches, or seasoned coaches, places listening skills at the top of the list, followed by empathy and a genuine interest in the person, the ability to deliver honest, direct feedback, having integrity, and being trustworthy.

I then ask these groups to list the qualities of a *great* coach. These lists typically include comments such as "really gets the person to reflect," "inspires people to want to change," "takes people to higher levels," "gets results," and "has a passion for helping others."

As the groups talk about what differentiates their two lists, they realize that their first list concentrates almost exclusively on traits and activities of the coach, whereas the second list highlights the person being coached and the outcomes that are achieved. Not surprisingly, workshop participants themselves are often so focused on the skills and techniques of coaching itself ("What am I supposed to do?") that they lose sight of the higher goal, which is to support the learner ("What is this person trying to achieve and how can I be most helpful to him?"). Through this simple exercise of exploring the difference between a good coach and a great coach, those attending the workshop often are able to find a more balanced perspective and become more intentional about their learning.

However, in all the years that I have asked these two questions, only three times has anyone mentioned the quality that I view as most important for an effective coach—an understanding of how people learn and develop. If the goals of coaching primarily include helping people learn new things, gain insight, be more effective, and improve performance, then it seems essential for coaches to have an understanding of how humans learn (Peterson, 2002).

Whether I am correct or the groups are correct or we are all missing some other essential variable, the research has not yet been done to answer this question definitively. In fact, very little is actually known about the knowledge or skills required to be a competent coach (Stober, 2010). Nonetheless, exploring how coaches can help people learn faster and better—and how coaches themselves can learn to be more effective coaches—can be a useful pursuit. This chapter explores what coaches can do to accelerate their journey towards great coaching by examining:

- What differentiates good coaching from great coaching
- Why it is relatively easy to become a good coach
- Why it is relatively difficult to become a great coach
- What is known about how experts in a variety of fields develop mastery and how that applies to coaching

Definitions and Distinctions

The terms *good coach* and *great coach* are used informally here, to some extent because the field of coaching has not yet converged on a clear understanding of what defines competence and mastery in coaching. For the purposes of this chapter, good coaching refers to the work of competent coaches who have successfully completed at least thirty coaching engagements. Great coaching refers to coaches who demonstrate mastery and deep expertise. Typically, great coaches have well over ten years of significant coaching experience and have successfully coached hundreds of clients. They are highly versatile and generally successful even with difficult, complex, and challenging coaching engagements.

Using Dreyfus and Dreyfus's (1986) five-stage model, good coaches are at level 3 (competent) and great coaches are at level 5 (expert):

1. *Novices* focus on accomplishing immediate tasks, typically requiring clear rules which they follow closely.
2. *Advanced beginners* begin to use the rules as guidelines, applying them in new situations, but are not able to handle exceptions or unforeseen problems.
3. *Competent* performers begin to create their own conceptual models of what they are doing and can handle more complex situations based on their experience.
4. *Proficient* performers have advanced beyond competence by experiencing a wide variety of situations and challenges and have developed the ability to see the big picture, monitor their own performance, and interpret underlying principles to adjust their behaviors as needed based on the context to effectively handle relatively novel situations.
5. *Experts* have such a high level of experience that they are able to identify and solve problems intuitively, with little explicit analysis or planning. They see underlying patterns effortlessly and they apply appropriate solutions, even to complex and unique situations, in such a way that they generate consistently superior performance. Lord and Hall (2005) note that expert performance is marked by the ability to see and interpret underlying principles instead of relying on heuristics or surface features, which is what most competent performers do. One of the ironies of this level of performance is that experts can be rather inarticulate in explaining how they arrived at a conclusion, a phenomenon explored in Gladwell's popular book *Blink* (2005).

When Expertise Makes a Difference

This distinction between competent and expert coaches has implications for coach training, development, and certification, as well as for how coaches are selected and matched to participants. Begley and Interlandi (2009) paint an interesting picture in the area of cancer treatment, which provides a useful analogy. They point out that for severe cancers, there is a very low survival rate regardless of the treatment or the expertise of the physician. For the relatively minor cancers, there is a high survival rate relatively independent of treatment. It is for the cancers that fall between these two extremes where expertise and judgment typically make a substantial difference in survival rates.

Similarly in coaching, some situations are relatively simple and straightforward (for example, a motivated learner, supportive environment, and straightforward development needs), so that even a beginning coach is likely to be helpful. Some situations are so complex (for example, multiple stakeholders with different expectations, highly political environment, or overwhelming business challenges that others have failed to overcome), so urgent (for example, there is simply not enough time for the person to develop what is needed), or so unfavorable (for example, a hostile, competitive environment where the boss or others are setting the person up to fail, significant substance abuse, or cognitive impairment) that the odds of any coach being successful are small. However, there are a number of situations that may be beyond the capabilities of a competent coach that an expert coach might handle quite capably.

Client Coachability

Focusing on the more difficult end of this spectrum, several authors have described what they refer to as uncoachable people. Goldsmith (2009), for example, provides four indicators: they don't think they have a problem, they are pursuing the wrong strategy for the organization, they're in the wrong job, or they think everyone else is the problem. Naficy and Isabella (2008) suggest that people with a fixed mind-set, who are forced into coaching, who lack trust and openness, or who feel manipulated by performance management in the guise of coaching are all uncoachable. Bacon and Spear (2003) propose seven levels of coachability, with the least coachable being those who are narcissistic, arrogant, impatient, resistant to feedback, defensive, or lacking in self-insight. Rather than simply labeling such individuals as uncoachable, it is more helpful to discuss under what conditions coaching might be useful and what type of coach, with what level of expertise, might be effective (Peterson, 2010).

The unfortunate irony in these discussions is that the people they describe as uncoachable are often the very people most in need of professional coaching. In contrast, the people that Bacon and Spear (2003) describe as most coachable are self-directed, insightful, motivated learners who are so committed to their own development that they may rarely need a coach. The real consideration is that the "coachability" of the person often depends on the coach's ability. Not all coaches are qualified to work with difficult or complex coaching situations, although some expert coaches are well qualified to work with narcissistic, defensive, distrustful, and difficult people (Ludeman & Erlandson, 2004; Mansi, 2009).

Easy to Be a Good Coach

Given the proliferation of new coaches entering the field (Liljenstrand & Nebeker, 2008) and that there are virtually no barriers to entry, there is some concern regarding the quality of coaching that is being delivered (Grant & Cavanagh, 2007; Platt, 2008; Sherman & Freas, 2004; Thomas, 2006). Certainly it is important for the credibility of the field to maintain minimum quality standards through improving training, coach supervision, and certification processes (Carroll, 2007; Hawkins & Smith, 2006; Lane, Stelter, & Stout Rostron, 2010).

On the other hand, there appear to be a surprising number of reasons why it is relatively easy to become an effective coach, especially for anyone with a solid base of intelligence, maturity, emotional intelligence, and basic social and communication skills (Bluckert, 2006). For one thing, people from a variety of backgrounds, such as human resources, training, consulting, management, and education, possess relevant knowledge and helping skills that readily transfer to coaching (Schein, 2009). Many simple components, such as the following, which require virtually no coaching experience or training, can potentially contribute to effective coaching (Peterson, 2010):

- Creating space and time for reflection (Burke & Linley, 2007) so that the person can step back from the situation and look at it more objectively.
- Offering an external, independent, objective perspective, especially if the coach takes the time to listen carefully to the person's situation.
- Identifying development goals and preparing an action plan.
- Sharing useful ideas, tips, tools, and models.
- Facilitating an accepting, positive, supportive, encouraging relationship (O'Broin & Palmer, 2007; Uhl-Bien, 2003). The therapeutic literature, for example, indicates that the relationship itself is often a significant factor in determining outcomes (Lambert & Barley, 2002; McKenna & Davis, 2009).
- Providing follow-up conversations that foster a sense of accountability, especially if the person makes a commitment to the coach to pursue a specific action (Goldsmith & Morgan, 2004).
- Simply asking the person what would be helpful to him or her and responding accordingly.

In addition, there are a number of other techniques that require minimal experience or training and yet can also enhance the effectiveness of coaching (Peterson, 2010):

- Asking questions that challenge assumptions and help reframe issues.
- Asking questions that encourage the person to clarify his or her goals and values and think about possible courses of action.
- Offering feedback, either directly or by seeking third-party feedback from interviews or multirater surveys (Levenson, 2009).
- Encouraging and providing opportunities for behavioral practice.
- Using simple coaching formulas such as the GROW model, a popular tool that consists of four steps: Goal setting, Reality checking, Options for action, and What is to be done (Alexander, 2006; Whitmore, 2009).

There is an additional factor inherent in the coaching process that makes it relatively easy for even novice coaches to achieve positive results. Coaches have the opportunity to get immediate feedback on their progress, through the other person's verbal and nonverbal cues, and adjust their approach, timing, language, and pace to more effectively meet the person's needs. If a coach's first attempt to be helpful misses the target, he routinely gets a second and even third chance to find something that works. This opportunity to learn and adapt in real time increases the odds that the participant will leave the session with at least some new insights and ideas.

Although this adaptive approach generally enhances outcomes, it makes it challenging to conduct definitive research on coaching, because it is more difficult to determine whether a given outcome is the result of one specific technique, some combination, or perhaps even the unique sequence of techniques that was used. Coaches, participants, and even trained observers may recognize that a specific technique was utilized but be unable to accurately determine its specific effect, if any, because of the unique context and the presence of so many other variables.

Easy to Remain a Good Coach

Once coaches reach a point where they are reasonably successful, they may be satisfied with their level of competence and not be motivated to advance beyond that level. Some consultants, for example, see coaching simply as one aspect of their broader consulting work and not as a specialty area that requires constant improvement. When it is a matter of weighing the options and consciously choosing to invest one's development efforts elsewhere, remaining at a basic level of competence makes perfect sense.

However, several factors may make it relatively easy for coaches to choose to remain merely good rather than seeking continual improvement. Some coaches reach a point where they value the relationship to such an extent that they are reluctant to challenge the client's perspective, raise sensitive issues, or discuss negative or difficult feedback. Other coaches enjoy a particular tool or model so much that they focus their practice around the methodology, rather than around meeting the client's needs. Even the best tool may not work in every situation, and coaches thus limit their own growth by such a narrow focus.

An even more insidious trap for some coaches is that it is so easy to place blame elsewhere when the coaching is not effective. Rather than asking themselves what they could have done differently to achieve a greater impact, coaches may point to the participant's low level of motivation, the organization's half-hearted support, or the lack of clear feedback and accountability from the boss. The fundamental attribution error can easily be a factor when coaches convince themselves that they did everything they could and simply place the blame on the participant or the circumstances. Given the complexity of most coaching situations, it is often easy for the coach to find supportive data and to ignore potentially disconfirming information. Conversely, of course, people tend to attribute success to their own efforts and to overestimate their personal contribution to successful endeavors, so coaches can easily conclude that their approach is highly effective. (See Kemp 2008a, 2008b, and Chapter Seven in this book for a discussion of these and other potential biases and heuristics that may be at work in the coaching process.)

Difficult to Be a Great Coach

In contrast to the proposition that it is relatively easy to be a good coach, it appears to be much more difficult to become a great coach. In a general sense, it is difficult to become a true expert in any complex endeavor (Colvin, 2008; Ericsson, 2006). Typically, the development of expertise in a complex activity such as chess, competitive sports, musical performance, or medicine requires at least ten years of experience or ten thousand hours of regular practice (Ericsson, 2006).

Experience Is Not Enough

Significantly, mere practice or repetition is not sufficient to develop expertise, and numerous studies across a variety of domains report that years of experience do not necessarily correlate with performance. In some cases performance may actually decline with additional experience after the end of formal training (Ericsson, 2006). What seems to differentiate those who continue to improve in performance with additional experience is engagement in what has become known as deliberate practice, a focused effort to repeatedly practice and improve specific, well-defined behaviors at an appropriate level of difficulty (Ericsson, Krampe, & Tesch-Romer, 1993). As Colvin points out, deliberate practice requires a great deal of effort and simply "isn't much fun" (2008, 71). Deliberate practice and specific implications for coaching are explored in more detail later in this chapter.

Relationship Between Coach Actions and Client Outcomes Is Not Always Clear

A second reason it is difficult to become a great coach is that developing expertise in any arena generally requires significant diligence, concentrated effort, and clear, specific feedback. It may even be more difficult in coaching, because the process takes place over an extended period of time, honest and systematic feedback is rare, and it is difficult to connect any particular coach behaviors—or even particular coaching conversations—to specific outcomes that occur months later. There are also many other events and activities occurring at the same time as the coaching is taking place, and pinpointing the causal link between coaching activities and distal outcomes is problematic. Further, some feedback on immediate outcomes may be misleading. For example, a client might express great appreciation for a coach's thoughtful advice on an issue, but take no action on the basis of that input. So a coach may reasonably assume that the guidance was useful, when in fact it was not.

In contrast, many of the endeavors for which expertise has been studied, such as musical performance, sports, and chess, operate under more clearly delineated and self-contained conditions. A sports coach, for example, will typically have a clear grasp of the rules of the game and detailed knowledge of the player skills and behaviors that contribute to success. There is a clear connection between player's activities and performance on key metrics, including scoring and winning (for example, see Lewis,

2003, in reference to baseball), and feedback is relatively immediate. Players are used to rehearsing specific behaviors during practice sessions and often receive detailed, immediate feedback on how they are doing.

In executive coaching, the rules of the game are less than transparent, the "games" themselves are lengthy, there are far more players on the field at any given time, with ambiguous and evolving roles, and players can enter, leave, or change in the middle of the action. Although at a global level there is little question that coaching can be an effective means for enhancing performance, sorting through all of this complexity to determine the value of any of the coach's actions is difficult, and coaches who are not diligently pursuing a goal of achieving expert levels of performance are likely to remain at the level of competent performer.

Requires Diverse Skills and Broad Knowledge

A third reason is that coaching, especially executive coaching, draws on many different skills and domains of knowledge, requiring a significant investment of time plus a level of curiosity and commitment to self-development that not all coaches have. The competency model developed by the Executive Coaching Forum (2008) is illustrative. They suggest that even a competent coach should be familiar with a wide range of topics within these four areas of knowledge:

- *Psychological knowledge*, including an understanding of personality, motivation, learning and behavior change, adult developmental theories, stress management, emotional intelligence, feedback, gender differences, and social psychology.
- *Business acumen*, including an understanding of basic business practices and financial concepts, management principles and processes, strategic planning, information technology, global business dynamics, and human resource management.
- *Organizational knowledge*, including an understanding of organizational structures and functions, organizational design, organizational culture, team effectiveness, leadership models,

systems theory, consulting theory and practices, business ethics, and leadership development.

- *Coaching knowledge,* including an understanding of executive coaching models and theories, coaching competencies, specific coaching practices (such as managing confidentiality, assessment, goal setting), various roles of a coach, coaching research, the history of coaching, and developing oneself as a coach.

Their competency model also includes two other detailed sections: the specific tasks and skills required for six phases of the coaching process (building and maintaining relationships, contracting, assessment, development planning, facilitating development and change, and ending formal coaching and transitioning to long-term development) and nine categories of general attributes and abilities:

- Mature self-confidence
- Positive energy
- Assertiveness
- Interpersonal sensitivity
- Openness and flexibility
- Goal orientation
- Partnering and influence
- Continuous learning and development
- Integrity

On a related note, in the fall of 2009 I surveyed fifty leading experts on professional coaching to get their recommendations on the three to five essential readings in the field. There was little consensus on the top choices, with only a handful of books receiving recommendations from three or more experts. However, the range of topics that people viewed as essential included, in addition to coaching per se, leadership and leadership development, management skills, consulting, counseling and therapy (including approaches to treating addictions), positive psychology, storytelling, strategy and strategic thinking, emotional intelligence, change management, phenomenological psychology, facilitation skills, the inner game of tennis, and organizational culture. Clearly, a field in which experts view such a wide range of topics as fundamental provides a certain challenge to anyone wishing to attain a level of mastery.

Requires Hard Work and Delay of Gratification

A fourth reason why it is difficult to become a great coach is that certain parts of the coaching process are relatively easy and generally result in immediate, positive feedback, making them rather seductive in nature. Thus they may dominate a coach's attention, preventing her from working on the difficult and less rewarding aspects of coaching that are part of the broad repertoire of skills and tools which characterize expert coaching. For example, asking powerful questions, giving feedback, and offering advice are relatively quick, straightforward behaviors that can provide tangible value to the participant. When they are on target, they can have an immediate impact and, rather significantly, the coach is perceived as the direct source of their value.

Other parts of the coaching process, in contrast, are slow, tedious, and often frustrating. Translating insights into action in the real world, for example, is much more difficult, as is working through the process of changing old habits and replacing them with new, more effective behaviors. In these instances, the credit for a successful outcome is much more likely to be attributed to the diligence and hard work of the participant. The coach's efforts to support this type of change, even when skillful and clever, are much less likely to be viewed as of equal importance. So coaches who feel good about the highly positive feedback they receive for their insightful feedback and advice may have little interest in pushing themselves to engage in the tedious and awkward parts of coaching where they may get little reward, but which are nonetheless absolutely essential for lasting results.

Developing Expertise in Coaching

There are many excellent books, workshops, training programs, and university courses available for those interested in learning the basics of coaching and achieving a level of competence. However, the key to developing expertise in coaching is likely to be found, as it has been in so many disciplines, in deliberate practice. Shadrick and Lussier (2009, 295–296) provide a detailed discussion of nine characteristics of deliberate practice in order to describe what it is and to help differentiate it from other types of training and practice.

- *Repetition.* Task performance is induced by presenting specific, designed tasks rather than waiting for these task demands to occur naturally, so that the behavior can be repeated and improved.
- *Focused feedback.* Task performance is evaluated by the coach or learner during performance against some target. There is a focus on elements of form that are critical parts of how one does the task.
- *Immediacy of performance.* After corrective feedback on how the task was performed, there is immediate repetition so that the task can be performed again to better match the process of experts or some other desired standard.
- *Stop and start.* Because of the repetition and feedback cycle, deliberate practice is typically seen as a series of short performances rather than as a continuous flow.
- *Emphasis on difficult aspects.* Deliberate practice explicitly focuses on more difficult aspects of the performance which might be encountered rarely in the real world.
- *Focus on areas of weakness.* Deliberate practice can be tailored to the individual and focused on areas of weakness. Allowing practice on one's weaknesses in a relatively safe environment and at an appropriate level of difficulty is much easier for most people than attempting it in actual performance contexts, where they may (appropriately) gravitate toward relying on their strengths.
- *Conscious focus.* Expert performance is characterized by many aspects being performed with little conscious effort. Once a behavior reaches this level of automaticity, it is difficult to improve it without significant conscious effort. By focusing on specific aspects of a performance, deliberate practice allows one to modify and adapt mental models one aspect at a time. After a number of repetitions attending to the desired element to ensure that it is performed as desired, the learner

may resume performance while focusing on the overall situation rather than on just the particular element.

- *Work versus play.* Characteristically, deliberate practice feels more like work and is more effortful than casual performance. The motivation to engage in deliberate practice generally comes from a commitment to improve in skills.

- *Active coaching.* Typically it is easier to engage in deliberate practice with the assistance of a coach who monitors performance, assesses adequacy, and controls the structure of the practice.

Coaches can apply many of these principles in structured deliberate practice in at least three ways.

Specific Learning Goals

First, in actual coaching conversations, coaches can consciously focus on specific learning goals, try new techniques, and vary their approach from what they've done in the past. They can also seek immediate feedback from their clients. For some skills, such as asking questions, they may even have opportunities to repeat a certain type of question with slight modifications to test which is most effective. They can deliberately focus for short periods of time on their weaknesses before moving back to areas of comfort and competence. By being deliberate about how they balance new behaviors with areas of proven competence, they often will have the opportunity to test several different approaches with each client. Of course, because of the variability in client needs and situations, coaches must be alert to the possibility that a given behavior might have been effective or ineffective with a given client for some particular reason.

Thus coaches need to systematically experiment with a given behavior across a range of different clients and situations in order to understand fully how and when it works. For example, a coach might systematically try to see how long, and under what conditions, clients can continue to generate options in a brainstorming exercise. Coaches might vary the type of questions they ask, the tone of their questions, and the amount of silence they provide. Such an activity is not necessarily measured against some specific criterion of excellence, as Shadrick and Lussier suggest, but on the basis of whether or not it seems to generate more and better responses and perhaps even greater client satisfaction with the process.

Focused Practice and Rehearsal

Second, coaches can work on certain skills and behaviors in solitary practice and rehearsal, such as generating a list of questions to pose to a particular client in order to elicit a deeply thoughtful response. Coaches can project how the client might answer each one and then test the best two or three in a later session with that client. In the spirit of deliberate practice, it is important to recognize the difference between merely generating a list of possible questions versus actively examining each question, repeating it in different ways to find the right tone and style, and comparing and contrasting different questions to gauge their appropriateness and fit in different circumstances.

Client Feedback

Third, coaches can schedule practice sessions with their own coaches, supervisors, or peers in order to work on specific skills. Although someone who is an expert on a particular technique might be optimal, even a relative novice can offer useful feedback on how effective a question, comment, or technique is from his or her personal perspective. The ultimate usefulness of such feedback, of course, rests on their similarity to the target client.

Self-Reflection

McGonagill (2002) provides a somewhat similar perspective in his discussion of the coach as reflective practitioner. Although he does not incorporate all the elements of deliberate practice, he highlights several critical aspects, including the role of specific learning goals and of conscious effort and attention in developing oneself as a coach. His approach adds some complementary elements to the literature on expertise in that reflective coaches are focused not just on their core practices, but on their vision, values, and assumptions. A common theme in virtually all of the literature on expertise and mastery (for example, Leonard, 1992) is the notion of self-awareness and self-discipline in the pursuit of excellence. In that spirit, I close this chapter with recommendations for a practice of self-reflection.

First, consider four basic directions of reflection:

- *Look inward:* What is most important to you? What values matter most and how are you manifesting them in what you are trying to achieve?
- *Look outward:* What matters most to others? What expectations do they hold that you need to address in order to be successful at your endeavors? How do they perceive you?
- *Look back:* What have you been trying to learn and what new things have you tried? What has worked well and what hasn't worked? What have you learned?
- *Look ahead:* What will you do differently? What do you need to keep learning? Where are your opportunities to try new things?

Second, consider reflection at six different levels of learning and development, corresponding to six natural time frames.

1. Daily (for about one minute): What new thing did I do today? How did it go? What one thing will I do differently tomorrow?
2. Weekly (3–5 minutes): What kind of progress did I make last week? What do I need to focus on this next week?
3. Monthly (5–10 minutes): How am I doing on my learning objectives? What do I need to do to keep learning? How will I get meaningful feedback?
4. Quarterly (10–15 minutes): How am I doing on my development? What is most important for my success going forward?
5. Annually (1 hour):
   - Where do I stand relative to what matters to me? What really matters to me? Where do I want to be a year from now and how do I get there?
   - What do I need to do to manage my learning more effectively? What do I need to do to make sure I'm not missing something important?

6. Decadely (Every 5–10 years or so, consider a personal retreat for a day or a quiet afternoon):
   • Who do I want to be? What values do I want to live by? How am I doing?
   • What do I need to do in the next five years to accomplish what matters most?

Conclusion

This chapter argues that it is easy to be a *good* coach. Many simple coaching tools and techniques can be quite effective in helping others grow and develop. At the same time, it is rather difficult to become a *great* coach and consistently perform at a high level, especially in the face of challenging and novel situations. To do so requires a clear commitment to learning, diligent practice, regular feedback, and disciplined self-reflection.

Regardless of whether you aim to be a great coach, a good coach, or simply seek to keep growing and learning on whatever path you are on, the words of Michelangelo offer some useful advice: "The greatest danger for most of us is not that our aim is too high and we miss it, but that our aim is too low and we reach it." Even to aim for a basic level of competence may be inadequate. For one thing, the number of practicing coaches continues to increase (Liljenstrand & Nebeker, 2008), creating a more competitive environment where even competent coaches must find ways to differentiate themselves and stand out from the crowd. Even more importantly, the science and practice of executive coaching is advancing rapidly and the bar for competent performance is continually being raised. Only those coaches who are self-reflective, intentional about their learning, and continually seeking to improve are likely to thrive.

References

Alexander, G. (2006). Behavioral coaching: The GROW model. In J. Passmore (Ed.), *Excellence in coaching: The industry guide* (61–72). Philadelphia: Kogan Page.

Bacon, T., & Spear, K. (2003). *Adaptive coaching: The art and practice of a client-centered approach to performance improvement.* Mountain View, CA: Davies-Black.

Begley, S., & Interlandi, J. (2009). What you don't know might kill you. *Newsweek, 154*(17), 42–46.

Bluckert, P. (2006). *Psychological dimensions of executive coaching.* New York: Open University.

Burke, D., & Linley, P. A. (2007). Enhancing goal self-concordance through coaching. *International Coaching Psychology Review, 2,* 62–69.

Carroll, M. (2007). Coaching psychology supervision: Luxury or necessity? In S. Palmer & A. Whybrow (Eds.), *Handbook of coaching psychology* (pp. 431–448). New York: Routledge.

Colvin, G. (2008). *Talent is overrated: What really separates world-class performers from everybody else.* New York: Portfolio.

Dreyfus, H. L., & Dreyfus, S. E. (1986). *Mind over machine: The power of human intuition and expertise in the era of the computer.* New York: The Free Press.

Ericsson, K. A. (2006). The influence of experience and deliberate practice on the development of superior expert performance. In K. A. Ericsson, N. Charness, R. R., Hoffman, & P. J. Feltovich (Eds.), *The Cambridge handbook of expertise and expert performance* (pp. 683–703). New York: Cambridge University Press.

Ericsson, K. A., Krampe, R. T., & Tesch-Romer, C. (1993). The role of deliberate practice in the acquisition or expert performance. *Psychological Review, 100,* 363–406.

Executive Coaching Forum. (2008). *The executive coaching handbook: Principles and guidelines for a successful coaching partnership* (4th ed.). Retrieved December 1, 2008, from www.executivecoachingforum .com.

Gladwell, M. (2005). *Blink: The power of thinking without thinking.* New York: Little Brown.

Goldsmith, M. (2009). How to spot the "uncoachables." Retrieved March 25, 2009, from http://blogs.harvardbusiness.org/gold smith/2009/03/how_to_spot_the_uncoachables.html? cm_mmc5npv-_-LISTSERV-_-MAR_2009-_-LEADERSHIP2.

Goldsmith, M., & Morgan, H. (2004). Leadership is a contact sport: The "follow-up factor" in management development. *Strategy + Business,* Fall, not paginated. Retrieved June 23, 2005, from www .strategy-business.com/press/article/04307?pg=0.

Grant, A. M., & Cavanagh, M. J. (2007). Evidence-based coaching: Flourishing or languishing? *Australian Psychologist, 42,* 239–254.

Hawkins, P., & Smith, N. (2006). *Coaching, mentoring and organizational consultancy: Supervision and development.* New York: Open University.

Kemp, T. J. (2008a). Coach self-management: The foundation of coaching effectiveness. In D. B. Drake, D. Brennan, & K. Gørtz (Eds.), *The philosophy and practice of coaching* (pp. 27–50). San Francisco: Jossey-Bass.

Kemp, T. J. (2008b). Self-management and the coaching relationship: Exploring coaching impact beyond models and methods. *International Coaching Psychology Review, 3,* 32–42.

Lambert, M. J., & Barley, D. E. (2002). Research summary on the therapeutic relationship and psychotherapy outcome. In J. C. Norcross (Ed.), *Psychotherapy relationships that work: Therapist contributions and responsiveness of patients* (pp. 17–32). New York: Oxford University Press.

Lane, D. A., Stelter, R., & Stout Rostron, S. (2010). The future of coaching as a profession. In E. Cox, T. Bachkirova, & D. Clutterbuck (Eds.), *The complete handbook of coaching* (pp. 357–368). Thousand Oaks, CA: Sage.

Leonard, G. (1992). *Mastery: The keys to success and long-term fulfillment.* New York: Plume.

Levenson, A. (2009). Measuring and maximizing the business impact of executive coaching. *Consulting Psychology Journal, 61,* 103–121.

Lewis, M. (2003). *Moneyball: The art of winning an unfair game.* New York: Norton.

Liljenstrand, A. M., & Nebeker, D. M. (2008). Coaching services: A look at coaches, clients, and practices. *Consulting Psychology Journal, 60,* 57–77.

Lord, R. G., & Hall, R. J. (2005). Identity, deep structure and the development of leadership skill. *The Leadership Quarterly, 16*(4), 591–615.

Ludeman, K., & Erlandson, E. (2004). Coaching the alpha male. *Harvard Business Review, 82*(5), 58–67.

Mansi, A. (2009). Coaching the narcissist: How difficult can it be? Challenges for coaching psychologists. *The Coaching Psychologist, 5,* 22–25.

McGonagill, G. (2002). The coach as reflective practitioner: Notes from a journey without end. In C. Fitzgerald & J. G. Berger (Eds.), *Executive coaching: Practices and perspectives* (pp. 59–85). Palo Alto, CA: Davies-Black.

McKenna, D. D., & Davis, S. L. (2009). Hidden in plain sight: The active ingredients of executive coaching. *Industrial and Organizational Psychology: Perspectives on Science and Practice, 2,* 244–260.

Naficy, K., & Isabella, L. (2008). How executive coaching can fuel professional and personal growth. *OD Practitioner, 40*(1), 40–46.

O'Broin, A., & Palmer, S. (2007). Reappraising the coach-client relationship: The unassuming change agent in coaching. In S. Palmer & A. Whybrow (Eds.), *Handbook of coaching psychology* (pp. 295–324). New York: Routledge.

Peterson, D. B. (2002). Management development: Coaching and mentoring programs. In K. Kraiger (Ed.), *Creating, implementing, and managing effective training and development: State-of-the-art lessons for practice* (pp. 160–191). San Francisco: Jossey-Bass.

Peterson, D. B. (2010). Executive coaching: A critical review and recommendations for advancing the practice. In S. Zedeck (Ed.), *APA handbook of industrial and organizational psychology: Vol. 2, Selecting and developing members of the organization.* Washington, DC: American Psychological Association.

Platt, G. (2008). *Coaching: A faster way to lose money than burning it.* Retrieved February 1, 2009, from www.trainingzone.co.uk/cgi-bin/item.cgi?id=179384.

Schein, E. H. (2009). *Helping: How to offer, give, and receive help.* San Francisco: Berrett-Koehler.

Shadrick, S. B., & Lussier, J. W. (2009). Training complex cognitive skills: A theme-based approach to the development of battlefield skills. In K. A. Ericsson (Ed.), *Development of professional expertise: Toward measurement of expert performance and design of optimal learning environments* (pp. 286–311). New York: Cambridge University.

Sherman, S., & Freas, A. (2004). The wild west of executive coaching. *Harvard Business Review, 82*(11), 82–89.

Stober, D. R. (2010). Continuing professional development for coaches. In E. Cox, T. Bachkirova, & D. Clutterbuck (Eds.), *The complete handbook of coaching* (pp. 405–415). Thousand Oaks, CA: Sage.

Thomas, J. C. (2006, December 6). Does coaching work? Who knows? [Review of the book *Evidence based coaching handbook: Putting best practices to work with your clients*]. *PsycCRITIQUES: Contemporary Psychology—APA Review of Books, 51*(49), Article 6. Retrieved December 14, 2006, from the PsycCRITIQUES database.

Uhl-Bien, M. (2003). Relationship development as a key ingredient of leadership development. In S. E. Murphy & R. Riggio (Eds.), *The future of leadership development* (pp. 129–148). Mahwah, NJ: Erlbaum.

Whitmore, J. (2009). *Coaching for performance* (4th ed.). London: Nicholas Brealey.

Chapter Five

THE CLIENT

Who Is Your Coachee and Why Does It Matter?

Anna Marie Valerio and Jennifer J. Deal

In today's global, fast, tumultuous environment our lives are changing in fundamental ways. The pace of both work and life has accelerated, and clients are bombarded with new demands at every turn. Today's environment has been affected by many factors such as globalization and the integration of the world economy, a fiercely competitive marketplace, demographic diversity in domestic and global workforces, and technological advances in communication that result in 24/7 work cycles.

Clearly, today's work climate affects who our clients are and what they need from coaching. Coaches must adapt their approach to meet the needs of the increasingly diverse clients who face these dynamic forces in their work. For example, what are the issues if the coachee is a thirty-two-year-old woman who grew up in Mumbai? Are they the same as those faced by a forty-year-old man who grew up in Johannesburg and was a teenager when Nelson Mandela was released from prison—and does it

Note: The authors would like to thank the following people for their assistance: Mariangela Battista, Erica Desrosiers, Jennifer Habig, Robert J. Lee, Lisette Manzi, David Oliver, Catherine Ruvolo, Denise Verolini, and Kym Ward.

matter if he is of English, Afrikaans, or Zulu background? What if it is a forty-six-year-old American woman who is taking a high level position in a male-dominated industry? What about a fifty-year-old man moving to Europe to lead a regional sales team? How a coach is able to relate to clients with such diversity in age, generation, gender, cultural background, and career/life goals is critical to the coach's success in helping clients achieve their leadership objectives. This chapter focuses on understanding the client, also termed "the coachee," the person who is being coached in the leadership coaching process.

Coaching is "a one-on-one development process formally contracted between a coach and a management level client to help achieve goals related to professional development and/or business performance" (Valerio & Lee, 2005). As the focus of the coaching process is the client, understanding the coachee is a key starting point for the coach. For coaching to have a successful outcome, it is most important to understand who the coachee is.

The chapter will start with wider focus on the evolving demographics in client populations and then move to a more narrow focus on the characteristics of the individual and the implications of those characteristics for coaching. We will consider the following key issues:

- The "traditional" population of coachees, the "new" evolving populations of coachees, and the implications that the shift in demographics has for coaching.
- The importance of viewing the coachee first and foremost as *an individual*, taking into account each person's uniqueness with respect to generation, gender, culture of origin, life stage, goals, and level in the organization.
- The challenges facing new populations of clients and the implications of these challenges for coaching.

The Evolving Population of Clients

The population of clients has been changing. In the past the population of coachees in the United States had traditionally been mid-to-upper-level white male executives. The changing demographics in the business world have led to increased numbers of women and other ethnic groups in the client population. To understand who our clients are now and the world of work that they face, it is helpful to take a brief historical perspective and better understand who the clients were and what were the coaching issues.

Historical Perspective of Coachees: 1990s to the Present

The Past

During the early 1990s, executive coaching gained popularity as a tool to develop leadership capability. During this period, successful companies focused on "e-business" and instantaneous technology to meet customer needs. The premium placed on information resulted in a new business sector that was characterized by informality, increased speed of change, "disruptive" technologies, and new products that made the old ones obsolete progressively faster. There was a proliferation of mergers and acquisitions, alliances, and joint ventures. "Downsizing" employees became a commonly used tool that enabled business to trim costs and meet Wall Street expectations for short-term business results. Workforces became flatter, leaner, and were required to make rapid decisions. Though more established business sectors (like banking) resisted this informality and speed, it began to infiltrate even the most buttoned-down environments (Valerio & Lee, 2005).

Who were the clients? Like the twenty years before, managers and executives were still primarily white men; in 1983, 13.5 percent of white men in the workforce were in managerial or executive roles, while only 8.3 percent of white women, 5.8 percent of black men, and 4.9 percent of black women (Bureau of Labor Statistics, 1983), but more women and nonwhites were moving up in the corporate ranks over time—as a percentage of employed people in 1991, 11.9 percent of women were in managerial or executive roles, as were 7.2 percent of black men and women, 6.0 percent of Hispanic men, and 7.0 percent of Hispanic women in comparison with 14.6 percent of white men (Bureau of Labor Statistics, 2003).

What were the issues? Coaching was often used for purposes of remediation, to help "fix" executives. This was needed because the trend in management style was moving from command and control toward a focus on teamwork and getting buy-in from subordinates, which meant many executives needed to improve their interpersonal skills.

The Present

Today, the ubiquity of portable devices and other improvements in remote technology allow work to happen anywhere at any time. The freedom that technology has given managers and executives to work outside of an office setting have translated into two new workplace assumptions: (1) that the workday is now 24/7, and (2) that vacation time no longer means time that is completely free of work. Globalization has brought more movement and exchange of people across countries and integration of the world economy (Valerio & Lee, 2005). The rapid growth of emerging markets in China, India, and other parts of the world requires managers to have a greater knowledge and understanding of the cultures and mores in different countries.

Who are the clients? Increasing numbers of women, nonwhites, and people from other cultures have been promoted to management and executive levels within large companies, although there continue to be more men than women in executive and management positions (Bureau of Labor Statistics, 2005). In 2008, the managerial workforce in the United States was 7.2 percent black, 7.5 percent Hispanic, 17.2 percent white male, and 14.3 percent white female (Bureau of Labor Statistics, 2008). A larger percentage (33 percent) of the women managers are single, compared to 18 percent of the men (McKinsey & Company, Inc., 2007).

Interestingly, for all the hype (Bunker, Kram, & Ting, 2002) about how people are being promoted at younger ages into management positions, there are fewer people under forty-five in executive and managerial positions than there were in 1994. In 1994, managers and executives aged 25–44 made up 56 percent of the managerial population, while in 2009 they only made up 41.7 percent of the managerial population (Bureau of Labor Statistics, 1994; Bureau of Labor Statistics, 2009).

What are the issues? Four general coaching challenges have arisen in the past few years as a result of the changing nature of work and demographic shifts in client populations: (1) competency attainment, (2) developing adaptability in leaders, (3) working in and leading virtual teams, and (4) work-life integration.

First, a greater emphasis is being placed on competency attainment. Organizations have developed leadership competency models that include descriptions of skills and behaviors that job incumbents need to be successful (Frisch, 1998). These models serve as guides, enabling organizations and their diverse—and changing—workforces to build consistent organizational capability because the models provide a common language that describes the behaviors that people in the organization need to demonstrate to be successful, *regardless* of gender, generation, or cultural orientation. Some commonly identified leadership competencies are: big picture thinking and a global perspective, motivating and inspiring others, building relationships with diverse groups of people, and demonstrating teamwork across lateral as well as vertical relationships.

Second, managers and executives need to be skillful at adapting themselves to changing environments. Leaders are now required to achieve results in highly complex, global environments, often with people from different countries and cultures. Most leadership models now contain competencies related to building global organizational capability across diverse cultures and geographic boundaries. To advance their careers, many men and women move to different countries and live in different cultures to take new job assignments. In doing this, to be successful, managers and executives must learn how to adapt to new rules of engagement, methods of decision making, and the language and communication norms of a different culture. Organizations and managers are finding solutions to these challenges by using a variety of diversity initiatives (Valerio, 2009). Leaders are expected to be business partners and to secure organizational support through collaborative efforts with others—all around the world.

Third, people do more of their work in teams virtually. Even teams from different cultures and societies find themselves having to work together, without knowing each other very well, or perhaps never even having the opportunity to meet each other face-to-face. The new emphasis on virtual work requires strong interpersonal and negotiating skills, both for working with people from the same culture and for working with people from other cultures. Effective distance collaboration is difficult, whether or not team members share a culture. At the same time it has become so common for organizations to have virtual teams at many levels that leading such teams has become a critical skill for leaders.

Fourth, work-life integration has become a major issue facing both men and women, regardless of marital status. The combination of a 24/7 work week and the greater numbers of women in the workforce has meant that many people face the complex challenges associated with child care and elder care. How can men and women create meaningful lives for themselves, their families, and their communities? Both men and women must find the equilibrium that is right for them, either as individuals or as couples or families, between how much of their energy and time is devoted to work and how much remains for "nonwork" activities. Many members of the workforce struggle with the stress and challenges of building their careers while having "quality time" with their loved ones. The issue of work-life integration has existed in all cultures and societies, but changes in workforce demographics and technological advances have made it a more prominent concern for today's workforce.

Implications of the Evolving Demographics on Coaching

In the past, coaches could walk into a coaching engagement with a good idea of the issues facing a client. Although each individual client was different, the homogeneity of the client population and the types of workplace challenges limited the possible variety of issues they were likely to encounter. In contrast, coaches today frequently walk into a coaching engagement with someone who differs from them in terms of generation, gender, cultural background, career expectations, pressures, and technical expertise. Though, of course, in the past coaches had to understand the client as an individual, this shift in demographics to a more culturally diverse and female managerial population potentially makes reaching this understanding more complex and challenging than it was in the past.

The next decade is likely to bring even greater global expansion, an increase in the importance of technology at work, and the retirement of many older workers from the Baby Boomer cohort. These shifts are likely to result in more executives from different countries and cultures, more women and nonwhites in executive positions, and more work taking place across different countries and cultures. Perhaps more than ever before, it is critical that coaches remember to begin at the beginning: the individual.

The Importance of the Individual

Part of the challenge and the excitement for the coach at the beginning of every new coaching assignment is that clients are unique in that they exhibit a unique blend of behaviors and characteristics, they are in a unique situation, and they have unique needs. The coach may use a variety of standard instruments and methods to better understand behavior and motivation, but all are in the service of understanding the special combination that comprises that individual. Although most coaches would agree that every client is a unique individual, coaches—like all humans—have a propensity to generalize and use stereotypes that may bias their judgment and decision making. Before considering characteristics such as gender, generation, and other factors of importance, it is critical for all coaches who wish to be successful to understand the dangers of stereotypical thinking.

The Danger of Stereotypes for Coaches

Stereotypes are generalizations about individuals' characteristics, most commonly made about membership in a particular demographic group such as gender, generation, or country of origin. The danger of stereotypes is that a coach may be influenced by these conventional, formulaic, and oversimplified conceptions of an individual. Stereotypes are particularly perilous for coaches because when they use them they run the risk of oversimplifying and misperceiving clients because the coach is making erroneous assumptions based on those stereotypes. Coaching based on false assumptions is bound to have unsuccessful outcomes. A coach needs to be as open-minded about the individual as possible in the very first meeting to be able to glean accurate information about the client and to create a good relationship from the outset. Both coach and client need to have a relationship built on trust and acceptance of each other, based on an accurate assessment of the client as an individual rather than based on generalizations that are made as a result of a demographic category.

Because coaching is not exempt from assumptions about gender, generation, and other categorizations and is likely influenced by them, the changing demographics of clients make it more important than ever to examine these issues.

Gender

Two themes that have special importance for understanding how gender stereotypes affect high-achieving women are "connection/communion" and "agency" (Ruderman & Ohlott, 2002). Connection/communion refers to behaviors that relate to our need to be close to others. Communal behaviors are associated with qualities associated with being feminine such as nurturing and empathy. Agency refers to behaviors that allow one to be self-sufficient and to act independently from others. Agentic behaviors are those typically associated with maleness such as assertiveness, dominance, and toughness. Gender role expectations for women are that they will be helpful and kind. Gender role expectations for men are that they will be aggressive and self-promoting.

One of the key findings from research studies on leadership has been that people rate managers as demonstrating more traits similar to men than to women (Schein, 2001). One major issue faced by female coachees is how to blend agentic (male) and communal (feminine) behaviors in their roles as leaders. It is important for coaches to recognize that when a female client is perceived by others as overly tough, ambitious, or aggressive, there may be negative consequences for her. Conversely, when a female client is perceived as showing more compassionate and nurturing behaviors, she runs the risk of being viewed by others as "too soft" and not tough enough to be a leader. Although males face similar issues, the band of acceptable behaviors is wider for them.

Leadership carries greater complexity for women, because each woman must find the right blend of agentic and communal behaviors to allow her to be an effective leader.

Generations

There is a general belief that each generation is distinct from others because they were born at about the same time and therefore were shaped similarly by shared historical and social life events such as technological advances, wars, and economic fluctuations (Kupperschmidt, 2000). The three generations currently in the workplace are Baby Boomers (born between 1946 and 1963), Generation X (born between 1964 and 1979), and Generation Y (born between 1980 and 2000). There has been a great deal of discussion regarding these generations, and much research describing the differences among them (Smola & Sutton, 2002; Zemke, 2001).

Some of the stereotypes associated with these three generations are that Gen X and Gen Y are more likely to be family-centric, that is, placing a higher priority on family or equally on both family and work. In contrast, Boomers are viewed as more work-centric. Some research has shown that Gen X fathers perform more child care than Boomer fathers and Gen Y fathers perform more than both of the other two generations (Families and Work Institute, 2005). Gen Y has been shown to be higher on positive traits such as self-esteem and assertiveness (Twenge & Campbell, 2001), as well as negative traits such as narcissism (Twenge, Konrath, Foster, Campbell, & Bushman, 2008) than were previous generations at the same age, leading people to call them narcissists.

Coaches work with clients from this multigenerational workforce. Because coaches themselves come from a particular generation, it is possible that they risk engaging in stereotypical thinking regarding generations other than their own. While there is much discussion about how different the generations are, other research finds that the differences aren't what they may first appear to be. Researchers have found substantial similarities among the generations with regard to their values, how engaged they are at work, how attached they are to their organization, what they want to learn, what they want in leaders, and how motivated they are to succeed (Deal, 2007; Gentry, Griggs, Deal, & Mondore, 2009;

Jurkiewicz, 2000; Yang & Guy, 2006). When coaches and clients are from different generations, therefore, it may be especially important for the coach to understand some other characteristics found to be of significance for clients.

Categorizations That Matter

In addition to considering the more standard demographic characteristics such as race, gender, and generation, in today's world (and for the foreseeable future) it may be equally useful for the coach to focus on factors such as life stage and goals of the client, the client's level in the organization, and the culture of origin of the client.

Life Stage

Research that has looked at generation, life stage, and level in the organization at the same time has suggested that life stage and level in the organization are better indicators of what is important to an individual than which generation he belongs to (Deal, 2007).

For example, when thinking about life stage, think about what happens when someone has a child—whatever her age. Whether twenty-four or forty-four (currently a Gen Y or a Gen Xer), when someone has a baby she is likely to have a different set of priorities than before. Those new priorities are a direct result of what is going on in life—what the life stage is—not the generation. Similarly, when a working person has a parent who has become infirm, he or she is going to have a new set of responsibilities and priorities are likely to shift. Whether the person is forty-four or sixty-four (a Gen Xer or a Boomer), those new priorities reflect a life stage rather than a generational difference.

Coaches can benefit clients more by obtaining information about life stage and goals because that information creates a more effective context for coaching than just knowing whether someone is a Baby Boomer or a Gen Xer. For example, if you know clients are members of Gen Y, you might be tempted to think (if we use the stereotype) that they are self-absorbed narcissists who love using the computer; they text, IM, Twitter, and use Facebook constantly; they are incapable of writing a thank-you note on paper, have at least one tattoo, and are likely to say they are going to quit work any day to go save the world somewhere (Twenge, 2006). Whereas if you know that they have three children and are interested in starting their own business (they're working for a large organization to learn the skills they need), you will have a very different idea of the coaching that would be most effective for them.

Level in an Organization

Similarly, what level an individual is within an organization often has a greater impact on an individual's beliefs and expectations than generation (Deal, 2007). For example, with regard to what competencies are needed to be successful at work, executives are more likely to choose strategic planning . . . than are people in lower levels of management . . . than are people who are individual contributors.

There is also a big difference by organizational level (rather than by generation) in what people believe about how people get ahead within an organization. Executives are significantly more likely than lower-level managers and professionals to say that people get ahead because of performance (Deal, 2007). The reverse is true with regard to whether people believe others get ahead because of politics at work: people lower in the organization are more likely than people higher in the organization to think people get ahead because of politics rather than because of performance (Deal, 2007). Thus, differences in attributions about the relationship between success and hard work is not a result of generational differences, it is a result of the level of success clients have attained—or the difficulty they are having reaching the level they want to attain.

A coach who knows the clients' current level, and which level they aspire to be (in both the short term and the long term) has a great deal of useful information to use to help them develop in the desired direction. Coaches can assist clients to create development plans that will help meet their career goals, whatever the level or organization.

Culture of Origin

Another relevant contextual variable is the individual's culture of origin. In contrast to thirty years ago, there are now many more people in executive positions who come from other countries. Knowing their country of origin and the conditions under which they moved are important to understanding the overall context that influenced them, because cultures differ in important ways. In brief, cultures differ on a number of different dimensions (Dalton, Ernst, Deal, & Leslie, 2002; Hoppe, 1998) including, but not limited to:

- Source and expressions of identity: emphasis on the in-group or emphasis on the self
- Source and expressions of authority: equality by birth or inequality by birth
- Means and goals of achievement: work to live or live to work
- Response to uncertainty and change: comfort with uncertainty or discomfort with uncertainty
- Means of knowledge acquisition: learning by observation or learning by experimentation
- Orientation to time: time as scarce or time is plentiful
- Response to natural and social environment: concern with harmony or concern with mastery

These types of cultural orientations are important to understand because they have a direct impact on behavior. For example, orientation to time is a common issue that can affect how attentive people are to being on time for meetings or how they prioritize making deadlines (Dalton et al., 2002; Hoppe, 1998). People who come from cultures that have a plentiful orientation toward time (such as Mexico, Indonesia, or Egypt) are likely to think of meeting times and deadlines as expressions of intent rather than as commitments. So when they don't appear on time for a meeting or miss a deadline, they don't see it as much of an issue, as might someone from a culture where time is scarce (such as the United States, the United Kingdom, or Germany).

Another issue that isn't as commonly understood is perceptions of equality in different cultures (Dalton et al., 2002; Hoppe, 1998). Some cultures (for example, Denmark, Sweden, or the United

States) perceive people as being existentially equal, regardless of their demographic characteristics or family background. These cultures tend to be characterized by informality, the belief that anyone can rise within the hierarchy regardless of gender, race, or birth family, that decision making should be consultative, and that managers should delegate and be supportive. Other cultures (for example, the Philippines, Saudi Arabia, or Mexico) tend to believe that people are not existentially equal. These cultures are characterized by the belief that managers should be directive, protective, and paternal, that decision making should be top-down, centralized, and driven by the person in charge, and that there should be greater opportunities for people based on their demographic or family characteristics. So a direct report's informality is likely to be perceived more negatively by a manager from a country where people are not perceived as being existentially equal than it would be in a country where they are perceived as being existentially equal. Therefore, to understand how the client perceives others' behavior, and how the clients' behavior might be affecting others, the coach must know what culture the client comes from and what the norms are in that culture.

Knowing this information can also help the coach have a better idea of what types of challenges the individual may be facing in the current position. For example, a coach may have a client who is German and has been recently expatriated to Mexico; she expresses a lot of frustration with timeliness of the people they are working with and the paternal attitude of their manager. Because the coach knows that the client's culture of origin scores differently on the dimensions of use of time and existential equality than does the culture where the client is now working, the coach will have a way of explaining the situation to the client and helping her through the difficulty, and thus improve her success.

Challenges Facing Current Client Populations

As mentioned at the start of the chapter, the recent changes in the work environment and the evolving categories of clients are creating new contexts in which coaches must help their clients successfully navigate. This section provides a client case example that illustrates some of the new challenges related to gender, life stage, level in an organization, and culture of origin.

Case Example

So, what *do* you do if the coachee is a forty-six-year-old American woman who is taking a high-level position in male-dominated industry? Mary, age forty-six, had been hired by a Fortune 500 company two months prior to the start of coaching and was viewed by her management as a likely candidate for the role of chief financial officer (CFO) in the future.

Who is the client? To obtain a better understanding of Mary as an individual, in the first several coaching sessions the coach asked about Mary's early education, family experiences, professional background, expertise, and current life stage.

Mary had grown up in the Midwest in a small, predominantly white, middle-class town where there was little cultural diversity. Both parents had a strong work ethic and encouraged their four children to work hard in school and be successful. She had few opportunities to travel to other countries when she was young, and, except for several vacations in Europe with her family, she had had little personal experience with people from different cultures.

Mary had many impressive achievements in a career that spanned more than twenty years. In her former organizations Mary had sought to build her professional expertise through a variety of experiences that included public accounting, corporate finance, and serving on committees and corporate boards. As a result of these experiences, Mary was viewed as a talented professional in her field. Regarding her current life stage, Mary's spouse was very supportive of her career aspirations and shared responsibility for the rearing of their two teenage children.

What are the issues? The purpose of the coaching was to enable Mary to make the behavioral adjustments in teamwork and adaptability as a leader. Although Mary's technical competence was excellent, she needed to demonstrate her ability to build relationships with peers in this company and to operate in a global role across cultures. Using the language of the company's leadership competencies, her coaching objectives targeted the development of teamwork and adaptability as a leader.

In addition to Mary, several of her peers, whose company tenure was, on average, eighteen years, were being considered for the role of corporate CFO. So she entered a company in which there were several male peers who had been working together for many years and were competing for the same promotion. Fortunately, Mary was appreciated for her competence, friendliness, and integrity, all of which were valued by the company. Mary entered the company as the second highest ranked woman and was viewed as a role model by other women. Mary's boss, Gary, and her HR manager were mindful of these facts and were interested in helping Mary succeed for the long term. They offered helpful advice to the coach's inquiry: "What does it take for a woman to be successful here?"

Mary's work as a member of teams suffered because, although she was generally liked, her peers viewed her as unacceptably assertive and ambitious, traits that are considered agentic and more acceptable for males to demonstrate. Her peers saw her as too "pushy" and trying to get ahead too fast, which resulted in them perceiving her as not being a team player. Further, they resisted her leadership and questioned her competence, ostensibly because she hadn't been at the company for as long as they had.

Gender Issues

Data from interviews with peers, corporate 360 feedback, employee opinion surveys, and individual assessments were used to help Mary improve her understanding of herself and how she was perceived by others. Coaching questions included: What behaviors do you demonstrate that may be classified as "agentic"? What behaviors would be perceived as "communal"? How will you blend both agentic and communal behaviors to be able to be accepted more by your peers? What do you need to do more of? Less of? How will you measure your success?

Although Mary's peers viewed her as highly competent, likable, and pleasant to work with, they thought she was too focused on her own success. They were negative about her behavior and viewed it as seeking to curry favor with upper management and the board of directors. For Mary to succeed in this organization, she needed to understand the perceptions of her peers and modify her behavior so that she could garner their support. Mary, her boss Gary, and the coach had several joint discussions about how Mary might combine her assertive style (agentic behaviors) with supportiveness towards peers (communal behaviors). In his role as boss, Gary provided feedback to Mary that was critical in allowing her to see how she was perceived by others in the organization. The coach encouraged Mary to continue with her natural tendency to be altruistic and to seek opportunities to help others to offset, through communal behaviors, some of the negative perceptions engendered by her agentic behavior.

During the coaching, the coach assisted Mary in leveraging her strengths by posing questions such as: How do you build support for yourself and your organization? How can you help your peers be successful in their jobs? What "roadblocks or hurdles" with each of your peers must you strive to overcome?

Level and Role in the Organization

In addition to the gender issues, other factors added to the complexity of the leadership challenge for Mary, who had entered the company at a senior management level with high visibility and global responsibilities. When Mary's predecessor had the job, his role was more of a domestic than global one and he remained more accessible to his peers than Mary had. As Mary had been hired specifically because of her knowledge and experience with global issues, she had some license to tailor the role to her background and interests. The coach encouraged her to discuss with her boss how the role might evolve under her leadership, paying specific attention to the results for the organization.

The coach's interviews with peers provided insights for the coach to help Mary learn what behaviors would lead to her success and which ones could result in derailment. The interviews revealed that the peers appreciated Mary's communal behaviors, namely her eagerness to help others achieve success in their jobs, as well as her high degree of integrity. For example, Mary's boss valued her willingness to engage in extensive travel to company locations in other countries to meet key people and to learn more about the business. During these visits, Mary often learned information that could help her peers in their respective areas of the business. Mary was diligent about passing along this information to her peers and often went out of her way to provide them with up-to-date information. Although Mary saw her actions as simply good business practice, the peer group viewed this behavior as helpful and altruistic and appreciated her efforts. Mary's helpful and kind behaviors toward others served to "compensate" somewhat for her assertiveness.

Culture

Mary's global role required managing and communicating with individuals and teams from other cultures, across different time zones, and with infrequent face-to-face contact. Despite her early limited experiences with different cultures, Mary was eager to learn about and adapt to the cultural practices of other countries.

To be successful, Mary had to listen to others' responses, understand the cultural practices of the people with whom she was working, and adapt her own behaviors accordingly. The coaching incorporated questions such as: How can you increase your knowledge of the different cultures of the countries in which you are operating? What are the stereotypes you hold about people from the countries you are working in? How can you enlist the help of others in learning how to interpret non-verbal behaviors that may have different meanings in the new context? Seizing on opportunities to better understand and adapt to different cultures on her business trips, Mary accepted all offers to socialize with her colleagues in other countries. She began to grow her relationships and networks of team members, receiving frequent invitations to visit in all global regions.

Coaching Outcome

Mary learned how to blend agentic and communal behaviors to improve her leadership, finding a comfortable and more effective blend of these behaviors to fit the corporate culture. Mary learned how to reduce the impact of her more agentic "politicking" behaviors that had been appropriate in a prior company with a different organizational culture but were causing her problems in the current organization. Although Mary had not had much experience with people from diverse backgrounds in her home town when growing up, she understood the importance of cultural adaptability for leaders in the global economy. She communicated how much she valued cultural differences by demonstrating teamwork with colleagues across different countries. Mary's ability to solicit ideas from her European and Asian colleagues enabled her to help her peers find better solutions for customers, which improved the organization's bottom line.

After a period of approximately thirty months in the company, Mary received the promotion into the role of CFO—ahead of her peers who had also been in contention for the role. Mary was well accepted in this new role by her peers, who recognized the value of her helpful behaviors in their own work efforts. Mary was viewed as a valuable team player whose skills and experience contributed to the company's global growth.

Implications for Coaching New Populations of Coachees

What are the implications for coaching these new populations? Being able to define clearly what it takes to be successful in an organization is critical for everyone. It is especially necessary if one is a member of a "nontraditional" or nondominant group. Asking the following question to coachees and others in the organization: "What does it take for a person with X characteristics (a female, person of color, male, Gen X, Boomer) to be successful here?" may elicit different responses depending on the subgroup membership. At the very least it will enable coachees to think about the behaviors that they need to demonstrate to achieve their goals. It may also be helpful for bosses and HR managers to consider the answers to this question so that they may provide guidance and feedback to coachees and coaches.

With greater diversity and less homogeneity in the evolving populations of coachees, there may be less familiarity with their cultural and educational backgrounds and, hence, their competency may be called into question by others. For example, one of the key challenges facing these "nontraditional" groups of people may be resistance to their leadership and the questioning of their competence by others. Information from both interviews and research with women leaders suggests that despite evidence of their effectiveness as leaders, women have been frequently called upon to repeatedly prove their qualifications (for a brief summary of research see Valerio, 2009, 79). Further research in this area might examine how the variables of generation, culture of origin, and life stage, in addition to gender, may affect perceptions of competency and resistance to leadership.

In conclusion, we have one final recommendation. Understand that your clients are increasingly likely to be different from you: from different generations, from different countries, from different cultures, and of a different gender. Enjoy helping them learn how their individual characteristics help them to bring a unique perspective to their work that will help them be successful . . . and their unique perspective will add creativity and fresh ideas to your work as their coach.

References

Bunker, T., Kram, K., & Ting, S. (2002) The young and the clueless. *Harvard Business Review, 80*(12), 80–87.

Bureau of Labor Statistics. (1983). *Handbook of labor statistics*, Bulletin 2175.

Bureau of Labor Statistics. (1994). Unpublished detailed occupation and industry tables, current population survey (CPS).

Bureau of Labor Statistics. (2003). *Employed persons by major occupation, sex, race, and Hispanic origin, annual averages 1983–2002.*

Bureau of Labor Statistics.(2005). *Women in the labor force: A databook.*

Bureau of Labor Statistics. (2008). *Employed persons by detailed occupation, sex, race, and Hispanic or Latino ethnicity.*

Bureau of Labor Statistics. (2009). *Employed persons by detailed occupation, sex, and age, annual average 2009 (current population survey).*

Deal, J. J. (2007). *Retiring the generation gap: How employees young and old can find common ground.* San Francisco: Jossey-Bass.

Dalton, M., Ernst, C., Deal, J. J., & Leslie, J. (2002). *Success for the new global manager.* San Francisco: Jossey-Bass.

Families and Work Institute. (2005). Generation and gender in the workplace. Retrieved January 6, 2008, from http://familiesandwork.org/eproducts/genandgender.pdf.

Frisch, M. H. (1998). Designing the individual assessment process. In R. Jeanneret & Silzer, R. (Eds.), *Individual psychological assessment: Predicting behavior in organizational settings* (pp. 135–177). San Francisco: Jossey-Bass.

Gentry, W. A., Griggs, T. L., Deal, J. J., & Mondore, S. P. (2009). Generational differences in attitudes, beliefs, and preferences about development and learning at work. In S. G. Baugh & S. E. Sullivan (Eds.), *Research in careers: Vol. 1. Maintaining focus, energy, and options over the life span* (pp. 51–73). Charlotte, NC: Information Age.

Hoppe, M. (1998). Cross-cultural issues in leadership development. In C.D. McCauley, R.S. Moxley, & E. Van Velsor (Eds.), *The Center for Creative Leadership handbook of leadership development* (pp. 336–378). San Francisco: Jossey-Bass and Center for Creative Leadership.

Jurkiewicz, C. L. (2000). Generation X and the public employee. *Public Personnel Management, 29*(1), 55–74.

Kupperschmidt, B. R. (2000). Multigeneration employees: Strategies for effective management. *The Health Care Manager, 19,* 65–76.

McKinsey and Company, Inc. (2007). Women matter: Gender diversity, a corporate performance driver. www.epwn.net/pdf/mcKinsey_gender_matters.pdf.

Ruderman, M. N., & Ohlott, P. J. (2002). *Standing at the crossroads: Next steps for high-achieving women.* San Francisco: Jossey-Bass.

Schein, V. (2001). A global look at psychological barriers to women's progress in management. *Journal of Social Issues, 57,* 675–688.

Smola, K. W., & Sutton, C. D. (2002). Generational differences: Revisiting generational work values for the new millennium. *Journal of Organizational Behavior, 23,* 363–382.

Twenge, J. (2006). *Generation me.* New York: The Free Press.

Twenge, J. M., & Campbell, W. K. (2001). Age and birth cohort difference in self-esteem: A cross-temporal meta-analysis. *Personality and Social Psychology Review, 5,* 321–344.

Twenge, J. M., Konrath, S., Foster, J. D., Campbell, W. K., & Bushman, B. J. (2008). Further evidence of an increase in narcissism among college students. *Journal of Personality, 76*(4), 919–927.

Valerio, A. M., & Lee, R. J. (2005). *Executive coaching: A guide for the HR professional.* San Francisco: Pfeiffer.

Valerio, A. M. (2009). *Developing women leaders: A guide for men and women in organizations.* Malden, MA: Wiley/Blackwell.

Yang, S. B., & Guy, M. E. (2006). GenXers versus Boomers: Work motivators and management implications. *Public Performance and Management Review, 29*(3), 267–284.

Zemke, R. (2001). Here come the Millennials. *Training, 38*(7), 44–49.

Chapter Six

MAXIMIZING IMPACT

Creating Successful Partnerships Between Coaches and Organizations

Erica Desrosiers and David H. Oliver

Executive coaching in organizations has the potential to bring value that far exceeds the sum of each individual coaching engagement in isolation. This added value is often the result of developing true partnerships between the coaches and the organization. As coaches and organizations work in partnership, coaching moves beyond just developing coachees into better leaders. There is the potential for the culture to be transformed, for practices learned through coaching to spread virally through the organization, to create an environment where development through coaching is accepted, even facilitated, and for leaders to take on the role of coaching.

In order to maximize the value of coaching in the organization, it is important to adopt a total systems perspective, thinking of coaching as a holistic intervention, and a set of interwoven

Note: A sincere thanks to Brandy Agnew, Brian Buford, Gisele Garceau, Carol Hedly, Marcel Henderson, Sarah Mankowski, Melinda Pearson, Chris Pollino, Steve Sass, Anita Stadler, Michael Tuller, Brian Underhill, Anna Marie Valerio, Shannon Wallis, Lee WanVeer, and all of the members of the Council for Executive Coaching for sharing their insights and experiences and offering valuable contributions to what we've shared in this chapter.

relationships and engagements. This is in contrast to a collection of one-off unrelated coach-leader pairings that happen to be occurring simultaneously within the organization. Coaching should also be treated as a broad development initiative, aligned with a strategy and goals, supported by the organization, with progress monitored throughout, and evaluated at key milestones. In doing so, the systems, processes, and practices that facilitate effective partnerships between coaches and leaders will become more salient, and a broader impact more achievable.

Our focus in this chapter is to enhance the value of coaching for the organization by emphasizing the critical partnership between the organization and coach at every phase of the process. As we move through our discussion, we will consider the three main phases of coaching that when viewed holistically have the power to facilitate coaching success throughout the organization: Alignment, Support, and Evaluation. Much of the focus in the coaching literature has been on the individual level, primarily between the coach and coachee. However, for the field and practice to continue a successful evolution, it's equally important to ensure there is alignment, support, and evaluation at the broader systems level.

Our perspective is that of a human resource (HR) leader or coaching practice leader charged with managing coaching throughout the organization. We will share what has worked for us, partnering with coaches in a large and complex global organization. Our discussion of best practices that we've learned and pitfalls that we've encountered (or, we hope, avoided) is based on our years of experience as we have worked to build a coaching practice and network in a Fortune 100 company and partner with coaches (and coachees) around the globe. We've also integrated our learnings from interviews and conversations with coaches and coaching practice leaders in other respected organizations (for example, Microsoft, Dell, Lockheed Martin, Target, EMC, John Deere) that set the bar for excellent coaching practices.

A Model for Coaching in Organizations

As mentioned above, we use an organizing framework (see Figure 6.1) to capture the best practices of coaching in organizations,

Figure 6.1. A Model for Coaching in Organizations

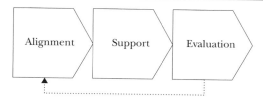

namely Alignment, Support, and Evaluation. Use of the model helps identify the critical issues throughout the process of coaching and of partnering effectively with coaches.

Within each section, we discuss the best practices and critical issues to consider both at the individual engagement level as well as at the organizational level. We focus on critical success factors for leveraging coaching within the organization, and discuss specifically how the partnership between the organization and the coach can help facilitate that success. In the Alignment section, we discuss the importance of partnering with coaches to ensure all key stakeholders within each engagement are aligned to a common purpose and goal. We discuss working with coaches to align not only on policies and procedures, but also the coaching philosophy and broader goals of the organization. In the Support section, we focus on how to best partner with coaches to ensure ongoing support for individual engagements, but also broader support for coaches working in the context of the organization. The organization should be a valuable resource for the coach, as the coaches should be for the organization. Finally, in the Evaluation section, we discuss practices used to evaluate coaching at both the engagement level and the system level, and how the partnership with coaches can be strengthened through the evaluation and how the overall process can be enhanced.

Alignment

For coaching to be effective in an organization, alignment between the coaches, the organization, and organizational representatives is required. Achieving that alignment is in large part the result of creating successful partnerships between coaches and the organization. Alignment begins with a clearly defined strategy and philosophy for coaching, one that is shared among senior leaders and HR professionals within the organization. External coaches (and the organization) also benefit tremendously from sharing that strategy and approach to coaching, as well as other relevant organizational information. Finally, within each engagement itself, the executive, his or her manager, HR representative, and coach all need to be aligned around expectations for the assignment—how it will progress and the intended outcome. In this section, we detail what the organization and coach should do to facilitate these multiple levels of alignment, and how to partner to achieve success.

Alignment at the Organizational Level

Compared to other development tactics at an organization's disposal, coaching is one of the most significant investments in terms of dollars and time (Corporate Leadership Council, 2003). Given that, it clearly makes sense for organizations to approach the use of coaching strategically and deliberately just as they would any other significant business initiative. Ideally, this starts with addressing the important questions of how and when an organization should use coaching. What is the organization's philosophy and plan for the use of coaching and how does it align with the broader talent management strategy and overall business imperatives? How does coaching support the organization's mission and values, how does it align to the leadership development strategy, who are the intended targets, and where are the most critical talent gaps where coaching should be leveraged for talent development?

In the past, coaching focused on what many refer to as "fix-it" situations (Coutu & Kauffman, 2009; Feldman & Lankau, 2005). Quite simply, the coach was called in because a leader was struggling, or even derailing, in his or her role. In recent years, many organizations have been evolving their use of coaching to a more proactive developmental focus as opposed to a reactive or remedial one (Feldman & Lankau, 2005; Peltier, 2009; Peterson & Little, 2008). As organizations develop an increased appreciation for the use of coaching as a proactive developmental approach, it is often used as part of a broader development strategy for proven and successful leaders and for recognized high potentials. The emphasis is on coaching great leaders to be even better.

As an organization positions coaching in a more positive light for key talent, HR and coaching practice leaders will likely distance coaching from the more traditional fix-it situations aimed at correcting performance concerns. In fact, we know of one large commercial banking organization that wouldn't refer to "fix-it" situations as coaching assignments. Instead, the coach was referred to as a consultant and was not managed or funded by the internal coaching practice. This was done to maintain the "purity" of the stated approach to coaching—that it was used to support the further development of high-potential leaders and key talent within the organization.

When the organizational strategy around coaching is focused on leveraging coaching as a developmental tool for strong leaders, the message becomes clear: coaching is a benefit or perk, reserved for the key leaders of the organization. Coaching begins to be seen as a positive rather than a negative, an indication that the organization is interested in and willing to invest in the executive's development. For example, in our own organization, we witnessed a very quick turnaround in the perception of coaching by providing coaches to very visible high-potential leaders who participated in a leadership development program. In less than a year, coaching went from being seen as a fix-it intervention to one that leaders were requesting. Further, proactive developmental coaching frequently catches leaders' performance problems at a time when small course corrections can be made to accelerate their development and keep them on track.

The partnership between the organization and coaches is strengthened to the degree that coaching is used as a developmental benefit. Coaches are more enthusiastic to work with organizations that position coaching as a positive, as this is a likely indication that an organization is progressive in its thinking about coaching. In addition, most coaches are usually excited to work with talented individuals with the ability and motivation to take their skills and career to the next level. The coach is also in a better position to be set up for success because the coachee understands that the organization is making an investment in his or her development and the coach is there to help facilitate that development. On the contrary, when coaching is used as a fix-it, the partnership can be more difficult. The coach may question the organization's motives for coaching. Do they really believe the person can be "saved," or is coaching just one more organizational process check on the coachee's way out the door?

In summary, how the organization positions coaching is critical for determining how coaching is viewed by leaders in the organization. This perception has implications for how well coaching is accepted and leveraged throughout the organization. Coaches must be aware of how coaching is perceived in the organization so they can manage those perceptions to achieve positive outcomes for both the coachee and the organization. The organization and coaches must be in sync so mixed messages are not sent. However, determining how coaching will be used in an organization is simply the first step. There is more work involved to leverage the true power of coaching as a system. There are decisions around processes and procedures, selecting and educating coaches, and matching coaches to executives. To the extent these decisions are aligned with the overall objectives of the coaching initiative, the more successful the coaching will be. In the next sections, we elaborate on several of the processes that contribute to strong alignment between coaches and the organization.

Selecting the Right Coaches

Identifying the most effective coaches for an organization requires not only an understanding of requisite coaching qualities, but the ability to recognize them in coaches, and overlay those qualities against the needs and culture of the organization. Other sources, even within this volume, examine coach qualities and competencies (for example, see Underhill's Chapter Two and Peterson's Chapter Four) and, clearly, there's a balance of education, experience, credibility, style, approach, flexibility, understanding of human behavior, and more. For example: What is the organizational culture like and would the coach be a good fit? Do leaders tend to have a strong bias towards coaches who know the business? What coach characteristics or experiences create credibility with leaders in the organization? Is the organizational culture generally consistent throughout, or are there subcultures within the main culture?

A key factor to consider is geography and local cultures. The essence of working well within a culture is having knowledge and experience with the culture. Coaches often specialize in particular cultures or geographies (such as Western Europe and the United States, or the Middle East and Africa), which are often tied to areas where they have lived or traveled extensively, giving them the familiarity with and understanding of the local culture, including in some cases speaking the language. As a result, coaches may have deep knowledge of a local culture, but still not have a broad enough perspective to fully understand (and coach others) relative to the larger global organization. However, those without the multicultural background may understand the broad aspects of a global organization, but may be ineffective in a particular culture (for example, China). In short, the best coaches possess a balance of deep local knowledge that enables them to be effective in a particular culture, as well as an appreciation of how things work across a global organization.

As the goal is to apply coaching strategically and consistently across the enterprise, effort is required to ensure that the right coaching partners are in place. Our approach, which worked quite well, was to communicate to regional HR teams that we were forming a global network of internally "approved" coaches. We advertised that we were seeking the best of the best to elevate within the organization and leverage their work more broadly. By partnering with the organizational leaders and considering the organizational goals, we were able to strategically identify and align coaches and avoid the negative outcomes associated with a more traditional "corporate takeover" approach.

Educating Coaches

Good coaches possess the skills needed to support development, and many coaches have extensive experience across a variety of organizations that they can draw upon. However, even the best coaches must be set up for success and know the rules of the road within an organization. For a true partnership to exist in which coaches are positioned to effectively help leaders, they must understand the context of the organization in which they are coaching. For an external coach, a significant challenge is lack of familiarity with the organization, its culture, and its norms. Basic background reading and research on the company is important, but it doesn't give the whole picture. Clarity from the organization around expectations, processes, and rules will help to bring consistency and point the collective coaching effort in the desired direction. We've found that coaches actually welcome this bit of structure.

So what can organizations do to help grow this knowledge and understanding in their coaches, short of hiring them as full-time employees? To provide this clarity, many successful organizations, including our own, find it useful to offer a form of orientation for external coaches. This tactic can be a very effective way to begin to align coaches and introduce them to the company's strategy and philosophy for coaching. Many companies take this approach and invite some or all external coaches (some even as a condition of hiring) to a one- or two-day orientation program, focused on learning about the organization. Topics covered often include:

- Organizational mission, vision, values
- Organizational structure, senior leadership
- Business model, current and key business initiatives
- Business challenges and opportunities
- Organizational culture
- Talent management strategy, philosophy, approach, and processes (including case studies to practice applying the information)
- Coaching philosophy and approach
- Ethics and confidentiality
- Roles and responsibilities, expectations

This information provides critical content to support the coach in the organization, but note it does not address "how to coach." Although some organizations are more prescriptive in the methodology or approach that coaches are expected to follow, we prefer to be more flexible, providing a certain level of structure, but not mandating specific details of the coaching process. In fact, experts in the field, generalizing from extensive research in psychotherapy, suggest that the specific coaching technique or method does not account for nearly as much variance in the coaching outcomes as other factors, such as the willingness and motivation of the coachee, or the coach-coachee relationship (see, for example, Feldman & Lankau, 2005; McKenna & Davis, 2009; Peltier, 2009). Of course, different coachees and situations may call for different approaches, and effective coaches are able to flex their approach accordingly (see Chapter One by Davis and McKenna). Therefore, the focus of a coach orientation is not to teach external coaches how to coach or tell them how they should be coaching, but rather to provide the context, tools, and resources they need to operate success-fully as a partner within the organization.

In addition to providing the needed context for the coaches, an orientation session can serve as a safe testing ground for HR to observe and assess new coaches. For example, an orientation may include a mock case study with actual data such as 360 feed-back, personality assessment data, and background information. This provides a great opportunity to watch the coaches in action and judge whether they are a good fit for the organization. We like to include HR leaders from our field organization to famil-iarize them with the processes and tools we're sharing with coaches, but also because they know their local businesses and leaders and will often play a critical role in matching coaches and leaders.

Orientation sessions are also a good forum to cover other relevant topics that the company deems important. One bank-ing and finance industry organization took this approach even a step further. At the time, diversity was a critical part of their strategy and they had specific initiatives in place to support that. One initiative was mandatory diversity training for all manag-ers and senior leaders. They extended that requirement to all external coaches with whom they worked because they felt it was important for the coaches to have the same level of understand-ing of where the organization was going with those initiatives and efforts.

Orientation sessions for the coaches need not be face-to-face sessions as just described. Organizations managing a global network of coaches, or those bringing in new coaches with less frequency or from dispersed locations, may be better served by either regional or individual orientation sessions for coaches. One large biotechnology company conducts one-on-one orientation sessions with every new coach selected to be in their preferred network of coaches. They spend time either in person or on the phone with the coaches to discuss and provide them with comprehensive supporting materials about the business, the culture, the contracting processes and expectations as a coach, and more. Although a different format, the intent is the same—to equip the coaches with the tools and information they need to be effective partners in leadership development.

Overall, the value of orientation programs is to set the coaches up for success within the organization. The better equipped they are with organization-specific knowledge, the more effectively they can coach within that context. Coaches we have spoken with have reinforced the value of such sessions, not only because of the opportunity to learn about the organization but because of the demonstration of the organization's commitment to the success of coaching through creating effective partnerships. So what is the coach to do when working with an organization that does not offer such an orientation for coaches? Our recommendation would be to spend time with the HR contact and ask questions that would help to better understand the organization as well as the specific context. This can be at the beginning of the engagement, but coaches should feel free to circle back with the HR representative throughout the engagement to seek clarity or have follow-up discussions, as the HR person can typically provide valuable perspective and insights not only into the organization but into the coachee's specific situation.

Setting Boundaries

Violating confidentiality or going outside the bounds of a coaching assignment are sure ways to damage or destroy the credibility of coaching in an organization. This can happen in one fell swoop, or over a period of time as leaders begin to realize they are not operating in a safe environment. Of particular focus is understanding what type of information is confidential between the coach and coachee, and what is shared with the organizational sponsors. What are the limits around topics to be discussed during the coaching engagement? Ultimately, the direction should come from the organization. But for an effective partnership to exist, the coaches need to clearly understand the organization's requirements and expectations, and the coaches need to be comfortable with those expectations and willing to abide by them.

The issue of what information to share or not share can be complicated for coaches and organizations. Many coaches come from the perspective of a clinical or counseling background and may believe the conversations they have with their clients should remain confidential. Many organizations, on the other hand, take the perspective that they are funding the assignment as an investment in their leaders, and they want reasonable assurance that the investment is paying off. This topic generates a variety of opinions by both coaches and organizations, and when the opinions are strongly held, they can be difficult to reconcile.

In our experience, there is a workable solution that addresses both the coach's interests in preserving confidentiality as well as organization's interests in progress. Confidentiality should be maintained for all contents of the "coaching conversations" between the coach and coachee. This might include topics related to a coachee's personal feelings, struggles in the current job, or challenges with difficult managers or coworkers. These limits should be upheld until the end unless topics arise that suggest the person or others are in immediate danger, similar to how a therapist would treat confidentiality (American Psychological Association, 2002; Natale & Diamante, 2005). For example, an organization is likely to want more information in the event that a serious crime or other ethics violation has been committed. Most organizations would expect to be notified if a coachee admitted to a coach that he had defrauded the company of thousands of dollars. Luckily, based on our experiences and what others have shared with us, extreme examples like these are rare. Nevertheless, companies should have clear policies about what is confidential between the coach and coachee, and they should review these with coaches up front, prior to any work taking place.

The concept of progress reporting addresses the organization's question about whether or not they are getting value from the investment. We believe the organization should receive periodic updates on the progress of the engagements. These should start with clearly articulated goals and key development themes and a coaching or development plan that outlines the action to be taken to address those needs. Progress reports should also be completed periodically throughout the engagement and at the end to summarize the progress against the objectives. This sharing of direction and progress will help both coachees and coaches to be more successful by keeping the engagement on track and keeping stakeholders aligned and informed. If the coach and coachee work together to prepare these documents, they can ensure nothing is reported that causes confidentiality concerns. We will also talk more about progress measurement in a later section.

The organization should also share with coaches their expectations of boundaries for engagements. For example, many organizations like to be clear that coaching should not focus on "out coaching," or any conversations regarding opportunities for the leader *outside* the organization. When leaders have a chance to step back and reflect on their careers and ultimately their lives, thoughts of "What do I do next?" or "Should I be doing something else?" can easily surface. Skilled coaches do not stop this conversation, but recognize that it can be a normal part of reflection. They also recognize when the boundaries are crossed and the conversation becomes more about helping the leader pursue other interests. It's a gray area, and it never hurts to remind coaches through policy that they are coaching leaders to be more effective leaders *at our organization*! Similar boundary problems exist when coaching moves towards therapy or counseling. Organizations should have policies to remind coaches to avoid these topics and refer clients with a serious problem to an employee assistance program or other appropriate service.

In summary, we have discussed how organizations can best partner with coaches to achieve alignment. Although the focus of the chapter is the system or organizational level, the three phases of coaching (Alignment, Support, Evaluation) must be addressed at the individual level as well if coaching is to be truly effective. In the next section, we will briefly discuss how organizations should partner with coaches at the individual engagement level to ensure success.

Alignment at the Engagement Level

Many coaches and coaching practice leaders have shared with us that a lack of alignment is one of the most common reasons they've seen for coaching engagements to fail. When the term "alignment" is used in this context, it is almost exclusively used to reference alignment at the individual level. This includes alignment between coach and coachee and alignment between this pair, the coachee manager, and any other key stakeholders in the organization sponsoring the particular assignment. This is a logical place to focus, because alignment at the engagement level is the foundation for a productive coaching engagement. For effective partnerships, everyone needs to understand at the outset what is expected of them and the end goals they're working against. When each stakeholder has a different definition of success, it's inevitable for the perception to be that the coaching did not accomplish the key objectives.

To the extent that the organization can help facilitate strong alignment, coaching can be more effective. This alignment process typically begins with a conversation between the HR representative and the coach. The HR representative should explain the issues and the reason for engaging with the coach. The HR person, particularly a more senior one, will often have an informed and more objective perspective on the situation that is critical for the coach to understand. If the organization deems it appropriate to proceed with the coach, we recommend the next meeting to be between the coach and the executive.

Matching

Because success will depend to a large degree on the partnership between the coach and coachee and their ability to create a collaborative and focused alliance (McKenna & Davis, 2009), it's important that both feel they will be able to develop an effective and trusting relationship (Marshall, 2006). This raises the issue of "matching"—how to go about the process of matching coaches and executives. Some organizations prefer to have HR or the coaching practice narrow the list of potential coaches down to two to three options and allow the executives to meet each and then decide who they would like to partner with for the engagement. An advantage of this approach is greater buy-in and commitment on the part of the executive for having taken part in the coach selection.

Other organizations prefer to have HR or the practice leader select the coach and then present him or her to the executive.

An advantage of this approach is that the process can often begin more quickly. The process can also be far more streamlined if a large number of engagements must be initiated at once, such as for a leadership program. If the HR person selecting the coach is familiar with the executive and the coach, he or she is likely to be a good judge of whether there will be a good fit between the two. In large global organizations where a central resource is less likely to know the executives as well, it becomes more important to rely on local HR to help narrow the pool to those coaches best suited to the executives.

We've found a modified approach to work well in many situations: HR selects the coach and the executive is notified that a coach has been carefully selected for him or her. Leaders are informed of their option to request a new coach in the event it doesn't work out. This still allows them some freedom in the decision, while keeping logistics much simpler. Most executives have stayed with the first coach selected for them and have been quite successful in their engagements.

Aligning with Stakeholders

Regardless of the approach taken to matching a coach, the first meeting between the client and coach is important to begin establishing trust and rapport, a requirement of effective partnerships (Natale & Diamante, 2005). This first meeting is also a valuable opportunity for the coach to hear the coachee's perspective of the situation. From there, the coach can decide who else to meet with to gain a more complete picture of the situation. For instance, if the coach was hired because the manager thought the coachee would benefit from working with a coach, the coach would be well-served to meet with the manager to better understand his or her perspective.

Every coach has his or her own particular approach and preferences, but ultimately in order to achieve alignment, the coach must partner with the coachee, his or her manager, HR representative, and other key sponsors to ensure all necessary parties agree on the coaching focus and how the engagement will progress. Although a simple idea, the importance of the role that HR can and should play in this process cannot be overstated. HR should partner with the coach to identify critical stakeholders with whom to speak, and even help to ensure that those meetings take place if scheduling gets in the way of progress and momentum.

Alignment Summary

In this section, we focused on alignment issues primarily at the organizational level, recommending that organizations take measures to ensure they select the best coaches, educate them regarding relevant aspects of the organization, and clarify issues of confidentiality and boundaries. Focusing on the individual engagement level, we briefly addressed issues of matching coaches to executives and ensuring that all parties are aligned on the overall goals for the engagement. In short, alignment is a critical success factor for the coaching to be effective, and establishing effective partnerships with coaches from the outset is necessary to achieve alignment.

Key Takeaways

- Clearly articulate a strategy around the use of coaching, and partner with coaches who will operate in line with those goals.
- Partner with coaches by helping them truly understand the organization, such as through a comprehensive orientation program.
- Establish organizational policies around confidentiality and boundaries and ensure coaches are aligned to those.
- Define a process for matching coaches to executives, recognizing that the quality of the relationship between coach and client will be a key driver of success.
- Ensure coaches partner with all key stakeholders in an engagement up front to align around expectations for the engagement—how it will progress and the intended outcomes.

Support

In this section, we address the next phase of our coaching model: Support. Like alignment, support occurs at multiple levels. Not only is support required for effective partnerships between coaches and coachees, but the organization must support the overall coaching practice to ensure its use as a valuable systemic developmental intervention. Once again, this is best achieved by creating and maintaining a true partnership between coaches and organizations. In this section, we will begin with how organizations and coaches can partner to support the effectiveness of ongoing coaching within the organization, followed by how such a partnership can ensure that each engagement is effectively supported.

Support at the Organizational Level

Earlier we described the best practice of bringing coaches together for an orientation program to align them to the organization's coaching strategy and philosophy, as well as to educate them regarding relevant aspects of the organization, its culture, and its processes. This type of orientation program also serves to support the long-term health of the coaching program, as it creates open lines of communication between the organization and the coaches, as well as among the network of coaches.

In order to build upon this kind of support for the coaching program, several best practice organizations (including Microsoft, Dell, John Deere, Capital One, EMC) conduct semi-regular group meetings with their coaches that serve as mutually beneficial sharing and learning sessions. In fact, when Microsoft conducted their first two-day "Coaches Forum" two years ago, they found it so beneficial that they decided to continue the practice, even conducting sessions virtually when in-person meetings were not an option. In these sessions, the organization learns from the coaches, coaches learn from the organization, and the communication and networks are strengthened and the partnership between the coaches and the organization is further cemented.

In these meetings, one primary topic the organization typically covers is business updates. In today's rapidly changing business environment, internal employees find it difficult to keep up with all of the business changes; it is even more difficult for external coaches to stay on top of such changes. Business topics include updates to the strategy, objectives, and major initiatives; how the broader external environment is affecting the business; and anything else the organization sees as relevant. The organization may also share insights into employee perceptions and the work environment, such as recent employee survey data and general talent management insights. These topics serve to build upon the partnership with coaches as true collaborators with the organization working toward the common goal of executive development. The sessions help to keep the coaches educated about the organization and up-to-date with relevant information and knowledge.

Furthermore, we know of several organizations that also use these types of sessions to continue to build the coaching skills of their coaches. As with any specialized practice, continuous improvement and honing one's skills are essential. Offering this developmental opportunity to help coaches continually grow their competence as coaches and their toolkit of techniques serves both the coaches and the organization well. Coaches you hire are having an impact within your organization, so it makes sense to invest in their continuous development as you would your own employees—like *true* partners.

These group sessions are also an ideal way to learn the coaches' perspectives about the organization. Coaches with multiple engagements over time within the organization will begin to develop an appreciation of the culture and its nuances, and will frequently recognize when change is occurring, themes that are emerging, or stresses that are present. They become a source of information that can provide valuable insights not otherwise available. An example of the benefits from this partnering activity involves Microsoft's Coaching Forum. They invited HR partners to participate in small group discussions with coaches working in their region. Coaches shared with HR the trends they were seeing with the clients they were supporting in that region, which HR found to be of tremendous value. The insights were also reported out by each group, enabling the organization to make enterprise-level revisions in their content and programs to enable significant year-over-year improvement.

Dell's coaching approach also exemplifies best practice in this area. In addition to hosting quarterly calls with their coaches to provide updates, feedback, and stay connected, they host a Worldwide Forum to bring their coaches together with the internal Global Learning and Development (L&D) team. The purpose of the forum is to bring together the coaches and the L&D team to collaboratively identify ways to improve the effectiveness of coaching at Dell, with a strengthened partnership between them as an explicit goal. The focus is to increase their coaches' deep knowledge of the company, including talent management tools and initiatives, as well as providing skill development opportunities. In the true spirit of the partnership, Dell also spends a significant amount of time gathering feedback from their coaches and exploring emerging coaching needs at the company.

Other examples of best practices include a large biotechnology company that hosts Coach Community meetings for all of their coaches three times per year with a high expectation of attendance. As with the other programs, the underlying purpose is to strengthen the partnerships and build a strong community of coaches who are passionate and engaged with their company. In addition to business updates and information sharing to better equip their coaches, the meetings incorporate a peer learning component to support coach development. Feedback from impact surveys conducted at the end of coaching engagements is also shared and discussed with the coaches. A specific example of an issue addressed in one of these sessions was stakeholder engagement. Participants collaborated on how to improve stakeholder (such as HR business partners and coachee's supervisor) involvement in the coaching, with a senior vice president in attendance to share his thoughts from the perspective of a coachee's manager. Further, recognizing the value of their coaches' insights, the organization asks coaches to share trends they're noticing in the organization, which are passed on internally. These events also provide networking opportunities, not only among coaches but also with HR business partners, to further strengthen relationships.

Some organizations elicit information and learnings from the coaches on an individual basis rather than in a group setting. For instance, Lockheed Martin conducts one-on-one meetings with all of their external coaches to solicit feedback on what the company can do to make the partnership more effective. Because the depth of experience varied greatly between coaches, the format evolved as the organization found that the one-on-one format, as opposed to group meetings, resulted in better feedback and fostered more effective partnerships. Whether done in groups or on a one-on-one basis, such programs' successes demonstrate that glossing over the potential added value coaches can offer would be a tremendous missed opportunity.

Last but not least, coaches can also be an invaluable link to the external environment (for example, through their coaching with other companies) that can help the organization stay up-to-date with external trends. External coaches can often see the organization more objectively, and can make good suggestions for changes or improvements across a variety of topics.

Support for Individual Engagements

As is the case with alignment, support at both the system level and the individual engagement level is critical. Once the coaching assignment is initiated, challenges can arise quickly. For example, the demands of the job might make it difficult for the leader to commit the time or there may be underlying resistance to the idea of coaching. This section considers support relative to each stakeholder in the engagement and his or her specific needs, including the coachee, the manager, and the coach.

Lockheed Martin provides an example of an innovative and proactive approach to supporting coaches. Lockheed Martin pairs each external coach with an internal senior coach embedded within the relevant business unit. Throughout the duration of the coaching engagement, the internal coach performs, not as a second coach, but rather as a support system for the external coach, offering knowledge and perspective on the organization, culture, and customer environment, as well as the coaching process within the company. In addition, the internal coach provides information about the business, its processes, and the complex organizational dynamics, including insights into the coachee and the context of the situation and the needs for the engagement. The internal partner also provides context and insight on feedback received on the coachee from organization members. Feedback from the external coaches indicates that this partnership is meaningful because it enriches their understanding and provides insight into the organization and the coachee, making their coaching more impactful. Coach partnering is one example of proactive practices to enhance partnerships.

Another practice is to increase coachee accountability. For example, Microsoft received feedback from their coaches that delays in engagement initiation and individual progress were often a result of coachee time constraints created by business and other priority conflicts. Equally frustrating for both the organization and the coaches, Microsoft created accountability mechanisms for their coachees, including specific deadlines for engagement start and deliverables in order for the engagement to continue. Marked improvement in the extent and efficiency of coaching was noticed.

Another approach Microsoft employs to support their coaches is to offer a "coach hotline" or key contact intended to fast-track any necessary support. For instance, scheduling and contacting busy executives can be burdensome and difficult for coaches. Coaches have a dedicated resource to provide assistance. As a result, the coaches can focus on progressing the coachee and not on time-consuming logistics, such as scheduling meetings or locating contact information. Both of these practices, coachee accountability and dedicated support for coaches, are further examples of how organizations can (and should) partner with coaches to achieve their joint objectives.

Support Summary

In this section we have discussed how organizations can support their coaches at the system level and at the individual level, how that support contributes to effective partnerships with coaches and, in turn, how those effective partnerships can maximize the value of the coaching for both the organization and the coachee. It is critical for the organization to share insights, information, and resources to help coaches navigate through the organization effectively. Equally important is for organizations to recognize that the coaches also have a wealth of information to share with the organization. This information can be leveraged for continuous improvement, positively impacting coaching effectiveness and other organizational programs and process.

Key Takeaways

- Coaches will be most effective when they have access to the proper tools, resources, and information, so organizations need to ensure that coaches have what they need to focus on developing leaders.
- Coaches have a unique view into individual leaders and the organization as a whole; organizations should solicit this information and use it for continuous improvement.
- Treat coaches as partners. Ask them what information or support they need to do their jobs better, and look for ways to provide it.

Evaluation

The last phase of the model is Evaluation. At first glance the value of a partnership between coaches and the organization may not be as readily apparent for Evaluation as it is for Alignment and Support. However, there are aspects of evaluation in which both the coach and the organization are best served by a solid partnership.

Evaluation at the Organizational Level

At the broad system level, the organization needs to know if coaching is having the desired impact on the business. Much is written elsewhere and even within this volume (see Steinbrenner and Schlosser, Chapter Fourteen) regarding detailed methodology for evaluation of coaching, so we will not address that here. The focus of this chapter is on how evaluative data can be leveraged to establish a partnership between coaches and organizations in order to maximize coaching impact.

One method of evaluation used by organizations is a post-engagement feedback survey, administered to the coachee, his or her manager, and the HR representative. At PepsiCo, we review feedback on a variety of aspects of the engagement as they relate to ratings of effectiveness to help us determine what contributes most directly to the success of engagements. For instance, one insight from our survey data was that immediate availability of the coach was a very important factor for our executives. When that type of information is shared with coaches, they are in a better position to meet the needs of their clients and increase the effectiveness of the coaching. Similarly, the biotechnology company previously mentioned conducts an impact and coach effectiveness survey following each engagement. The high-level themes and insights are shared with their coaches at their Coach Community meetings to ensure a constant feedback loop that allows real-time adjustments to the coaching process.

Aggregate evaluation data can also be used to determine which coaches are most effective within the organization, and whether there are some with a niche in which they are particularly effective. Some coaches may be better suited for a particular region or with particular types of leaders, whereas others are better in certain functions or with certain levels of the organization. In this regard, organizations can essentially determine how coaches can best be utilized, which partnerships should be reevaluated, and which should be maintained and strengthened. The stronger coaches can also be leveraged in other ways, such as in helping to orient newer coaches to the organization by providing an external perspective and serving as a resource for these coaches. In the spirit of true partnership, those coaches can facilitate a more seamless relationship between the external coaches and the internal organizational representatives.

Evaluation of Individual Engagements

Whereas coaches are less likely involved in the evaluation process at the organizational level, there is far more opportunity to partner meaningfully with the organization to evaluate coaching at the individual engagement level. This evaluation can and should include progress checks throughout the engagement and a final evaluation at the conclusion of the engagement. The coach and the organization can partner to conduct these evaluations, or one of the parties can take the lead, but key is for the coach and organization to partner in a review of the results and determination of go-forward plans.

Organizations may have a clear and established process for measuring progress at set points throughout the duration of an engagement. Such checks may be formal or informal, qualitative or quantitative. Sometimes the organization has a less centralized process, but the coaches are accountable for measuring and reporting progress. Who actually conducts the evaluation is not the most important consideration. The key is that the organization and coach review the information together and evaluate whether the coaching is on course or if adjustments need to be made. In that regard, mid-engagement progress checks are even more important than final evaluations because they can ensure that an engagement is on track and steer it toward more successful outcomes.

Earlier we discussed Lockheed Martin's use of internal senior coaches to support ongoing engagements with external coaches. As an established part of that partnership, the senior coach conducts an evaluation at the midpoint and the conclusion of the engagement. Part of that evaluation consists of a personal discussion with stakeholders around an evaluation of the coach. Such discussions and feedback are invaluable not only to ensure that the engagements are headed in the right direction and making progress, but that the coach is being effective in that role. That feedback is then shared with the coach in the spirit of the partnership and to maximize the value of the coaching for the organization.

Summary of Evaluation

Partnerships in the evaluation stage are centered on the notion of sharing insights and information with coaches. This information is useful to help coaches understand where they are excelling in the development of leaders and where they have opportunities for improvement. Likewise, it helps the organization determine the best way to leverage coaches for various locations and assignments. This approach optimizes the effectiveness of the partnership, and ensures that the organization is getting the most out of its investments in coaching.

In turn, coaches are able to provide the organization with invaluable information regarding the progress of broader coaching initiatives including systemic barriers and supports that may have an impact on the initiative's effectiveness. In addition, coaches often have insight into the degree of progress being made toward desired coaching outcomes, beyond individual behavior change.

Key Takeaways

- At the engagement level, evaluate by checking progress part-way through and at the conclusion of engagements.
- At the aggregate level, define evaluation criteria that are aligned with expected outcomes of the coaching program, including feedback on the coaches.
- To create effective partnerships that will maximize the benefits of coaching within your organization, share the data with coaches to enable continuous improvement.
- Leverage this data to determine the best ways to use specific coaches, whether based on location, type of assignment, or type of executive.

Concluding Thoughts

In this chapter, we discussed the importance of partnerships between coaches and organizations following a three-phase model: Alignment-Support-Evaluation. Though each phase of the model has relevance at both the individual engagement level and the broader system level, we focused at the broader level to emphasize the value of a collective, systemic initiative. With this focus, we intended to clearly communicate that there are many activities an organization can do beyond simply hiring coaches and setting them loose in the organization. The first step is adopting a mind-set that the coaches are and should be treated as extended and valuable assets of the organization. This includes taking steps toward orientation, education, continuous development, resource allocation, removal of barriers, and feedback. It also includes respecting the value of the coaches' experience and insights gained within the organization as a means to continuously improve the organization. All of this is best achieved through effective partnerships to ensure that coaches and key organizational stakeholders are aligned to common goals, that engagements and the coaching practice are effectively supported, and that evaluative information is shared and leveraged. With this mind-set and approach, organizations can truly benefit from coaching that far exceeds the sum of the parts.

References

American Psychological Association. (2002). *Ethical principles of psychologists and code of conduct.* Washington, DC: American Psychological Association.

Corporate Leadership Council. (2003). *Maximizing returns on professional executive coaching.* Washington, DC: Corporate Executive Board.

Coutu, D., & Kauffman, C. (2009, January). What can coaches do for you? *Harvard Business Review, 87*(1), 91–97.

Feldman, D. C., & Lankau, M. J. (2005). Executive coaching: A review and agenda for future research. *Journal of Management, 31*(6), 829–848.

Marshall, M. K. (2006). *The critical factors of coaching practice leading to successful coaching outcomes.* Unpublished doctoral dissertation. Yellow Springs, OH: Antioch University.

McKenna, D. D., & Davis, S. L. (2009). Hidden in plain sight: The active ingredients of executive coaching. *Industrial and Organizational Psychology: Perspectives on Science and Practice, 2,* 244–260.

Natale, S. M., & Diamante, T. (2005). The five stages of executive coaching: Better process makes better practice. *Journal of Business Ethics, 59,* 361–374.

Peltier, B. (2009). *The psychology of executive coaching: Theory and application* (2nd ed.). New York: Routledge.

Peterson, D. B., & Little, B. Growth market: The rise of systemic coaching (2008, January-February). *Coaching at Work, 3*(1) 44–47.

The Journey: Processes and Practices of Leadership Coaching

Chapter Seven

BUILDING THE COACHING ALLIANCE

Illuminating the Phenomenon of Relationship in Coaching

Travis Kemp

John is an experienced and successful executive coach whose client, Peter, a senior executive in a top tier business consulting firm, presented for coaching wanting to find greater work-life balance. His self-expressed motivation for achieving this objective was to enable him to spend more time with his three children. For Peter, spending four out of five days each week travelling out of state had taken its toll on his family, but equally concerning was the impact that the situation was having on his performance at work. His growing irritability and impatience with his team was having a heavy impact on his leadership performance; his talent and capability were now being questioned. To make his situation more stressful, he saw his wife, Sarah, as being unsupportive and critical of his parenting ability, often accusing him of being an "absent" father. In Peter's eyes, Sarah was self-centered, unreasonable and inattentive to his needs. According to him, this was a function of her tangible resentment of him leaving her alone to manage and care for their

(Continued)

children during his regular and extended absences. He was frustrated by his feelings of being "taken for granted" by not only his wife but also his leader and peers at work.

John found himself becoming increasingly agitated and judgmental about Peter's behavior and, while John refrained from overtly and openly expressing his emotional responses to Peter, John found his reactions to Peter's dialogue were becoming overtly agitated and aggressive. Most concerning though was that John could sense that Peter was now feeling judged in the coaching relationship and was progressively withdrawing. The coaching engagement was deteriorating, and Peter's likelihood of success was diminishing.

Considerable discourse has been devoted to the formulation and application of a multitude of coaching models and methods (for example, Cavanagh, Grant, & Kemp, 2005; Dembkowski & Eldridge, 2008; Stober & Grant, 2006; Whitmore, 2002) as an informing body of practice-based evidence (Barkham & Mellor-Clark, 2000) within coaching has emerged. Intriguingly, it is only relatively recently that interest in the coaching *relationship* itself has surfaced as a focus for theoretical exploration (Bluckert, 2005; Gyllensten & Palmer, 2007; Kemp, 2008a, 2009; O'Broin & Palmer, 2006, 2007, 2009). The current chapter seeks to explore the phenomenon of the coaching relationship through a set of theoretical lenses that serve to illuminate the developmental alliance built phenomenologically between coach and client and, through a case study window, will illustrate the utility and application of these lenses.

By approaching our understanding of the coaching intervention from the context of *relationship* rather than *method*, this chapter will openly challenge the arguably axiomatic presupposition that coaching clients present with a clear, informed, and well-articulated understanding of their desired goals and objectives. Though this premise is often touted throughout the broader coaching industry as fact, in practice this assumption is rarely accurate, nor is the assumption that all coaching clients bring to coaching the self-understanding, resilience, and capability to implement the desired changes they articulate (Kemp, 2006). Indeed, for many coaching clients, the outcome of their coaching experience may well be a deeper understanding and clarity of their internal drivers and desires and an ability to accurately *conceptualize, construct,* and *articulate* their goals. Hence, the current chapter will explore the experiential, emergent, and iterative nature of the coaching engagement and the importance that the subjective quality of the collaborative alliance that is built between client and coach plays in supporting the client's growth and development.

Specifically, authors such as Burdett (1998), McKee, Boyatzis, and Johnston (2008) and Kemp (2009), among others, have proposed that coaching within the organizational context can be more broadly conceptualized as an evolved form of *leadership*. Greenleaf (1970) suggested that leaders who demonstrated values and behaviors such as acceptance, empathy, listening, and understanding were more effective than those who demonstrated the more directive, command-and-control style of leader-follower behaviors. Hence, when coaches and leaders alike demonstrate a more engaging, introspective, and self-managed style of interpersonal relationship building, those affected by these behaviors appear more likely to successfully attain their own personal goals.

The lenses presented in this chapter support coaches' deeper explorations of themselves and their coaching relationships. They provide a reflective process designed to guide and inform coaches as they build a robust foundation for their coaching relationships and engagements. Implicit in the theoretical construct of these lenses is the criticality of coaches' own commitment to continuous development, the deepening of their understanding of "self," and the importance that this has on their ability to effectively apply any particular coaching model.

Challenges to Building Coaching Relationships

Conceptually, the coaching relationship can be viewed as a "helping" relationship, similar in structure to that described by Egan (2002). Of specific interest to the emerging discipline of coaching psychology are the many structural similarities observable between therapeutic relationships and those established within the practice of coaching (see Chapter One by McKenna and Davis; Kemp, 2008a). In addition to this, previous comparisons of professional practice within the counseling and therapeutic fields have highlighted the educational, developmental, and essentially nonclinical nature of these practices in many situations (Corey, 2004; Egan, 2002).

The *working* or *therapeutic alliance* are terms often used to describe the relationship that is established between counselors and therapists and their clients in their therapeutic engagements. This alliance has been found to be a strong predictor of efficacious outcomes in individual psychotherapy across a broad range of treatment methods and modalities (Horvath, 2000, 2001, 2006; Horvath & Bedi, 2002; Horvath & Symonds, 1991). As the practice of coaching continues to build its body of knowledge upon the evidence-based literature within psychology, education, and business, these findings compel us to apply these insights to the investigation of the *coaching* alliance. This approach is arguably validated by the expanding body of theoretical literature highlighting the relationship between coach and client itself as being a vital change agent within the coaching intervention (Bachkirova, 2007; Bluckert, 2005; De Haan, 2008; Gyllensten & Palmer, 2007; Jones & Spooner, 2006; Kampa-Kokesch & Anderson, 2001).

To illustrate the importance of utilizing these related informing bodies of knowledge in exploring the coaching alliance, we need only conduct a cursory examination of the discipline of social psychology to highlight the wealth of contextual understanding it provides for the coaching relationship. For example, Jones and Davis (1965) highlighted that we often incorrectly assume that people's intentions and dispositions match their actions and behavior. The implications of this *attribution bias* in the initial stages of the coaching relationship can be that the coach assumes that his client's behaviors and interactions accurately reflect internalized intentions, desires, and broader personality. However, these potentially inaccurate assumptions may become problematic as the relationship develops and may ultimately compromise the client's developmental outcomes if the coach is not actively managing their impact on the coaching engagement.

Another pertinent contribution is provided by Ross (1977). The *fundamental attribution error* is the tendency one has when observing a situation to underestimate the situational factors contributing to the outcome and overestimate the dispositional factors of the individuals within that situation as being contributory to the overall outcome. This phenomenon can present a unique challenge for coaches when coaching individuals who are grappling with undesirable circumstances, situations, or relationships. This cognitive bias often manifests behaviorally for coaching clients in the form of blaming others for their unwanted circumstances or outcomes. Within the coaching relationship, many situations and developmental events surface that tempt clients to attribute blame to someone or something external to themselves rather than examining and challenging their own contribution to the situation. A reactive or defensive cognitive framework rather than a proactive and solution focused one (Kemp, 2005) can constrain successful coaching outcomes. These are but a small sample of the numerous cognitive biases that humans, and hence coaches, fall victim to on a daily basis and which inherently challenge the development of a strong working alliance.

In addition to these cognitive biases, Kilburg (2004) has argued that psychodynamic factors also impact on the coaching relationship in a number of ways. In our case study, John's ability to act as an effective change agent within the coaching engagement was compromised by his historic and current familial structure, experiences and accumulated learning surfacing and having an impact on his relationship with Peter.

John grew up in what many would consider an underprivileged environment. He was cared for from the age of eighteen months by his mother after his father had left their marriage. John's mother struggled to support both him and his brother in their early childhood years and, being largely unskilled, she often juggled two or three part-time jobs at once to survive financially. In his early adolescent years, John was often left to care for his sibling in his mother's absences and he vividly recalls his memories of feeling resentful, angry, and unjustly burdened by having this responsibility thrust upon him at such an early age. His anger was not solely directed at his mother, however; John still articulates a strong sense of bitterness towards his father for "abandoning" his family and forcing John to have to "grow up before his time."

Transference can be described as the tendency for the client to perceive and respond to the coach with a pattern that matches the way in which he responds to others who demonstrate similar personality characteristics and styles as those of the coach. The client's projections of these perceptions, beliefs, and attributes toward the coach may have considerable impact on the ability of the coach to establish the intimacy and trust crucial to building an effective coaching alliance. Similarly, the reciprocity of this transference, or countertransference, on the part of the coach toward the client creates barriers to maintaining a client-centered engagement. Though failing to explore and surface these psychodynamic influences can be destructive for the client, they can also be seen as a natural consequence of all human relationships. When utilized intentionally and insightfully by the coach, these influences may become a valuable tool for client growth.

John had maintained a supervisory relationship with an experienced psychologist since first becoming licensed. He had always been prone to becoming intolerant, judgmental, and agitated when confronted by executives expressing what were, in John's words, "dubious" and "questionable" values. In particular, John struggled with senior male executives who had disclosed and, in some cases were openly boastful about, their extramarital affairs and infidelities. When John reflects on a possible source of these emotional responses, he acknowledges that his mother still nurtures a resentment of his "absent" father's indiscretions during the earlier years of their marriage and she continues to seize every opportunity to remind John of the selfish and uncaring man his father was.

Over several supervision sessions, John actively explored these issues to the point where he was better able to maintain a position of unconditional positive regard and respect for Peter. More important, however, his introspection surfaced the need to address his early life experiences more deeply within a therapeutic relationship and, as a result, John sought out the support of highly regarded counseling psychologist. This therapy resulted in a number of courageous and challenging conversations with his mother and current wife, Anne, resulting in the resolution of a number of long-standing issues within these two relationships.

In John's case, he used his introspective reflections and explorations to develop a broader perspective and understanding of Peter's behavior. He then utilized this understanding by applying self-management within his coaching conversations with Peter to more deeply understand and empathize with Peter's *intentions* beyond his demonstrable behavior. This enabled John to nurture higher levels of trust and mutual respect with Peter, which subsequently allowed for John's contribution to Peter's development to be supportive rather than judgmental and self-serving. It was through John's active commitment to his continuing process of inquisitive self-reflection and introspection that he was better able to identify his own psychodynamic patterns and the negative impacts that these were having on the coaching relationship.

In summary, the efficacy of the coaching engagement is enhanced as a result of the coach's awareness and management of her own subjective psychodynamic context and, as a result, coaches are better able to support the creation of what Wesson and Boniwell (2007) refer to as "flow-enhancing" coaching relationships (see Moore, Drake, Tschannen-Moran, Campone, & Kauffman, 2005, on relational flow).

It is apparent that coaches' awareness of the broader informing bodies of knowledge from the fields of psychology, counseling, and psychotherapy is important in enabling them to effectively and safely support their clients' achievement of efficacious developmental outcomes. A coach's inability to effectively identify and manage his cognitive biases and interpersonal dynamics and maintain appropriate boundaries compromises the trust, empathy, and shared insight that can be achieved within the alliance. Hence, it is vital for coaches to develop the ability to identify how these unique dynamics surface and manifest within their coaching relationships and subsequently establish a robust and accountable mechanism for adjusting and managing these biases when engaging with the client. To assist this process, the *human factors lens* (HFL) and the *coaching alliance lens* (CAL) provide a valuable framework for guiding and structuring the self management challenge.

Beginning the Process of Self-Calibration

It is helpful at this point to remind ourselves that human change is complex (Gilbert, 2002) and that this axiom presents a unique dilemma for coaches. To become effective change partners for their clients, coaches must develop more than just an extensive understanding of the science of human learning and change; they must develop a unique personal experience, understanding, and appreciation of change by participating in the same change and learning processes that they facilitate for their clients.

In an effort to provide a structured framework for coaches to explore their unique perspectives and experiences, Kemp (2007, 2008a, 2008b) proposed an introspective framework for coaches. Refinements made to the original framework emphasize four key human factors that contribute to one's own unique understanding of and interaction with our environment. The HFL provides a guiding framework through which coaches reflect upon their own unique "self" (see Figure 7.1 below) and, in particular,

Figure 7.1. The Human Factors Lens

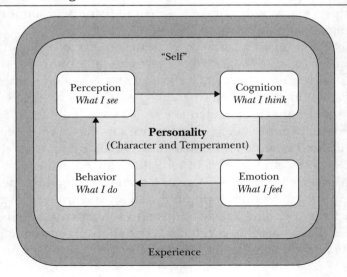

develop a deeper understanding of both the inherent and learned components of their personality (Sperry, 2006) and formative life experiences.

When applying the HFL to the introspection process, we begin by reflecting on our own unique *cognition*, or thinking patterns, through which we are able to observe the myriad cognitive biases mentioned previously. In addition, deeper reflection on our thoughts and thinking patterns effectively surfaces our own unique biases in the context of our past and present experiences. This process of "thinking about our thinking," or metacognition, serves to interrogate the accuracy of our habitual, automatic, or conditioned thinking and surfaces our own unique biases and schemas.

Next, by reflecting on our *emotion*, or feelings, we begin to develop a deeper insight and awareness of the powerful impact that emotions have on the other three human factors. If we can better understand how we respond and behave in the face of frustration, anger, elation, and a myriad of other emotions that surface in coaching relationships, we are more able to notice and manage the impact of these responses synchronously within the coaching conversation.

As our *behavior* has the most overt impact within the coaching relationship, and is normally the most easily observable by the client within the coaching interaction, it is imperative that the coach understands her behavioral patterns and refines her behavioral response repertoire, especially in relation to personally challenging situations and events when these surface in the coaching engagement. If, for example, it is the coach's tendency to withdraw when confronted with strong interpersonal conflict, it is important that the underlying causes of this behavior be explored and addressed outside of the coaching engagement to ensure that client outcomes are not jeopardized by the coach's personal developmental challenges.

Finally, coaches are called upon to reflect upon their *perceptions* of others, their situations, and their environments in their day-to-day life. The way we see our environment and make sense of this is subjectively unique. By identifying and exploring these perceptions through a process of data gathering and feedback, potential discrepancies in the coach's perceptual acuity can be highlighted and adjustments made. For example, if a coach perceives withdrawal and disengagement in her client as aloofness or arrogance rather than contemplation and reflection, her response may be one of direct challenge and confrontation rather than of allowing silence and reflective space in support of the client's process. Each of these two potential responses may have a markedly different impact on the client's coaching experience and outcomes.

Supervision and Its Contribution to Coaching Alliance

The continuous surfacing, reflection, and management of these intrapersonal and interpersonal insights can be confusing and confronting for coaches if conducted in isolation from professional supervision. The continuing engagement in a supervisory relationship is an important professional foundation of the practice of coaching and also provides a solid platform for the coach's continuing personal and professional growth. This supervisory relationship may also serve the purpose of surfacing, illuminating, and monitoring the "blind," "hidden," and "unknown" selves (Luft & Ingham, 1955) to further deepen the coach's self-insight and understanding.

The specific purpose of the supervision process within the coaching context is predominantly twofold; through the structured process of sharing private coaching interventions in strict professional confidence, the coach's strengths, weaknesses, and challenges can be identified, surfaced, and discussed with a professional, impartial, and confidential third party. This provides professional integrity and accountability to clients. In addition, this supervisory relationship offers an opportunity for the coach to identify those methods and practices that yield the most effective client outcomes and subsequently enable the coach to determine how best to generalize these methods to similar situations and clients in the future.

Though personally challenging, John's investment in supervision paid dividends for Peter's coaching outcomes. John found himself listening more openly and without judgment, even in the face of his well-ingrained and automated resistance to some of Peter's expressed perspectives. He was becoming more tolerant, patient, and accepting of Peter and he was beginning to understand him with a new level of "wholeness." For the first time, John could also see that Peter's underlying intentions and motivations were far more "honorable" and well-intentioned that what he had originally believed and, as a result of this shift in the relationship, John had noticed a marked increase in Peter's openness to input and level of trust and mutual respect that they both demonstrated in their coaching conversations.

By actively pursuing his own growth and development, while concurrently refining and implementing his Self-Management Plan (Kemp, 2008b), John was better able to listen to, observe, and illuminate Peter's "blind spots" and challenge him appropriately and empathetically with positive regard and without unresolved anger. John was able to identify the triggers for his automatic reactions and behaviors to situations similar to what he was experiencing with Peter more effectively and, by appropriately self-managing, John was able to modify his behavior within the coaching relationship.

The Coaching Relationship Dynamic

While the HFL can be drawn upon to understand how we as individual coaching psychologists experience and respond to a broad range of client relationships, and can also serve as a guiding framework for supervision, the framework may also illustrate the unique challenges that these individual dynamics play when first establishing a coaching relationship at the commencement of the coaching engagement (see Figure 7.2).

The relationship that is created in the coaching engagement is underpinned by the client's unique context, purpose, and motivation for commencing coaching. When these unique personal and experiential factors combine with those of the coach, the complexities in this dynamic are amplified. In addition, when the coaching engagement is conducted within an organizational setting, the complexity and variability of these dynamics increase considerably (see Figure 7.3).

Figure 7.2. The Coaching Relationship Dynamic

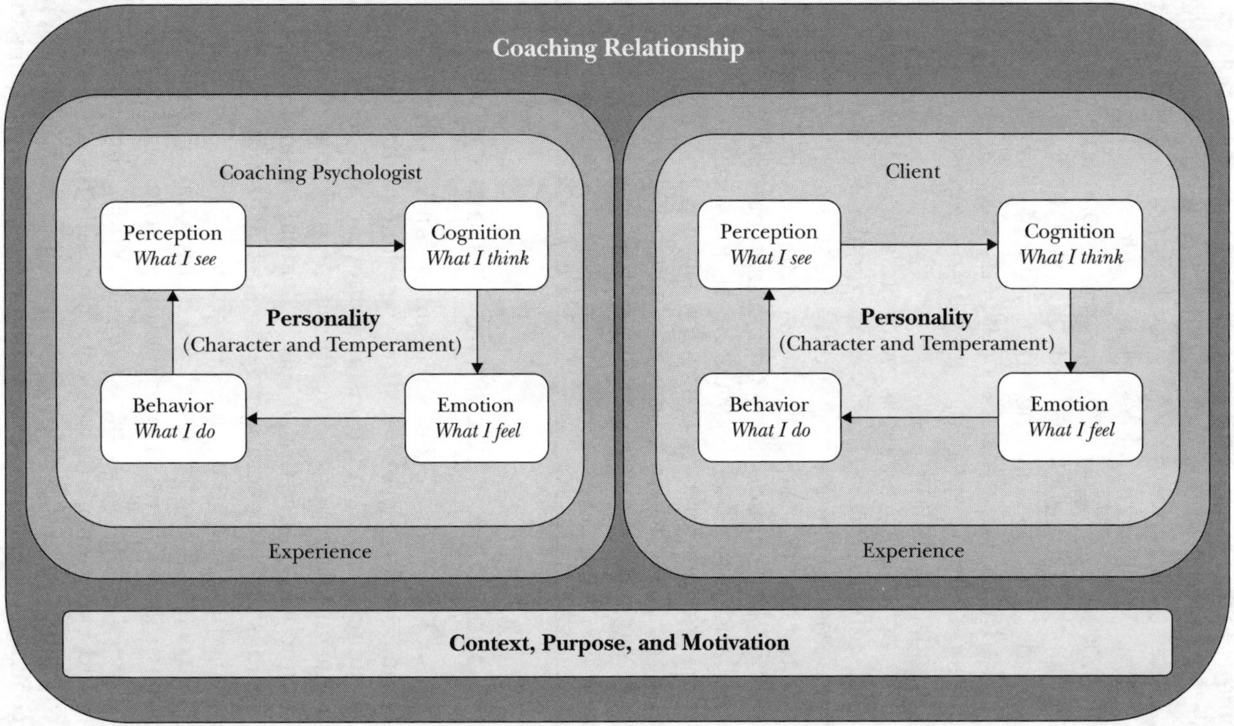

Figure 7.3. The Organizational Coaching Dynamic

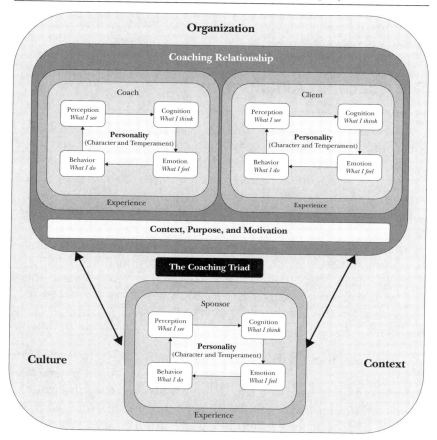

Within organizational settings, the importance of coaches' ability to manage the manifestations of their own unique human factors and their impact on the client and the client's organization is vividly highlighted. As the number of stakeholders increases, the potential confounding impacts of poor self-management also increase, as do one's subjective biases, political, and personal dynamics. In addition to creating an alliance between coach and client, there are other implications and impacts of the "inferred" alliance created between the organizational sponsor, the wider organization, and its stakeholders. This introduces yet another layer to the client's motivational drivers for entering into the coaching engagement. Hence, the need for a robust and standardized template for managing these multiple competing demands is vital to achieving valuable individual and organizational outcomes.

The Coaching Alliance Lens

> After Peter's second consecutive coaching appointment cancellation, John realized something was wrong. Most important, he realized that he needed to explore this relationship at a deeper level and so he reconnected with his supervisor. This time, though, he recognized the need to invest in his own personal reflective process. As a result, he focused his explorations on the emotional and cognitive responses that were surfacing for him in his relationship with Peter. In collaboration with his supervisor, John began to make connections between his biases in his perception of Peter and his situation and the way in which he was presenting and "occurring" for Peter as his coach in the coaching engagement.

The Coaching Alliance Lens (CAL) is a reflective template that guides coaches' self-development and applied practice. The lens highlights the critical importance of the processes of introspection and self-management as the cornerstones of maximizing positive client outcomes and captures the experiential antecedents necessary for establishing impactful and productive coaching relationships. Figure 7.4 diagrams this alliance-building process.

Introspection and Surfacing for Awareness

Although it is tempting, and arguably comforting, to begin the challenge of coaching with a model as a foundation for the coaching engagement, the coaching alliance is most impactful when the coach makes a significant investment in deeply exploring and reflecting upon her "self" prior to engaging in any formal coaching process with a client. This phase is vital in building the

Figure 7.4. The Coaching Alliance Lens

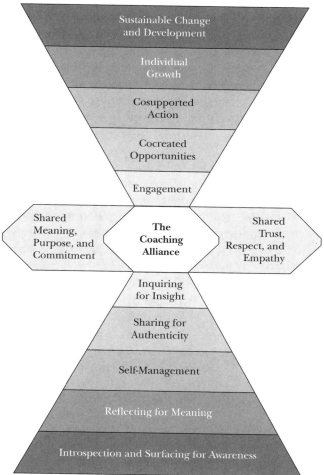

foundations for the coaching alliance and ideally occurs prior to the commencement of all coaching interventions. Most important, this stage is critical to establishing a sound personal foundation for effective self-management later in the alliance-building process.

During this phase, the coach progressively reflects upon and surfaces her own existing beliefs, values, biases, and prejudices that are occurring in relationship to her presenting client.

If these unique factors are not identified and surfaced prior to the commencement of the coaching engagement, the potential impact on the client's developmental direction and process can be significantly compromised. For example, a coach whose early life experiences were accumulated within a soundly adjusted and highly functioning "traditional" family consisting of mother, father, and one sibling living together in a suburban setting in an average suburb with sound community infrastructure may be quite different from a client whose early experiences were as an institutionalized orphan within state care as a result of a traumatic parental separation.

A coach's unique life context and experiences influence her perceptions of her client's life context and, as a result, the coach must actively surface these subjective biases to prevent them from actively confounding the content and direction of the coaching engagement. Though surfacing these biases is critical, it is the subsequent exploration and understanding that emerges from this process that galvanizes the platform for effectively managing her cognitive behavioral patterns within the coaching alliance.

It is this foundational introspective and surfacing phase that enables the coach to first identify and then to develop a deeper understanding and awareness of her unique strengths and weaknesses as a professional helper. Utilized in collaboration with a trusted supervisor, this framework provides a valuable process for coaches to deepen their personal understanding of how they "occur" or present for their clients in the coaching engagement and, subsequently, establishes the foundation of trust, openness, and authenticity that has been identified by Bluckert (2005) and others as being critical to the achievement of successful coaching outcomes.

Reflecting for Meaning

Once the coach has begun the process of introspection and is progressively surfacing her unique "self" within cognitive awareness, the opportunity for deeper understanding and meaning emerges. It is in this phase that the coach may make the most significant breakthroughs in self-understanding and, subsequently, the most significant increases of awareness relating to specific areas of the "self" that may require management in building the client-coach relationship to ensure that the client and her needs remain free of the coach's potential biases. As the coach becomes aware of his unique thinking, behavior, emotions, and perceptions, these insights provide the basis for continuing reflection and inquiry within supervision to further refine his self-management repertoire. With the supervisor's support, meaning and insights emerge for the coach, and it is through this process that she is able to actively explore and confront her biases and underlying drivers of her current behavior. With this knowledge, understanding, and skills at hand, the coach is free to engage with the client purely on behalf of his needs and desires and free of any potential confounding effect of her own motivators and drivers. The coach is hence able to be "present" and "selfless" in the process of supporting her client's developmental process.

During this phase, the skill and experience of the professional supervisor is crucial. The supervisor listens deeply and actively challenges inconsistent or random dialogue within the coach's reflective process, and the trust and accountability established within the supervisory relationship provides a foundation for the coach's continuing growth and personal transformation. As a unique form of helping relationship in its own right, the supervisor-coach relationship is founded on both positive personal regard and professional respect and this in turn allows for high levels of accountability of professional practice.

Self-Management

Self-management has been described as a process through which an individual develops a deep understanding of her own unique cognitive, behavioral, perceptual, and emotional patterns and subsequently refines the skills necessary to effectively manage these patterns' externalized impact on her client (Kemp, 2008b). Having commenced the process of developing deeper insight and understanding of the self, the progressive process now allows for the coach to begin to mold this awareness into what has been referred to previously as a "Self-Management Plan" (SMP) (Kemp, 2008b). Through this process, the coach captures and records her potential biases, beliefs, insights, strengths, and weaknesses; indeed any cognitive, behavioral, perceptual, or emotional insight that may influence the coaching intervention is highly valuable to the coaching alliance. The coach actively designs the solutions, actions, and responses to these phenomena that will be applied within the coaching engagement should the need arise.

The SMP may include such elements as the identification of preemptive cues or the identification of a set of positive and productive cognitive responses to these potentially challenging elements of the relationship. By way of example, a coach who has surfaced a persistent pattern of avoidance with her clients when they demonstrate anger or frustration may choose to explore this in her SMP. She may then design a response to this situation that disrupts her automatic behavioral responses and which could include such actions as verbalizing the emotion with the client—in fact, experiencing this in the moment—then deepening her empathy and understanding of the source and experience of this emotion by consciously taking three deep breaths, relaxing in the moment, and allowing the space and time for the client to articulate the source of his frustration in a safe and supported conversation. This strategy is important for both the client's growth and development and also that of the coach as she broadens her capability in supporting a wide range of clients.

Sharing for Authenticity

Listening deeply to the client's unique narrative of the emergent realities and sharing authentically with them within the appropriate boundaries of the client-coach relationship is an important part in the relationship-building process. As the coach continues to develop a deeper understanding of herself and a subsequent ability to more purposefully calibrate her cognitive-behavioral responses and mediate her subjective biases, the coach begins to develop a capability to deeply listen to the *intent* behind the client's overt language and literal dialogue.

This process of "listening with the third ear" (Macran, Stiles, & Smith, 1999, 426) allows the coach to begin to develop a more complete picture of the client's unique goals and challenges. As the coach's perceptual filters and processing biases are more mindfully managed within the coaching conversation, less data from the client's unique perspective and context is lost through the coach's filtering process, thus harnessing more richness for the client's experience within the development process. In short, the coach is able to listen, hear, and respond to the client and her unique goals and aspirations in a way that seeks to reduce the subjective influence of the coach's life experiences and personal values, opinions, and judgments on these responses. Hence, the client's experience in the coaching relationship is one that is, as much as possible, of her own creation and authentic to his own desires and goals.

Inquiring for Insight

During the *inquiring for insight* phase of establishing the coaching alliance, the coach maintains the position of "curious collaborator," respectfully and appropriately deepening her understanding of the client's unique experience through rich dialogue, empathy, and deep listening. Adopting this position of "humble learner" allows the coach to maintain and nurture her intention of genuine interest, concern, and unconditional positive regard for the client. By maintaining this position, the coach creates the reflective space within the relationship to allow for the client's needs and insights to progressively synthesize into clear intent and action.

With the coach now actively self-managing the intrapersonal dynamic between herself and the client, she is now able to pursue progressively more refined and evocative inquiry through the use of sophisticated questioning that can facilitate new insight on the client's presenting challenges and opportunities. Much more than simply a set of well-crafted questions, though, insight-focused questioning stimulates a self-generative environment for the client and nurtures motivation for deepening his personal awareness and understanding of both himself and his organizational context. Questions such as "If you were to change your view of the current situation, what would that allow for?" and "What may be possible if you were to make the change you are describing?" compel the client to free himself of what Ellis (1967) describes as the "irrational shoulds and musts" that lead to self-limiting cognitions.

The Emergence of the Coaching Alliance

The cumulative outcome of moving through these foundational phases within the relationship-building process is the emergence of the coaching alliance. It is important to emphasize this important conceptual distinction. The alliance forms, or emerges, as a result of the coach's extensive efforts on her own introspection and reflective understanding of the way that she occurs for her client in the relationship.

Though a transactional and functional relationship can be built mechanically, the deeper phenomenological qualities of the relationship that define it as an *alliance* surface as a result of the coach's contributing her own unique awareness of herself as a change agent within the coaching process and, subsequently, by actively nurturing the relational antecedents necessary for the alliance to germinate and flourish. This proposition supports previous suggestions that the coaching alliance emerges through an organic process and not simply through the controlled and replicable application of any specific model or method. Once realized, the coaching alliance becomes a pivotal point in the coaching process whereby the relatively transactional coaching relationship transforms into an intimate, influential, and impactful alliance that supports the subsequent goal-focused action phases of the coaching intervention.

Client Outcomes—The Results of Effective Coach Calibration

By the conclusion of the coaching relationship, Peter had made several important developmental leaps forward from both a business and personal perspective. He had put in place the necessary changes that supported a better work-family balance and, as a result, was reporting significantly higher levels of satisfaction with his life and his role as father to his three young children. His leadership relationships had improved markedly and feedback that he was receiving from his team members indicated that his support and accessibility had improved significantly. He was now more approachable and engaged with them authentically. Peter had also been able to articulate his deeper desires and objectives more accurately and now understood that the original objective that stimulated his request for coaching—improved work-life balance—was a symptomatic response to a much deeper and complex developmental challenge.

As a result of engaging fully in the five foundational phases of the alliance-building process, the coach effectively *calibrates* herself as a "tool" for client development and is now able to build and sustain the self-generating environment for the client. In moving forward from a place of shared meaning, a high level of trust within the coaching relationship evolves, openness increases, and defensiveness dissipates. This broadening movement toward client growth allows for a rapid expansion of possibilities and opportunities to surface within and for the client and, with further clarity, the client can strengthen his commitment and resolve to achieving these goals.

As the client maintains his focus and action within coaching and moves into the maintenance phase of the change process (Prochaska, Norcross, & DiClemente, 1994), the probabilities of a new level of performance and self-mastery become visible and achievable and further serve to nurture the client's motivation for continued effort. For some clients, new emerging possibilities that may have been previously perceptually unachievable may now be possible.

Client Outcomes of the Alliance

It is from this point that the outcomes of the alliance-building process emerge freely and authentically. Without the coach's efforts to calibrate effectively through the five reflective stages, these outcomes may either fail to manifest at all, in the case of coaching relationship breakdown, or may manifest in inherently biased or diluted outcomes. For example, if a client experiences that the coach has been driving a specific personal agenda not aligned to his, his commitment to action and goal attainment may be marginal or variable, preventing him from engaging fully in the alliance. Equal *engagement* of both the client and the coach ensures that a focus and commitment to the client's continuing efforts toward achieving desired outcomes are sustained. This engagement nurtures the collective creativity of the coach and client within the alliance and new *cocreated opportunities* for client action emerge. Again, without effective coach calibration, opportunities for the client's development that may be identified by the coach may not be authentically cocreated and hence the client's commitment to these may be marginal. When the coach is calibrated accurately, both she and the client actively collaborate to support the client's continuing efforts and *action*, with the coach providing continuous feedback and generative dialogue to empower the client's developmental efforts. These efforts are designed by and sustained by the client himself and not by the perspectives, desires, or directions of the coach. It is this key point that highlights the ultimate impact of poor coach calibration and the importance of professional supervision.

Finally, at the conclusion of the coaching engagement, the client works with the coach to review and evaluate progress made and to discuss future developmental directions. This often results in the establishment of a broad plan to ensure the sustainability of the client's achievements in the coaching intervention. Likewise, this termination phase begins the retrospective process of analysis for the coach in her supervisory relationship to ensure her continuing professional development.

Conclusion

In its broadest sense, this chapter has sought to deepen our theoretical understanding of the human relationship formed within a coaching engagement. Further, it highlights the critical importance of the inherent intimacy and complexity of this relationship and its impact on coaching clients' ability to achieve positive and efficacious outcomes. In support of this intention, the chapter has offered a set of theoretical lenses that can be utilized by practitioners to explore the critical core elements that surface both from within the coach and from within the client during the coaching process, and how these elements influence the outcomes of coaching.

By deepening our understanding of broad human predispositions to bias using an ongoing, structured process of introspection and progressive surfacing of our own unique idiosyncrasies and foibles, coaches are better equipped to maintain their role as calibrated, balanced, and "neutral" facilitators in the coaching engagement and are also better prepared to interact and respond to their clients in ways that maintain the primacy of clients' goals and objectives at the forefront of the coaching intervention.

References

Bachkirova, T. (2007). Role of coaching psychology in defining boundaries between counselling and coaching. In S. Palmer & A. Whybrow (Eds.), *Handbook of coaching psychology: A guide for practitioners* (pp. 351–366). Hove, UK: Routledge.

Barkham, M., & Mellor-Clark, J. (2000). Rigour and relevance: Practice-based evidence in the psychological therapies. In N. Rowland & S. Goss (Ed.), *Evidence-based counselling and psychological therapies: Research and applications* (pp. 127–144). London: Routledge.

Bluckert, P. (2005). Critical factors in executive coaching: The coaching relationship. *Industrial and Commercial Training, 37*(7), 336–340.

Burdett, J. O. (1998). Forty things every manager should know about coaching. *Journal of Management Development, 17*(2), 142–152.

Cavanagh, M., Grant, A. M., & Kemp, T. J. (Eds.) (2005). *Evidence based coaching, Vol. 1. Theory, research and practice from the behavioural sciences.* Queensland: Australian Academic Press.

Corey, G. (2004). *Theory and practice of counseling and psychotherapy* (7th ed.). New York: Wadsworth.

De Haan, E. (2008). *Relational coaching: Journeys towards mastering one-to-one learning.* Chichester, UK: Wiley.

Dembkowski, S., & Eldridge, F. (2008). Achieving tangible results: The development of a coaching model. In D. Drake, D. Brennan, & K. Gortz (Eds.), *The philosophy and practice of coaching: Insights and issues for a new era* (pp.195–212). West Sussex, UK: Wiley.

Egan, G. (2002). *The skilled helper: A problem-management and opportunity-development approach to helping* (7th ed.). Pacific Grove, CA: Brooks Cole.

Ellis, A. (1967). Goals of psychotherapy. In A. R. Mahrer (Ed.), *The goals of psychotherapy* (pp. 206–220). New York: Macmillan.

Gilbert, R. L. (2002). *How we change: Psychotherapy and the process of human development*. Boston: Allyn & Bacon.

Greenleaf, R. (1970). *The servant as leader*. Indianapolis: The Robert K. Greenleaf Center.

Gyllensten, K., & Palmer, S. (2007). The coaching relationship: An interpretive phenomenological analysis. *International Coaching Psychology Review, 2*(2), 168–177.

Horvath, A. O. (2000). The therapeutic relationship. From transference to alliance. *Journal of Clinical Psychology, 56*(2), 163–173.

Horvath, A. O. (2001). The alliance. *Psychotherapy, 38*(4), 365–372.

Horvath, A. O. (2006). The alliance in context: Accomplishments, challenges and future directions. *Psychotherapy: Theory, Research, Practice, Training, 43*(3), 258–263.

Horvath, A. O., & Bedi, R. P. (2002). The alliance. In J. C. Norcross (Ed.), *Psychotherapy relationships that work: Therapist contributions and responsiveness to patients* (pp. 37–69). New York: Oxford University Press.

Horvath, A. O., & Symonds, D. (1991). Relation between working alliance and outcome in psychotherapy: A meta-analysis. *Journal of Counseling Psychology, 38*(2), 139–149.

Jones, E. E., & Davis, K. E. (1965). From acts to dispositions: The attribution process in social psychology. In L. Berkowitz (Ed.), *Advances in experimental social psychology, Vol. 2* (pp. 219–266), New York: Academic Press.

Jones, G., & Spooner, K. (2006). Coaching high achievers. *Consulting Psychology Journal: Practice and Research, 58*(1), 40–50.

Kampa-Kokesch, S., & Anderson, M. Z. (2001). Executive coaching: A comprehensive review of the literature. *Consulting Psychology Journal: Practice and Research, 53*(4), 205–228.

Kemp, T. J. (2005). The proactive behaviour framework: A reflective process for exploring thinking, behaviour and personal insight. In M. Cavanagh, A. M. Grant, & T. J. Kemp (Eds.), *Evidence based coaching, volume 1: Theory, research and practice from the behavioural sciences* (pp. 49–56). Sydney: Australian Academic Press.

Kemp, T. J. (2006). An adventure-based framework for coaching. In D. R. Stober & A. M. Grant (Eds.), *Evidence based coaching handbook*. Hoboken, NJ: Wiley.

Kemp, T. J. (2007). Simplifying evidence-based practice: Applying the human factors lens to the coaching process. *Opening Keynote Address*. 3rd Australian Evidence-Based Coaching Conference, Sydney, July.

Kemp, T. J. (2008a). Coach self-management: The foundation of coaching effectiveness. In D.D. Drake, D. Brennan, & K. Gortz (Eds.), *The philosophy and practice of coaching: Insights and issues for a new era* (pp. 27–50). Chichester, UK: Wiley.

Kemp, T. J. (2008b). Self-management and the coaching relationship: Exploring coaching impact beyond models and methods. *International Coaching Psychology Review, 3*(1), 32–42.

Kemp, T. J. (2009). Is coaching an evolved form of leadership? Building a transdisciplinary framework for exploring the coaching alliance. *International Coaching Psychology Review, 4*(1), 105–110.

Kilburg, R. R. (2004). When shadows fall: Using psychodynamic approaches in executive coaching. *Consulting Psychology Journal: Practice and Research, 56*(4), 246–268.

Luft, J., & Ingham, H. (1955). The johari window, a graphic model of interpersonal awareness. *Proceedings of the Western Training Laboratory in group development.* Los Angeles: UCLA.

Macran S., Stiles, W. B., & Smith, J. A. (1999). How does personal therapy affect therapists' practice? *Journal of Counseling Psychology, 46*(4), 419–431.

McKee, A., Boyatzis, R., & Johnston, F. (2008). *Becoming a resonant leader: Develop your emotional intelligence, renew your relationships, sustain your effectiveness.* Boston: Harvard Business School Press.

Moore, M., Drake, D. B., Tschannen-Moran, B., Campone, F., & Kauffman, C. (2005). *Relational flow: A theoretical model for the intuitive dance.* Paper presented at the Coaching Research Symposium, San Jose, CA.

O'Broin, A., & Palmer, S. (2006). The coach-client relationship and contributions made by the coach in improving coaching outcome. *The Coaching Psychologist, 2*(2), 16–20.

O'Broin, A., & Palmer, S. (2007). Re-appraising the coach-client relationship: The unassuming change agent in coaching. In S. Palmer & A. Whybrow (Eds.), *Handbook of coaching psychology: A guide for practitioners* (pp. 295–324). Hove, UK: Routledge.

O'Broin, A., & Palmer, S. (2009). Co-creating an optimal coaching alliance: A cognitive behavioural coaching perspective. *International Coaching Psychology Review, 4*(2), 184–194.

Prochaska, J. O., Norcross, J. C., & DiClemente, C. C. (1994). *Changing for good: A revolutionary six-stage program for overcoming bad habits and moving your life positively forward.* New York: Avon.

Ross, L. (1977). The intuitive psychologist and his shortcomings: Distortions in the attribution process. In L. Berkowitz (Ed.),

Advances in experimental social psychology, Vol. 10 (pp. 173–240). Orlando, FL: Academic Press.

Sperry, L. (2006). *Cognitive behavior therapy of DSM-IV-TR personality disorders: Highly effective interventions for the most common personality disorders.* New York: Routledge.

Stober, D. R., & Grant, A. M. (2006). *Evidence based coaching handbook: Putting best practice to work for your clients.* Hoboken, NJ: Wiley.

Wesson, K., & Boniwell, I. (2007). Flow theory—its application to coaching psychology. *International Coaching Psychology Review, 2*(1), 33–43.

Whitmore, J. (2002). *Coaching for performance: Growing people, performance and purpose* (3rd ed.). London: Nicholas Brealey.

Chapter Eight

COACHING PROGRAMS

Moving Beyond the One-on-One

Lorraine Stomski, Janis Ward, and
Mariangela Battista

The practice of executive coaching has grown rapidly in recent years (Corporate Leadership Council, 2003). Research has found that though there is a preference for executive coaching among executives, this developmental tool was found to be more costly than other leadership development activities and organizations were rarely managing coaching investments in a coordinated or consistent manner (Corporate Leadership Council, 2003).

Coaching engagements in organizations can be quite unfocused in that coaching is provided based on the merits of an individual request rather than the business needs and requirements. An organization can be running a number of different coaching engagements for different leaders, each with a different purpose and intended outcome and none of the outcomes necessarily tied to business initiatives or needs. With such haphazard purposes it is difficult to document success or any kind of return on this investment.

Further, some of the ad hoc engagements can take on a nature of secrecy, especially if the purpose is to assist a potentially derailing executive. Because these engagements are cloaked in secrecy the coaching goals do not necessarily correspond to business or organizational goals and they fail to create any impact for the business. They often fail to create an impact for leaders as well because they may be working on individual issues in isolation from the bigger organizational issues that may impede their personal success.

In summary, though executive coaching has become more prevalent in many organizations, we often see coaching engagements as ad hoc solutions to a leader's immediate skill gap or need versus a more comprehensive and enterprise-wide initiative that is focused on broader strategy alignment and culture change. This chapter will focus on strategic uses of executive coaching. More specifically we will discuss the development of a "coaching culture" in organizations, and the use of executive coaching in action learning programs, succession planning programs, and organizational on-boarding programs. To the extent available, we employ and therefore share our evidence-based practices and, where applicable, we offer case studies to bring the specific executive coaching application to life. Our nearly hundred years of combined experience in developing coaching cultures in multinational organizations have taught us the exponential value of aligning organization strategies with coaching practices.

Creating a Coaching Culture

The practice of executive coaching can be used to help establish a culture of feedback and coaching in organizations. A coaching culture is one where feedback is shared openly among members of work groups, teams, and organizations to improve or sustain high performance. In organizations that have well-developed coaching cultures, feedback flows fairly freely across levels and divisions with a goal of continuous process improvement. These organizations have invested time and training to prepare their members to give feedback effectively and receive it in an open, nondefensive manner. They also often use tools such as performance appraisals, 360 surveys, or employee satisfaction and organizational climate surveys to initiate the feedback discussions.

Although the use of these tools and practices is prevalent among large organizations, there are still many organizations that have not embraced them or have done so in a very limited or traditional manner. For whatever historic, organizational, cultural, or industry reasons, many of these organizations have a very strong performance culture where an individual's success is the individual's own responsibility and one either sinks or swims on his or her own merit. These organizations may provide a fair amount of training and support for the technical and functional expertise connected to the business and industry, but leadership development is left to evolve on its own. Often the assumption is that if one was successful at the job he or she would be a successful leader and manager of others performing that job.

As decades of leadership development research and practice tells us (Charan, Drotter, & Noel, 2000), functional expertise can carry a leader only so far. As organizations begin to recognize a need to provide better guidance to their leaders, they may engage in coaching engagements that are designed to help a manager who is failing in his or her current role. These one-off, incidental engagements do not, however, help solve the more endemic problem of lack of feedback, coaching, and leadership support organization-wide. Instead, they address an immediate management need but not the larger, more strategic approaches to leadership development. Creating a coaching culture can help transform an organization into a high-performing one with a focus on continuous process improvement.

Start at the Top

When creating a coaching culture, coaching engagements are part of a more comprehensive and strategic leadership development plan. These coaching engagements usually start at the top of an organization or functional part of an organization and then cascade to the next level of the organization. If the organization already uses tools for feedback, such as performance appraisal or 360 surveys, these can be used to initiate the process. If the organization currently does not implement such practices, a good place to start is a well-constructed, well-implemented 360 survey that gathers and delivers feedback anonymously. A coach would work individually with each senior leader to interpret the results and to put an action plan in place to address the feedback.

Typically, the engagements cascade down to the next level every year so that over a few years, most of the organization's management has participated in executive coaching and the coaching and feedback practice becomes commonplace.

Promote a Public Program

Coaching engagements that are more individually oriented often are not public, although there are a number of key stakeholders who sponsor and are aware of the coaching engagement. Strategic, enterprise-wide programs that are trying to create a coaching culture need to be public programs. Everyone in the participating organization should know the coaching program is occurring and that it has the buy-in and participation of the most senior leaders of the organization. Whenever possible, senior executives should be encouraged to share their developmental goals with their team so that the team can witness the process of coaching firsthand prior to their own participation as a coaching recipient. This transparency builds trust in the process and preempts much of the resistance that starting a coaching program can create. Of course, sharing the developmental focus of a senior executive must be carefully thought out so as to avoid undermining the executive's credibility and power. However, it is possible to strike a good balance between an open and transparent process and revealing too much information.

Align with Business Strategy

Coaching cultures require that enterprise-wide coaching programs be aligned with the business strategy. Coaching programs built around a strategic need, such as alignment with the organization's goals and strategy, can have a large impact on the executives' buy-in and motivation to fully avail themselves of the coaching engagement opportunity. Executives may be skeptical of the need for and benefits of working with a coach and may believe they are fine just the way they are. Though there is no benefit in forcing someone to participate in a coaching engagement, some developmental opportunity usually surfaces through the initial assessment of leadership skills and ability (usually through a 360 feedback assessment) of which they were completely unaware. This type of "blind spot" is often the case in organizations without a feedback culture. When a case can be made that developing a set of skills or focusing on particular areas for development will allow them to better execute strategy and deliver results on organizational goals, the executives are more likely to buy in.

Focus on Feedback

The coaching engagements in these enterprise-wide coaching programs often center on similar development areas as one-off individual engagements, but they also address much more. The senior executives receive an assessment of their own leadership talent and are given coaching that focuses on their leadership abilities and areas for improvement. In addition, the coaching also focuses on the senior leaders' ability to deliver feedback to their direct reports. The coach becomes a role model of how to coach others; while working with the executives, the coach is modeling the skills needed to be an effective coach. Thus, these enterprise-wide coaching programs are providing executives a firsthand experience on the benefits of giving feedback and coaching. Such an experience is more vivid and immediately pragmatic for them, as opposed to attending a training program or reading about how to be a good manager and coach.

Creating a Coaching Culture: Bank of New York Case Study

The Bank of New York was founded in 1784, making it the oldest bank in the United States, and existed until its merger with the Mellon Financial Corporation in 2007 to form Bank of New York Mellon. In 2004, a new senior executive was hired to head the Corporate Trust Division. She brought with her rich personal experience with coaching, feedback, 360 assessment, and formal performance appraisal processes from her previous employment experiences. As a result, she felt

(Continued)

Creating a Coaching Culture: Bank of New York Case Study (*Continued*)

that the lack of these formal programs at Bank of New York needed to be addressed and therefore enlisted our services.

This is not to suggest there were no effective leaders in this division prior to her arrival, but there were no formal programs and processes to ensure and support the development and success of these leaders moving forward. Under our guidance, the senior executive initiated a program of 360 feedback and coaching starting with herself and her immediate direct reports. An initial kickoff event was created and the senior executive and her direct reports held a strategy session. During this meeting the strategic initiatives were announced and the coaching program was introduced as a supporting part of strategy attainment. Much communication, information, and training were provided to both educate and "sell" the leaders on the 360 feedback process and the benefits of feedback and coaching, especially as it was cascaded throughout the organization. All of her direct reports received confidential 360 feedback surveys and assigned coaches to help them interpret the data and hone in on developmental opportunities. The developmental opportunities were addressed through ongoing coaching sessions over a six-to-nine-month time period. Once the direct reports of the senior executive had completed the process, their direct reports were the focus of the next round of 360 feedback and coaching engagements approximately a year later. For consistency, and as a result of the credibility established by the original cadre of coaches, the same coaches worked with this next round.

As a result of the same coaches being used throughout the initiative, it was critical that the comfort level of participants at all levels and the confidentiality of each coaching engagement were taken into consideration in making coaching assignments. This process continued for a number of successive rounds of direct reports until all levels of leaders had received 360 feedback and coaching. As the organization became more comfortable with receiving and delivering feedback, the senior executive of Corporate Trust felt the organization was ready to begin a formal performance appraisal process. The executive coaches were available to the leaders to help them with this process.

Given the experience with executive coaches and delivering and receiving feedback, moving to a formal performance appraisal process was a very smooth transition. The leaders and members of their teams were given an opportunity to experience firsthand the benefits of effective feedback and coaching of their own performance first and then were supported by their coaches as they appraised and coached the performance of their direct reports and teams.

By following these steps we were able to assist the senior executive in creating a coaching culture where feedback was a more regular event and coaching became a way in which leaders helped their direct reports and teams become more effective. This organization thus transformed into one where feedback and coaching is a regular event with fewer surprises at year's end. This process also enabled the organization to implement the strategy needed to compete and succeed in their industry. This case study illustrates how to create a coaching culture within an organization that previously had no formal process for delivering feedback.

Action Learning Coaching

Action learning coaching is another way in which coaching is moving beyond one-on-one engagements. This coaching initiative focuses on a learning team, providing a unique learning approach. The participants are a learning cohort who can provide feedback to one another in real time while the coach can observe both individual and group performance simultaneously and provide feedback accordingly. Action learning is a process by which individuals develop leadership skills while working with others to solve important problems for their organization. Action learning has been used for almost sixty years and has gained popularity in the last decade or so as a means of helping executives ramp up quickly to address today's complex leadership demands (Marquardt, Leonard, Freedman & Hill, 2009.) This learning process can accelerate the development of strategic leadership skills in a very pragmatic and hands-on way.

Today's action learning teams are more likely to be a part of larger, high-potential leadership development experiences. As a result, they are usually not an intact team. This distinguishes action learning team coaching from team coaching. Action learning teams are also not the same as ad hoc task forces because the action learning team's primary purpose is learning. The learning occurs as a result of reflecting on team performance that is facilitated by a trained coach. The business issue the action learning teams undertake is often one that has cross-functional roots and shared ownership and that has not been easily solved by their organizational "owners." Their deliverable is to make a recommendation to the sponsor(s) and stakeholders on how to resolve the problem posed to the team.

Action Learning Projects

Effective action learning programs are typically linked to the organization's business strategy. This can be done in several ways. One way is to ensure that the problem the team is working on is directly linked to the company's strategic focus. This is a function of the relevance of the project—will it have an impact on the advancement of the company's business strategy? The potential projects must be vetted at a very high level in the organization to ensure choosing a worthwhile endeavor that will receive organizational support. These business issues usually have great importance and urgency for resolution, hence giving the action learning team's work huge significance and visibility in the organization.

This also suggests a second link—senior executive involvement. Successful action learning programs have top executives participate as sponsors who submit potential project ideas to be addressed by the action learning teams. They review and approve which projects are worked on. They are also key stakeholders who are affected by the recommendations made by the teams. Each project has at least one sponsor and usually several stakeholders in the organization. These stakeholders tend to be senior leaders who either own the problem the team is trying to resolve or will own the solution the team will recommend.

This high-level visibility gives the action learning projects the gravitas needed to keep the team members focused and motivated to deliver a successful solution recommendation. Solutions may or may not be implemented based on many organizational factors, but the success of the solution recommendation is judged by the panel of sponsoring executives in such terms as how well it solves the problem, its viability and innovation, and so on. This high-level sponsorship and visibility also provides access to senior leaders in the organization that team members might not ordinarily have, as well as exposure to more strategic initiatives and problems. This exposure also provides insight into how decisions are made at the most senior levels of the organization and provides an opportunity to influence senior decision makers. Participation in action learning teams becomes a key lesson of experience for these emerging leaders.

This exposure and opportunity to work with senior leadership help participants broaden their perspective and develop their strategic thinking very quickly. They also develop a more sophisticated understanding of organizational politics and the role that politics plays in their organization, as well as how to work within these organizational parameters. For instance, it is not uncommon for particular sponsors and stakeholders of a given project to be at odds with each other in terms of how the "problem" should be resolved, what scope the project should take, and who owns the resolution or implementation. Working through this type of organizational conflict is an invaluable education in leadership effectiveness.

Action Learning Coach

The role of the executive coach in these action learning engagements is to help the team quickly become self-managing and fully functioning. In addition to aiding them in resolving an organizational problem, the coach also helps the participants learn about themselves and their leadership abilities, develop effective group process skills, and provide strategies on how to accomplish tasks in their organizational system. The coach's role evolves and changes as the action learning team develops and matures. For example, in the beginning, it may be more beneficial for the coach to be more directive and active in helping the participants shape their team functioning. Coaches are particularly valuable in assisting members navigate through the stages of group development (Tuckman, 1965).

Forming

Typically team participants also have individual coaching available to them to work on their individual leadership needs. Therefore they have received feedback from their personal coaches from various assessment sources, usually 360 feedback, a personality measure, and simulation experiences. The individual assessment work is usually completed prior to the action learning team meeting to begin their team forming process. This timing is deliberately set so that individuals are primed with fairly comprehensive feedback about their own strengths and developmental opportunities, which they then bring to the team process and project. During initial team meetings, participants are encouraged to share their leadership areas of strength so that their strengths can be leveraged for accelerated team functioning and to also share their developmental opportunities so that the action learning team experience can be turned into a safe place to try out new behaviors and approaches or practice new and developing skills.

Norming

The sharing of feedback requires that norms of trust, respect, and confidentiality are quickly established. A safe learning environment is one of the initial action learning team norms that the team is encouraged to adopt. Team members often have complementary strengths and developmental opportunities, namely one person's strength is another's developmental opportunity. Out of these conversations often comes the group identity—the "who we are." Their collective values of "hard work" "achievement" and "making a difference" or "impressing senior management" emerge. One can also begin to get a sense of the group's personality as it is just starting to formulate. This helps them establish their vision for their work together. Here is where their excitement about the project starts to build.

Coaches can encourage these team members to "buddy up" and help one another to leverage their strengths and develop new ones. This is more likely to take place in a symbiotic fashion in a safe action learning situation than to occur in an existing and intact team where competition and individual performance results attainment is the currency of the land. Individual team members are more likely to be generous in sharing their skills with less accomplished colleagues when there are no individual gains to be made on either side of the partnership. It's all about learning and improved team performance. Action learning teams tend to sink or swim together.

Storming

Coaches also need to set expectations for how the team will handle conflict. At the honeymoon stage of team bonding it is hard for team members to envision ever having to deal with conflict but the team will definitely face instances of this. An effective coach will ask them how they want to conduct themselves around this issue. Will it be direct and in the moment or will it be handled off-line? The coach should ask team members what their comfort level is with conflict and their preferred way of handling it to help them come to agreement and keep the team at a high functioning level. Coaches may also offer themselves as mediators if the time comes when the team cannot resolve a conflict on their own and introduce tools that help them understand the various approaches to handling conflict and what approach works best in a given situation.

An effective coach can get participants to value the unique contributions of their teammates and to leverage these contributions to derive a superior solution. Participants may be driven to achieve the common goal, but they do have differing styles and leadership capabilities that have to be understood and leveraged in a constructive way. Coaches can help to nurture that insight. As participants become more attuned to their own performance, both individually and as a functioning team, coaches take a more observational role, interjecting only if needed or solicited.

Providing Feedback

Finally, coaches model how to debrief team processes and how to provide feedback to each other. Typically, either as a one-on-one coach or as a result of some simulation exercises, coaches will have had the opportunity to deliver feedback prior to the participants working as a team. At the end of the initial coaching session the coach may ask what worked well and what could be done differently so that the coaching experience is more effective. Often this is modeled in a round-robin format where multiple rounds of soliciting and providing feedback help the team view its functioning in a reflective and critical way. It also opens the floor for giving and receiving feedback from each other. This contracting and discussion of norms and expectations up front helps the team become fully functioning more quickly and helps facilitate team learning.

Challenges in Action Learning

Although action learning programs can benefit both the participant and the organization, many times the action learning coach is not fully utilized. Participants are typically accomplished and driven emerging leaders—they are not used to seeking help. They assume they can solve their own problems. This sense of independence and responsibility should be applauded; however, an experienced coach can help guide them in ways the team could never discover on its own. It is important to encourage and remind participants to take advantage of their coach resource and to use coaches at key junctures when the team is in conflict or becomes stuck.

Global Issues in Action Learning

Working with action learning teams on global issues for global companies adds an extra level of complexity and richness to the work with action learning teams. In these situations, the coaches work with team members from different regions of the world who are assembled on a team to work on strategic projects with global impact. These team members learn the same forming, storming, and norming lessons of team functioning, how to handle and resolve conflict, as well as how to give and receive feedback, but they also learn how their different cultural norms, language challenges, and time zone differences affect team functioning.

These differences of expectations and assumptions need to be openly addressed as part of the team chartering process in establishing team norms, and dealt with throughout the team's work together as differences pop up. For some team members this may be their first foray into working on a global scale and for others it is business as usual. These differences in experience provide the team members a chance to stretch their skills (and patience) as well as an opportunity to think seriously about how their own cultural expectations differ from those of others and how their expectations are likely to play out when working with people from a different region or experience set. The insights and reflections on learning for these team members can accelerate the development of global acumen that many multinational companies wish to instill in their leaders.

Linking Action Learning to an Organization's Talent Strategy: A High-Potential Program

Targeting high potential is one opportunity to employ an action learning approach in leadership programs. When the action learning team project is embedded in a larger leadership development program, the coaches encourage team members to share their individual leadership strengths and developmental opportunities that may pertain to team functioning. This enables each group member to derive the most out of this learning experience by targeting particular areas for growth as well as contribute to the development of their peers on the team through sharing ongoing feedback.

Individual Versus Project-Based Approaches: An Added Bonus

In the context of high-potential programs, coaches may act as action learning team coaches where their only role is to facilitate team learning and functioning. These same coaches have the unique opportunity to act as individual leadership development coaches to some or all of the members of the action learning team they were coaching. Working with a group of individuals assembled for the purposes of action learning is a great opportunity to have an impact on each developing leader's skills, insights, and abilities. It's doubly beneficial if the participant can be coached by the same coach on both an individual one-on-one skill development basis and as part of the team's functioning. Admittedly this requires a unique contracting of confidentiality and creation of a safe and trusting learning environment in order for the engagement to be successful, but once established and strictly adhered to, this can lead to considerable developmental growth in the allotted time. Coaches can leverage the observations from the action learning team time to inform the work done at an individual coaching level and vice versa. Coaches can take the insights gleaned from the one-on-one work to accelerate team learning and functioning.

Action learning team projects can be a significant value-add to traditional high-potential programs to help facilitate learning around individual, team, and organizational leadership skills that might not otherwise be addressed at an accelerated learning pace in a practical and time-sensitive manner. Further, high-potential developing leaders are presented an opportunity to contribute at strategic levels to resolve organizational problems and on a larger stage much earlier in their careers. Thus, action learning coaching serves as a strategic initiative that approaches leadership development from a systemic perspective.

Succession Planning Coaching

Having a future focus on the development and coaching of talent is critical. Unfortunately, many organizations increase transition failures due to the common practice of making promotion decisions based on current performance in isolation of the criteria associated with potential. Given the failure rates in a newly transitioned role (over 50 percent; Downey, March, & Berkman, 2001), the organization's involvement in readying the individual *before* he takes on the role is a wise strategy.

Succession Planning as a Strategic Advantage

There are four areas of strengths and gaps that should be examined in order to determine readiness for the next role: the *competencies* needed, the *relationships* within and outside of the organization that need to be built or strengthened, *personality attributes* associated with fit to the role and organizational culture, and the *on-the-job experiences* necessary for success in the new role (Yost & Plunkett, 2009). The output of the assessment can serve as a strong outline for the coaching plan. The coaching plan should be considered a succession planning tool and should involve key members of the organization, including internal business leaders and human resources (HR) partners.

Coaching can be a strategic advantage when used in conjunction with a succession planning process. When the talent review process is completed, an aggregated review of the talent pool can help the organization understand where critical gaps still exist. Coaches can then help address those gaps by working with individuals to develop the critical behaviors and competencies required for the new role, identify and build key relationships, understand how personality attributes can facilitate or hinder transition into the role, and create on-the-job opportunities that will contribute to success in the new role. If an internal coach is used, it is recommended that he or she be from the business, and not the HR function. Though the HR partner is an important member of the team, having a business leader serve as the coach provides direct insight into the business and helps create and reinforce a coaching culture within the organization.

Overcoming Managerial Fear of Talent Loss

Another interesting aspect of coaching in the succession planning process is helping managers overcome some of their own fears they feel when developing their talent. There are three common fears that we see on a regular basis: (1) talent loss, (2) redundancy, and (3) competition (for their jobs).

One common fear is that if an individual is coached to the "next level," there is a probable loss of a valuable member of the team. With the increased focus on results and constant streamlining of organizations, losing someone who is an "A" player can be a significant blow to the team, productivity, and business results.

Another fear is the potential creation of redundancy. We have all heard the refrain of managers who say, "My focus is to develop my people so I am out of a job." Though in spirit this is a noble intent, in reality it rarely plays out this way. Here, the risk for the manager is in developing someone strong enough so he can actually be the successor to his position *or* the direct report can become the competition. Given these potential risk factors, how can you incentivize and motivate a manager to take on the role of a coach when it could eventually mean talent loss or potential redundancy in his own role?

There are two approaches that have proven to be successful at reducing those fears. First, a robust succession plan will help the manager see his *own* potential and career path. Second, building in accountabilities for managing organizational talent effectively helps counter some of the potential "bad behaviors" such as hoarding talent and failing to grow leaders. Oftentimes, these managers are perceived as career killers, given their failure to build teams, and as a result fail to attract the top talent. Creating the expectation of managers to coach and mentor their talent and rotate them in the organization will, in turn, attract talent to the manager's team, thus reinforcing the right behaviors that help retain top talent.

Succession Planning Coaching: New York Presbyterian Hospital Case Study

New York Presbyterian Hospital is the largest employer in New York City. The hospital is also a teaching hospital, therefore it should come as no surprise they adopt the "Leader as Teacher" concept in their talent development and coaching strategy.

In 2006, the Chief Learning Officer identified a skill gap with their top two hundred in the hospital: no one knew how to have a "talent conversation" with direct reports. Distinct from a performance management discussion, the emphasis in the talent conversation is on an individual's career aspirations. Using a framework adapted from the Corporate Leadership Council's work with high potentials, talent was segmented into three categories: promotional, professional, and essential talent:

- *Promotional Talent* was defined as an individual who has the ability and aspiration to succeed at a more senior level. These individuals are characterized as possessing qualities essential to advance to the next level, having a clear record of outstanding achievement, and as a widely respected person whose capabilities no one questions. In traditional succession planning language, this is a "ready now" candidate.
- *Professional Talent* was defined as someone who is a recognized functional/technical expert; has a depth of organizational knowledge; can be counted on, especially in tough times; is a consistent top performer year after year; is committed to organizational goals and vision; works independently with little or no direction; is a trusted source and resource in the organization; and works with the informal network. This category of talent is often ignored or mislabeled as these individuals do not always desire to move up into a more senior level in an organization, but instead want to deepen their technical skills. As such, managers are often confused as to how to have a talent conversation, given that promotion is not necessarily their motivation, but growth in their role is a deeply held desire.
- *Essential Talent* was defined as an individual who is currently stable in role and responsibility but does have minor gaps or development needs that must be addressed. These individuals are often labeled as "Ready in 1–3 years (with development)."

Though managers were effective at having performance management conversations with their direct reports, they were less effective in speaking to them about their career aspirations. To some degree, this was attributed to the challenge that the hospital faced in having very few opportunities for advancement once you reached a particular level, as the

(Continued)

Succession Planning Coaching: New York Presbyterian Hospital Case Study (*Continued*)

hospital's organizational structure flattens near the top positions. As such, managers became concerned that they had seemingly nothing to offer their top talent with respect to promotional opportunities. Therefore, the strategy became to avoid the conversation.

To help equip the managers to address the development needs of their top talent they wished to retain, NYPH developed a workshop for all senior leaders in the organization called "The Talent Advantage." The focus of the workshop was to help create a common framework and language for the hospital to use in working with their talent. The opening of the workshop focused on creating a compelling business case for the senior leaders as to why focusing on this subject is critical to the success of the hospital. Then the framework and definitions of talent were presented and discussed (as discussed earlier). Using a template, the managers then identified which category each of their team members fell into (in addition, a category called "talent not keeping pace" was used, but was not the focus of the workshop).

Not surprisingly, some managers felt they could not easily categorize all of their talent. Why? Because managers never had the conversation about aspirations. In fact, one of the most powerful insights that managers had was the assumption that each of their direct reports had a strong desire to be promoted when in fact they never even had the conversation with them. In addition, managers were asked to provide supporting evidence of their categorizations. In other words, if you stated that a direct report had high promotional aspirations, you were asked: How do you know this? When was the last time you spoke to him about this? This kept the managers from making assumptions about the abilities and aspirations of their talent.

The final segment of the workshop addressed the actual talent conversation. The facilitators demonstrated both a poor example and a good example to illustrate the differences. The workshop ended with managers creating an action plan for each of the talent conversations to be held over the next two months. To help support the managers in their conversations, an external coach was assigned to help them prepare for the sessions with their direct reports. Coaches spent a few hours with them to discuss how they categorized their talent and what the agenda of the meeting would look like. Role plays were conducted to anticipate and deal with the likely obstacles and challenges the managers would face. Following the conversations managers had with their direct reports, the external coaches would debrief with the managers on how it went. As a result of the feedback from those coaching sessions, the managers would readjust their approach or reinforce the messages that worked.

New York Presbyterian Hospital represents an organization that proactively addressed the complex issues associated with succession planning. Though many organizations recognize the importance of succession planning, the actual "how to" is often missing for those responsible for its implementation. The NYPH case study provides a notable example of how coaching can be used in a succession planning context.

Coaching in Executive On-Boarding

Grow Within/Buy Outside: The Business Case

With the increased emphasis on growth and change, it seems only natural that when filling critical positions a company looks to use the approach of "buy" as opposed to growing from within when there are apparent talent gaps. However, this strategy should be used with caution. The statistics are stacked against new executives brought in from the outside. It has been estimated that 50 percent of leaders will be fired or quit within the first three years and most will fail within the first eighteen months in their role (Downey, March, & Berkman, 2001). Nadler (2007) makes the case that companies are wise to grow their leaders from within to avoid exorbitant costs of replacement, upwards of $500,000 a year. This calls for strong talent management strategies and succession planning processes embedded in the organization to anticipate gaps and begin building talent from within to avoid these costly mistakes. Regardless of whether you bring someone in from the outside or promote from within, you need a strong on-boarding process to help increase the chances of success in the new role.

Figure 8.1. Executive On-Boarding Model

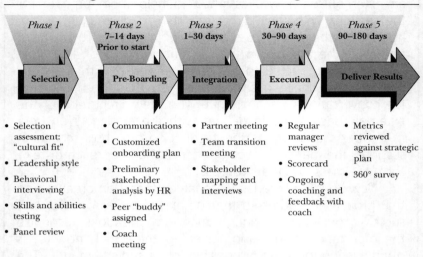

Source: Adler and Stomski, 2009.

Executive On-Boarding Model

The model in Figure 8.1 illustrates the entire life cycle of on-boarding, from the point where the individual goes through the selection process through successful transition into a fully productive executive.

The Coach's Role in Executive On-Boarding

When on-boarding new executives, the majority of the executive's focus is on learning, not doing. Given this, a coach can be a tremendous asset in guiding the new executive through the five key tasks involved in the learning process (Adler & Stomski, 2010):

1. Mastering the position—learning about the requirements of the role the individual is being placed in
2. Mapping the organization—understanding who the key stakeholders are and how the executive's role drives the success of the business

3. Building relationships—with key stakeholders and team members
4. Understanding the culture—understanding the social framework and norms that guide behavior
5. Using the tools—navigating the technology and systems used by the organization

Increasingly, organizations are drawing upon the expertise of executive coaches to help accelerate time to productivity and increase the odds that newly promoted individuals or external hires will thrive in their new roles. The role of the coach can be critical, particularly in the early stages of the on-boarding process when the risk of derailment is high. A coach can serve several purposes:

- Accelerate the executive's personal development
- Identify and coach the executive through key transition milestones
- Guide the participant away from potential derailer situations
- Act as a sounding board for the new executive
- Facilitate the team alignment process

Often, the individual who takes on the role of coach is an external coach who comes with specific expertise on on-boarding new executives. However, more and more organizations are drawing upon the organization's internal HR professionals to serve as coaches to new executives. The HR insider has unique and deep knowledge regarding the organization, and this can be extremely helpful as new executives navigate through the various challenges they will encounter.

Nevertheless, the value of an outside, objective perspective cannot be overlooked. One of the key derailers that new leaders face when coming from the outside is the failure to adapt to the new organizational culture. In fact, Watkins (2007) found that 75 percent of HR leaders attributed the failure of new leaders to "poor cultural fit." With the support of HR, an outside coach can help bring perspective to the new executive. An external coach can bring unique insight to help the individual navigate through the organization, anticipate challenges, and learn how to operate within the rules and norms of the organization.

In the on-boarding process, an external coach should be introduced early in the process, even prior to the start date, if possible. In fact, one of the first meetings a coach should have is with the manager and HR professionals to identify the key strengths this individual brings to the role and any potential risk factors. In other words, were there any concerns or issues identified in the hiring process that the organization was willing to take on and agreed to monitor closely? By proactively addressing these issues up front, the HR leader, manager, and coach can create strategies for addressing the gaps before they become too big to overcome. Creating discipline around the on-boarding process can help organizations save significant money by providing the appropriate level of support and resources to those new in the role.

Rapid Alignment Coaching

As organizations are asked to more quickly show results, one of the greatest challenges they face is to ensure that their employees understand the strategy, how they fit into that strategy, and what their role is in implementing it. Further, they must align quickly in order to execute against the strategy. Unfortunately, most organizations are not well equipped to deal with this pace of change in a fast, efficient, and aligned manner. Traditional learning solutions such as individual coaching engagements and leadership development programs by themselves are not making enough impact. They don't do a thorough job of aligning people to strategy. As a result, organizations frequently lament that they are too slow, fragmented, and siloed to create the speed, agility, and alignment needed to execute strategic change.

Obviously, organizations can benefit greatly if they can align more quickly. However, one of the barriers to this alignment is the failure to provide appropriate support to an important layer in the organization—middle management. A 2009 global survey of leaders (McKinsey, 2009) stated that although executives emerged from the economic crisis relatively well, middle managers did not. They reported lower levels of satisfaction and enthusiasm with their jobs and they stated they were less committed to staying with their organizations. Why have middle managers seemed to be hit the hardest? The McKinsey study reported that middle management has taken on additional responsibilities in their current roles, thus increasing their dissatisfaction with not only their own performance, but with their managers as well.

Often referred to as the "rubber bumper" in the organization, the middle of the organization is where change must be translated into new ways of operating. Here, change needs to transcend beyond a "fuzzy notion" and become the new reality. However, at this layer and the layer below, understanding the reason for strategic change and what that means to managers in their day-to-day reality is not often clear. While senior leaders are formulating the next strategic move the company will make, middle managers continue to look inward at the work that needs to get done today. This inward focus is not necessarily an active resistance to change, it is simply the fact that leaders need to figure out how it affects the work their teams do. By simultaneously coaching middle managers and their teams to execute strategy faster, we are concurrently up-skilling a large portion of the organization that has a significant role in achieving the priorities and goals set for the organization.

By implementing coaching as a mechanism to help drive change and strategy, not only at the individual level but also at the team level, alignment can be more readily achieved. By having a team of coaches focusing the organization's key leaders on moving in the same direction, we can leverage the coaches' expertise and up-skill entire teams at the same time.

This approach to coaching is unique in that it is an individual *and* team-based approach. Drawing on the insights that the coaches gain from the coachees, this feedback is circled back to the organization to help inform the need to shift their approach to the strategy or change initiative. This approach is illustrated in Figure 8.2 and described below.

Figure 8.2. Rapid Alignment Model

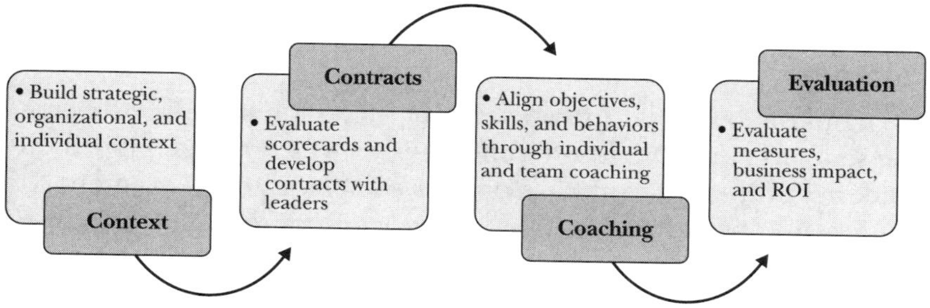

Rapid Alignment Model

At its core, rapid alignment is a business coaching process designed to be customized to the company's strategies, priorities, and the leader's needs. There are four stages in the process:

1. Understanding the context
2. Contracting with leaders and their teams
3. Coaching them to achieve their individual and organizational goals
4. Evaluating the learning achieved as a result of going through this process.

Following are details of each stage.

Context

The first stage in the model requires the coach to understand the business strategy and what the organization is trying to achieve in a more rapid time frame The coach should also fully understand the organizational culture and context in which the leaders and their teams are operating.

Contracts

The second stage is to understand how the strategy or change effort is cascaded down. Here, a tool for alignment is created through the use of a scorecard showing how enterprise change goals are stepped down to goals at each organizational level and finally translated into team and individual goals. The scorecard provides the basis for an ongoing dialogue between the coach, the individual leader, the leader's team, and the leader's immediate boss. The scorecard is used for each coaching engagement, but is customized to the team and individual leader's goals.

Coaching

Coaching is provided in two ways: (1) through scheduled coaching sessions and (2) a just-in-time basis, in which a coach helps the leader capture and capitalize on *moments of leadership*. Moments of leadership are defined as how a leader reacts to daily challenges such as how a manager responds to a missed goal, what she says when an employee presents an obstacle, and how she approaches the weekly team meeting. These moments of leadership may seem small, but they occur multiple times a day in an organization. It is here where change is reinforced and realized as well as where leaders' values are communicated. To the manager, it feels like an individual coaching session, but when there is an entire coaching team providing help on these moments of leadership, it becomes a transformational effort for the entire organization. The coach serves as a catalyst in ensuring the individuals and teams understand their roles in the change process.

Evaluation

There are four metrics examined in this coaching approach: on the *initiative* itself, the impact on the *business*, on the overall *organization*, and the *individual*. Measurement comes from business goals and outcomes, self-assessment, 360 feedback surveys, and progress against the scorecard (see earlier section on Contracts). By having dialogue with the business leaders through regular progress reports, the sponsor organization will know if the coaching is not generating the intended impact, and steps can be taken in real time to correct the process. The unique aspect of this coaching approach is that while each leader is working at an individual level, the coach is also working with the team. This helps create efficiencies of the coaching process by achieving critical mass of change, increasing the chances of success. With everyone working from the same scorecard, rapid alignment is achieved.

Though a manager may be a critical resource in providing feedback, not all managers are good coaches. Rather than pushing managers to enhance their coaching skills, another approach is to deploy a coordinated team of expert external coaches or a trained internal group. Here, the coaching team not only supports individual managers and their teams, it also acts as an alignment and coordination mechanism. The individual coaches, who each support several managers and their teams, provide feedback and organizational insight to the lead coach, who liaises with the organizational sponsor. This communication, enabled by the coaching team, is a powerful feature that enables rapid alignment and feeds back key insights to the organization.

Part of what makes rapid alignment coaching effective is achieving change more rapidly than before. Before using this approach to coaching, an organization should determine how important it is to achieve their initiatives in a quicker time frame. How much more valuable is the change if it occurs in three months as opposed to six months? It's when people actually see the value of speed, and they understand it is achievable, that they fully embrace the sense of urgency that makes the rapid alignment approach work. Another element of value is the increase of capability and capacity within the individual managers and team members. While the organization is implementing change, it is also improving individual leadership skills. The impact of having a greater number of capable leaders is that the organization will have a deeper succession pool, more flexibility in deploying talent, and the ability to take on more work. In essence, the role of the coaches is to help leaders accomplish work in new and different ways that benefit the individual, the team members, and, ultimately, the organization.

Conclusion

Coaching can have a tangible impact on individuals, teams, and organizations, helping each to reach their potential. Strategically designed, enterprise-wide coaching programs—versus ad hoc coaching engagements—have the potential to transform an organization by fundamentally aligning all leaders to a common mission and goals. Action learning, succession planning, and on-boarding programs are examples where strategically focused coaching can galvanize and shift how an organization operates. These enterprise-wide programs can provide participants with strategic alignment between their personal developmental goals and the business direction.

The future of such large-scale endeavors is, however, in question. As organizations continue to cut funding and resources, they are sacrificing the investments needed to create alignment and transformation. Thus, we may continue to see more of the immediate need, ad hoc coaching, than of the enterprise-wide strategic programs. This is unfortunate because, as evidenced in the prior discussion, organizations that move beyond the one-on-one of coaching and align their leadership development efforts with organizational goals will have a greater return on their investment and a greater probability of organizational success.

References

Adler, S., & Stomski, L. (2010). Ropes to skip and ropes to know. In R. Silzer & B. E. Dowell (Eds.), *Strategy-driven talent management: A leadership imperative* (pp. 159–211). San Francisco: Jossey-Bass.

Corporate Leadership Council. (2003). *Maximizing returns on professional executive coaching.* Washington, DC: Corporate Executive Board.

Charan, R., Drotter, S., & Noel, J. (2000). *The leadership pipeline: How to build the leadership powered company.* San Francisco: Jossey-Bass.

Downey, K., March, T., & Berkman, A. (2001). *Assimilating new leaders: The key to executive retention.* New York: AMACOM.

Marquardt, M. J., Leonard, H. S., Freedman, A. M., & Hill, C. C. (2009). *Action learning for developing leaders and organizations.* Washington, DC: American Psychological Association Press.

McKinsey Global Survey. (2009). *Leaders in the crisis.* Retrieved December, 16, 2009, from www.McKinsey.com.

Nadler, D. A. (2007). The CEO's second act. *Harvard Business Review, 85*(1), 66–72.

Tuckman, B. W. (1965). Development sequence in small groups. *Psychological Bulletin, 63,* 384–399.

Watkins, M. (2007). Help newly hired executives adapt quickly. *Harvard Business Review, 85*(6), 26–30.

Yost, P., & Plunkett, M. (2009). *Real time leadership development.* Chichester, UK: Wiley-Blackwell.

Chapter Nine

ETHICS IN COACHING

Jonathan Passmore and Lance Mortimer

Though less discussed than models and theories, ethics is a critical aspect of leadership coaching. Despite its critical nature, it is rarely featured in research papers or in coaching conference papers when compared with evaluation of programs or coaching models. Its relatively low profile in the coaching literature and in conversations between coaches may be because by its very nature ethics is unclear and ambiguous. Almost everyone thinks he or she is acting ethically. We suspect that this view applied equally to many of the people at Enron and Worldcom, where ethical mismanagement led to corporate disaster.

Professional bodies in coaching (for example, International Coach Federation, Association for Coaching, European Mentoring and Coaching Council) have offered some guidance, but in a sector that is largely unregulated, many coaches operate outside of the professional codes of practice set by coaching trade bodies. In psychology, there is clearer and stronger ethical guidance which reflects the more highly regulated nature of the domain. However, such guidance is often written with the clinical practitioner in mind and thus does not always consider the ethical issues which arise within organizational contexts and specifically within the tri-client nature of executive coaching— coach, coachee, and organizational client

In this chapter we explore the issue of ethics in coaching, starting with a review of the nature of ethics. In the second section, we explore how other professions try to manage ethical issues and specifically draw on practices from clinical areas, such as counseling and nursing, as well as from business. In the third section, we review the limited literature on coaching ethics and reflect on what steps we might take to improve current practice. In the final section of this chapter, we consider ethical decision making and offer a model of decision making designed specifically for coaching practitioners.

Exploring Ethics

The development of ethical thinking dates back centuries. Trager (1979), has suggested that ethics can be traced back as far as 38,000 years, to the time when people began to organize life and assign tasks among each other. Weiner (2004) has highlighted the evolution of ethics, which is based on the early work of Greek philosophers such as Socrates, Plato, and Aristotle. Even in these early times, there appeared to be a divide between the great thinkers. Plato advocated that the denial of bodily pleasure was the best course to achieve happiness. He argued that real life is only achieved through ideas and not what can be experienced through the senses. This proved to be a foundation for later religious moral codes. Others, such as Socrates, advocated moderation as opposed to denial. Here we begin to witness the beginnings of a divide that encapsulates the issues we tussle with today. What are ethics and what do they mean when we try to apply them to real-world, complex problems?

Society in modern times is besieged by uncertainty as to the "right" or "wrong" of decisions and answers. We live in a multicultural world with multiple and cross-cultural ideas of what morality is. As a result the psychologist and coach need to navigate these in their work. Before we move to explore ethical standards in various domains, let us review what we mean by ethics.

What Is Ethics?

As alluded to in the introduction to this chapter, ethics means different things to different people. In a business sense, it may be as simple as "learning right from wrong, and then doing the right thing" (McNamara, 2008). Others (Bailey & Schwartzberg,

1995) have defined ethics as the systematic study of the nature and science of morality.

Morality may be seen as a set of standards and guidelines that are aspired to as ideals within the social norms (Thompson, 2005) for the protection and adherence of values. Ethics is a practice that determines what we consider to be good or bad, right or wrong, in social relations. As de Jong (2006) notes, this is about the virtue of helping others, keeping the interests of the individual at the heart of the matter, honoring the trust placed in the practitioner and promoting autonomy. All of these are important in the leadership coaching relationship.

Ethical theory (Thompson, 2005) states that there are four basic approaches. *Descriptive ethics* concern the values and beliefs that are held in relation to particular societies. As an example, some societies may believe that multiple marriage is acceptable, but in other countries such a practice is illegal. Descriptive ethics do not examine issues, they merely serve to provide us data about situations that exist throughout the world and how different people respond to them.

Second, *normative ethics* examine how social norms exist and materialize. What are the "ought to do's" and the "mustn't do's"? These normative beliefs give rise to moral standards, which serve to inform ethical judgment. Social norms tend to change, sometimes at alarming speed, depending on the alacrity of the environment, so what may have been acceptable a few years ago may be inappropriate today. Consider the examples of wearing seatbelts in cars or hitting children.

Third, *meta ethics* takes the view that when people make assertions that some things are right or wrong, then there is a reason for saying so. Meta ethics considers the language and linguistic representation behind what it means to actually *say* something is right or wrong.

Finally, *applied ethics* uses scenarios to test thinking and the application of principles in practice. The applied stance gives rise to debate and in the right circumstances, ethical and personal development.

Rowson (2001), draws a different picture of approaches to ethics. He bases his model on three classifications for understanding an individual relationship with ethical decision making: consequentialist, deontological, and pluralist. These are summarized in Table 9.1.

Table 9.1. Classification of Ethical Approaches

Approach	Summary and Example
Consequentialist	The end result determines the course of action and rules are viewed as flexible. For example, a situation where the coach may seek to shame the coachee into actions that may ultimately help them achieve their goal.
Deontological	Determines actions to be either good or bad; provides little or no room for flexibility or individual interpretation. This approach is efficient, however, challenging the individual to make a choice given two options. An example of this may be when the coach reflects back what he or she heard and paints a picture of two scenarios, one clearly positive, the other clearly negative.
Pluralistic	Seeks to balance the above two approaches to arrive at the best result for the client. This is a collaborative situation between coach and client that is led by the coach, who will shift between flexible and rigid as is believed to be best at the time. Kelly (1955) recommends a "creative cycle," whereby both parties think over the problem several times from different angles until a satisfactory understanding is reached. This can lead to the development of new perspectives.

Ethical Codes

In the first section we set out a number of different ways in which writers have thought about ethics and sought to categorize ethics. In this section we will briefly explore how professional bodies have developed ethical thinking into codes of practice. The American Psychological Association (APA, 2003) suggests a list of five general principles in its code of practice. These cover the themes of beneficence (promotion of the client's best interests), fidelity (faithfully to clients), integrity, justice, and respect for people's rights. These are summarized in Table 9.2.

Table 9.2. APA Ethical Principles

Principles	Summary
1. Beneficence and Non-Maleficence	To strive to benefit those with whom they work and take care to do no harm. In professional actions, seek to safeguard the welfare and rights of those with whom they interact professionally and other affected persons. When conflicts occur, they attempt to resolve these conflicts in a responsible fashion that avoids or minimizes harm.
2. Fidelity and Responsibility	Establish relationships of trust with coworkers. To be aware of their professional responsibilities to society and to the specific communities in which they work.
3. Integrity	Seek to promote accuracy, honesty, and truthfulness.
4. Justice	Recognize that fairness and justice entitle all persons to access and benefit from the contributions, processes, procedures, and services being conducted.
5. Respect for People's Rights and Dignity	Respect the dignity and worth of people, and rights of individuals to privacy, confidentiality, and self-determination.

It might be assumed that English-speaking psychologists, operating in similar environments and with the same organizational clients, would adopt very similar ethical codes. As a comparison, we have included the British Psychological Society's (BPS) ethical code. The BPS (2005), however, manages to set out its ethical approach in just four areas. These are summarized in Table 9.3 and, as will be seen, whereas the APA code makes explicit the aspect of benefits to clients this is more implicit within the BPS code. However, both codes stress the rights of individuals and the integrity of psychologists to practice.

Table 9.3. BPS Ethical Principles

Principle	Summary
1. Respect	Value the dignity and worth of all persons, with sensitivity to the dynamics of perceived authority or influence over clients. Particular regard to people's rights including those of privacy and self-determination.
2. Competence	Value the continuing development and maintenance of high standards of competence in their professional work and the importance of preserving their ability to function optimally within the recognized limits of their knowledge, skill, training, education, and experience.
3. Responsibility	Value their responsibilities to clients, to the general public, and to the profession and science of psychology. Including the avoidance of harm and the prevention of misuse or abuse of their contributions to society.
4. Integrity	Value honesty, accuracy, clarity, and fairness in their interactions with all persons and seek to promote integrity in all facets of their scientific and professional endeavors.

Reviewing Ethics in Parallel Domains

In this section, we explore how other sectors have tried to manage ethical issues. We draw especially on practices from clinical areas such as counseling and nursing to areas that others may consider to be closer to executive coaching, that of business ethics.

Counseling

As in coaching, counseling has numerous professional bodies representing the interests of counselors. In the United Kingdom the main body is the British Association for Counseling and Psychotherapy (BACP, 2010). It provides six ethical principles, which are fidelity (honoring the trust relationship), autonomy (respect for client's right to self-determination), beneficence, non-maleficence, justice (impartial and fair treatment of clients), and self-respect (promotion of practitioner's care for self and self-knowledge

What is interesting are the discrepancies between the contents of the codes established by different organizations; take, for example, the British Association for Counseling (BACP), the Confederation of Scottish Counseling Agencies (COSCA), both of which exclusively deal with counseling, the British Psychological Society (BPS), and the United Kingdom Council for Psychotherapy (UKCP), both of which include counseling as one of many positions. BACP prioritizes the principle of autonomy, with the exception of possible situations of self or public harm. The BPS assumes a similar stance, giving priority to fidelity, whereas UKCP and COSCA give precedence to the principle of beneficence (Bond, 2000).

This, as Bond (2000) notes, leads to a difference in the power relations experienced by the client. A greater prominence on the respect for client autonomy is likely to result in the sharing of power, whereas a more controlling relationship exists when beneficence is exercised. These discrepancies between bodies are hardly ideal, as they lead to client and counselor confusion. In addition, practitioners belonging to more than one of these bodies are left with ethical dilemmas as a consequence of conflicting guidelines.

Counselors and coaches alike must also devise strategies to deal with dilemmas between contractual duties and ethical principles. Consider the scenario where a client confides in the coach about having suicidal thoughts due to the fear about the financial collapse of the business. The coach may be faced with the conflict between promoting autonomy and client welfare and avoidance of harm. Legal requirements to report may be unenforceable by law and the executive coach may be faced with the decision whether to report (and if so to whom) the problem or to try and work with it.

It has been argued (Cross & Wood, 2005) that ethical standards are developed through experience. In essence, ethical dilemmas are a route to personal and professional development. We draw on Kelly's personal construct theory (1955) as a way to understand the impact of ethical practice. They suggest that dilemmas are developmental and that they help us to consider what is right and wrong. However, we will often open ourselves up to conflict and confusion. Such states may lead to cognitive dissonance—the uncomfortable feeling caused by holding two conflicting ideas at the same time. Doing the right thing may not always feel right. In returning to our definition, this is the very thing that makes it a "dilemma."

Nursing

The principle underlying the ethical basis of medical practice is to "prevent abuse of power by the medical practitioner" (Kelly, 1996). No universal code has been established for medical practice. However, medical practitioners adhere to four main principles; justice, autonomy, non-maleficence (avoidance of harm to the client), and beneficence (promotion of the client's best interests). These principles, however, are frequently ignored, as an over-adherence to a code may restrain nurses' autonomy and prove detrimental to the standard of care (Chadwick & Tadd, 1992).

In many instances nurses and therapists may be instructed by their employers or managers what actions to take. Such instructions, however, may go against these principles or the interests of the patient. As independent and competent professional adults, it is the nurses who must aim to consider the situation and apply the principles and live with the consequences of their actions (Bailey & Schwartzberg, 1995).

Writers in the sector have noted that, although codes are a catalyst for moral thinking and are useful in that they provide a means of discipline and quality control, they cannot replace the individual ethical decisions which practitioners need to make (Bailey & Schwartzberg, 1995). Such decisions require practitioners to be able to review situations and the interests of patients to come to the best decision in that moment. This requires nurses to develop skills as effective ethical decision makers, guided by a mental model of the decision-making process. A similar situation is required in coaching. An overreliance on codes cannot help practitioners as much as a framework for ethical decision making which they can apply in the moment and thus which is more responsive to clients and individual situations a code can never be expected to cover.

Business

A considerable amount has been written on the topic of business ethics (Ciulla, Martin, & Soloman, 2007; Crane & Matten, 2004; De George, 2006; Ferrell, Fraedrich, & Ferrell, 2002; Fisher & Lovell, 2009; Trevino & Nelson, 1999). The work in this area can be divided into two broad themes. The first focuses on case studies and scenarios of ethical issues. The second considers ethical models and ethical decision-making processes. Though there are some references to the later, the majority of work focuses on ethical dilemmas and case studies which reflect the business-school approach to learning from observing and reflecting on real-life cases. This contrasts with the psychological model of learning and research which is focused on research studies using empirical methods.

In business, the dilemma at the heart of ethics is balancing competing interests. Ferrell, Fraedrich, and Ferrell (2002) suggest that ethics in business is essentially about a tradeoff between interests of profit and consumer and stakeholders. Businesses which push the profit aspect too far are likely to be short lived; considering only the needs of stakeholders will lead to financial disaster.

Given the diffuse nature of business, the focus has been on ethical decision-making models as opposed to codes of practice. The most interesting work has been in the area of ethical decision making in business. Ford and Richardson (1994) have suggested that models of ethical decision making divide the influencing factors into two groups: individual factors and situational factors. At the individual level are factors such as age, gender, education, personality, and attitudes. At the situational level factors include work context, organizational culture, and job role. Crane and Matten (2004) have highlighted differences between U.S. and European approaches. European approaches have tended to focus on the situational factors such as the institution and the wider system, whereas U.S. approaches have tended to focus more on the individual factors.

Several authors have offered models to help managers resolve ethical dilemmas. Ferrell, Fraedrich, and Ferrell (2002) have suggested that to understand ethical decision making we need to consider three aspects in framing business ethical decisions. (See Figure 9.1.) The first is the intensity of the issue itself.

Figure 9.1. Framework for Understanding Business Ethical Decision Making

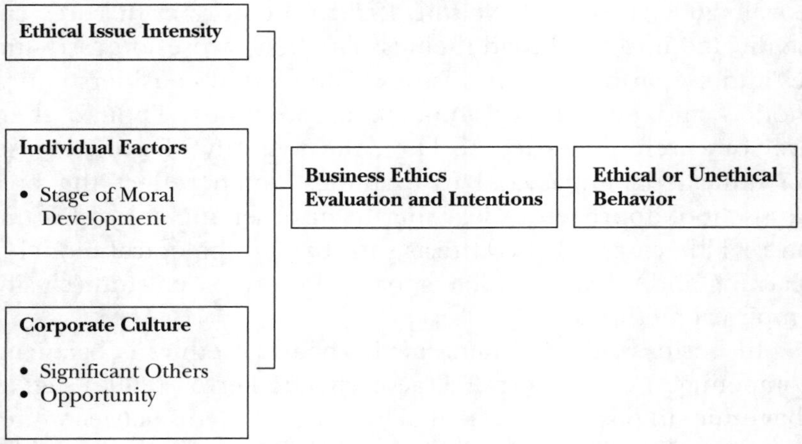

Source: Adapted from Ferrell, Fraedrich, and Ferrell, 2002, 104.

This is the perceived importance of the issue, which may be affected by personal values and organizational circumstances. The second is the stage of the moral development of the individual making the decision. This factor within the model draws on the work of Kohlberg (1969), who suggested that individuals have different levels of moral development, the lowest being punishment and obedience, the highest being universal ethical principles, which include inalienable rights that apply to all. The third element is the culture of the organization, which sets its own ethical framework about the way stakeholders are regarded and treated. When combined, these three elements influence the intended behavior and thus the ultimate actions of the organization.

Other writers have suggested alternative models. Jones (1991), drawing from earlier work by Rest (1986), has argued that individuals move through four stages of a process for ethical decision making:

- Recognize the moral issue.
- Make a moral judgment about that issue.
- Establish an intention to act upon that judgment.
- Act according to intention.

In Table 9.4 we have summarized the codes from two different sectors, nursing and business, and compared them with coaching. The comparison makes interesting reading. For example, we find that codes place the client at the center in person-centered work such as nursing and coaching; however, this is missing in business, with a lack of certainty about who is placed at the center. This raises interesting questions when we consider ethical dilemmas in leadership coaching about who is the client—is the client the individual in the room or the organization? Whose needs should be put first if there is a conflict between them? A second interesting difference is collaboration. Though this is featured in nursing and business codes, it is missing in coaching. However, it could be argued that to make the biggest difference leadership coaches need to collaborate with those running the organizational change plan and those delivering management training.

Table 9.4. Comparing Ethical Codes Across Sectors

Ethical Code	Nursing[Source: ANA]	Business[Source: ERC]	Coaching[Source: ICF]
Responsible/ Accountable	Responsible and accountable for patient care and rights of the patient	Obligation or willingness to accept responsibility	Client centered/development of client. Appropriate services offered
Competence	Owes the same duties to self as to others, to maintain competence and to continue personal and professional growth	The state or quality of being adequately or well qualified	The need to enhance their experience, knowledge, capability, and competence on a continuous basis through continual personal development
Cooperation	Participates in establishing, maintaining, and improving health care environments	The willing association and interaction of a group of people to accomplish a goal	Personal pledge to abide by codes of ethics and conduct set out by their own representative body
Education	Participates in the advancement of the profession through contributions to practice, education, administration, and knowledge development	Obtaining or developing knowledge or skills through a learning process	Recognize their own limitations of competence and the need to exercise boundary management and learn or acknowledge different approaches to coaching which may be more effective for the client

Collaboration	Collaborates with other health professionals and the public in promoting community, national, and international efforts to meet health needs	To work cooperatively, especially in a joint intellectual effort	
Integrity	Responsible for articulating nursing values, for maintaining the integrity of the profession and its practice, and for shaping social policy	Identification of and adherence to core values and beliefs that guide and motivate attitudes and action	Confidentiality and standards: Apply high standards in their service provision and behavior
Reputation			Every coach will act positively and in a manner that increases the public's understanding and acceptance of coaching
Law		Abiding by the encoded rules of society	Act within the laws of the land within which they practice and also acknowledge and promote diversity at all times

Codes of Practice in Coaching

As we have noted, coaching is an unregulated sector. It has a wide number of different professional bodies, all of which publish ethical codes. Though these are similar, as Brennan and Wildflower (2010) note, there are important differences. Such differences in wording or emphasis, as we noted above in counseling, can provide room for confusion.

In an attempt to minimize this problem a group of bodies came together to start the process of agreeing on the *First UK Statement of Shared Professional Values* (Association for Coaching, 2010). The coaching bodies involved were the International Coach Federation (ICF, 2010), the Association for Coaching (AC), Association for Professional Executive Coaching and Supervision (APECS), and the European Mentoring and Coaching Council (EMCC).

The agreement prepared a statement of shared professional values. These are

- Every coach, whether charging fees for coaching provided to individuals or organizations or both, is best served by being a member of a professional body suiting his or her needs.
- Every coach needs to abide by a code of governing ethics and apply acknowledged standards to the performance of his or her coaching work.
- Every coach needs to invest in ongoing continuing professional development to ensure that the quality of his or her service and his or her level of skill are enhanced.
- Every coach has a duty of care to ensure the good reputation of our emerging profession.

The agreement further breaks down into a series of seven guiding principles:

Principle One—Reputation. Every coach will act positively and in a manner that increases the public's understanding and acceptance of coaching.

Principle Two—Continuous Competence Enhancement. Every coach accepts the need to enhance his or her experience, knowledge, capability, and competence on a continuous basis through continual personal development.

Principle Three—Client-Centered. Every client is creative, resourceful, and whole and the coach's role is to keep the development of that client central to his or her work, ensuring that all services provided are appropriate to the client's needs.

Principle Four—Confidentiality and Standards. Every coach has a professional responsibility (beyond the terms of the contract with the client) to apply high standards in his or her service provision and behavior. He or she needs to be open and frank about methods and techniques used in the coaching process, maintain only appropriate records and to respect the confidentiality of (a) the work done with clients, and (b) the representative body's members' information.

Principle Five—Law and Diversity. Every coach will act within the laws of the jurisdictions within which he or she practices and will also acknowledge and promote diversity at all times.

Principle Six—Boundary Management. Every coach will recognize his or her own limitations of competence and the need to exercise boundary management. The client's right to terminate the coaching process will be respected at all times, as will the need to acknowledge different approaches to coaching which may be more effective for the client. Every endeavor will be taken to ensure the avoidance of conflicts of interest.

Principle Seven—Personal Pledge. Every coach will undertake to abide by the above principles that will complement the principles, codes of ethics, and conduct set out by the representative body to which he or she adheres. Any breach would require them to undergo due process from the body.

However, even when professional bodies come together in this way to collaborate and develop best practice, the issue remains, as in nursing, that codes are only a starting point. Codes can never offer a solution for all situations, but only principles to consider in making a decision. The alternative route is to help practitioners develop ethical decision-making frameworks which can guide them in making more conscious and informed ethical decisions.

Exhibit 9.1. Three Key Questions When Appointing a Coach

1. What arrangements do you have in place for supervision?
2. What ethical codes do you adhere to?
3. How would you resolve an ethical dilemma which occurred during your coaching work at this organization?

We would also argue that the existence of ethical codes in itself has not fully imposed itself in the world of coaching. Spence, Cavanagh, and Grant (2006), researching Australian coaches, found that 11 percent of them had not provided clients with ethical information or guidelines when formulating the relationship and contracting. Our experience of delivering coach training and supervision in the United Kingdom is similar. In fact we are surprised that the figure is this low. We would estimate from our own experience that less than half of coaches regularly set out the ethical or complaint guidelines to coachees and organizational clients. This must raise a concern regarding possible negligence and may leave the coachee or organizational client confused as to how to recognize whether they may have been violated in the first place.

This situation may change as clients become more experienced in procuring coaching. It is likely that clients will demand an insight into the coach's ethical standards, framework, and model for ethical decision making. In fact we would suggest that clients, when selecting, should include three key questions about supervision, ethical codes, and resolving ethical dilemmas (see Exhibit 9.1).

Ethics in Coaching

The next section focuses on how coaches might use codes, their personal values, and insight to resolve ethical dilemmas in their own practices through using a heuristic decision model.

Sources of Ethical Dilemmas

Sources of ethical dilemmas can stem from four sources; issues with the coachee, issues with the coach, boundary issues, and issues stemming from the multiple relationship nature of coaching in organizations.

Issues with the coachee. These may be emotional, personality, or behavioral issues. Each of these may be a precursor to the client being a danger to himself, those around him, and the organization within which he works. When this is the case a coach must decide how to act upon it, if at all. An example is the tragic case of a British civil servant, who was in the media spotlight over his advice on weapons of mass destruction during the lead up to the Iraq War. The individual felt under intense pressure and committed suicide by hanging himself from a tree.

Issues with the coach. These may be personal, emotional, or behavioral. The coach may have a personal problem or find it difficult to cease coaching when it seems it may be the correct step to take. A example may be the coach who continues to identify new issues and challenges for the coachee to work on, thus prolonging the relationship for commercial gain.

Boundary issues. Boundaries may be crossed by anyone in the coaching relationship. These boundaries may be written explicitly in the form of professional codes or may be presented as standards of practice implicit within coaching. The dilemmas faced as a result of someone crossing certain boundaries are further exacerbated by the fact that there is a large degree of uncertainty in the new field of coaching. Guidelines often prove inadequate and regulations are weak. An example might be where the coach and coachee, having finished the coaching session, continue their discussions over drinks and dinner.

Issues stemming from multiple dyadic relationships. These dilemmas present themselves as a result of the coach working for many individuals and bodies at the same time. The coach may be asked to partake in something ethically questionable by favoring one particular stakeholder. In these instances the coach must assess who the client is, who should be given favorability, and what principles would be broken and boundaries crossed by acting one way or another. An example of this would include the dilemma of whether to share information with the organization's representative regarding the individual client's decision to leave the organization, given that the manager is working on a business critical project and the client's departure would have an impact on the firm's financial future.

Multiple sources. Frequently, dilemmas cross between one or more of these source categories, which adds to both their complexity and the "stuckness" the coach can feel when facing the situation.

Ethical Decision-Making Models in Coaching

Ethical decision making is a nonlinear process that is principally cognitive in nature. Recurrent ethical thinking should be at the forefront of the coach's mind and fundamental to the operation of ethical decision making. Therefore it is reasonable to say that ethical decision making is intertwined with the process of coaching.

Many models have been proposed to help the executive coach make ethical decisions, some of which have been critiqued. For ethical decision making, it is advisable that one adopt or devise a framework of the series of processes necessary to analyze the problem. It is likely that the personal principles already developed will be used as part of this process, yet as the dilemma has not arisen and the context is not yet known, these personal principles may require revisiting several times. Furthermore, different dilemmas may compel the coach to access different resources to inform a decision.

Carroll and Walton (1997) devised a linear framework for use in counseling. Stage one involves creating ethical sensitivity, such as understanding one's own list of moral principles and reflecting on case studies on ethical dilemmas. Stage two involves formulating an ethical course of action, such as identifying the problem, reviewing the guidelines, and considering the course of action. Stage three entails implementing an ethical decision by anticipating potential difficulties in implementation, exploring fears and limitations, and ensuring necessary support. Finally, stage four involves living with the ambiguities of having made a decision, through such activities as self-reflection, acceptance of the limitations of the decision, and formulating a learning experience from the situation.

In reality, solving an ethical dilemma is a messy process and rarely unidirectional, requiring evaluation and reevaluation of actions before a final resolution is reached. Therefore, ethical decision making can be construed as an important and complicated process that involves making decisions of ethical concern, based largely on ethical principles and guidelines. It should be a nonlinear process involving an iterative process. For example, we would argue that ethical thinking is fundamental to the operation of ethical decision making and needs to be intertwined all the way through the process of coaching.

A Model for Ethical Decision Making in Coaching

Given the issues with ethical codes of practice and the limits of such codes, our attention has focused on the development of decision-making frameworks that could aid the individual coach in his or her work. The model consists of six stages to ethical decision making and, in contrast to previous models which have been largely linear, the model aims to offer both iteration and flexibility for coaches to incorporate their own vales and beliefs as part of the decision process. The six stages of the ACTION model (Passmore, 2009) are set out in Figure 9.2. The stages are briefly summarized.

Awareness. Being aware of one's own coaching position and the ethical code of the professional body that they are affiliated to. Second, awareness of one's own personal values and beliefs.

Classify. Identification of the issue as it emerges in practice and the ability to classify the issue as a "dilemma."

Time for reflection, support, and advice. The coach takes time to personally reflect using a combination of experience, peer support networks, and accessing professional journals and diaries. We recognize that different coaches will use different approaches to suit their own personal styles and needs. One difference is the route taken by experienced coaches versus novices or coaches in training. The experienced coach is likely to have a wide network of support, may have a co-coaching relationship in place, or be a member of a peer network. For the novice coach and those in training, the role of the supervisor is more important and the coach is likely to discuss the issue with a supervisor as part of training.

Initiate. Through the previous stage, the coach may be able to start building a number of solution options to the ethical dilemma. It is advisable to take a period of time to fully explore all of the options available, both self-generated and generated by the coach's support network, including through discussions with peers or a supervisor

Option evaluation. Through this stage, coaches must give time and space to each of the options generated in the Initiate stage. This will include checking with ethical codes and reflecting on how the decision fits with their own values (revisiting stage 1). It is also likely to involve checking for any multiple relationship issues that may arise when being hired by an organization to coach its staff, and finally reflecting on whether the decision is consistent with the contract established at the start of the relationship with the organizational client and the coachee.

Novate. Once the decision has been made, the coach must incorporate this scenario into his or her ethical journal or experiences. It may also be prudent to share such a scenario (in a confidential manner) with those within one's own network or coaching body, so that colleagues can benefit from the situation.

Figure 9.2. The Action Model for Ethical Decision Making in Coaching

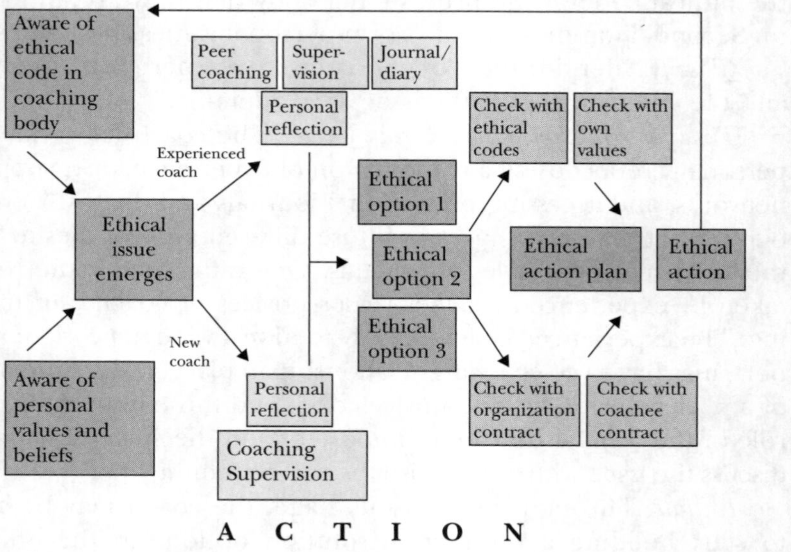

Source: Passmore, 2009.

Conclusions

In reviewing professions parallel to coaching, ethical codes offer both benefits and also limits to how we think about ethical decision making in coaching. Alternatives include developing ethical sensitivity through scenarios and ethical decision-making models. We have argued that subtle differences can lead to confusion. Further ethical standards are also only guidelines for action and do not lead us to be able to make ethical decisions. In the final section we offered a model for ethical decision making in coaching—the ACTION model, which aims to offer a specific tool for decision making for those working in leadership coaching. The model takes into account previous research and models developed in parallel domains and seeks to offer a flexible, nonlinear approach to the resolution of dilemmas. As a coach-centered approach, ACTION provides a useful heuristic for coaches in their real-life practice. We recognize that such a model is not definitive and we encourage others to critically reflect on this work and through research to enhance our understanding of the dilemmas and ethical challenges faced by coaches and also to build more comprehensive models to guide coaches in resolving ethical problems.

References

ANA. (2001). Code of ethics. Retrieved 20 February, 2010, from http:// nursingworld.org/ethics/code/protected_nwcoe813.htm.

APA. (2003). Ethical code. Retrieved 2 February, 2010, from www.apa .org/ethics/code/index.aspx.

Association for Coaching. (2010). Shared values statement. Retrieved 20 February, 2010, from www.associationforcoaching.com/news/ M80221.doc.

Bailey, D. M., & Schwartzberg, S. L. (1995). *Ethical and legal dilemmas in occupational therapy*. Philadelphia: F. A. Davis.

BACP. (2010). Ethical framework for good practice in counseling and psychotherapy. Retrieved 3 March, 2010, from: www.bacp .co.uk/ethical_framework/.

Bond, T., (2000). *Standards and ethics for counseling in action* (3rd ed.). London: Sage.

BPS. (2005). BPS *code* of conduct, *ethical* principles & guidelines. Retrieved 3 March, 2010, from www.bps.org.uk/downloadfile.cfm? file_uuid56D0645CC-7E96-C67F-D75E2648E5580115&ext5pdf.

Brennan, D., & Wildflower, L. (2010). Ethics in coaching. In E. Cox, T. Bachkirova, & D. Clutterbuck (Eds.), *The complete handbook of coaching* (pp. 369–380). London: Sage.

Carroll, M., & Walton, M. (1997). *Handbook of counseling in organizations.* London: Sage.

Chadwick, R., & Tadd, W. (1992). *Ethics and nursing practice: A case study approach.* London: MacMillan Press.

Ciulla, J., Martin, C., & Soloman, R. (2007). *Honest work: A business ethics reader.* Oxford: Oxford University Press.

Crane, A., & Matten, D. (2004). *Business ethics: A European perspective.* Oxford: Oxford University Press.

Cross, M., & Wood, J. (2005). The person in ethical decision making: Living with choices. In R. Tribe & J. Morrissey (Eds.), *Handbook of professional and ethical practice for psychologists, counsellers and psychotherapists* (pp. 47–60). Hove, UK: Brunner Routledge.

De George, R. (2006). *Business ethics.* Upper Saddle River, NJ: Pearson.

De Jong, A. (2006). Coaching ethics: Integrity in the moment of choice. In J. Passmore (Ed.), *Excellence in coaching: The industry guide* (pp. 191–202). London: Kogan Page.

ERC. (2010). Ethics toolkit. Retrieved 4 June, 2010, from www.ethics.org/page/ethics-toolkit.

Ferrell, O., Fraedrich, J., & Ferrell, L. (2002). *Business ethics: Ethical decision making and cases.* Boston: Houghton Mifflin.

Fisher, C., & Lovell, A. (2009). *Business ethics & values: Individual, corporate and international perspectives.* Harlow, UK: Pearson.

Ford, R., & Richardson, W. (1994). Ethical decision making: A review of the empirical literature. *Journal of Business Ethics, 13*(3), 205–221.

ICF. (2010). Code of ethics. Retrieved 3 March, 2010, from www.coachfederation.org/about-icf/ethics-&-regulation/icf-code-of-ethics/.

Jones, T. (1991). Ethical decision making by individuals in organizations: An issue contingence model. *Academy of Management Review, 16,* 366–395.

Kelly. G. (1955). *The psychology of personal constructs.* London: Routledge.

Kelly, M. (1996). A code of ethics for health promotion. London: The Social Affairs Unit.

Kohlberg, L. (1969). Stages and sequences: The cognitive developmental approach to socialisation. In D. A. Goslin (Ed.), *Handbook of socialization theory and research* (pp. 347–480). Chicago: Rand McNally.

McNamara, C. (2008). Complete guide to ethics management: An ethics toolkit for managers. Retrieved on 8 November, 2009 from www.managementhlep.org/ethics/ethxgde.htm.

Passmore, J. (2009, October 15). Looking after yourself as a coach. Paper presented at West Midlands Local Government Annual Coaching Conference, Coventry, UK.

Rest, J. (1986). *Moral development: advances in research and theory.* New York: Praeger.

Rowson, R. (2001). Ethical principles. In F. Palmer Barnes & L. Murdin (Eds.), *Values and ethics in the practice of psychotherapy and counseling* (pp. 6–22). Buckingham: Open University Press.

Spence, G. B., Cavanagh, M. J., & Grant, M. (2006). Duty of care in an unregulated industry: Initial findings on the diversity and practices of Australian coaches. *International Coaching Psychology Review, 1*(1), 71–85.

Thompson, M. (2005). *Ethical theory.* London: Hodder-Murray.

Trager, J. (1979). *The people's chronology: A year by year record of human events from prehistory to the present.* New York: Holt, Rinehart and Winston.

Trevino, L., & Nelson, K. (1999). *Managing business ethics.* New York: Wiley.

Weiner, K. (2004). *The little book of ethics for coaches: Ethics, risk management, and professional issues.* Bloomington, IN: Author House.

Chapter Ten

TOOLS AND TECHNIQUES

What's in Your Toolbox?

Ann M. Herd and Joyce E. A. Russell

Research indicates there may be as many tools and techniques for coaching as there are coaches. As Bono, Purvanova, Towler, and Peterson (2009) noted in a review of executive coaching practices, "there is little uniformity in the practices of executive coaches. Coaches seem to use a variety of assessment tools, scientific or philosophical approaches, activities, goals, and outcome evaluation methods in their coaching" (361). The goal of the current chapter then is to pull together in one place many of the tools, techniques, and frameworks that have been used in the practice of leadership coaching. To date, there hasn't been a single source that has described all of these resources; thus, this chapter should serve as an important resource for coaches of all levels of experience.

We will briefly describe various frameworks, techniques, and tools in the context of the various phases of the coaching process. The specific tools and techniques identified in this chapter were chosen based on extensive reviews of the academic and

Note: The authors contributed equally to this chapter.

practitioner literature on executive coaching. In addition, we conducted discussions with more than a dozen other coaches regarding the frameworks, tools, and techniques they found most valuable when coaching leaders for varying purposes. These are briefly described in the appendixes at the end of this chapter.

Defining Coaching Frameworks, Techniques, and Tools

The terms coaching "frameworks, techniques, tools" have been used interchangeably in the literature on executive coaching. For the purposes of this chapter we define a coaching "tool" as a specific assessment instrument with measurement properties, a coaching "technique" as a specific interchange process between the coach and client used to facilitate agreed-on coaching goals, and a "framework" as a conceptual model that may be used by a coach in guiding a coaching discussion or in suggesting specific activities for a unique coaching purpose.

Coaching experts agree that the use of tools and techniques requires a great deal of judgment and discernment on the part of the coach to take into account the unique context of each coaching engagement, including cultural considerations and the unique needs of each client (Megginson & Clutterbuck, 2005; Rosinski, 2003). In addition, special training, practice, or certification may be required with various tools and techniques before a coach can effectively use them. Throughout this chapter, we provide sources where additional information about each tool and technique can be found, and we note cross-cultural considerations.

Because a coaching *tool* is a measurement instrument, it must be evaluated in the context of its measurement properties and the relevance of this measurement to specific coaching goals. Questions that must be considered when deciding whether to use a particular coaching tool include: What construct does the tool purport to measure? Is this construct a competency, skill, or characteristic that is important for meeting the client and/or organization's goals? How well does the tool measure what it purports to measure? Ease of use and cost are further considerations when deciding whether to use a particular assessment tool. Coaches are encouraged to examine these issues when determining which particular tools to use. We have provided brief descriptions of the various tools in the appendixes. Coaches are also encouraged to refer to the specific tools' Web sites to learn more details (for example, costs, certifications required, translations into multiple languages).

Because the coaching relationship is considered an important factor in successful coaching outcomes (Bluckert, 2005), an evaluation of various coaching *techniques* or *frameworks* must be made in the context of the specific coaching relationship and the goals for that unique coaching engagement. Questions that must be considered include: Does the use of the technique or framework promote a positive coaching experience and relationship? and Does it meet an important objective of the coaching process at that point in time? Does the use of the framework or technique add value to the coaching process over and above the use of alternatives? Is the use of the technique or framework appropriate in light of cultural factors that may be influencing the coaching process? Although a detailed examination of each framework and technique in terms of these issues is beyond the scope of the current chapter, it is critical for coaches to answer these questions.

Organizing Framework

The coaching process often progresses through five phases: (1) establishing the coaching relationship, (2) gathering feedback, (3) setting goals, (4) progressing toward goals, and (5) transitioning out of the coaching engagement. Figure 10.1 illustrates these phases and the primary objectives of each phase. The frameworks, tools, and techniques will be discussed in terms of these phases. Because these phases are not discrete, and because the coaching objectives that are predominant during each phase carry over into all other phases, it should be noted that tools and techniques discussed as appropriate for use during one phase may also be appropriate for use in other phases of the coaching process.

Goldsmith and Lyons (2006) have suggested that the systems concept of equifinality may apply in recognizing that a variety of

Figure 10.1. Phases and Objectives of the Coaching Engagement

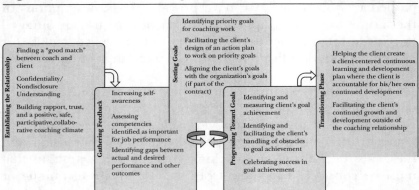

personal styles could be useful to achieve the same learning or business objective during coaching, and we suggest that this concept may also apply to some choices of techniques as well. On the other hand, some coaching frameworks are overarching and can serve to structure the coaching process across all phases, such as the GROW framework (Whitmore, 2009). Coaches should also consider the global context relevant to their clients and those with whom they interact, because, as noted by Rosinski (2003), "Too often, unfortunately and despite good intentions, (coaching) models are presented without any hint of the underlying implicit cultural assumptions and without the necessary care one needs to exercise when trying to implement the models across cultures" (128).

Phase 1: Establishing the Coaching Relationship

As noted in Figure 10.1, when establishing the coaching relationship, the key objectives are to find a good match between coach and client, gain an understanding of issues around confidentiality and nondisclosure, and build rapport, trust, and a positive coaching climate. An intake interview form is one technique that coaches might use to meet these objectives. Newer coaches might want to refer to Coach U's books which provide numerous forms for use in starting a coaching practice (Coach U, 2005a, 2005b). Regardless of the form used or the unique background of the coach, there are three critical steps that need to be accomplished in that first coaching session (Poteet et al., 2009):

1. *Determine the client's readiness for coaching.* Coaches often use a coaching readiness assessment to determine what previous experiences the executive has had with coaching and, if any, what his or her view of this coaching was. In addition, it is helpful for the coach to find out if the client has any previous experience having received feedback from any type of assessment, such as an assessment center or 360, and if so, what those experiences were like.

2. *Agree on the contract.* A written agreement or contract is used during the initial stage to help establish a clearly understood coaching engagement. Key components in this contract include defining the parameters of the coaching engagement, time frame, objectives, expectations, ground rules, and confidentiality (Kilburg, 1997; Natale & Diamante, 2005).

3. *Collect initial information about the client.* It is important for the coach to learn about the client's background, current work situation, career goals, and perceived strengths and developmental needs.

Phase 2: Gathering Feedback

The second stage in the coaching process consists of gathering information from the client and other appropriate sources regarding the client's current situation in the context of his/her goals for the future. As noted in Figure 10.1, the major objectives of this phase are to increase clients' self-awareness (Kilburg, 1997), assess their competencies, and identify gaps between their actual and desired performance. Feedback is a necessary and useful tool for achieving these goals (Church, 1997; Yammarino & Atwater, 1993).

Frameworks

To gather feedback during the second phase and throughout the coaching engagement, a coach may be guided by any of several frameworks. Appendix A presents a brief description of thirteen frameworks used in leadership coaching. For example, one powerful framework is the **GROW** model (Whitmore, 2009), which provides structure to the coaching process by starting with visioning and feedback-gathering as major steps in the model. **Appreciative inquiry**, or appreciative coaching, is another strong framework which is useful throughout all phases of coaching (Moore & Tschannen-Moran, 2010; Orem, Blinkert, & Clancy, 2007), beginning with questions about the client's strengths, values, and learning goals to then lead the client through stages of change. Other coaching frameworks may prove valuable during the feedback gathering phase, depending upon the individual coaching context and the presenting issues discussed during Phase 1 (Wahl, Scriber, & Bloomfield, 2008).

Techniques

Appendix B provides a brief description of more than thirty coaching techniques from which coaches might choose during all phases of the coaching engagement. During the feedback gathering activities of Phase 2, for example, coaches find storying and time line exercises particularly useful in enhancing awareness of key themes on which to focus.

Tools

Appendix C presents a list of more than fifty assessments tools commonly used in executive coaching, which are especially useful during the Gathering Feedback stage. As shown in the Appendix, the tools have been categorized according to the coaching goal (for example, to enhance self-awareness, communication, empathy) or the construct being measured (for example, critical thinking, personality, conflict management). Details illustrating the psychometric qualities (for example, reliability, validity) of the tools can be found in the *Buros Mental Measurements Yearbook* (Vol. 10) as well as from the tools' Web sites. All of these tools can be useful during Phase 2 when gathering feedback to enhance the clients' self-awareness, assess their competencies, or identify performance gaps.

Tools which are particularly useful in the early stages of coaching include assessments of *self-awareness and life values, work values and motivation, career interests, learning styles, innovative problem-solving style*, and *personality*. These self-report tools provide insights into the clients' general "makeup," including strengths, blind spots, behavioral tendencies, what they consider to be important in their lives, as well as the types of jobs, industries, or careers to which they are best suited. A specific personality assessment gaining in popularity are tools which measure personality attributes that can potentially *derail* executives (see, for example, Chappelow & Leslie, 2001; Dotlich & Cairo, 2003; Goldsmith, 2007). Because *critical thinking and reasoning* skills are important for leadership performance, tools which measure these abilities are also useful for improved self-awareness.

A particularly useful tool with which to begin gathering feedback is one which measures the client's preferences among various cultural dimensions (that is, *cultural styles and adaptability*). An underlying assumption of such a tool is that individuals vary in their cultural preferences regardless of the general culture of the country in which they live and work (Schmitz, 2006). Knowing a client's cultural preferences on dimensions such as time (monochromic or polychromic), communication (low context or high context), collectivity (group or individual), structure (predictability or uncertainty), and power (egalitarian or hierarchical) provides useful insights in understanding how the client responds to, and processes, feedback and other coaching activities throughout the coaching engagement (Moran, Harris, & Moran, 2007). In addition to the cultural preference measures described in Appendix C, the Center for Creative Leadership has also developed suggestions and short assessments to help executives develop cultural adaptability (Deal & Prince, 2003).

Most coaches find performance feedback tools helpful in motivating clients to set goals and improve performance. The coach might shadow the executive in meetings with his or her team or use interviews whereby the executive's supervisor, coworkers, subordinates, customers, or other relevant work associates serve as sources for feedback (Goleman & Boyatzis, 2008; Orenstein, 2002). Coaches may also choose among a variety of *multisource or 360-degree assessments* available (Conway & Huffcutt, 1997). Some are customized for the particular executive coaching program or client firm (see Appendix C). Advantages of 360-degree tools include the ability to gather large amounts of quantifiable as well as qualitative data in an efficient manner. Ratings across sources can be explored for convergence in identifying clients' strengths and developmental areas. Cross-culturally, one caveat to using 360-degree assessment tools is that leaders with a strong hierarchical orientation may experience reluctance about giving and receiving feedback across hierarchical levels (Rosinski, 2003). Coaches may also use specific measures of a client's *strengths* when helping them to set goals or examine how they are seen in terms of *general leadership* dimensions.

In contrast to multisource performance ratings which provide a "sign" of past performance, assessment centers and exercises provide actual current samples of job-related behavior (Thornton & Byham, 1982). Assessment center exercises are a powerful feedback tool in coaching because the exercises serve as a snapshot of the client's job-related behavior, with interpersonal skills and leadership process behaviors among the dimensions commonly measured (Meriac, Hoffman, Woehr, & Fleisher, 2008). The exercises are usually videotaped for rating purposes, and the coach and client can then review the videotape together. Studies consistently report high client acceptance of feedback from the exercises compared to 360-degree ratings (Hermelin, Lievens, & Robertson, 2007; Meriac et al., 2008). A disadvantage to assessment center exercises is that they are relatively expensive in comparison to 360 tools.

Coaches often work with clients on *managing conflict* and *stress* in their lives, so assessments to measure these are especially helpful as they set goals to improve their individual leadership skills and their work in teams. Teamwork is, in fact, another area often targeted in executive coaching (that is, how leaders work in teams and can get their teams to work more effectively). To aid clients in understanding their own style when working in teams or how their teams work together, coaches can use a variety of *team orientation or decision-making* tools described in Appendix C. Coaches might also use Lencioni's five dysfunctions of teams (2005) to teach clients about problems with workplace teams and strategies for improving team effectiveness.

Finally, one of the most popular areas of assessment in coaching today is *emotional intelligence* (Bar-On, 2004). Kunnanatt (2004) and Adkins (2004) both noted that EI or EQ training has grown into a multimillion dollar training industry. As noted in Appendix C, there are several well-developed tools for assessing EQ. Readers are also referred to McEnrue and Groves (2006) for a detailed comparison of the psychometric attributes (such as validity) of various EQ measures.

Phase 3: Setting Goals

The third stage in the coaching process is one of setting goals based on feedback gathered in the previous stage. The coach's objectives are to work with the client to identify his or her priority goals, help the client develop an action plan, and possibly align the identified goals with the organization's goals. Like Phase 2, this phase can be an ongoing activity throughout the coaching engagement, as the coach and client prioritize and reprioritize the goals. Kilburg (1997) suggests that a coach must continuously work at focusing the client's attention on the areas most important for that client's growth and development. This may include external events or performance issues in the client's professional or personal life, or internal states, conflict, or emotions the client is experiencing, such as those revolving around the concept of self (Drath & Van Velsor, 2006; Kegan, 1994).

One objective of the goal-setting stage is a written action plan on which the client will work during the coaching process. In the executive coaching program at the Robert H. Smith School of Business, this action plan is called an "Individual Development Plan (IDP)," which serves as a template for the goal-setting process as well as a "living document" for all subsequent coaching sessions. A sample IDP can be found in Appendix D. IDP outcome and action goals are best written using the SMART structure of specific, measurable, achievable, realistic, and time bound. Along with action goals and deadlines, potential barriers and ways to overcome barriers should be identified in the IDP. Resources for helping the clients develop their goal-setting plans include *Successful Manager's Handbook, Successful Executive's Handbook, FYI For Your Improvement*, and the Center for Creative Leadership's Guidebooks. Homan and Miller (2008) also present an example of a Coaching Development Plan which includes SMART goals.

Frameworks, Techniques, and Tools

A first step in developing an IDP is to help a client identify desired goals and outcomes. Any of the frameworks, techniques, and tools described in Appendixes A, B, and C may be useful in this endeavor. For example, coaching using an *appreciative inquiry* framework (Moore & Tschannen-Moran, 2010) often begins the process with a *visioning* technique (Seligman, 2004). To use this technique, the coach has the client relax (for example, by using deep-breathing exercises) and then visualize all aspects of his or her ideal life or performance. The client is encouraged to visualize the various details of this ideal scenario, including sights, sounds, actions, location, setting, and other people. The client is asked to write down the details of this ideal visual or use artwork, such as a *collage*, to explore with the coach the most important aspects of this visualization (for example, motives, performance outcomes, long-term and short-term goals, relationships with others, "being" aspects versus "doing" aspects, and so forth) (Rosinski, 2003). The ideal scenario, and its underlying aspects, serves as the springboard for the client's goal-setting process, usually as a long-term goal around which specific action plans can be built.

Other techniques that are especially helpful to help clients to set goals are the use of *story* and *time line* exercises (Echols, Gravenstine, & Mobley, 2008; Loehr, 2007; Rosinski, 2003). Using these techniques, the coach encourages clients to identify, analyze, and reframe stories, key experiences, or metaphors about their life experiences and goals. *Role model analysis* is another technique which is useful in helping the client identify "vital behaviors," upon which to focus for positive change (Patterson, Grenny, Maxfield, McMillan, & Switzler, 2008).

During the goal-setting phase, it is important for the coach to be aware of cross-cultural differences in assumptions about goal setting (Rosinski, 2003). For example, in individualistic cultures such as the United States, more weight is typically given to self-actualization, personal achievement, and "doing" goals, whereas in more collectivistic cultures such as Japan there may be more emphasis on group achievement, harmony, and "being" goals (Chittum, 2008; Peterson, 2007; Rosinski, 2003).

Clients also vary in their cultural orientations toward time, whereby those with a "single focus" may prefer focusing on one task or goal at a time, while those with a "multifocus" orientation may prefer attending to multiple goals simultaneously (Schmitz, 2006). In terms of setting deadlines for goal accomplishment, clients with a more "fluid" time orientation may attend less to specific coaching deadlines than those with a "fixed" time orientation, while those with a "present" time orientation may prefer to focus on short-term and quick results, in contrast to clients with a more "future" time orientation. Clients with a more "private" as opposed to "public" cultural orientation toward space may be less comfortable acknowledging or verbalizing their personal goals publicly (Peterson, 2007). A suggestion made by Peterson regarding personal space preferences is to ask clients alternative types of questions when trying to help a client ascertain motivations and goals, such as "What values do you want to uphold in the work that you do?" (267). Tools for measuring *values* (see Appendix C) can also be helpful during this goal-setting process.

Phase 4: Progressing Toward Goals

The primary objectives of the fourth phase of the coaching process are to identify and measure the client's goal achievement, identify obstacles, and celebrate any successes. Most coaching frameworks, techniques, and tools listed in Appendices A, B, and C can be used to support the client during his or her work in this stage.

Frameworks and Techniques

When discussing the client's goal-oriented behavior and progress toward goals during this stage, it is important to recognize the context in which the client is working (Orenstein, 2002), including the organizational culture and specific working relationships involved (Rosinski, 2003). Many of the most useful coaching techniques for this phase focus on discussing with clients, and helping the client reframe their thinking about, their actions, circumstances, goals, strategies, and developmental stage. For example, the GROW model (Whitmore, 2009), *action-observer-reflection* model (Hughes, Ginnett, & Curphy, 2008), *brief solution-focused* coaching (Wakefield, 2006), *constructive-developmental* framework

(Drath & Van Velsor, 2006), and *motivational interviewing* (Moore & Tschannen-Moran, 2010) are particularly useful techniques during this stage of the coaching process.

Areas which often receive particular emphasis as part of the executive client's IDP include energy management, emotional intelligence skills, and executive presence skills (Blattner & Bacigalupo, 2007; Goleman & Boyatzis, 2008; Scriber, 2008). Energy management skills can be fostered by *time* and *energy management, somatic,* and *balance* activities (Ebner, 2008; Echols & Mobley, 2008; Loehr & Schwartz, 2001; Richardson, 2009; Zeman, 2008). *Role play* and *role model analysis* are useful for developing skills related to emotional intelligence and executive presence, for identifying specific "vital" behaviors for achieving goals (Patterson et al., 2008), and for practicing challenging conversations (Echols & Mobley, 2008; Scott, 2004).

Tools

To identify progress on goals, many coaches use general performance data or multisource ratings (for example, *Benchmarks, PDI Profiler*) to compare the client's initial behavior with his or her recent behavior (that is, after working for some period of time on certain behavioral goals). For managers, measures of leadership (such as *LPI* and *MLQ*) also prove useful to measure any gains in leadership skills or behaviors.

Cross-culturally, the coach needs to be aware of differing assumptions regarding locus of control (Rosinski, 2003; Schmitz, 2006). For example, in Western cultures and indeed in most coaching practices, there is an assumption that the individual determines his or her own destiny, whereas in Eastern and Middle-Eastern cultures the clients may wish to focus more on living in acceptance of their circumstances rather than changing them (Peterson, 2007). A client who places a high value on structure, control, collectivism, and hierarchy may not feel comfortable being "empowered" to come up with plans and solutions completely on his or her own (DeLay & Dalton, 2006; Walker, Walker, & Schmitz, 2003), while a client with a "private" versus "public" orientation may prefer practice activities within the coaching session before experimenting in the work setting (Kram & Ting, 2006).

For developing one's own cross-cultural coaching skills as well as coaching clients who wish to develop their cross-cultural skills, the initial step involves developing a "global mindset" (Zucal, 2008) and gaining knowledge of cultural orientations and "basic cultural prototypes" (DeLay & Dalton, 2006, 126). Techniques and tools for developing global awareness include assessment (for example, using a cross-cultural assessment tool such as the *COI*) and review of major cultural dimensions involving the following: environment, time, action, communication, space, power, individualism, competitiveness, structure, and thinking (Dorfman, Hanges, & Bordbeck, 2004; Hofstede, 2001; Rosinski, 2003; Schmitz, 2006; Trompenaars & Hampden-Turner, 1998). Coaching techniques for developing skills in leading others from other cultures include *style switching, communication patterns* role play analysis, and *modes of thinking* problem-solving exercises (Rosinski, 2003; Schmitz, 2006).

Phase 5: Transitioning Out of the Coaching Engagement

The final stage of the coaching process is the transitioning phase, where the client exits the coaching process and becomes solely responsible for his or her own lifelong development. One of the major objectives of coaching is for the clients to develop the tools they need so they can essentially coach themselves without needing the coach (Bartlett, 2007; Peterson & Hicks, 2006; Rosinski, 2003). The coach can facilitate a client's feelings of self-efficacy and self-sufficiency throughout the coaching process by asking questions that encourage the client to take responsibility for his or her progress on IDP goals, and by highlighting the role the client has played in making progress (Poteet et al., 2009).

Coaching tools and techniques used during the transitioning phase pertain mainly to helping clients develop a clear picture of how far along they have come in achieving their goals, and plans for follow-up contact with the coach and for using coaching resources (Megginson & Clutterbuck, 2009). Learning journals can be used as a technique for review of progress and insights. In addition, the IDP, which has ideally served as a "living document" tool throughout the coaching process, can be used to help the client review continued and future goals, action steps, anticipated challenges, and support tools (see Appendix D). In addition, the coach should help clients see the shift from receiving "coaching" to becoming lifelong learners and getting more involved in creating their own long-term development plan, including continuing involvement in professional networks, leadership development opportunities, and multiple developmental relationships (Higgins & Thomas, 2001).

Conclusion

This chapter has presented a comprehensive reference for many of the popular assessment tools, techniques, and frameworks that are being used by executive coaches today. It appears likely, however, that as the field of executive coaching and the number of coaches continue to grow so too will the tools and techniques that are available for coaches' use. As noted earlier, care must be taken to discern the validity of the assessment tools and usefulness of the coaching techniques for the particular needs and goals of each client in the context of each unique coaching engagement. Further research is needed to evaluate the extent to which each tool and technique has been found useful by coaches and executive clients in various contexts and for various purposes, and for clients and coaches with various cultural orientations.

References

Adkins, S. (2004, February). Beneath the tip of the iceberg: Technology plumbs the affective learning domain. *Training and Development Magazine*, 28–33.

Bar-On, R. (2004). The Bar-On Emotional Quotient Inventory (EQ-i): Rationale, description and psychometric properties. In G. Geher (Ed.), *Measuring emotional intelligence: Common ground and controversy* (pp. 115–145). Hauppauge, NY: Nova Science.

Bartlett, J. E. (2007). Advances in coaching practices: A humanistic approach to coach and client roles. *Journal of Business Research, 60*, 91–93.

Blattner, J., & Bacigalupo, A. (2007). Using emotional intelligence to develop executive leadership and team and organizational development. *Consulting Psychology Journal: Practice and Research,* *59*(3), 209–219.

Bluckert, P. (2005). Critical factors in executive coaching—the coaching relationship. *Industrial and Commercial Training, 37*(7), 336–240.

Bono, J. E., Purvanova, R. K., Towler, A. J., & Peterson, D. B. (2009). A survey of executive coaching practices. *Personnel Psychology, 62*(2), 361–397.

Buros Mental Measurements Yearbook. (2009). Vol. 10. Lincoln, NE: O.K. Buros Institute of the University of Nebraska.

Center for Creative Leadership. *Ideas into action guidebooks.* Available from www.ccl.org/guidebooks.

Chappelow, C., & Leslie, J. B. (2001). *Keeping your career on track: Twenty success strategies.* Greensboro, NC: Center for Creative Leadership.

Chittum, R. (2008). Eastern influence on coaching. In C. Wahl, C. Scriber, & B. Bloomfield (Eds.), *On becoming a leadership coach: A holistic approach to coaching excellence* (pp. 21–28). New York: Palgrave Macmillan.

Church, A. H. (1997). Managerial self-awareness in high-performing individuals in organizations. *Journal of Applied Psychology, 87,* 281–292.

Coach U, Inc. (2005a). *Coach U's essential coaching tools: Your complete practice resource.* Hoboken, NJ: Wiley.

Coach U, Inc. (2005b). *The Coach U personal and corporate coach training handbook.* Hoboken, NJ: Wiley.

Conway, J. M., & Huffcutt, A. I. (1997). Psychometric properties of multisource performance ratings: A meta-analysis of supervisor, peer, and self ratings. *Human Performance, 10,* 331–360.

Deal, J. J., & Prince, D. W. (2003). *Developing cultural adaptability.* Greensboro, NC: Center for Creative Leadership.

DeLay, L., & Dalton, M. (2006). Coaching across cultures. In S. Ting & P. Scisco, *The CCL handbook of coaching: A guide for the leader coach* (pp. 122–148). San Francisco: Jossey Bass.

Dorfman, P. W., Hanges, P. J., & Brodbeck, F. C. (2004). Leadership and cultural variation. In R. J. House, P. J. Hanges, M. Javidan, P. W. Dorfman, & V. Gupta (Eds.), *Culture, leadership, and organizations: The GLOBE study of 62 societies* (pp. 669–720). Thousand Oaks, CA: Sage.

Dotlich, D. L., & Cairo, P. C. (2003). *Why CEOs fail.* San Francisco: Jossey-Bass.

Drath, W., & Van Velsor, E. (2006). Constructive-developmental coaching. In S. Ting & P. Scisco. *The CCL handbook of coaching: A guide for the leader coach* (pp. 312 – 343). San Francisco: Jossey-Bass.

Ebner, K. (2008). Coaching for leverage: Helping clients to manage priorities, time, energy, and resources. In C. Wahl, C. Scriber, & B. Bloomfield (Eds.), *On becoming a leadership coach: A holistic approach to coaching excellence* (pp. 189–197). New York: Palgrave Macmillan.

Echols, M., Gravenstine, K., & Mobley, S. (2008). Using story in coaching. In C. Wahl, C. Scriber, & B. Bloomfield (Eds.), *On becoming a leadership coach: A holistic approach to coaching excellence* (pp. 53–60). New York: Palgrave Macmillan.

Echols, M., & Mobley, S. (2008). Using somatics to coach leaders. In C. Wahl, C. Scriber, & B. Bloomfield (Eds.), *On becoming a leadership coach: A holistic approach to coaching excellence.* (pp. 81–90). New York: Palgrave Macmillan.

Gebelein, S. H., Lee, D. G., Nelson-Neuhaus, K. J., & Sloan, E. B. (1999). *Successful executive's handbook.* Minneapolis: Personnel Decisions International.

Gebelein, S. H., Nelson-Neuhaus, K. J., Skube, C. J., Lee, D. G., Stevens, L. A., Hellervik, L. W., & Davis, B. L. (Eds.) (2004). *Successful manager's handbook* (7th ed.). Minneapolis: Personnel Decisions Corporation/ePredix.

Goldsmith, M. (2007). *What got you here won't get you there.* New York: Hyperion.

Goldsmith, M., & Lyons, L. (2006). *Coaching for leadership: The practice of leadership coaching from the world's greatest coaches.* San Francisco: Pfeiffer.

Goleman, D., & Boyatzis, R. (2008). Social intelligence and the biology of leadership. *Harvard Business Review,* 74–81.

Hermelin, E., Lievens, F., & Robertson, I. T. (2007). The validity of assessment centers for the prediction of supervisory performance ratings: A meta-analysis. *International Journal of Selection and Assessment, 15*(4), 405–411.

Higgins, M. C., & Thomas, D. A. (2001). Constellations and careers: Toward understanding the effects of multiple developmental relationships. *Journal of Organizational Behavior, 22*(3), 223–247.

Hofstede, G. (2001). *Culture's consequences: Comparing values, behaviors, institutions and organizations across nations.* Thousand Oaks, CA: Sage.

Homan, M., & Miller, L. J. (2008). *Coaching in organizations: Best coaching practices.* Hoboken, NJ: Wiley.

Hughes, R. L., Ginnett, R. C., & Curphy, G. J. (2008). *Leadership: Enhancing the lessons from experience.* New York: McGraw-Hill/Irwin.

Kegan, R. (1994). *In over our heads: The mental demands of modern life.* Cambridge, MA: Harvard University Press.

Kilburg, R. R. (1997). Coaching and executive character: Core problems and basic approaches. *Consulting Psychology Journal: Practice and Research, 49*(4), 281–299.

Kram, K. E., & Ting, S. (2006). Coaching for emotional intelligence. In S. Ting & P. Scisco (Eds.), *The CCL handbook of coaching: A guide for the leader coach* (pp. 179–202). San Francisco: Jossey-Bass.

Kunnanatt, J. (2004). Emotional intelligence: The new science of interpersonal effectiveness. *Human Resources Development Quarterly, 15,* 489–495.

Lencioni, P. (2005). *Overcoming the five dysfunctions of a team: A field guide.* San Francisco: Jossey-Bass.

Loehr, J. (2007). *The power of story: Rewrite your destiny in business and life.* New York: The Free Press.

Loehr, J., & Schwartz, T. (2001). The making of a corporate athlete. *Harvard Business Review, 79*(1), 120–128.

Lombardo, M. M., & Eichinger, R. W. (2009). *FYI for your improvement* (5th ed.). Minneapolis: Lominger International: Korn/Ferry.

McEnrue, M. P., & Groves, K. (2006). Choosing among tests of emotional intelligence: What is the evidence? *Human Development Quarterly, 17*(1), 9–42.

Megginson, D., & Clutterbuck, D. (2005). *Techniques for coaching and mentoring.* Oxford, UK: Butterworth-Heinemann.

Megginson, D., & Clutterbuck, D. (2009). *Further techniques for coaching and mentoring.* Oxford, UK: Butterworth-Heinemann.

Meriac, J. P., Hoffman, B. J., Woehr, D. J., & Fleisher, M. S. (2008). Further evidence for the validity of assessment center dimensions: A meta-analysis of the incremental criterion-related validity of dimension ratings. *Journal of Applied Psychology, 93*(5), 1042–1052.

Moore, M., & Tschannen-Moran, B. (2010). *Coaching psychology manual.* Baltimore, MD: Lippincott Williams and Wilkins.

Moran, R. T., Harris, P. R., & Moran, S. V. (2007). *Managing cultural differences.* New York: Elsevier Butterworth-Heinemann.

Natale, S. M., & Diamante, T. (2005). The five stages of executive coaching: Better process makes better practice. *Journal of Business Ethics, 59,* 361–374.

Orem, S. L., Blinkert, J., & Clancy, A. L. (2007). *Appreciative coaching: A positive process for change.* San Francisco: Jossey-Bass.

Orenstein, R. L. (2002). Executive coaching: It's not just about the executive. *Journal of Applied Behavioral Science, 38,* 355–374.

Patterson, K., Grenny, J., Maxfield, D., McMillan, R., & Switzler, A. (2008). *Influencer: The power to change anything.* New York: McGraw-Hill.

Peterson, D. B. (2007). Executive coaching in a cross-cultural context. *Consulting Psychology Journal: Practice and Research, 59*(4), 261–271.

Peterson, D. B., & Hicks, M. D. (2006). *Leader as coach: Strategies for coaching and developing others.* Minneapolis: Personnel Decisions International.

Poteet, M. L., Kudisch, J. D., Stevens, C. K., Gettman, H. J., Wouters, K., Edinger, S. K., Tesluk, P. E., & Russell, J. E. A. (2009, June). Preconference workshop. *Bridging the science and practice of executive coaching: A playbook for unleashing leadership talent.* Presented at The University of Maryland, Robert H. Smith School of Business, College Park, MD.

Richardson, C. (2009). *The art of extreme self-care.* Carlsbad, CA: Hay House.

Rosinski, P. (2003). *Coaching across cultures: New tools for leveraging national, corporate, and professional differences.* London: Nicholas Brealey.

Schmitz, J. (2006). *Cultural orientations guide: The roadmap to cultural competence.* Princeton, NJ: Princeton Training Press.

Scott, S. (2004). *Fierce conversations.* New York: Berkley.

Scriber, C. L. (2008). Coaching for leadership presence. In C. Wahl, C. Scriber, & B. Bloomfield (Eds.), *On becoming a leadership coach: A holistic approach to coaching excellence* (pp. 177–187). New York: Palgrave Macmillan.

Seligman, M. (2004). *Authentic happiness: Using the new positive psychology to realize your potential for lasting fulfillment.* New York: The Free Press.

Thornton, G. C., & Byham, W. C. (1982). *Assessment centers and managerial performance.* New York: Academic Press.

Trompenaars, F., & Hampden-Turner, C. (1998). *Riding the waves of culture: Understanding diversity in global business.* New York: McGraw-Hill.

Wahl, C., Scriber, C., & Bloomfield, B. (2008). *On becoming a leadership coach: A wholistic approach to coaching excellence.* New York: Palgrave Macmillan.

Walker, D. M., Walker, T., & Schmitz, J. (2003). *Doing business internationally: The guide to cross-cultural success.* New York: McGraw-Hill.

Wakefield, M. (2006, Summer). New views on leadership coaching. *Journal for Quality and Participation,* 9–12.

Whitmore, J. (2009). *Coaching for performance: Growing human potential and purpose.* London: Nicholas Brealey.

Yammarino, F. J., & Atwater, L. E. (1993). Understanding self-perception accuracy: Implications for human resource management. *Human Resource Management, 32,* 231–247.

Zeman, S. (2008). *Listening to bodies: A somatic primer for coaches, managers and executives.* Richmond, CA: Shasta Gardens.

Zucal, B. (2008). Global mindset: An essential ingredient for the successful assignee. *The Expatriate Observer, 31*(1), 9–11.

Appendix A: Examples of Coaching Frameworks

Source	Framework	Description
1	**ABCDE Model**	Used in cognitive behavioral coaching to deal with psychological blocks in coaching. The ABCDE model (Activating event, self-limiting Beliefs, Consequences, Disputing the self-limiting beliefs, Effective new outlook) stresses that a self-limiting belief can be changed to help produce more positive consequences.
2	**ACT Model**	ACT (Awareness, Choice, and Trust) is a model for improving focus and believing in one's inner resources in order to make desired changes.
3	**Action-Observer-Reflection Model**	Used to help clients observe and reflect on the outcomes from newly practiced behaviors. Also useful for developing coaching skills and awareness.
4	**ALIFE Model**	ALIFE (Authenticity, Leadership, Intentionality, Fear/Courage, and Execution) is a coaching management tool model, part of the holistic coaching approach.
5	**Appreciative Inquiry Model**	Used to establish a reflective and positive dialogue about what has worked well for the client and in what circumstances. Uses the five-step process of "define, discover, dream, design, destiny" to help clients "flourish."

Source	Framework	Description
6	**Cognitive Behavioral Change Techniques**	Based on cognitive behavior therapy assumptions that perceptions influence actions and that changing one's perceptions can lead to changes in behavior. Useful for developing executives in targeted areas (e.g., listening, public speaking, stress management).
7	**Constructive-Developmental Framework**	Provides an analysis of stages or "webs of belief" (Kegan, 1994) which affect how the client responds to feedback from others and how the client defines the "self." Used to help the client become more self-authoring and self-revising in their definition of self.
8	**FLOW Model**	FLOW (Fast, Linked, Outcome, Worthwhile) is a model for reviewing the effectiveness of a coaching session as it proceeds.
9	**GRACE Model**	GRACE (Goodwill, Results, Authenticity, Connectivity, and Empowerment) refers to five key components in powerful relationships that provide affirmation, inspiration, and personal transformation.
10	**GROW Model**	GROW (Goal—Current Reality—Options—Will/Way Forward) is used throughout all stages of coaching to help identify goals, compare to current situation, identify and brainstorm options for change, and taking action to move forward.
11	**Solution-Focused Model**	Tactical questions (e.g., miracle, exception, what else, scaling, coping, relationship questions) are used to help clients focus their attention on building solutions and replacing ineffective behaviors with goal-directed behaviors.
12	**Thinking Path**	A change model which leads the client to understand how thinking, feeling, actions, and results can be changed in that order.

(Continued)

Source	Framework	Description
13	**Transtheoretical Model of Behavior Change**	Used to diagnose the client's readiness for change, in terms of stages: precontemplation (not ready for change), contemplation (thinking about change), preparation (preparing for action), action (taking action), and maintenance (maintaining a positive behavior).

Sources

1. Neenan, M. (2006). Cognitive behavioral coaching. In J. Passmore (Ed.), *Excellence in coaching: The industry guide* (pp. 91–105). Philadelphia: Kogan Page.
2. Gallwey, W. T. (2000). *The inner game of work: Focus, learning, pleasure, and mobility in the workplace.* New York: Random House.
3. Hughes, R. L., Ginnett, R. C., & Curphy, G. J. (2008). *Leadership: Enhancing the lessons from experience.* New York: McGraw-Hill/Irwin; Orem, S. L., Blinkert, J., & Clancy, A. L. (2007). *Appreciative coaching: A positive process for change.* San Francisco: Jossey-Bass.
4. Wahl, C., Scriber, C., & Bloomfield, B. (2008). *On becoming a leadership coach: A wholistic approach to coaching excellence.* New York: Palgrave Macmillan.
5. Cooperider, D. L. (1996). The child as agent of inquiry. *OD Practitioner, 28*(1 & 2), 5–11; Moore, M., & Tschannen-Moran, B. (2010). *Coaching psychology manual.* Baltimore, MD: Lippincott Williams & Wilkins; Orem, et al. (2007).
6. Ducharme, M. J. (2004). The cognitive-behavioral approach to executive coaching. *Consulting Psychology Journal: Practice & Research, 56*(4), 214–224; Neenan (2006).
7. Ball, F. (2008). Continued development: Self-authorship and self-mastery. In C. Wahl, C. Scriber, & B. Bloomfield (Eds.), *On becoming a leadership coach: A holistic approach to coaching excellence* (pp. 29–35). New York: Palgrave Macmillan; Drath, W., & Van Velsor, E. (2006). Constructive-developmental coaching. In S. Ting & P. Scisco (Eds.), *The CCL handbook of coaching: A guide for the leader coach* (pp. 312–343). San Francisco: Jossey-Bass; Fitzgerald, C., & Berger, J. G. (2002). Leadership and complexity of mind: The role of executive coaching. In C. Fitzgerald & J. G. Berger (Eds.), *Executive coaching* (pp. 27–57). Palo Alto, CA: Davies-Black, Rock, D., & Page, L. J. (2009). *Coaching with the brain in mind.* Hoboken, NJ: Wiley.

8. Alexander, G. (2006). Behavioral coaching—The GROW model. In J. Passmore (Ed.), *Excellence in coaching: The industry guide* (pp. 61–72). Philadelphia: Kogan Page.

9. De Nijs (2008). G.R.A.C.E. at work—strong relationships for powerful results. In C. Wahl, C. Scriber, & B. Bloomfield (Eds.), *On becoming a leadership coach: A holistic approach to coaching excellence* (pp. 43–51). New York: Palgrave Macmillan.

10. Whitmore, J. (2009). *Coaching for performance: Growing human potential and purpose.* London: Nicholas Brealey.

11. Grant, A. M. (2006). Solution-focused coaching. In J. Passmore (Ed.), *Excellence in coaching: The industry guide* (pp. 73–90). Philadelphia: Kogan Page; Wakefield, M. (2006). Brief solution-focused coaching. In S. Ting & P. Scisco (Eds.), *The CCL handbook of coaching: A guide for the leader coach* (pp. 286–311). San Francisco: Jossey-Bass.

12. Caillet, A. (2008). The thinking path. In C. Wahl, C. Scriber, & B. Bloomfield (Eds.), *On becoming a leadership coach: A holistic approach to coaching excellence* (pp. 149–166). New York: Palgrave Macmillan.

13. Prochaska, J. O., Norcross, J. C., & DiClemente, C. C. (1995). *Changing for good: A revolutionary six-stage program for overcoming bad habits and moving your life positively forward.* New York: Harper Collins.

Appendix B: Examples of Coaching Techniques

Source	Techniques	Description
1	**Action Learning Conversations**	Used to enhance transformative reflection and learning. Uses action learning questioning and reflection techniques to analyze real problems, situations, and critical incidents. Can be used for clients in a group setting and as a heuristic to guide coach development.
2	**Alignment Coaching**	Focuses on the beliefs, values, and purposes of the executive, to help clients align their goals and actions with their values within a variety of specific contexts.
3	**Building Alliances to Leverage Organizational Arrangements Exercise**	Used to help the client increase cross-cultural skills and self-awareness relating to hierarchy vs. equality, universalist vs. particularist, stability vs. change, and collaborative vs. competitive cultural dimensions.
4	**Challenging Deeply Held Assumptions Exercise**	Used to help clients do a cost-benefit analysis of deeply held beliefs, declare limiting beliefs, and replace limiting beliefs with new positive ones. Asks clients to identify their ten most important "moving toward" values as well as "moving away from" values, and the rules associated with each.

Source	Techniques	Description
5	**Cards**	Used for a variety of coaching purposes (e.g., to clarify values, perceptions of team or organizational culture, goals, obstacles) and in a variety of ways (e.g., cards with visual images or words from which a client must choose; notecards on which to write or draw, and/or arrange in mind-mapping exercises).
6	**Collage**	Used in conjunction with visualization activities to depict aspects of their ideal life or goals. A "common purpose collage" is a technique used in a team situation to help the client increase cross-cultural skills and self-awareness.
7	**Core Coaching Techniques**	Powerful questions: used to clarify, uncover, and reframe a client's assumptions, motivations, values, goals, resistance to change factors; to foster creativity, problem solving, and innovation; to show empathy and understanding. Active Listening, Strategizing, Messaging, Acknowledging, Mindfulness used throughout the coaching process in conjunction with powerful questions.
8	**"Compelling" Vision; Visualizing Ideal**	Used for goal setting and for uncovering the underlying dimensions of the client's goals by having the clients visualize and write down all aspects of their visualized "ideal life."
9	**Decisional Balance Exercise**	A reflective listening technique and a quantitative rating system, often used in conjunction with motivational interviewing, to help clients think through the pros and cons of changing and not changing.
10	**Energy Management and Balance Activities**	Activities for improving energy and balance include: creating rhythms and routines; developing "Absolute Yes" and "Absolute No" lists based on priorities; practicing presence, mindfulness, and protecting sensitivity; managing technology; practicing forgiveness; and energy activity analysis.

(Continued)

Source	Techniques	Description
11	**Feedback and Self-Disclosure Exercise**	Used to help clients increase cross-cultural skills and self-awareness relating to feedback and self-disclosure cultural dimensions.
12	**Feedforward Exercises**	Used in behavioral change coaching, to provide ideas for positive behavioral change that the client can do in the future, rather than reliving negative feedback regarding past behavior.
13	**Fieldwork and Experiments**	Used to test hypotheses, make decisions, or try out new behaviors.
14	**Gratitude Exercises**	Include writing and presenting a letter of gratitude, keeping a gratitude journal listing up to five things each day for which one is grateful, in conjunction with assessments to measure life satisfaction and general happiness.
15	**Guided Imagery**	Used to explore thoughts, perceptions, and feelings about a particular issue. May take many forms, such as the coach using a script and eliciting the client's inputs through an imagined scenario.
16	**Inner Critic Exercises**	Useful when clients believe their inner critic is keeping them from fully achieving their goals. Might use drawing or clay to depict the inner critic and then ask questions about or of the inner critic, converse with the inner critic, and then do the same with the compassionate self.
17	**Insight and Motivation Grid**	Used in evidence-based coaching to guide the coach's questions and the client's synthesis of new awareness regarding insights and motivations by incorporating appreciative inquiry and Johari window elements.
18	**Learning Journal/ Journaling**	Used by clients to track observations, reflections, and progress toward a variety of learning goals and purposes. Can include letters sent and unsent, and scriptwriting to explore difficult conversations and work relationships.

Source	Techniques	Description
19	**Logic Trees**	Used to break down complex goals into specific steps, starting with a SMART definition of the goal, then definition of competencies needed to achieve the goal, and specific action steps and timelines for developing the competencies.
20	**Modes of Thinking Exercise**	Problem-solving exercise used to help clients increase cross-cultural skills and self-awareness relating to inductive vs. deductive and analytic vs. systemic modes of thinking cultural dimensions.
21	**Motivational Interviewing**	Uses principles of empathy, developing discrepancy, rolling with resistance, and supporting self-efficacy to help clients explore and resolve ambivalence. Useful when clients are stuck in reaching their goals.
22	**Neuro-Linguistic Programming**	Used to increase awareness of the client's perceptual processes, such as which senses are most relied on by the client (e.g., visual, auditory, kinesthetic), and for building rapport.
23	**Reflected Best Self Exercise**	Based on appreciative inquiry and positive psychology, clients collect examples from 20 to 30 people of when they were at their best and the specific strengths they displayed.
24	**Rituals**	Used by the client to affirm changes or transitions, such as rituals to celebrate successes, release negative emotions, affirm next steps, solidify commitment.
25	**Role Model Analysis**	Used to help clients identify specific behaviors they may want to emulate in achieving their behavioral goals (e.g., developing executive presence, specific leadership styles).
26	**Role Play Exercises**	Useful for a variety of purposes, including practicing emotional competence skills such

(Continued)

Source	Techniques	Description
26	**Role Play Exercises**	as those relating to managing conflict and empathy, or having difficult conversations and making requests. Somatic activities can be used in conjunction with these exercises. For cross-cultural analysis, a communication patterns role-play analysis can be used to help the client increase cross-cultural skills and self-awareness.
27	**Rulers**	Has clients rate on a 0–10 scale "ruler" (with 0 = not at all, and 10 = most) their willingness, confidence, and readiness for change.
28	**Somatics/Body Work**	Used to help clients develop greater awareness of the connections between their body, perceptions, feelings, language, actions, and impact.
29	**Use of Story; SCAN Model**	Used to help clients edit and reframe their stories and add new positive chapters. The SCAN model stands for Story—Commitment—Authentic Self—New Story and Action.
30	**Style Switching Exercise**	Role-playing exercise used to develop cross-cultural skills in practicing the cultural dimension that is different from the client's own cultural preference.
31	**Timeline Exercises**	Used to help the client increase self-awareness in diagnosing key formative events and successes from the past in relation to present and future goals for leadership.
32	**Transpersonal Coaching**	Used to help the client integrate various aspects of self, including quantitative achievement and qualitative values.
33	**Videotaping**	Useful in providing feedback for a variety of client goals, including presentation skills, team skills (e.g., during leaderless group discussions and other assessment center activities), and executive presence.

Sources

1. Marsick, V. J., & Maltbia, T. E. (2009). The transformative potential of action learning conversations. In J. Mezirow & E.W. Taylor (Eds.), *Transformative learning in practice* (pp. 160–171). San Francisco: Jossey-Bass.

2. Lazar, J., & Bergquist, W. (2003). Alignment coaching: The missing element of business coaching. *International Journal of Coaching in Organizations, 1*(1), 14–27.

3. Rosinski, P. (2003). *Coaching across cultures: New tools for leveraging national, corporate, and professional differences.* London: Nicholas Brealey.

4. Hill, G. (2005). Committing to action. In D. Megginson & D.Clutterbuck (Eds.), *Techniques for coaching and mentoring* (pp. 139–143). Oxford: Butterworth-Heinemann.

5. Palus, C. J. (2006). Artful coaching. In S. Ting & P. Scisco (Eds.), *The CCL handbook of coaching: A guide for the leader coach* (pp. 259–285). San Francisco: Jossey-Bass; Schwarz, D., & Davidson, A. (2009). *Facilitative coaching: A toolkit for expanding your repertoire and achieving lasting results.* San Francisco: Pfeiffer.

6. McCauley, C. D., & Van Velsor, E. (2004). *The Center for Creative Leadership handbook of leadership development.* Hoboken, NJ: Wiley; Rosinski (2003).

7. Coach U, Inc. (2005a). *Coach U's essential coaching tools: Your complete practice resource.* Hoboken, NJ: Wiley; Coach U, Inc. (2005b). *The Coach U personal and corporate coach training handbook.* Hoboken, NJ: Wiley; Moore, M., & Tschannen-Moran, B. (2010). *Coaching psychology manual.* Baltimore, MD: Lippincott Williams & Wilkins. Stoltzfus, T. (2008). *Coaching questions: A coach's guide to powerful asking skills.* Virginia Beach, VA: Tony Stoltzfus.

8. Coach U, Inc. (2005a; 2005b); Moore & Tschannen-Moran (2010); Seligman, M. (2004). *Authentic happiness: Using the new positive psychology to realize your potential for lasting fulfillment.* New York: The Free Press.

9. Botelho, R. (2004). *Motivate healthy habits: Stepping stones to lasting change.* Rochester, NY: MHH Publications; Moore and Tschannen-Moran.

10. Kommor, P. (2002). Learn mindfulness to boost performance. *Business First of Louisville,* Jan. 4; Loehr, J., & Schwartz, T. (2001). The making of a corporate athlete. *Harvard Business Review,* (1), 120–128, Richardson, C. (2009). *The art of extreme self-care.* Carlsbad, CA: Hay House; Zeman, S. (2008). *Listening to bodies: A somatic primer for coaches, managers and executives.* Richmond, CA: Shasta Gardens.

11. Rosinski (2003).
12. Goldsmith, M. (2006). Try feedforward instead of feedback. In M. Goldsmith & L. Lyons (Eds.), *Coaching for leadership: The practice of leadership coaching from the world's greatest coaches* (pp. 45–49). San Francisco: Pfeiffer.
13. Schwarz & Davidson (2009).
14. Seligman (2004).
15. Schwarz & Davison (2009); Whitmore (2009). *Coaching for performance: Growing human potential and purpose.* London: Nicholas Brealey.
16. Schwarz & Davison (2009).
17. Hauser, L. (2009). Evidence-based coaching: A case study. *OD Practitioner, 41,* 8–13.
18. Haji, S. (2008). In the spirit of coaching. In C. Wahl, C. Scriber, & B. Bloomfield (Eds.), *On becoming a leadership coach: A holistic approach to coaching excellence* (pp. 37–42). New York: Palgrave Macmillan; Rosinski (2003); Schwarz & Davidson (2009).
19. Megginson, D., & Clutterbuck, D. (2005). *Techniques for coaching and mentoring.* Oxford: Butterworth-Heinemann.
20. Rosinski (2003).
21. Moore & Tschannen-Moran (2010).
22. McDermott, I. (2006). NLP coaching. In J. Passmore (Ed.), *Excellence in coaching: The industry guide* (pp. 106–118). Philadelphia: Kogan Page.
23. Pace, A. (2010). Unleashing positivity in the workplace. *Training and Development, 64*(1), 40–46.
24. Schwarz & Davidson (2009).
25. Gebelein, S. H., Nelson-Neuhaus, K. J., Skube, C. J., Lee, D. G., Stevens, L. A., Hellervik, L. W., & Davis, B. L. (Eds.) (2004). *Successful manager's handbook* (7th ed.). Minneapolis: Personnel Decisions Corporation/ePredix.
26. Echols, M., & Mobley, S. (2008). Using somatics to coach leaders. In C. Wahl, C. Scriber, & B. Bloomfield (Eds.), *On becoming a leadership coach: A holistic approach to coaching excellence* (pp. 81–90). New York: Palgrave Macmillan; Rosinski (2003); Patterson, K., Grenny, J., McMillan, R., & Switzler, A. (2002). *Crucial conversations: Tools for talking when stakes are high.* New York: McGraw-Hill; Scott, S. (2004). *Fierce conversations.* New York: Berkley; Weeks, H. (2001). Taking the stress out of stressful conversations. *Harvard Business Review,* 112–119.
27. Moore & Tschannen-Moran (2010).
28. Echols & Mobley (2008); Schwarz & Davidson (2009); Zeman (2008).
29. Echols, M., Gravenstine, K., & Mobley, S. (2008). Using story in coaching. In C. Wahl, C. Scriber, & B. Bloomfield (Eds.), *On becoming a leadership coach: A holistic approach to coaching excellence*

(pp. 53–60). New York: Palgrave Macmillan; Loehr, J. (2007). *The power of story: Rewrite your destiny in business and life.* New York: The Free Press.
30. Schmitz, J. (2006). *Cultural orientations guide: The roadmap to cultural competence.* Princeton, NJ: Princeton Training Press.
31. Hughes, R. L., Ginnett, R. C., & Curphy, G. J. (2008). *Leadership: Enhancing the lessons from experience.* New York: McGraw-Hill/Irwin; Rosinski (2003); Schwarz & Davidson (2009).
32. Whitmore, J., & Einzig, H. (2006). Transpersonal coaching. In J. Passmore (Ed.), *Excellence in coaching: The industry guide* (pp. 119–134). Philadelphia: Kogan Page.
33. Guthrie, V. A., & King, S. N. (2004). Feedback-intensive programs. In C. D. McCauley & E. Van Velsor (Eds.) (2nd ed.), *The Center for Creative Leadership handbook of leader development.* San Francisco: Jossey-Bass.

Appendix C: Examples of Coaching Assessment Tools

Source	Framework	Description
Self-Awareness and Life Values Tools		
1	**Johari Window**	Used to help clients understand how they communicate with themselves and with others, how they perceive their place in the world, and how they present themselves. Often used to enhance clients' current reality (i.e., to help them consider their behavior and reaction patterns).
2	**The Inner Theatre Inventory**	A 360-degree survey instrument to help clients understand the drivers in their inner theatre—the values, beliefs, and attitudes that guide their behavior. Used to help clients identify the primary life anchors that drive them and develop a lifestyle more congruent with their values and belief systems.
3	**Riso-Hudson Enneagram Type Indicator (RHETI)**	Used to examine: external behaviors underlying attitudes, one's characteristic sense of self, conscious and unconscious motivations, emotional reactions, defense mechanisms, object relations, what people pay attention to, and spiritual potentials. Coaches can help clients understand their self-defeating habits and reactions and their unconscious motivations and defenses.

Source	Framework	Description
4	**SCTi Assessment "MAP"**	Also called *The Leadership Development Profile.* Assesses leadership maturity level and personal integration. Used to identify where the most leverage exists for positive transformation so that resources can be optimally targeted to the capacity of the client.

Work Values and/or Motivation Tools

5	**eCF Personal Work Values**	Measures eighteen work values (e.g., achievement, autonomy, creativity, integrity). The report describes the importance of personal work values in career transitions, the client's results, including their top five work values, and a discussion of their top five work values in relation to his or her career. Used to help clients make better career choices.
6	**Motives, Values, & Preferences Inventory (MVPI)**	Measures ten core values (e.g., recognition, power, tradition, commerce, science), goals, and interests. The report indicates which type of position, job, and environment will be most motivating for the client and when he/she will feel the most satisfied and find job/value fit.
7	**Personal Values Questionnaire (PVQ)**	Measures the importance an individual attaches to three social motives—achievement, affiliation, and power—and what this can mean for the person in the workplace. Coaches can also highlight a mismatch between a person's values and the requirements of the job. A mismatch can be acted upon before it results in tension for an individual, or productivity or turnover issues for an organization.
8	**The Work Engagement Profile**	Measures four intrinsic rewards from work (meaningfulness, choice, competence, and progress) to help clients understand the intrinsic rewards they are receiving from work. Used to help clients identify options to increase either their own or their employees' engagement in work.

(Continued)

Source	Framework	Description

Career Interest Inventories

9	**The Work Expectations Profile**	Measures ten work expectations (e.g., regarding recognition, autonomy, career growth, diversity). Coaches use the tool to help clients: (1) discover which expectations they consider most important, (2) learn how to communicate, initiate action, and adjust expectations, (3) get feedback on managing their expectations, (4) improve their outlook and enhance their attitude toward work, and (5) enjoy the benefits of increased job satisfaction and improved performance.
10	**Career Anchors**	Used to help clients identify their Career Anchor, which encompasses their primary areas of competence, motives, and career values. Coaches help clients understand their values, what they really want out of a career, and make better decisions regarding the career best suited to them.
11	**Strong Interest Inventory**	Measures career interests in four main categories of scales: General Occupational Themes (GOTs), Basic Interest Scales (BISs), Personal Style Scales (PSSs), and Occupational Scales (OSs). The six GOTs measure categories of occupational interests—Realistic, Investigative, Artistic, Social, Enterprising, and Conventional (RIASEC) while the thirty BISs measure clusters of interest related to the GOTs in areas such as Athletics, Science, and Sales. The five PSSs (e.g., Work Style, Learning Environment, Leadership Style, Risk Taking, Team Orientation) measure preferences for styles of living and working, and the OSs measure the extent to which a person's interests are similar to those of the same gender working in many diverse occupations.

Source	Framework	Description

Measures of Learning and Innovation

12	The Learning Style Inventory (LSI)	Measures learning preferences along two continua: active experimentation-reflective observation and abstract conceptualization-concrete experience. The LSI identifies preferred learning styles (e.g., converger, accommodator, assimilator, diverger) and explores their implications for problem solving, teamwork, and conflict resolution.
13	Honey and Mumford Learning Styles Questionnaire (LSQ)	Measures, as a variation on the Kolb model, clients' inclinations toward: activist (having an experience), reflector (reviewing the experience), theorist (concluding from the experience), or pragmatist (planning the next steps). For coaches, a benefit of knowing a client's preferred learning style is to improve his/her learning skills and processes, which can open up the coaching process to improvement.
14	Kirton Adaptive Innovation (KAI) Inventory	Measures creativity in problem solving. An overall score is comprised of three dimensions: originality, detail-minded, and rule conformity. Coaches use the KAI to help clients understand how they prefer to contribute to team work, what type of fit they have with their job, and how they interact with others at work and home. Also used in the training of managers and key teams as part of an organizational change.

Personality Inventories

| 15 | California Personality Inventory (CPI) Assessments | The CPI 434 Profile measures seven scales including: Creative Temperament, Managerial Potential, Work Orientation, Leadership Potential, Amicability, Tough-Mindedness, and Law Enforcement Orientation. The CPI 260 Coaching Report for Leaders helps clients identify their strengths and blind spots in order to plan action steps to increase their effectiveness as leaders. |

(Continued)

Source	Framework	Description
16	**DISC Profile**	Measures behavioral styles as grouped in four categories: Dominance, Influence, Steadiness, and Conscientiousness. The DISC report can be used to help clients gain an understanding about their personal behaviors, the needs of others, and to build positive relationships and teams.
17	**Fundamental Interpersonal Relations Orientation (FIRO-B)**	Measures three interpersonal needs: Inclusion, Control, and Affection. Measures the extent to which each of these interpersonal needs is expressed or wanted. Expressed needs refer to behaviors that individuals demonstrate toward others, whereas wanted needs refer to behaviors individuals prefer to have exhibited toward them by others. The report addresses how behaviors driven by these needs can affect one's interactions with others.
18	**Hogan Personality Inventory (HPI)**	Measures seven personality dimensions: Adjustment, Ambition, Sociability, Interpersonal Sensitivity, Prudence, Inquisitive, and Learning Approach. Used to help clients understand their strengths and shortcomings, better manage their careers, understand the characteristics relevant for success in many work environments, and see the fit between their style and various jobs.
19	**Life Styles Inventory (LSI)**	Measures personal orientations (Constructive, Passive/Defensive, and Aggressive/Defensive) and twelve specific thinking and behavioral styles associated with these orientations. Most frequently used by coaches to promote self-understanding and guide self-development, improve capabilities as a team member or individual contributor, and provide feedback for stress management programs.

Source	Framework	Description
20	**Myers-Briggs Type Indicator (MBTI)**	Measures personality preferences along four dimension: Extraversion (E) and Introversion (I), Sensing (S) and Intuition (N), Thinking (T) and Feeling (F), and Judging (J) and Perceiving (P). Available in twenty-one languages, it is used to improve individual and team performance, explore careers, and reduce workplace conflict. Booklets useful for coaches include those dealing with Type in Organizations, Teams, Emotional Intelligence, Change, and Leadership. There is also a booklet illustrating the international type table distributions based on data gathered from more than 340,000 individuals representing sixty countries and regions.
21	**Revised NEO Personality Inventory (NEO PI-R)**	Measures personality based on the Five-Factor Model of personality (e.g., Neuroticism, Extraversion, Openness to Experience, Agreeableness, Conscientiousness) and the six facet traits that define each domain. Contains both a self-report (Form S) which can be used with clients and an observer report (Form R) that can be used with others to get feedback on the client. Coaches can also use the report which is generated to help clients understand their coping and defense mechanisms, somatic complaints, interpersonal characteristics, cognitive processes, and personal needs and motives. A shortened version NEO Five-Factor Inventory (NEO-FFI) is available if time is limited.
22	**16-PF**	Measures sixteen personality factors (e.g., warmth, reasoning, emotional stability, dominance, rule-consciousness). Used for a variety of applications requiring insights into personality, including vocational guidance.

(Continued)

Source	Framework	Description
Executive Derailers		
23	**Hogan Development Survey (HDS)**	Measures eleven potential personality derailers (e.g., excitable, skeptical, cautious, reserved, leisurely) that can impede success in careers, relationships, education, and life. The detailed report is helpful for outlining the leadership implications of the derailers and suggested developmental steps.
24	**Benchmarks**	Measures sixteen skills and perspectives critical for managerial success (e.g., meeting job challenges, leading people, respecting self and others) and five potential derailers (interpersonal relationships, difficulties building or leading a team, difficulties adapting, failure to meet business objectives, narrow functional orientation). This 360-degree tool is available in eight languages.
Critical Thinking and Reasoning Measures		
25	**Hogan Business Reasoning Inventory (HBRI)**	Measures two kinds of problem solving in reasoning ability: tactical and strategic reasoning. Tactical Reasoning concerns solving problems and coming to sensible conclusions once the facts are known. Strategic Reasoning refers to the ability to detect errors, gaps, and logical flaws in data. Used to guide clients in how to enhance their critical thinking.
26	**Watson Glaser Critical Thinking Appraisal (WGCTA)**	Measures critical thinking skills for sound decision making. Used by coaches to understand how well an executive will make accurate inferences, recognize assumptions, properly deduce, interpret information, and evaluate arguments—skills crucial to enhancing organizational performance, and especially important for executive positions.

Source	Framework	Description

Cultural Styles and Adaptability

| 27 | **Cross-Cultural Adaptability Inventory (CCAI)** | Measures behavioral, emotional, and problem-solving skills that are related to successful cross-cultural adaptation, specifically: Emotional Resilience (i.e., the degree to which an individual can rebound and react positively to new experiences); Flexibility/Openness (i.e., the extent to which a person enjoys the different ways of thinking and behaving that are typically encountered in the cross-cultural experience); Perceptual Acuity (i.e., the extent to which a person pays attention to and accurately perceives various aspects of the environment); and Personal Autonomy (i.e., the extent an individual has evolved a personal system of values and beliefs and at the same time respects others and their value systems). Used to gain insights about potential for cross-cultural effectiveness. |
| 28 | **Cultural Orientations Index (COI)** | Measures preferences on ten cultural dimensions (environment, time, action, communication, space, power, individualism, competitiveness, structure, thinking). The COI is offered within the context of the Cultural Navigator, which offers tools designed to prepare expatriates, frequent business travelers, short-term assignees, localized employees, and third-party nationals and their families to function effectively and efficiently in a new environment. Tools include person to country, country to country, and within team comparisons of cultural preferences. Available in nine languages. |

(*Continued*)

Source	Framework	Description
Source	*Framework*	*Description*

General Performance Measures or Multisource Ratings

29	**Benchmarks**	See above. A 360 tool for experienced managers which measures the skills learned through development or on-the-job leadership experiences that are critical for success (e.g., meeting job challenges, leading people, respecting self and others). The report is accompanied by a Development Planning Guide which coaches may use in action planning.
30	**Executive Dimensions**	A 360 tool to assess leadership effectiveness at the highest levels of an organization. Used to examine the unique issues faced by top-level senior executives (e.g., CEOs, COOs, EVPs). Dimensions assessed include: Leading the Business (e.g., strategic planning, leading change, results orientation, global awareness); Leading Others (e.g., inspiring commitment, forging synergy, developing and empowering, leveraging differences); Leading by Personal Example (e.g., courage, executive image, credibility).
31	**PDI Profiler and Time2Change tools**	A 360 tool for training and development purposes, customized to an organization's development goals and business objectives. Profiler assesses development needs while the Time2Change tool assesses whether the client is changing. With Time2Change clients can customize a survey to reflect areas they are working on, receive feedback on the amount of change that has occurred, and track their development progress. Employers can use it to: check progress and increase ROI for development initiatives.

Source	Framework	Description
32	**Prospector**	A 360-degree online feedback tool that measures a person's openness to growth opportunities. Designed to be used specifically with high-potential managers, executives, and managers with global responsibilities, and high-level individual contributors. Useful in individual assessment, coaching, and planning with clients. It also comes with a Development Planning Guide which coaches can use with managers to develop action plans.
33	**The Leadership Circle Profile (TLCP)**	A 360 tool that measures Creative Competencies (e.g., brings out the best in others, leads with vision) and Reactive Tendencies (e.g., caution over creating results, aggression over building alignment) and identifies key opportunities for development. Used to put clients in touch with what is working, what is not, and why.

Measures of Strengths

Source	Framework	Description
34	**Clifton Strengths Finder (CSF)**	Based on positive psychology, Gallup introduced an online measure of personal talent that identifies which of thirty-four possible areas (e.g., achiever, developer, empathy, learner) an individual's greatest potential for building strengths exists. The newest version from Gallup is the StrengthsFinder 2.0 online assessment. Once taken, individuals receive reports of their top five themes (talents), a discussion of fifty ideas for action (ten for each of their top five themes), a Strengths Discovery Interview to help them think about how their experiences, skills, and knowledge can build strengths, and a Strength-Based Action Plan to help them set specific goals in applying their strengths. Recently, the tool has been more closely linked to leadership whereby leaders can receive a highly customized Strengths-Based Leadership Guide which

(*Continued*)

Source	Framework	Description
		identifies their top five themes and offers suggestions for leading with each theme.
35	**Values in Action Inventory of Strengths (VIA-IS)**	Measures character strengths and consists of 240 questions which reveal a person's constellation of strengths and identify his or her top five signature themes. Measures six classes of virtue (e.g., wisdom and knowledge, courage, humanity, justice, temperance, transcendence) which consist of twenty-four measurable character strengths. The twenty-four traits (e.g., leadership, creativity, integrity, social intelligence) are defined behaviorally with psychometric evidence demonstrating that they can be reliably measured and have appropriate validity. Coaches use the tool to help clients enhance their signature strengths and build up lesser strengths.
General Leadership		
36	**The Global Executive Leadership Inventory (GELI)**	A tool that coaches use to understand clients' leadership abilities and the steps they would need to take to improve. Consists of one hundred action-and-behavior-based questions that are designed to measure competency within twelve dimensions or characteristics of successful global leaders (e.g., visioning, empowering, energizing, team building, global mindset, emotional intelligence, life balance). Includes a self-assessment tool as well as a 360° component, and results in a workbook that guides the client through the feedback to create a leadership development plan.
37	**The Leadership Archetype Questionnaire (LAQ)**	A questionnaire used by coaches to help clients identify their salient leadership behavior through eight leadership archetypes. These include: Strategist, Change-Catalyst, Transactor, Builder, Innovator, Processor, Coach, and Communicator.

Source	Framework	Description
38	**Leadership Cube**	Addresses six key areas that have impact on a person's leadership capabilities and potential: effective communication, emotional management, stress recovery, positive perspective, belief adjustment, and personal awareness. A combination of Emotional Intelligence (EQi) Testing, NLP Techniques, and Business Coaching is used.
39	**The Leadership Practices Inventory (LPI)**	A 360-degree assessment based on the leadership challenge. LPI Online is primarily designed for management consultants, human resource executives, and department managers in charge of leadership development. The LPI is given to participants as part of their pre-work for The Leadership Challenge Workshop. Coaches can use it to help leaders assess the extent to which they actually use those practices so that they can make plans for improvement.
40	**Multifactor Leadership Questionnaire (MLQ)**	Based on the Full Leadership Model and measures: Transactional Leadership (e.g., fights fires, monitors mistakes, rewards achievements) and Transformational Leadership (e.g., acts with integrity, encourages innovative thinking, and coaches people). The profile report enables a mapping of the leader-managers' own self-perceptions in terms of the Full Range Leadership Model and a comparison of their self-profiles with their estimations of how others would collectively see them on these leadership styles. The results are also linked to a development plan for leaders.

Stress Management Measures

41	**Personal Resilience Profile**	Measures seven dimensions of effective adaptation to disruptive change, using a seventy-five-item Web-based questionnaire. Coaches use this tool to provide feedback

(Continued)

Source	Framework	Description
		to clients about how they handle disruptive change and to facilitate goal setting regarding steps to take for improved resilience in change situations. The tool can also be used with intact teams to facilitate discussion about team effectiveness in responding to change.
42	**Personal Stress Navigator (PSN)**	Measures the stresses caused by the demands and pressures of everyday life. Consists of three sections that measure: *Susceptibility to Stress*—twenty-two items sampling health behaviors, lifestyle issues, and coping resources (social, financial and spiritual); *Sources of Stress*—six scales measuring stress from job, family, personal, social, environmental, and financial areas; *Symptoms of Stress*—seven scales sampling the most commonly occurring stress symptoms within a given physiological subsystem (e.g., muscular, endocrine system, immune system). Individuals receive a Personal Stress Report that coaches can use to help understand the stress patterns for the client. This is useful for coaches as they work with their clients to set goals and action plans.

Conflict Management Measures

43	**Strength Deployment Inventory (SDI)**	Measures a person's underlying motivation, based on Relationship Awareness Theory, when things are going well (calm style) and when they are in opposition (conflict style). There are four basic styles (altruistic, assertive, analytic, and flexible) and three blended styles (assertive-altruistic, assertive-analytic, altruistic-analytic) that people use in calm or conflict when dealing with others. Coaches can have clients complete the self-assessment tool and also get others to give them feedback using the *Feedback Edition* so they can see how others view them.

Source	Framework	Description
44	**Thomas-Kilmann Instrument Conflict-Mode**	Measures preferences for five different styles of handling conflict: Competing, Collaborating, Compromising, Accommodating, and Avoiding. The five modes are described along two dimensions—assertiveness (i.e., extent one tries to satisfy his/her own concerns) and cooperativeness (i.e., extent one tries to satisfy the concerns of another). Used to help clients improve their conflict management behaviors.

Team Orientation and Decision Making

Source	Framework	Description
45	**Belbin Team Role Inventory**	Measures how strongly a client expresses traits on nine different team roles (e.g., coordinator, monitor, implementer). Includes 360-degree feedback from observers as well as self, to contrast colleagues' perceptions versus self-perceptions of team behavior.
46	**The Group Styles Inventory (GSI)**	Assesses the way team members interact with one another and approach problems and decisions. Used most frequently by coaches for enhancing the impact of team-building sessions based on survival or business simulations, assessing the styles and processes of teams as they work to solve "real-life" problems, improving team dynamics to enhance the quality of team decisions, increasing team members' satisfaction, and integrating team development with individual, leadership, and organizational development.
47	**The Team Dimensions Profile**	Helps teams identify individual strengths and approaches to teamwork, clarify team members' roles, reinforce the contributions of every team member, reduce project cycle time, and increase productivity. Identifies four key team performance roles: creator, advancer, refiner, and executor. Uses the "Z Process" to map the flow of assigning roles, completing tasks, and handing off tasks to other members. Used to get new teams moving forward quickly and to get current teams unstuck.

(Continued)

Source	Framework	Description
48	**The Team Management Profile**	Offers a framework that helps team members work both individually and together to realize their full potential. Based on a self-assessed questionnaire, each report focuses on a person's strengths within a team, relationships with team members, and the way they prefer to influence and lead. Used to uncover a person's major roles and preferences, revealing untapped potential as well as identifying and matching the client's personal energies with the work they do and their role within a team.
49	**Team Survival Exercises**	A line of survival simulations and business simulations and a challenge series of exercises which combine team building with learning opportunities around strategic planning, performance management, and other organizational processes. The simulations are designed to teach the interpersonal (people) and rational (task) behaviors involved in successful teamwork. Coaches have clients work in a team on these simulations and videotape their performance to provide them with meaningful feedback on their team performance and style.

Emotional Intelligence

Source	Framework	Description
50	**Bar-On Emotional Quotient Inventory EQ-i**	Measures fifteen emotional skill areas that have been shown to contribute to proficiency in complex business activities. Scales consist of intrapersonal (e.g., self-regard, self-actualization); interpersonal (e.g., empathy, social responsibility), stress management (e.g., stress tolerance, impulse control); adaptability (e.g., reality testing, flexibility); general mood (e.g., optimism, happiness); positive impression, and an inconsistency index. Coaches might want to use both the self-assessment as well as the multirater assessment to gain more information for clients.

Source	Framework	Description
51	**Emotional Competence Inventory (ECI)**	Measures eighteen competencies organized in four clusters: self-awareness, self-management, social awareness, and relationship management. Provides a report that gives both aspiring and current leaders insights into areas they can develop and leverage to improve their performance, competence, results, and well-being. In addition to having a self-assessment and multi-rater assessment, there is a university edition.
52	**Emotional and Social Competence Inventory (ESCI)**	Measures twelve competencies organized into four clusters: self-awareness (e.g., recognizing one's emotions and their effects), self-management (e.g., emotional self-control, adaptability, achievement orientation, positive outlook); social awareness (e.g., empathy, organizational awareness), and relationship management (e.g., coaching and mentoring, inspirational leadership, conflict management, teamwork). It offers a way to assess the strengths and weaknesses of individuals.
53	**Mayer-Salovey-Caruso Emotional Intelligence Test MSCEIT**	Measures the four branches of the EI model: perceiving emotions—ability to perceive emotions in oneself and others as well as in objects, art, stories, music, and other stimuli; facilitating thought—ability to generate, use, and feel emotion as necessary to communicate feelings or employ them in other cognitive processes; understanding emotions—ability to understand emotional information, to understand how emotions combine and progress through relationship transitions, and to appreciate such emotional meanings; and managing emotions—ability to be open to feelings, and to modulate them in oneself and others so as to promote personal understanding and growth. The ability-based test consists of 141 items and provides fifteen main scores: Total EI score, two Area scores, four Branch scores, and eight Task scores and three Supplemental scores.

(Continued)

Sources

1. http://kevan.org/johari. See also: Luft, J., & Ingham, H. (1955). The Johari window: A graphic model of interpersonal awareness. *Proceedings of the western training laboratory in group development.* Los Angeles: UCLA. See also: Riso, D. R., & Hudson, R. (1999). *The wisdom of the Enneagram: The complete guide to psychological and spiritual growth for the nine personality types.* New York: Bantam Books.

2. http://ketsdevries.com/instruments/iti/iti.html.

3. www.enneagraminstitute.com/. See also: Riso, D. R., & Hudson, R. (1999). *The wisdom of the Enneagram: The complete guide to psychological and spiritual growth for the nine personality types.* New York: Bantam Books.

4. www.cook-greuter.com/. See also: Cook-Greuter, S. (2006). 20th Century background for integral psychology. *AQAL: Journal of integral theory and practice, 1*(2), 144–184; Cook-Greuter, S. (2006). AQ as a scanning and mapping device. *AQAL: Journal of integral theory and practice, 1*(3), 142–157.

5. http://info.ecareerfit.com/eCareerFit/workvalues.htm. See also: Lounsbury, J. W., Moffitt, L., Gibson, L. W., Drost, A. W., & Stevenson, M. W. (2007). An investigation of personality traits in relation to the job career satisfaction of information technology professionals. *Journal of Information Technology, 22,* 174–183; Lounsbury, J.W., Loveland, J., Sundstrom, E., Gibson, L., Drost, A., & Hamrick, F. (2003). An investigation of personality traits in relation to career satisfaction. *Journal of Career Assessment, 11*(3), 287–307.

6. www.hoganassessments.com. Hogan, R., Hogan, J., & Warrenfeltz, R. (2007). *The Hogan guide: Interpretation and use of Hogan inventories.* Tulsa, OK: Hogan Assessment Systems.

7. www.haygroup.com.

8. www.cpp.com. See also: Thomas K. W. (2009). *Intrinsic motivation at work: What really drives employee engagement* (2nd ed). San Francisco: Berrett-Koehler.

9. www.corexcel.com.

10. www.careeranchorsonline.com. See also: Schein, E. H. (1996). *Career anchors: Discovering your real values.* San Francisco: Pfeiffer.

11. www.cpp.com/products/strong. See also: Strong, E. K., Jr. (1935). Predictive value of the Vocational Interest Test. *Journal of Educational Psychology, 26,* 332; Strong, E. K., Jr. (1955). *Vocational interests 18 years after college.* Minneapolis: University of Minnesota Press; Holland, J. L. (1959). A theory of vocational choice. *Journal of Counseling Psychology, 6,* 35–45; Dirk, B. J., & Hansen, J. C. (2004, February). Development and validation of discriminant functions for the Strong

Interest Inventory. *Journal of Vocational Behavior, 64*(1), 182–197; Donnay, D. A. C., & Borgen, F. H. (1996). Validity, structure, and content of the 1994 Strong Interest Inventory. *Journal of Counseling Psychology, 43,* 275–291.

12. www.haygroup.com. See also: Kolb. D. A., & Fry, R. (1975). Toward an applied theory of experiential learning. In C. Cooper (Ed.), *Theories of group process* (pp. 33–58). London: Wiley.

13. www.peterhoney.com/. See also: Honey, P., & Mumford, A. (2006). *The Learning Styles Questionnaire* (revised). London: Peter Honey Publications.

14. www.kaicentre.com. See also: Kirton, M. J. (1976). Adaptors and innovators: A description and measure. *Journal of Applied Psychology, 61*(5), 622–629; Kirton, M. J. (1978). Field dependence and adaptation innovation theories. *Perceptual and Motor Skills, 47,* 1239–1245; Kirton, M. J. (2003). *Adaptation and innovation in the context of diversity and change.* London: Routledge; Kirton, M. J., & Ciantis, S. (1986). Cognitive style and personality: The Kirton adaption-innovation and Cattell's sixteen personality factor inventories. *Personality and Individual Differences, 7*(2), 141–146. See also: Gough, H. G., & Cook, M. (1996). *CPITM-434 manual.* Oxford: Oxford Psychologists Press; Gough, H. G., & Bradley, P. (1996/2002). *CPITM manual* (3rd ed.). Mountain View, CA: CPP, Inc. Gough, H. G. & Bradley, P. (2005). *CPI 260TM manual.* Mountain View, CA: CPP, Inc.

15. https://www.cpp.com/products/cpi. See also: Gough, H. G., & Cook, M. (1996). *CPITM-434 manual.* Oxford: Oxford Psychologists Press; Gough, H. G., & Bradley, P. (1996/2002). *CPITM manual* (3rd ed.). Mountain View, CA: CPP, Inc; Gough, H. G., & Bradley, P. (2005). *CPI 260TM manual.* Mountain View, CA: CPP, Inc.

16. www.corexcel.com/html/disc-profile.htm.

17. www.cpp.com/products/firo-b/. See also: Hammer, A. L., & Schnell, E. R. (2000). FIRO-B® technical guide. Mountain View, CA: CPP, Inc.; Schnell, E. R., & Hammer, A. L. (2004). *Introduction to the FIRO-B instrument in organizations,* Mountain View, CA: CPP, Inc.

18. www.hoganassessments.com.

19. www.humansynergistics.com/products/lsi.aspx.

20. https://www.cpp.com/products/mbti/index.aspx. See also: Myers, I. B., McCaulley, M. H., Quenk, N. L., & Hammer, A. L. (1998). *MBTI Manual: A guide to the development and use of the Myers Briggs type indicator* (3rd ed). Mountain View, CA: CPP, Inc.

21. www.parinc.com See also: Costa, P. T., Jr., & McCrae, R. R. (1985). *The NEO personality inventory manual.* Odessa, FL: Psychological

Assessment Resources; Costa, P. T., Jr., & McCrae, R. R. (1992). *NEO PI-R professional manual.* Odessa, FL: Psychological Assessment Resources, Inc.

22. www.pearsonassessments.com/HAIWEB/Cultures/en-us/Product detail.htm?Pid5PAg101&Mode5summary. See also: Cattell, R. B., Cattell, K., & Cattell, H. E. P. *16PF.* (5th ed). Upper Saddle River, NJ: Pearson.

23. www.hoganassessments.com. See also: Hogan, R., Hogan, J., & Warrenfeltz, R. (2007). *The Hogan guide: Interpretation and use of Hogan inventories.* Tulsa, OK: Hogan Assessment Systems; Dotlich, D. L., & Cairo, P. C. (2003). *Why CEOs fail.* San Francisco: Jossey-Bass; Goldsmith, M. (2007). *What got you here won't get you there.* New York: Hyperion.

24. www.ccl.org/leadership/assessments/360-degreesurvey.

25. www.hoganassessments.com. Hogan, R., Barrett, P., & Hogan, J.(2007). *Brief technical manual: Hogan business reasoning inventory.* Tulsa, OK: Hogan Assessment Systems.

26. www.pearsonassessments.com. See also: Watson, G., & Glaser, E.M. (1952). *Watson-Glaser critical thinking appraisal.* New York: Harcourt, Brace & World.

27. www.vangent-hcm.com. See also: Deal, J. J., & Prince, D. W. (2003). *Developing cultural adaptability.* Greensboro, NC: Center for Creative Leadership.

28. www.culturalnavigator.com.

29. www.ccl.org/leadership/assessments/360-degreesurvey.

30. www.ccl.org/leadership/assessments/360-degreesurvey.

31. www.personneldecisions.com.

32. www.ccl.org/leadership/assessments.

33. www.theleadershipcircle.com. See also: Anderson, R. J., & Vechio, R. P. (2009). Agreement in self-other ratings of leader effectiveness: The role of demographics and personality. *International Journal of Selection and Assessment, 17*(2), 1–15.

34. www.strengthsfinder.com and http://sf2.strengthsfinder.com. See also: Buckingham, M., & Clifton, D. O. (2001). *Now, discover your strengths.* New York: The Free Press; Buckingham, M. (2007). *Go put your strengths to work.* New York: The Free Press; Rath, T. (2007). *Strengths finder 2.0.* New York: Gallup Press; Rath, T., & Conchie, B. (2008). *Strengths based leadership.* New York: Gallup Press.

35. www.valuesinaction.org. See also: Peterson, C., & Seligman, M. E. P. (2004). *Character strengths and virtues: A handbook and classification.* Oxford: Oxford University Press; Seligman, M. (2004). *Authentic happiness: Using the new positive psychology to realize your potential for lasting fulfillment.* New York: The Free Press.

36. http://ketsdevries.com/instruments/geli/geli.html.
37. www.leadershiparchitect.com *or*http://ketsdevries.com/instruments/laq/laq.html.
38. www.leadershipcube.com/home.html.
39. www.leadershipchallenge.com *or* https://www.lpionline.com/. See also: Kouzes, J. M., & Posner, B. Z. (2007). *The leadership challenge* (4th ed.). San Francisco: Jossey-Bass.
40. www.mlq.com. See also: Avolio, B. J., Bass, B. M., & Jung, D. I. (1999). Re-examining the components of transformational and transactional leadership using the Multifactor Leadership Questionnaire. *Journal of Occupational and Organizational Psychology, 72,* 441–462. Bass, B. M., & Avolio, B. J. (1997). *Full range leadership development: Manual for the Multifactor Leadership Questionnaire.* Palo Alto, CA: Mind Garden.
41. www.resiliencealliance.com/. Hoopes, L., & Kelly, M. (2004). *Managing change with personal resilience: 21 keys for bouncing back & staying on top in turbulent organizations.* Raleigh, NC: Mark Kelly Books.
42. www.stressdirections.com.
43. https://www.personnelstrengths.com. See also: Porter, E. (1973, 2005). *SDI: Standard Edition.* Carlsbad, CA: Personal Strengths Publishing.
44. https://www.cpp.com/products/tki/index.aspx. See also: Thomas, K. W., & Kilmann, R. H. (1974). *Thomas Kilmann conflict mode instrument.* Tuxedo, NY: Xicom.
45. www.belbin.com/. See also: Belbin, R. M. (2010). *Management teams: Why they succeed or fail* (3rd ed). London: Butterworth Heinemann.
46. www.humansynergistics.com/products/gsi.aspx.
47. www.internalchange.com/disc_profile_store/mall/teams_online.asp.
48. www.tmsdi.co.uk/profiles/team_management.cfm. See also: McCann, D., & Mead, N. (1998). *Team management systems research manual* (3rd ed.). www.tms.com.
49. www.humansynergistics.com/.
50. www.mhs.com. See also: Bar-On, R. (2004). The Bar-On Emotional Quotient Inventory (EQ-i): Rationale, description and psychometric properties. In G. Geher (Ed.), *Measuring emotional intelligence: Common ground and controversy* (pp. 115–145). Hauppauge, NY: Nova Science.
51. www.haygroup.com *or* www.eiconsortium.org. See also: Boyatzis, R. (2007). *The creation of the Emotional and Social Competency Inventory (ESCI).* Boston: Hay Group; Boyatzis, R., Goleman, D., & Rhee, K. (1999). Clustering competence in emotional intelligence: Insights from the Emotional Competence Inventory (ECI). In R. Bar-On and

D. Parker (Eds.), *Handbook of emotional intelligence* (pp. 343–362). San Francisco: Jossey-Bass; Goleman, D. (1998). *Working with emotional intelligence.* New York: Bantam Books; Goleman, D. & Boyatzis, R. (2008). Social intelligency and the biology of leadership. *Harvard Business Review,* 74–81.

52. www.haygroup.com *or* www.eiconsortium.org. See also: Boyatzis, R. (2007). *The Creation of the Emotional and Social Competency Inventory (ESCI).* Boston: Hay Group; Boyatzis, R., Goleman, D., & Rhee, K. (1999). Clustering competence in emotional intelligence: Insights from the Emotional Competence Inventory (ECI). In R. Bar-On & D. Parker (Eds.), *Handbook of emotional intelligence* (pp. 343–362). San Francisco: Jossey-Bass.

53. www.eiconsortium.org/measures/msceit. See also: Mayer, J. D., Salovey, P., & Caruso, D. R. (2002). *Mayer-Salovey-Caruso Emotional Intelligence Test (MSCEIT).* Toronto, Ontario: Multi-Health Systems, Inc; Mayer, J. D., Salovey, P., & Caruso, D. R. (2004). Emotional intelligence: Theory, findings, and implications. *Psychological Inquiry, 15,* 197–215. Mayer, J. D., Salovey, P., Caruso, D. R., & Sitarenios, G. (2003). Measuring emotional intelligence with the MSCEIT V2.0. *Emotion, 3,* 97–105. Palmer, B., Gignac, G., Manocha, R., & Stough, C. (2005). A psychometric evaluation of the Mayer-Salovey-Caruso emotional intelligence test version 2.0. *Intelligence, 33,* 285–305.

Appendix D: Sample Individual Development Plan

Employee: Catherine Belle	Supervisor: Julia Hannah	Date Created: 5/1/2010
Target Area for Change #1	*Development Objectives*	*Specific Situations*
Judgment and Decision Making	To slow the speed at which I made decisions in order to allow myself to consider a greater range of alternative actions, assess the pros and cons of those actions, and think through how those decisions impact others.	Apply to issues, problems, assignments, etc., that are "A" priority (determined by prioritizing each issue according to criticality and urgency).

Specific Actions	Resources and Support	Deadline	Status
1. Each week, read about one decision-making technique from the Web site: www.mindtools .com/pages/main/ newMN_TED.htm. Practice each applicable technique for one month and review results.	1. Time to review Web site and read book.	1. 5/31/10	Not started
	2. Supervisor to help identify and introduce me to executives who make sound decisions.	2. 7/31/10	Not started
2. Identify 2–3 executives respected for their decision making, and seek out a coaching relationship to learn from them the processes and techniques they use to make decisions.	3. Supervisor support to accommodate slower decision whiles techniques are being learned.	3. 9/30/10	Not started
3. Read *Smart Choices: A Practical Guide to Making Better Decisions* by John Hammond. Identify 4–5 techniques to apply.			

Internal & External Obstacles and Ways to Overcome	Measures of Success	Tracking Progress/Rewards
External: Time will be an obstacle. Will overcome by sacrificing some pleasure reading on own time, and at work by delegating more mundane tasks to staff. Internal: Tendency to act quickly and move on to the next issue. Overcome by reminding myself to slow down; by having boss regularly remind me of this development objective, and to create feedback loops with colleagues and staff to alert me when I may be jumping to conclusions too quickly.	Improved scores on Judgment and Decision Making dimensions of annual 360 survey from all respondents. Prioritizing decisions regularly into A, B, and C categories in order to make quicker decisions on easy issues and more reflective decisions on difficult issues.	Will assess progress toward goals every two months. Successful completion of three success measures will result in a new bike. Each decision (and how it was made) will be noted in a journal; Two-three weeks after each decision is made, it will be reviewed and evaluated as to its effectiveness. What went right, what went wrong, and what contributed to the decision's outcome, will be noted and acted upon.

Source: Modified from Poteet, M. L. June, 2009, President, Organizational Research & Solutions, Inc. 7223 Wareham Drive, Tampa, Florida 33647. Phone: 813-972-8189, e-mail: mlpoteet@verizon.net. Web site: www.orgsol.com.

Chapter Eleven

E-COACHING

Accept It, It's Here, and It's Evolving!

Lisa A. Boyce and David Clutterbuck

> It's after midnight and I'm still struggling with the length of my skirt and hair, the color of both as well as my eyes, and wondering if I should make my lips a bit thicker. In reality, that should be the least of my worries as I prepare my avatar for her first virtual coaching experience in Second Life. Sure, first impressions count, but I have deeper concerns with building rapport, establishing trust, and integrating the novel tools that are available in this virtual world. Well, at least I've mastered flying, sort of.

Nearly 75 percent of distinguished practicing executive coaches indicate that they are coaching in media other than face-to-face using tools ranging from e-mail to virtual simulations. If you are reading this chapter, you or someone you know is likely involved in e-coaching. Perhaps you or your organization has been employing e-practices for several years or you are interested in becoming more virtual and realize there are many issues to consider. Personally, I can remember a coaching brown bag over fifteen years ago where a dozen internal coaches debated if we should allow the use of e-mail in our coaching engagements, with several coaches adamantly objecting on grounds that there would be a decrease of quality of interaction which would degrade the relationship and have a negative impact on the leadership coaching experience. Interestingly, the technology has evolved but many of the fundamental issues have not.

David, too, has been thinking and writing about these issues for nearly two decades, and together we hope to offer a foundation for thinking about e-coaching, including practical considerations with incorporating e-practices. To the extent we can offer supporting research, we will, but unfortunately e-coaching-related literature is even less available than executive coaching research in general. Therefore, we borrow liberally from our sister practices (such as mentoring, counseling, education, and so on) and adamantly emphasize the need for systematic research to promote evidence-based practices.

Laying the Foundation

At recent executive coaching conferences attended by both seasoned and novice leadership coaches, we were excited by the number of individuals interested in e-coaching but a bit surprised with our general lack of awareness and consensus regarding foundational matters, such as a definition of e-coaching, technologies of e-coaching, and even the state of e-coaching. Therefore, we feel that laying a foundation, a common ground, is critical to building an understanding of e-coaching.

Definitions of E-Coaching

Unlike coaching in general, there is relative consistency in how e-coaching or its close synonyms (such as blended coaching, distance coaching, online coaching, telecoaching, or virtual coaching) are defined. Most definitions (see Boyce & Hernez-Broome, 2010; Clutterbuck & Hussain, 2010; Dixon, 2008; Frazee, 2008; Marino, 2005; Pulley, 2007) incorporate three key elements: (1) a coach-client relationship, (2) the utilization of technology, and (3) the purpose of facilitating client growth. For example, we compare and contrast two popular definitions,

> a "formal one-one" relationship between a coach and client, in which the client and coach collaborate using technology to assess

and understand the client and his or her leadership development needs, to challenge current constraints while exploring new possibilities, and to ensure accountability and support for reaching goals and sustaining development (Boyce & Hernez-Broome, 2010, 141; adapted from Ting & Hart, 2004, 116).

A developmental partnership, in which all or most of the learning dialogue takes place using email, either as the sole medium, or supplemented by other media (Clutterbuck & Hussain, 2010).

These two definitions, devised independently and on opposite sides of the pond, clearly highlight the integration of technology in supporting a developmental relationship. Though David's definition is more general, both focus on three key components: the relationship, the developmental purpose, and the use of technology. In addition, the broad reference to "technology" and "media" without specific details hint at the evolving nature of the technologies employed. For example, telephone coaching, which is perhaps the earliest and most common form of distance coaching, is synchronous in that conversations occur in real time (hence, aka "synchronous audio"). E-mail, now a staple of e-coaching, is asynchronous with conversations often occurring at different times and even different days.

However, the most fashionable coaching technologies do not necessarily reflect the most sophisticated applications nor are asynchronous judged as superior to synchronous to or vice versa. Released in 2003, Skype, which is now nearly synonymous with desktop video conferencing, supports synchronous conversations. Also launched in 2003, Second Life, the 3-D virtual world, provides synchronous interactions. The two fastest-growing social networking tools, Facebook and Twitter (founded in 2004 and 2006, respectively), support asynchronous text-based conversations (Kazeniac, 2009). There is obviously no one best way to communicate.

Technologies of E-Coaching

The integration of technology presents both benefits and challenge to leadership coaching. As we foreshadowed above, the advances in technology are not necessarily sequential but an evolution of differing factors that affect the nature of coaching. Though there are many criteria to examine when considering specific technology (for example, usability, security, accessibility, and so on), media richness theory (MRT) (Daft, Lengel, & Trevino, 1987) provides us with a framework to focus our understanding of how technology affects communication.

Media richness refers to a continuum of related functions, including immediacy of feedback, amount of information transferred during a given time interval, and the number of communication channels. For example, face-to-face conversation is considered to have high richness because immediate feedback is possible, the amount of information that can be transferred verbally is high, and multiple cues (visual, auditory, and so forth) are available. Text-based e-mail, on the other hand, has a relatively lower level of richness because asynchronous communication allows delay in feedback, the amount of information transferred in a given time period is low, as the message has to be typed, sent, and then read, and e-mail relies on a single communication channel.

Although an initial reaction might be to rank order technology on such criteria and be done with the chapter, we feel that doing so would imply that one is better or the best. Instead we suggest that different technologies are more appropriate for different needs and contexts. For example, there are benefits and challenges to speed of transmission. Synchronous conversations (such as face-to-face) offer greater potential for spontaneity and emergence of unidentified issues or uncensored self-disclosure. But synchronous discussions do not naturally provide opportunities for reflective thinking; the ability to reflect is built into asynchronous discussions (such as e-mail) (Pulley, 2007). Further, text-based interactions support the seamless collection and maintenance of written records, which is particularly helpful for indentifying patterns in thinking and behavior and tend to be power-neutral because of the absence of other cues (Hamilton & Scandura, 2003).

Our intention in consolidating various communication technologies in terms of media richness is to frame not only current technologies for future discussions but also to provide a mechanism to think about future technologies or those not specifically discussed in this chapter. Borrowing on communication researchers (such as Newberry, 2001; Sitkin, Sutcliffe, & Barrios-Choplin,

1992; Trevino, Lengel, & Daft, 1987), Table 11.1 places seven different types of communication technology into three categories (low, medium, high) based on the mediums ability to support immediate feedback, large amounts of information transfer, and multiple communication channels or cues, as well as the ability to relay feelings or emotions and to tailor the message to the individual recipient.

Table 11.1. Media Richness of Communication Technology Types

	Low	*Medium*	*High*
Feedback Immediacy	E-Mail Asynchronous Audio Threaded Discussion		Face-to-Face Video Conferencing Synchronous Audio Text-Based Chat
Information Transfer	Text-Based Chat E-mail Asynchronous Audio	Threaded Discussion	Face-to-Face Video Conferencing Synchronous Audio
Multiple Cues	Synchronous Audio Asynchronous Audio Text-Based Chat E-mail Threaded Discussions	Video Conferencing	Face-to-Face
Share Emotions	Text-Based Chat E-mail Threaded Discussions	Video Conferencing Synchronous Audio Asynchronous Audio	Face-to-Face
Message Tailoring	Text-Based Chat Asynchronous Audio Threaded Discussions	Video Conferencing Synchronous Audio E-mail	Face-to-Face

Obviously face-to-face communication is high across all five criteria and we've already acknowledged there is some resistance to e-coaching. So perhaps an even more fundamental issue is to understand whether and why coaches are employing technology in their practice.

State of E-Coaching

E-coaching is definitely occurring. Two recent surveys provide insights on the extent of e-coaching practices. Nearly 1,300 respondents worldwide indicated that 51 percent of coaching communication is not "in person," and instead use technology to deliver coaching without any personal contact (Corbett, Corbett, & Colemon, 2008, 6). A second survey of nearly two hundred coaches reported that only 8 percent of coaching was occurring entirely face-to-face. Twenty-six percent of coaching was primarily or entirely occurring at a distance with technology-supported communication and resources (Frazee, 2008).

The interest in and use of e-coaching is likely a response to the popularity and evolution of leadership coaching in general. In addition, the changing nature of organizations and work demands leaders to lead a diverse workforce, develop cross-cultural competencies, respond swiftly and effectively to novel situations, and to be continuous life-long learners. E-coaching is well suited to meet these needs providing greater flexibility, accessibility, and availability required of today's dynamic cost-savings environment.

Integrating technology into coaching practices presents many advantages (Marino, 2005; Olson, 2001; Rossett & Marino, 2005). These advantages can be grouped into three client-centered categories: Convenience, Service, and Support. Convenience incorporates the advantages technology provides regarding coaching logistics, such as accessibility, flexibility, and affordability. Service addresses the ability of the coach to meet the client's dynamic just-in-time needs. Support encompasses the availability of digital data, tailored resources, and performance metrics to support coaching assessment, performance, and evaluation. Table 11.2 presents a list of thirty benefits associated with e-coaching within the three client-centered categories (Boyce & Hernez-Broome, 2010).

Table 11.2. Advantages of E-Coaching

Convenience	*Service*	*Support*
Accessible	***Just-in-Time***	***Assessment and Performance***
Coach and client can be globally separated as geographical boundaries are no longer a constraint	Client issues can be addressed as they emerge	Client assessments can be electronically collected and data digitally stored
Coaches can reach clients in situations typically unable to receive coaching (such as business travel, military deployment, third-world countries)	Guidance and feedback can be provided in real time as the client performs	Synchronous sessions and asynchronous communications can be unobtrusively and effortlessly stored and later used to chart milestones, review goals and progress, and identify trends
	Coaches can act as sounding-boards so client's decision is validated or challenged before implemented	Tracking mechanisms support longitudinal assessments as well as comparative summative reports
		Coaches can review homework assignments online and provide feedback in preparation for sessions
Available	***Rapid Response***	***Resources***
Multinational leadership coaches can support cultural and expatriate needs	Coaches can provide immediate feedback on assessments or assignments	Coaches can provide client access to resources, including tools to help set goals, record and track progress
Coaches are able to grow boutique practices or provide specialized service	Coaches can link clients with experts from different information domains	Coaches can direct clients to appropriate online learning assignments to prepare for coaching sessions
Single coaches can work with multiple clients with differing needs as greater coach-client ratios are possible	Coaches can link clients with peers having similar challenges	Clients can access electronic support systems, such as knowledge bases and data repositories as needed

(*Continued*)

Table 11.2. Advantages of E-Coaching (*Continued*)

Convenience	Service	Support
Flexible	*Administrative Ease*	*Evaluation*
Clients can coordinate synchronous coaching, complete assignments, and respond to asynchronous feedback according to their dynamic schedules	Interactive calendars allow clients and coaches to log-on and schedule or reschedule sessions efficiently	Individual metrics of engagement, use, and satisfaction can be tracked and monitored
Clients can view, store, and process coaches' responses as convenient and appropriate	Coaches can tailor and time reminders to provide support and reinforcement	The ability to track organizational metrics by quantitatively measuring and aggregating data supplies info to ROI and productivity improvement studies
		Organizations can analyze aggregate information to identify organizational strengths, gaps, and trends
Affordable	*Practical Pauses*	
E-coaching reduces costs of travel, time away from the job, and so on	Asynchronous conversations allow clients to pause and reflect on feedback before responding	
Assessment tools, such as 360-degree feedback and self-assessments, can be administered, at low cost, and as needed	Asynchronous conversations support advance thinking time, which allows coaches and clients to prepare and focus during a synchronous coaching session	

Despite these many advantages, we are not advocating that e-coaching replace face-to-face coaching. Both face-to-face and virtual approaches have advantages and disadvantages. Both have added value in leadership coaching and should be considered in a context based on the particular client-coach relationships and each unique situation. Therefore the real issue is not whether technology should be integrated into leadership coaching practices but rather *how* it should be integrated. This practice is already occurring and is likely to expand to support the growing coaching demand and needs of future leaders. We propose that the issue is to understand the context and conditions most appropriate for employing various types of technology.

Building the E-Coaching Practice

Three major considerations to incorporating technology into a coaching practice include the coach, the client, and the organization. As stated earlier, the practice of e-coaching is in its infancy with research to support such practices nearly nonexistent. Therefore, we do not purport to have all the answers. Quite to the contrary, we don't even suggest that we have all the questions. But having systematically thought, presented, and written on the topic, we'd like to offer a series of propositions based on experience and the limited research to frame key issues. Our submissions are designed to help collectively scaffold our thinking about today's virtual coaching needs as well as about the evolving needs and capabilities of tomorrow. We'll begin by examining the client, coach, and organizational challenges.

Organization Challenges

Strategically, we must ask ourselves whether certain types of organizations are more suited and receptive to e-coaching. If you paused to answer this thought, a likely response would be *multinational companies*. Expatriate executives benefiting from local coaches prior to relocation more efficiently adjust to the culture and enter their new roles more prepared to work. Charities and nongovernmental agencies also have staff located at numerous sites, particularly around the developing world in small offices in remote locations. E-coaching affords expatriates continuous development as well as provides a source of social networking. Small business owners find that e-coaching provides the flexibility to balance professional growth with the time and effort in running and growing their business with the coaches' broader perspective particularly valued in their often isolated situations.

These three types of organizations spotlight a need that e-coaching can support, particularly the ability to cross cultural and distal barriers as well as the flexibility to support solitary or isolated leaders. When organizations recognize they have a need that can most effectively be met through technology, they are more likely to be receptive, invest, and support the practices, such as organizations with globally isolated leaders. Establishing that e-coaching is needed by leaders in a particular organization but also benefits that organization creates an environment conducive to support the practice. As organizations integrate coaching into their business strategies (see Stomski, Ward, and Battista's Chapter Eight and Riddle and Pothier, Chapter Fifteen) the coaching culture promotes coaching, including e-coaching, as a means for improving organizational performance as well.

The support of both the client and coach organizations is no minor issue. Depending on the complexity of the technology base needed and the number of clients and coaches supported, an e-coaching program could be cost and labor intensive. For example, a packaged IT support platform used to mediate between participants and monitor coaching program progress will often require modifications and tailoring, which is generally cheaper than building customized software. Further, a virtual coaching program needs oversight, which, on average, requires one day per week for every twenty to twenty-five coach-client pairs for the duration of the relationships. Both the client and coach organizations need to determine the appropriate level of technology required to meet the program objectives and ascertain the source of support in terms of resources, influence, and commitment to ensure the program is sustainable.

Client Challenges

Tactically, we must also ask ourselves whether there are certain types of clients or client characteristics that are more suited or receptive to e-coaching. Clearly, the globally isolated leader high-lighted in the previous discussion constitutes a population with a high need. Interestingly, collegial conversations identified a range of professionals that were particularly suited for e-coaching ranging from women on maternity leave to technical "geeks" moving into management roles to senior executives whose time and preference required an alternative to scheduled face-to-face sessions. The needs of the client appear to be as much a requisite for e-coaching as the need of the job.

Clients require a level of motivation and readiness to be coached in an e-environment. E-coaching requires relatively greater commitment and accountability from the client. For example, busy leaders find it easier to procrastinate in responding to an automated message reminder or to multitask during an asynchronous conversation. Further, potential e-clients must be open to the use of technology. Individuals have different preferences for face-to-face versus virtual communication. Virtual mentoring research has found that introverts are more likely to engage in electronic communication, perceiving it as less risky (Hamilton & Scandura, 2003), and demonstrate greater response patterns with higher achievement in virtual versus face-to-face communication (Hubschman, 1996). Therefore motivations to be coached as well as a desire to incorporate technology are strong prerequisites for e-coaching.

The most relevant readiness factor focuses on clients' technology competence. Age, education, and geographical location all influence individuals' speed of assimilation of new technology. Previous experience with technology is also related to success with new technologies, including communication disclosure satisfaction, perceived knowledge gain, and behavioral improvements (Calvin, 2005; Carey, Wade, & Wolfe, 2008; Shelton, 2004). Further, individuals with strong literacy skills may be more adept at written communication and e-coaching may be more suited for those communicating in a second language. Research suggests gender and age differences in e-based communications, with men and older persons using fewer emotional cues and expressions. The impact of these gender differences in e-mail conversations includes the ability to build bonds and to be influenced or persuaded (Guadagno & Cialdini, 2002). Therefore, the comfort and skill with the technology encompasses both the familiarity with the medium as well as the underlying mechanism for communicating.

An interesting implication is that e-coaching may not be appropriate for certain clients. For example, e-coaching may not be satisfactory for an older male executive lacking both the time and interest to learn a new but relevant application. Additionally, certain conditions may be inappropriate. Consider an individual suited for e-coaching but whose developmental goals are incongruent to the medium, such as an introverted technology analyst with low interpersonal skills positioning to become a vice president. Though research suggests training can increase virtual skills (see, for example, Jonas, Boos, & Sassenberg, 2002; Rosen, Furst, & Blackburn, 2006; Warkentin & Baranek, 2001) and evolving technology may support developmental objectives traditionally requiring face-to-face interaction, we would be wise not only to stay current on the research and these advances but also to consider each client and his or her situation uniquely when integrating e-coaching practices.

Coach Challenges

The characteristics and requirements of a successful e-coach are considered to differ from those of the traditional face-to-face coach (Dixon, 2008; Goldsmith, Govindarajan, Kaye, & Vicere, 2002; Rossett & Marino, 2005; Triad, 2001). Of the coach characteristics, the coach's readiness factors, specifically coaching philosophy, experience, and competencies, may be the most relevant to coaching in an e-environment.

Employing technology and removing or reducing the face-to-face interaction is a coaching choice, one that each individual coach needs to evaluate within his or her own coaching philosophy. We are familiar with senior leadership coaches who are less than receptive to incorporating technology, especially as a primary means of communication. Their coaching philosophy, grounded in counseling, is based on the belief that face-to-face interaction is necessary to be most effective. In addition to believing relationship-based practices need the information gained from nonverbal as well as verbal cues, reticent coaches are concerned with the lack of opportunity to observe their clients.

Interestingly, counseling itself is moving towards a virtual practice with e-counseling gaining popularity and research support (see, for example, Mallens, Day, & Green, 2003; Ritterband et al., 2009; Tate, Jackvony, & Wing, 2003). Nonetheless, coaches must assess their personal beliefs and values to assess not only their desire but comfort with e-coaching.

Other coaches reluctant to integrate technology into their practice feel they lack the experience to meet the needs of the younger and more technologically savvy client. As discussed earlier, experience breeds confidence and ability to communicate more effectively in different media. Pulley (2007, 355) describes the "learning curve" associated with technology-supported communication in which coaches who initially experienced apprehension and discomfort later reported a positive experience after learning and adjusting to the technology. Research has demonstrated that experience with technology positively relates to technology appreciation (see, for example, Czaja & Sharit, 1998; Ellis & Allaire, 1999; Melenhorst & Bouwhuis, 2004), including appreciation for enhanced and extended communication capabilities (Melenhorst, Rogers, & Bouwhuis, 2006), and ability to translate skills to other technologically complicated devices (Kang & Yoon, 2008). Fortunately, gaining experience is not limited to work practice with opportunities available through social networking sites (such as Facebook, LinkedIn) and Internet protocols (such as Skype). In fact, a study of Facebook users by iStrategyLabs found that 28 percent of United States users are between the ages of thirty-five and fifty-four, making it the biggest age group using the Web site (Kopytoff, 2009). Any discomfort or perceptions of deficiency is, however, relevant as the skills needed to perform e-coaching may differ from traditional coaching.

Multiple coaching organizations, including The Society for Industrial and Organizational Psychology (SIOP), the International Coach Federation (ICF), and the European Mentoring and Coaching Council (EMCC), as well as the published literature (see, for example, Brotman, Liberi, & Wasylyshyn, 1998; Graham, Wedman, & Garvin-Kester, 1994; Hall, Otazo, & Hollenbeck, 1999) provide relatively similar lists of core coach requirements and competencies. Unfortunately, we can only speculate on the extent these requirements need to be adapted to support e-coaching.

The most obvious competency requirements are associated with working with technology. For example, coaches must become adept at using technology to accommodate their clients' preferred technology support and communication tools. Because leaders seeking coaching generally do not have the time or inclination to learn a new technology, the onus is on the coach to understand the basic technology (such as capabilities, bandwidth, information security, and so forth), maximize its effectiveness, and leverage its capabilities to advance the relationship, as well as monitor technological innovations that might be appropriate to gradually introduce later in the coaching program.

E-coaches will also need to be more adept at communicating their thoughts and emotions in writing. In addition to explaining complex issues in simple terms, e-coaches will need to translate nonverbal messages virtually. Whyman, Santana, and Allen (2005, 6) offered several specific techniques to support e-coaching communication, such as

- Consciously use language that invites further interactions (such as "I'm looking forward to receiving your update next Friday. Please let me know how I can be helpful").
- Keep responses short to accommodate the tendency of people to skim the computer screen.
- Make the main point first, then add supporting information, which contradicts a common coaching technique of first giving the supporting information, then building to a conclusion (that is, *B*ottom *L*ine *U*p *F*ront—BLUF).
- Use capitals to emphasize a single word, and typographical devices, known as emoticons (such as :-), :@,=O) and symbols (*, !) to express emotion and emphasis.
- Though these guidelines are not comprehensive, they clearly illustrate that an e-coach will need to understand and possess a unique skill set to effectively communicate with clients online.

Perhaps not exclusive to an e-coach, the reality that an e-coach is more likely to encounter cross-cultural coaching opportunities suggests a need to emphasize the importance of cross-cultural coaching skills. In addition to the increased probability of a client needing skills and support to adapt to other cultures, clients from across the globe may seek e-coaching to support their integration into different countries and cultures. Therefore, knowledge of cultural behavioral change models and intercultural communication seems essential.

Building the Future

We highlighted organizational, client, and coach challenges for us to consider as we develop e-coaching programs and practices. We proposed that certain types of organizations have a greater need and therefore are more likely to invest in and support e-coaching. In addition, clients with both a particularly strong and appropriate development focus, as well as technology experience and competence, are more motivated and disposed for e-coaching. Finally, a harmonized e-coaching philosophy with successful technology experience and competence is needed to successfully coach in a virtual environment. As technology and research to support e-coaching practices evolves and purveys, such requirements may evolve or even be minimized. However, until that futuristic time, we encourage those entering or reflecting on their e-coaching practices to consider these key issues and for researchers to systematically examine the requirements in terms of understanding the impact on coaching processes as well as individual and organizational outcomes.

Supporting the E-Coaching Process

E-coaching is not simply an extension of coaching or an add-on to established processes. Technology and coaching have "synthesized into something new and exciting" (Clutterbuck & Hussain, 2010). Understanding e-coaching and determining who should coach and be coached are prerequisites to building an e-coaching practice. Once this foundation has been established, the practicalities of conducting e-coaching require a focused examination. This section examines many such key issues, including matching coaches with clients, logistical issues, the actual technology, building and maintaining relationships, and evaluation and transitioning. We again offer the caveat

that coaching through technology is a relatively new phenomenon with minimal applied or empirical support. We therefore
share these ideas to identify and frame the discussion to further
our collective thinking as well as to support current e-coaching
processes.

Matching

A good match or fit between a client and coach is critical to the
development of a quality coaching relationship (CCL, 2009; ICF,
1999; TECF, 2008). While matching attempts to identify a coach
tailored to meet the needs of an individual client, the process
occurs with varying degrees of rigor (Hernez-Broome, Boyce, &
Ely, 2009). In addition, the factors critical to successful pairing
are debatable (Boyce, Jackson, & Neal, 2010) as is the influence
of these factors in virtual relationships (Clutterbuck & Hussain,
2010).

Possible factors to consider when aligning coaches with clients include commonalities in demographic, professional and
personal backgrounds, compatibility in behavioral preferences,
such as personality and work styles, and coach's capability and
credibility relative to the client's needs based on his or her competence and experience (Boyce & Hernez-Broome, 2010). For
example, matching on similarity may help achieve rapid rapport
(Wycherley & Cox, 2008) and the mentoring literature suggests
that personality mismatches result in premature termination
of the relationship (Gerstein, 1985; Hunt & Michael, 1983).
However, should the relationship survive, the differing tempera-
ments may result in more complex interactions leading to higher
performance outcomes (Boyce et al., 2010; Scoular & Linley,
2006).

While it could be argued that virtual relationships are less
or more influenced by similarity or differences, our view is perhaps
more conservative and practical. Organizations should examine
match factors and systematically match using those they consider relevant, seek formative feedback, and adjust accordingly.
Reporting of systematic research is also encouraged, particularly as the matching impact may be related to less direct factors
(such as coaching experience, type of technology employed, client

readiness). Regardless of the current state of affairs, we are confident that virtual coaching offers greater matching potential as the coaching pool increases, because location is no longer a key factor of consideration.

Practical considerations for e-coaching focus on automating the matching process. Personal experience and interview responses attest to how tedious and time-consuming it is to create matches by hand (such as with paper-and-pencil, index cards, Excel spreadsheets). Automated options range from centrally managed software that supports coordinators' identifying potential pairings to fully automated systems where matching software identify best-fit matches on specified criteria. An example of the latter is a software program that first compares coach and client values compatibility based on research indicating that values compatibility was a significant predictor of rapport in dyadic learning relationships (Hale, 2000) and then sorts by demographic factors (including age, gender, academic discipline, and so on). Regardless of the level of automation, coaching coordinators must clearly articulate the key factors in terms of similarities and complementary stretch characteristics. Further, consider initially piloting with a control group and assess if the matches that emerge meet the criteria determined. Also, periodically assess that the resulting matches intuitively make sense.

Other practical considerations include the potential value of allowing clients to make the final decision in selecting their coaches. In organizations that launch coaching on singular dates this option is logistically difficult, but for programs with staggered entrance and a large coach pool, mutual selection could be an option. However, we note that in situations where coaches are matched, the need to rematch is quite low, perhaps because both coaches and clients are provided an opportunity to detail the type of person with whom they would prefer to be paired and not paired. Regardless, as with face-to-face relationships, procedures for rematching should also be established.

Logistics

Perhaps a bit more mundane, a virtual environment increases the complexity of logistical issues. Therefore, aspects of the mechanics of coaching such as contracting, scheduling, and confidentiality are considered. As the reasoning behind these practices is the same as conventional coaching, our discussion intentionally focuses on the unique considerations.

Contracting

Contracting is an opportunity to manage expectations. Think of that busy client who could gain more from the coaching experience if he or she would invest more time and effort into coaching "homework"—then imagine that individual not faced with an imminent face-to-face meeting. The virtual environment supports flexibility at a price. Clients are perceived as often less prepared, communication gaps may be longer, and cancellations more frequent. Some coaches have also indicated they feel as if they are always "on call" with clients expecting immediate response and availability. Therefore, establishing and managing expectations and boundaries is critical in a virtual environment.

When considering the ground rules, possible issues to discuss include clear guidelines regarding the terms of communication, use of support technology, and implications for violating mutually agreed-on conditions. Misunderstandings, delayed reaction, and duplication of effort are associated with gaps in communication (Dixon, 2008). Therefore, establish rules regarding the frequency and length of communication. For example, with increased accessibility (via BlackBerries and iPhones) coach and client need to determine requirements for acknowledging asynchronous communications and a maximum response time. Likewise, both parties need to establish limitations to their availability as office hours become even more relevant with time zone differences. Further, mutually agree on rules of communication. Netiquette provides general rules of social online communication that facilitate virtual interactions and can serve as baseline.

Scheduling

Scheduling is another opportunity to manage expectations and increase preparation. Drawing on our e-mentoring colleagues, we know that involvement or frequency and duration of e-mentoring interactions are consistently related to positive outcomes (Single & Single, 2005). Therefore, determine a schedule that creates a rhythm regarding the number, frequency, and duration for both synchronous and asynchronous communications. Further, coordinate technology to take advantage of interactive scheduling tools and auto reminders. Finally, detail policies regarding billing (for example, per contact, per time spent, flat rate over time) and policy violations (such as cancellations, reschedules) to maximize involvement while appreciating that virtual coaching provides flexibility and, as a result, communication varies (for example, several short e-mail interactions, a longer Skype conversation). Of major importance is ensuring that the client and coach both have personal responsibility to the coaching arrangement.

Confidentiality

Confidentiality, security, and data protection are of particular concern in virtual coaching. With many organizations monitoring and storing computer communications, clients need to be aware that their conversations may not be confidential. In addition to making strong statements on confidentiality, coaches and clients can minimize risk by communicating by telephone or personal e-mail accounts. Mechanisms to safeguard storage and retrieval of data need to also be established. Finally, protocols need to be developed for sharing data within the relationship and third parties (such as client organization, coach supervisor, professional referral) and need to be articulated.

The Technology

Let us refocus briefly on the technology in terms of the support it can provide in the development of relationships and the practical considerations for program directors and participants in using them in a coaching context.

As we discussed earlier, media richness provides a framework to aid our understanding of how technology affects communication, which is useful in determining which communication tools to use. Considering the limitations of less rich communication, including delayed feedback, slower information transfer, fewer cues, and reduced ability to relay emotions or tailor messages, your gut response might be to use the richest possible medium. In addition to the pragmatic issues with always selecting media-rich technology, Walther (1994, 18) cites several studies in which "experienced CMC [computer mediated communication] users rated text-based media, including e-mail and computer conferencing, 'as rich or richer' than telephone conversations and face-to-face conversations." One possible explanation of such perceptions resides in Social Presence Theory (Gunawardena, 1995).

Social presence theory (Short, Williams, & Christie, 1976) is a seminal theory of the social effects of communication technology. Social presence theory assumes an interaction involving two parties, in which both are concerned with developing or maintaining a personal relationship. Short et al. (1976, 65) define social presence in relation to a medium and describes it as an "attitudinal dimension of the user, a 'mental set' towards the medium" and as the "subjective quality of the communication medium." Research has demonstrated that social presence has a significant impact on online interaction, persistence, satisfaction, improved learning and motivation (Garrison, Anderson, & Archer, 2000; Gunawardena & Zittle, 1997; Lobry de Bruyn, 2004; Picciano, 2002; Richardson & Swan, 2003; Rourke, Anderson, Garrison, & Archer, 2001; Tu & McIssac, 2002).

Researchers and practitioners have also offered advice regarding how to facilitate social presence (for example, Aragon, 2003; Russo & Campbell, 2004; Stacey, 2002; Swan, 2003). Examples include automating assessment and feedback, restating or paraphrasing, using emoticons, and viewing a photo of your client when communicating. Aragon (2003) categorized various strategies which serve as a useful organizer for determining tactics to increase social presence using different technologies. Translated to e-coaching, the categories are program design (for example, incorporating audio), instructor (for example, sharing personal stories and experiences), and client (for example, using emoticons).

Several practical issues also need to be considered in identifying optimal technology. We are not technology experts, but our experiences suggest several issues are particularly relevant. The two general factors to consider are the logistics (such as cost, accessibility, technical support, and confidentiality/security) and the applications (including evaluation, monitoring, feedback, linking into other resources such as learning logs, learning sets, and closed subgroups) and there are generally always tradeoffs. For example, widely available, low-cost options are not always reliable and often do not support tailored applications, such as multirater feedback tools (see Clutterbuck & Hussain, 2010, for more in-depth discussion). In designing virtual coaching programs, identifying technology requirements upfront will minimize the frustrations and costs later.

Building and Maintaining Relationships

Perhaps the greatest resistance to e-coaching is the lack of face-to-face communication (Boyce & Hernez-Broome, 2010); however, researchers have found no significant differences in learning outcome between online and face-to-face practices and provide support that communication technology facilitates the formation of new relationships and strong social bonds (see, for example, McKenna, Green, & Gleason, 2002; Parks & Roberts, 1998; Russell, 2001; Walther, 1993, 1995, 1996; Walther & Burgoon, 1992). Perhaps the preference for face-to-face interactions is a result of familiarity (Bornstein, 1989; Zajonc, 1968). But with communication remaining the dominant use of home computer systems and domestic Internet access quadrupling every three years (Kraut et al., 2002), familiarity may soon be an outdated argument.

As discussed in the introductory chapter, the four key relationship processes are building and maintaining rapport, establishing and maintaining trust, encouraging commitment, and promoting collaboration. These four social constructs involve a mutual responsibility between a coach and client and as a result may present additional challenges in a virtual environment, particularly as the coach cannot accomplish these processes alone. Rapport and trust take longer to establish virtually (Bierema & Merriam, 2002; Buche, 2007). Commitment and cooperation are more fragile as participants are more likely to disengage because of lower emotional social embarrassment (Whiting & de Janasz, 2004) and the nonverbal behaviors useful in building and maintaining these relationship-based processes are often unavailable virtually (Bernieri, Gillis, Davis, & Grahe, 1996; Dimatteo & Taranta, 1979).

Therefore, we provide example practices to support each of the four processes. Many of these recommendations are examples of good coaching techniques in general, but the notable difference is that the lack of performing the behavior may not have as severe an impact on the traditional coaching relationship. Those involved in e-coaching programs will benefit from understanding the inherent limitations of technology and consciously adjusting their efforts to complement their use.

Practical techniques to build and maintain rapid rapport in an e-environment include both partners initially sharing professional and personal information to quickly identify commonalities and then incorporate those commonalities, in addition to feelings and comments from session to session. By continuing to share experiences and discussing similar and dissimilar perceptions of those experiences, each partner is further able to appreciate the other's frame of reference. Further, specific behaviors are needed more frequently than in face-to-face interactions, including asking open-ended questions, rephrasing, and using names to demonstrate personalized and focused attention. Also, similar to face-to-face, coaches can mirror communication by matching level of information, key words and phrases, and preferences for visual, auditory, or kinesthetic learning modalities.

Practical techniques for establishing swift trust include creating and promoting a safe and supportive environment through contracting and confidentiality behaviors, scheduling the first two to four sessions close together, and identifying an individual you both know and trust (trust link) to build a foundation for trust. Establishing communication rules to increase awareness and clarify miscommunication, emotions, or misunderstandings, and addressing perceived discontent or unsatisfactory dialogue as early as noticed, are critical maintenance factors. Further, providing substantive and timely responses and following up on deliverables with explanations for any delays are key behaviors for sustaining trust virtually.

Commitment can be encouraged by identifying in writing goals and milestones, establishing clear lines of responsibilities, holding each other accountable, and maintaining a regular pattern of communication. Each dyad should also identify external influences that could impede goal achievement and employ technology to reduce or remove barriers to success, such as interactive calendars, databasing with organizational metrics, and video-based analysis systems. And though often overlooked in virtual environments, highlight early successes, focus on the milestones accomplished of an overall goal, and celebrate successes by sending an e-card or scheduling a virtual celebration. It is also important to share the success with the client's organization, particularly as he may be geographically separated from his parent office.

Collaboration can be promoted by candidly discussing the need to collaborate in a virtual environment and employing collaboration tools, such as SharePoint, GoogleApps, LinkUAll, Info Workspace, Lotus Notes, WebEx, and so on. Obviously, do not rely solely on e-mail. Both partners need to openly share information and resources, but in moderation to reduce information overload and allow time for thoughtful reflection and ideas to incubate. Coaches can develop an atmosphere of learning by demonstrating a learner-centered focus, responding to different learning styles. Further, incorporating a completion ritual, such as reviewing the *Four I's* (*I*ssues, what did we discuss?; *I*deas, what creative thinking occurred?; *I*nsights, what changed?; and *I*ntentions, what are we going to do?) at the end of each session builds an emotionally connected relationship.

Evaluation and Transition

Monitoring and evaluating coaching processes is particularly critical as virtual programs are less politically visible and have less empirical research demonstrating their success. Fortunately, assessing formative and summative coaching outcomes are relatively easier in e-environments. As highlighted in Table 11.2, a major advantage of e-coaching is that data, such as frequency, length, and content of interactions are often digitally stored. Results of online assessment tools are often maintained in a centralized database which can be aggregated to provide benchmarks and organization-level outcome feedback.

One example of a successful low-cost evaluation system involves administering three automated questionnaires, one at the beginning of the relationship and then again six and twelve months later. Response rates tend to be higher because of the accessibility and the imbedded reminders to nonresponders. Practical considerations again mirror those in face-to-face practices (see Ely and Zaccaro, Chapter Twelve) but appreciate that certain activities, such as identifying stakeholders and securing confidentiality, may be more challenging; others, such as collecting and analyzing data, may be less demanding.

Finally, an often neglected process is transitioning. In addition to reviewing the coaching experience, use the opportunity to place closure on the relationship. If the client entered the program and continued to collaborate with colleagues, hold a collective virtual celebration—perhaps a virtual party complete with virtual games and virtual food. At a minimum, establish expectations and rules for future contacts and consider presenting a reward (for example, a certificate or small goal-related gift), and publicizing achievement and program completion in organizational newsletters.

Conclusion

During a recent pilot study examining issues with virtual rapport, undergraduate participants nearly unanimously shared that they have been establishing and maintaining relationships virtually for years. Watching my seven-year-old effortlessly maneuver his blue hippo around Webkinz World®—including gaining skills so that his hippo could get a job and meeting up with friends to virtually play—I'm convinced that our next generation of leaders will not only want but expect coaching to occur virtually with technology seamlessly integrated.

As the technology continues to evolve, our understanding of how to integrate it into our coaching practices must also continue to evolve. However, that does not preclude us to think in advance about issues that may have an impact on the effectiveness of a coaching engagement and practice. By offering a common language and understanding of e-coaching, we provided a foundation for examining technology. By offering a series of propositions, we highlighted key issues to consider in building an e-coaching practice. By focusing on the unique aspects of the e-coaching process, we shared practical tactics to support e-coaching practices. Altogether, we hope this chapter presents a structure with a foundation to build and support the future needs of e-coaching.

Finally, we would again emphasize the need for research to support practice. For leadership coaching to continue to grow and be recognized as a critical method for developing and supporting current and future leaders, scientist-practitioners must systematically examine the individual components (for example, the coach, client, mechanics, relationships) as well as the interactions between them. We must learn to walk before we can fly; perhaps we must understand how to walk while we are learning to fly.

References

Aragon, S. R. (2003). Creating social presence in online environments. *New Directions for Adult and Continuing Education, 100,* 57–68.

Bernieri, F. J., Gillis, J. S., Davis, J. M., & Grahe, J. E. (1996). Dyad rapport and the accuracy of its judgment across situations: A lens model analysis. *Journal of Personality and Social Psychology, 71*(1), 110–129.

Bierema, L. L., & Merriam, S. B. (2002). E-mentoring: Using computer mediated communication to enhance the mentoring process. *Innovative Higher Education, 26*(3), 211–227.

Bornstein, R. F. (1989). Exposure and affect: Overview and meta-analysis of research, 1968–1987. *Psychological Bulletin, 106,* 265–289.

Boyce, L. A., & Hernez-Broome, G. (2010). E-coaching: Consideration of leadership coaching in a virtual environment. In D. Clutterbuck & A. Hussain (Eds), *Virtual coach/virtual mentor* (pp. 139–174). Charlotte, NC: Information Age Publishing.

Boyce, L. A., Jackson, R. J., & Neal, L. J. (2010). Building successful leadership coaching relationships: Examining impact of matching criteria in a leadership coaching program. *Journal of Management Development.*

Brotman, L. E., Liberi, W. P., & Wasylyshyn, K. M. (1998). Executive coaching: The need for standards of competence. *Consulting Psychology Journal: Practice and Research, 50*(1), 40–46.

Buche, M. I. (2007). Development of trust in electronic mentoring relationships. *International Journal of Networking and Virtual Organisations, 5*(1), 35–50.

Calvin, J. (2005). Explaining learner satisfaction with perceived knowledge gained in Web-based courses through course structure and learner autonomy. *Dissertation Abstracts International Section A: Humanities and Social Sciences, 66*(5–1), 1632.

Carey, J. C., Wade, S. L., & Wolfe, C. R. (2008). Lessons learned: The effect of prior technology use on web-based interventions. *CyberPsychology and Behavior, 11*(2), 188–195.

CCL (Center for Creative Leadership). (2009, March 23). *Transcript: The coaching relationship.* Center for Creative Leadership Leading Effectively Podcast Series. Retrieved March, 28, 2009, from http://www.ccl.org/leadership/podcast/transcriptTheCoachingRelationship.aspx

Clutterbuck, D., & Hussain, Z. (2010). The technology in practice. In D. Clutterbuck & Z. Hussain (Eds), *Virtual coach/virtual mentor.* Charlotte, NC: Information Age.

Corbett, B., Corbett, K., & Colemon, J. (2008). *The 2008 Sherpa executive coaching survey.* West Chester, OH: Author.

Czaja, S. J., & Sharit, J. (1998). Age difference in attitudes towards computers. *Journal of Gerontology, 53*, 329–340.

Daft, R. L., Lengel, R. H., & Trevino, L. (1987). Message equivocality, media selection, and manager performance. *MIS Quarterly, 11*, 355–366.

Dimatteo, M. R., & Taranta, A. (1979). Nonverbal communication and physician-patient rapport: An empirical study. *Professional Psychology, 8*, 540–547.

Dixon, K. (2008). *Ecoaching: How it works.* Retrieved April 21, 2008, from www2.academee.com/html/news-case/articles/article-3.html.

Ellis, R. D., & Allaire, J. C. (1999). Modeling computer interest in older adults: The role of age, education, computer knowledge, and computer anxiety. *Human Factors, 41*, 345–355.

Frazee, R. V. (2008). *E-coaching in organizations: Mapping the terrain.* Presentation conducted at the 2008 EDTEC Alumni Conference, San Diego, CA.

Garrison, D. R., Anderson, T., & Archer, W. (2000). Critical inquiry in a text? based environment: Computer conferencing in higher education. *The Internet and Higher Education, 2*(2/3), 87–105.

Gerstein, M. (1985). Mentoring: An age old practice in a knowledge-based society. *Journal of Counseling and Development, 64*, 156–157.

Goldsmith, M., Govindarajan, V., Kaye, B., & Vicere, A. A. (2002). *The many facets of leadership* (pp. 211–212). New York: Financial Times Prentice Hall.

Graham, S., Wedman, J. F., & Garvin-Kester, B. (1994). Manager coaching skills: What makes a good coach. *Performance Improvement Quarterly, 7*(2), 81–97.

Guadagno, R., & Cialdini, R. (2002). Online persuasion: An examination of differences in computer-mediated interpersonal influence. *Group Dynamics Theory, Research and Practice, 6*, 38–51.

Gunawardena, C. N. (1995). Social presence theory and implications for interaction and collaborative learning in computer conferences. *International Journal of Educational Telecommunications, 1*(2), 147–166.

Gunawardena, C., & Zittle, F. (1997). Social presence as a predictor of satisfaction within a computer mediated conferencing environment. *American Journal of Distance Education, 11*(3), 8–26.

Hale, R. I. (2000). To match or mismatch? The dynamics of mentoring s a route to personal and organizational learning. *Career Development International, 5*(4/5), 223–234.

Hall, D. T., Otazo, K. L., & Hollenbeck, G. P. (1999). Behind the closed doors: What really happens in executive coaching. *Organizational Dynamics, 27*(3), 39–53.

Hamilton, B. A., & Scandura, T. A. (2003). Implications for organizational learning and development in a wired world. *Organizational Dynamics, 31*(4), 388–402.

Hernez-Broome, G., Boyce, L. A., & Ely, K. (2009). The coaching relationship: A glimpse into the black box of coaching. In L. A. Boyce & G. Hernez-Broome (Chair), *The client-coach relationship: Examining a critical component of successful coaching.* Symposium conducted at the 24th Annual Conference of the Society for Industrial and Organizational Psychology, New Orleans, LA.

Hubschman, B. G. (1996). The effect of mentoring electronic mail on student achievement and attitudes in a graduate course in education research (Doctoral dissertation, Florida International University, 1996). *Dissertation Abstracts International, 57–08A,* 3417.

Hunt, D., & Michael, C. (1983). Mentorship: A career training and development tool. *Academy of Management Review, 8*(3), 475–485.

ICF (International Coach Federation). (1999). Selecting a coach. Retrieved March 28, 2009 from www.coachfederation.org/find-a-coach/selecting-a-coach/.

Jonas, K. J., Boos, M., & Sassenberg, K. (2002). Unsubscribe, pleeezz!!!: Management and training of media competence in computer-mediated communication, *CyberPsychology and Behavior, 5*(4), 315–329.

Kang, N. E., & Yoon, W. C. (2008). Age- and experience-related user behavior differences in the use of complicated electronic devices. *International Journal of Human-Computer Studies, 66*(6), 425–437.

Kazeniac, A. (2009, February). Social networks: Facebook takes over top spot, Twitter climbs. Retrieved February 17, 2009 from http://blog.compete.com/2009/02/09/facebook-myspace-twitter-social-network/.

Kopytoff, V. (2009). Most Facebook users are older, study finds. Retrieved July 8, 2009, from www.sfgate.com.

Kraut, R., Kiesler, S., Boneva, B., Cummings, J., Helgeson, V., & Crawford, A. (2002). The Internet paradox revisited. *Journal of Social Issues, 58*, 49–74.

Lobry de Bruyn, L. (2004). Monitoring online communication: Can the development of convergence and social presence indicate an interactive learning environment? *Distance Education, 25*(1), 67–81.

Mallens, M. J., Day, S. X., & Green, M. A. (2003). Online versus face-to-face conversations: An examination of relational and discourse variables. *Psychotherapy: Theory, Research, Practice, Training, 40*(1/2), 155–163.

Marino, G. (2005). *E-coaching: Connecting learners to solutions.* Retrieved June 21, 2008 from http://edweb.sdsu.edu/people/ARossett/pie/Interventions/ecoaching_2.htm.

McKenna, K. Y. A., Green, A. S., & Gleason, M. E. J. (2002). Relationship formation on the Internet: What's the big attraction? *Journal of Social Issues, 58*(1), 9–31.

Melenhorst, A. S., & Bouwhuis, D. G. (2004). When do older adults consider the internet? An exploratory study of benefit perception. *Genontechnology, 3*, 89–101.

Melenhorst. A. S., Rogers, W. A., & Bouwhuis, D. G. (2006). Older adults' motivated choice for technological innovation: Evidence for benefit-driven selectivity. *Psychology and Aging, 21*(1), 190–195.

Newberry, B. (2001). Raising student social presence in online classes. *World Conference on the WWW and Internet Proceedings,* Orlando, FL: ED466611, 2–7.

Olson, M. L. (2001, September). *E-coaching.* Retrieved April 21, 2008, from www.learningcircuits.org/2001/sep2001/olson.html.

Parks, M., & Roberts, L. (1998). Making MOOsic: The development of personal relationships on-line and a comparison to their off-line counterparts. *Journal of Social and Personal Relationships, 15*, 517–537.

Picciano, A. (2002). Beyond student perceptions: Issues of interaction, presence, and performance in an online course. *Journal of Asynchronous Learning Networks, 6*(1), 21–40.

Pulley, M. L. (2007). Blended coaching. In L. A. Boyce and G. Hernez-Broome (Chair), *E-coaching: Supporting leadership coaching with technology*. Symposium conducted at the 22nd Annual Conference of the Society for Industrial and Organizational Psychology, New York, NY.

Richardson, J. C., & Swan, K. (2003). Examining social presence in online courses in relation to students' perceived learning and satisfaction. *Journal of Asynchronous Learning Networks, 7*(1), 68–88.

Ritterband, L. M., Thorndike, F. P., Gonder-Frederick, L. A., Magee, J. C., Bailey, E. T., Saylor, D. K., & Morin, C. M. (2009). Efficacy of an Internet-based behavioral intervention for adults with insomnia. *Archives of General Psychiatry, 66*(7), 692–698.

Rosen, B., Furst, S., & Blackburn, R., (2006). Training for virtual teams: An investigation of current practices and future needs. *Human Resource Management, 45*(2), 229–247.

Rossett, A., & Marino, G. (2005, November). If coaching is good, the e-coaching is. . . . *Training and Development*, 46–49.

Rourke, L., Anderson, T., Garrison, R. D., & Archer, W. (2001). Assessing social presence in asynchronous text-based computer conferencing. *Journal of Distance Education, 4*(21), 50–71.

Russell, T. L. (2001). *The no significant difference phenomenon: A comparative research annotated bibliography on technology for distance education*. Montgomery, AL: IDECC.

Russo, T., & Campbell, S. (2004). Perceptions of mediated presence in an asynchronous online course: Interplay of communication behaviors and medium. *Distance Education, 25*(2), 215–232.

Scoular, A., & Linley, P. A. (2006). Coaching, goal-setting and personality type: What matters? *The Coaching Psychologist, 2*(1), 9–11.

Shelton, J. A. (2004). Technology-mediated interactions: An exploration of the effects of previous technology experience and comfort on self-disclosure in virtual environments. Paper presented for the PsiChi Research Grant 2003–2004 Winners. Retrieved August 17, 2008, from www.psichi.org/awards/winners/summer_03_04grant.asp.

Short, J. A., Williams, E., & Christie, B. (1976). *The social psychology of telecommunications*. New York: Wiley.

Single, P. B., & Single, R. M. (2005). E-mentoring for social equity: Review of research to inform program development. *Mentoring and Tutoring, 13*(2), 201–320.

Sitkin, S., Sutcliffe, K., & Barrios-Choplin, J. (1992). A dual-capacity model of communication media choice in organizations. *Human Communication Research, 18*(4), 563–598.

Stacey, E. (2002). Social presence online: Networking learners at a distance. *Education and Information Technologies, 7*(4), 287–294.

Swan, K. (2003). Developing social presence in online discussions. In S. Naidu (Ed.), *Learning and teaching with technology: Principles and practices* (pp. 147–164). London: Kogan Page.

Tate, D. F., Jackvony, E. H., & Wing, R. R. (2003). Effects of internet behavioral counseling on weight loss in adults at risk for Type 2 diabetes. *Journal of the American Medical Association, 289,* 1833–1836.

TECF (The Executive Coaching Forum). (2008). *The executive coaching handbook: Principles and guidelines for successful coaching partnership* (4th ed.). Retrieved March 28, 2008, from www.theexecutive coachingforum.com/.

Ting, S., & Hart, E. W. (2004). Formal coaching. In C. D. McCauley & E. Van Velsor (Eds.), *The Center for Creative Leadership handbook of leadership development* (pp. 116–150), San Francisco: Jossey-Bass.

Trevino, L., Lengel R., & Daft R. (1987). Media symbolism, media richness, and media choice in organizations. *Communications Research, 14*(5), 553–574.

Triad. (2001, October). Executive summary impact evaluation on the Coaching.com Intervention for [Client Company]. Retrieved June 21, 2008, from www.workplacecoaching.com/pdf/Coaching. ComReport.pdf.

Tu, C. H., & McIssac, M. S. (2002). An examination of social presence to increase interaction in online classes. *American Journal of Distance Education, 16*(2), 131–150.

Walther, J. B. (1993). Impression development in computer-mediated interaction. *Western Journal of Communication, 57,* 381–398.

Walther, J. (1994). Interpersonal effects in computer mediated interaction. *Communication Research, 21*(4), 460–487.

Walther, J. B. (1995). Relational aspects of computer-mediated communication: Experimental observations over time. *Organization Science, 6*(2), 186–203.

Walther, J. B. (1996). Computer-mediated communication: Impersonal, interpersonal, and hyperpersonal interaction. *Communication Research, 23*(1), 3–43.

Walther, J. B., & Burgoon, J. K. (1992). Relational communication in computer-mediated interaction. *Human Communication Research, 19,* 50–88.

Warkentin, M., & Beranek, P. M. (2001). Training to improve virtual team communication. *Information Systems Journal, 9*(4), 271–289.

Whiting, V., & Janasz, S. C. (2004). Mentoring in the 21st century: Using the internet to build skills and networks. *Journal of Management Education, 28,* 275–293.

Whyman, W., Santana, L., & Allen, L. (2005). Online follow-up: Using technology to enhance learning. *Leadership in Action, 25*(4), 14–17.

Wycherley, M., & Cox, E. (2008). Factors in the selection and matching of executive coaches in organizations. *Coaching: An International Journal of Theory, Research and Practice, 1*(1), 39–53.

Zajonc, R. B. (1968). Attitudinal effects of mere exposure. *Journal of Personality and Social Psychology, 9,* 1–27.

"Recalculating" Directions: Evaluating the Effectiveness of Leadership Coaching

Chapter Twelve

EVALUATING THE EFFECTIVENESS OF COACHING

A Focus on Stakeholders, Criteria, and Data Collection Methods

Katherine Ely and Stephen J. Zaccaro

As executive coaching continues to become a popular approach to leadership development, researchers and practitioners have become more interested in evaluating the effectiveness of coaching engagements in order to better understand the coaching process, and determine how coaching engagements can be improved. In addition, as organizations tighten their budgets, they are becoming increasingly concerned about the effectiveness of coaching engagements relative to their costs as they make decisions about resource allocations.

Although there is a high level of interest in evaluating coaching, guidance on conducting systematic evaluation remains scarce. In response to this lack of guidance, Ely et al. (in press) offered an integrated conceptual framework for evaluating coaching interventions. That framework included several premises about such evaluation, which involves the collection of both formative and summative data. Formative data are used to improve an ongoing development program, while summative data are used to evaluate the overall effectiveness of a program (Beyer, 1995; Brown & Gerhardt, 2002). In addition, Ely et al. suggested that a comprehensive coaching evaluation should reflect the multiple stakeholders that are networked together in a typical program (for example, clients, coaches, the clients' organizations, and the coaches' organization), that coaching evaluations include a wide range of criteria based on Kirkpatrick's four-level taxonomy (1994) (with extensions and other criteria suggested by Kraiger, Ford, & Salas, 1993), and that a comprehensive coaching evaluation include multiple data collection methodologies and sources.

In this chapter, we provide additional examination of three elements in Ely et al.'s framework (in press): (a) identifying the full range of *evaluation stakeholders*, (b) identifying *relevant evaluation criteria*, and (c) identifying *appropriate data collection* methodologies. These factors are functionally related to one another—the identification of relevant stakeholders determines what kinds of criteria need to be gathered, and both contribute to specifying how and from whom data is to be acquired and aggregated (see Figure 12.1). The goals of this chapter are to define and describe several key issues regarding these three elements of Ely et al.'s integrated framework for evaluating coaching.

Figure 12.1. A Multi-Stage Approach to Coaching Evaluation

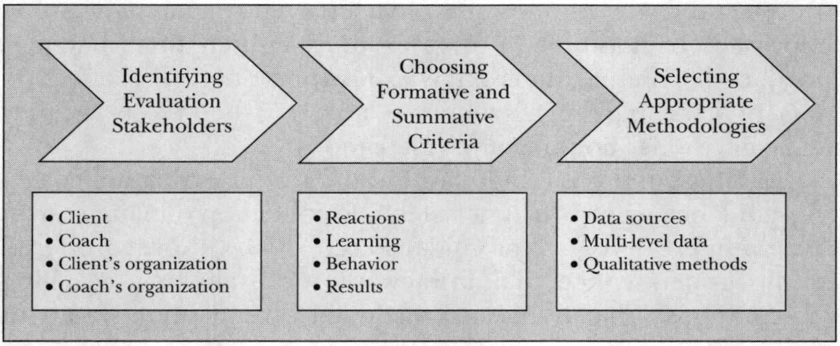

Identifying Evaluation Stakeholders	Choosing Formative and Summative Criteria	Selecting Appropriate Methodologies
• Client • Coach • Client's organization • Coach's organization	• Reactions • Learning • Behavior • Results	• Data sources • Multi-level data • Qualitative methods

Identifying Evaluation Stakeholders

We argue that stakeholders may be inextricably bound in terms of connected processes and outcomes. Thus, the client's growth from coaching has implications for his or her organization; the coach's professional effectiveness and learning have implications for organizations and institutes that include him or her on their roster of coaches; and clients' and coaches' organizations are bound by the implications of successful coaching for their mutual strategic plans and goals. Because stakeholders are participants in a system of learning and performance, the evaluation of coaching should reflect that system quality (Grove, Kibel, & Haas, 2006).

The first step in building an integrative framework for evaluating coaching entails identifying the full range of evaluation stakeholders—those constituencies that have an interest in the outcomes of a coaching program. This step involves not only specifying all participants in the coaching enterprise, but also the types of information they are interested in gleaning from an evaluation. Ely et al. (in press) identified four key coaching evaluation stakeholders: the *client*, the *coach*, the *client's organization* and the *coaching organization*. Although they defined these stakeholders as separate entities, we would add that they could have multiple ties among them. Thus clients and coaches are obviously entwined, as are the client and his or her organization. Moreover, the goals of the client's organization and the coaching organization are linked; and the characteristics of the coach, along with the success of the client, may bear heavily on the interests of the coaching organization. We define the number of stakeholders and the nature of their ties as reflecting the degree of *inter-stakeholder complexity* in a coaching enterprise.

We also suggest that each stakeholder reflects internally a number of other possible constituencies, issues, and agendas that may be related to each other in systematic ways. For example, the client can bring issues and agendas to coaching that are not only related to leadership growth, but also to the client's work and family contexts. Put another way, some goals that a client may pursue in coaching can have consequences not only for his or her subordinates and peers at work, but also for family members and friends. We label the number of constituencies, issues, and agendas reflected within a stakeholder and the nature of ties among them, *intra-stakeholder complexity.* We contend that the degree of both inter- and intra-stakeholder complexity in a coaching enterprise will influence the amount, nature, and source of evaluation data to be collected. In the next sections we elaborate on Ely et al.'s four stakeholder groups and the kinds of intra-stakeholder complexity each might reflect.

Clients

Clients are those individuals who engage in coaching efforts to improve leadership-related competencies, behaviors, attitudes, perspectives, and strategies, with the hopes of translating their efforts into effective job performance and organizational outcomes (Feldman & Lankau, 2005; Kampa-Kokesch & Anderson, 2001). The typical coaching client can reflect a number of constituencies that may have varying degrees of stakes in the client's growth. Figure 12.2 indicates these aspects of the client that can

Figure 12.2. Client as Coaching Stakeholder

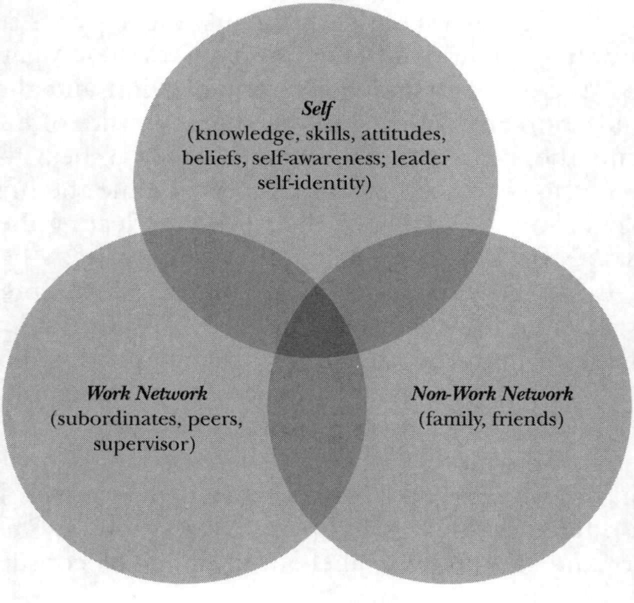

Self
(knowledge, skills, attitudes, beliefs, self-awareness; leader self-identity)

Work Network
(subordinates, peers, supervisor)

Non-Work Network
(family, friends)

weave through, influence, or be affected by the coaching process. They can be broadly grouped into (a) aspects of the "leader self-concept" of the client, (b) the client's work network, and (c) the client's social network outside of work.

The client as "self," particularly growth in the client's understanding and representation of self, represents a prime target of coaching (Drath & Van Velsor, 2006), and therefore coaching evaluation. Self theory (Markus & Nurius, 1986) suggests a number of ways a client can be represented as a stakeholder in coaching. For example, a client can hold both an "actual self" and "a possible self," the latter reflecting the kind of person the client would like to become (Markus & Nurius, 1986). Murphy (2002) described how an individual can hold an idea or prototype of what kind of leader he or she should be as well as "an assessment of their specific leader abilities against this prototype" (p. 165). Thus, the leader prototype could be termed the possible self as leader while the latter could be labeled the actual self as leader (see Murphy, 2002). Coaching fundamentally entails helping clients develop specific attributes (knowledge, skills, abilities, attitudes) in a way that narrows the difference between some aspect of their possible and actual leader selves (Van Velsor & McCauley, 2004). As such, coaching evaluations should focus specifically on assessing whether such a narrowing has occurred.

The work and non-work networks of clients reflect those elements in their social contexts that may be influenced by the learning goals they pursue and the learning gains they accrue in the coaching process. The client's subordinates, peers, and supervisor all have a stake in the client's growth as a leader through coaching. Thus, as clients work on developing leadership competencies, any learning and skills gains should be reflected in the perceptions, and in some cases the behaviors, of their work colleagues. This means that as members of the client's work network become prominent as stakeholders in his or her coaching, their perceptions and behaviors need to be considered in a comprehensive coaching evaluation. For example, if a manager is working on delegation skills, then the subordinates to whom tasks are to be delegated are stakeholders in the coaching process, and their subsequent performance and motivation become necessary components of evaluations of that process. Similarly, for managers working on peer collaboration skills, peers become prime stakeholders, and their perceptions—as well as assessments of their subsequent collaborative work with the client—need to be included in coaching evaluations.

A client's work constituents are not the only social stakeholders in his or her coaching; concerns of friends and family can be reflected in the learning goals pursued by leaders in their coaching. For example, balancing work and family concerns can become an important issue in leader development, especially for women (Ruderman, 2004). Accordingly, the struggle to define and maintain an appropriate balance, or coming to terms with the failure to have such balance, can become a primal focus point in coaching (Grubb & Ting, 2006). As an example of this focus, Grubb and Ting (2006, 174) described a CEO in a coaching program who, in terms of receiving feedback, "was most anxious to learn if, in his children's eyes, the sacrifices he made to support his ambitions and their lifestyle were worth it. And with regard to his wife, he speculated nervously whether enough of their original relationship remained to survive their now empty nest." For this CEO, his family became important stakeholders in his coaching process; accordingly, they would need to be integrated in any assessment and evaluation of this executive's progress in coaching.

Coaches

Coaches are professionals who work one-on-one with clients for the purpose of improving clients' leadership effectiveness and job performance (Feldman & Lankau, 2005; Ting & Hart, 2004). As shown in Figure 12.3, the coach may have several proximal and distal stakes in a coaching engagement that would need to be considered in evaluations. First and foremost, coaches are present in such engagements as facilitators of client growth. Accordingly, coaching evaluation as a formative process should provide information that allows them to assess the progress that clients have made toward their goals and determine next steps for the coaching engagement (Ely et al., in press). Second, coaches are also present as personal business enterprises; they have an interest in building their own coaching portfolios in

Figure 12.3. Coach as Coaching Stakeholder

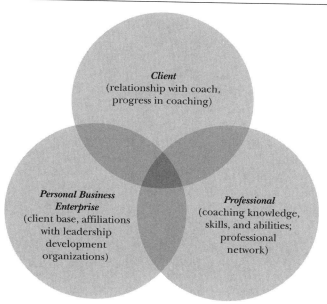

terms of a client base and affiliations with different leadership development organizations that may contract for their services. Thus, for coaches, a more longitudinal perspective in a coaching evaluation, or one that occurs across multiple clients, could focus on business growth and progress.

Coaches also bring to coaching engagements an amount of professional capital that includes their professional reputation as well as their knowledge, skills, and abilities in fostering leader development. This capital can also include their professional network of other coaches. Such capital can grow as coaches interact with and across multiple clients—they build their professional reputation based on clients' satisfaction with and results from the coaching engagements. However, they too can gain new knowledge and understanding from interactions with different clients. Each client may represent a new kind of leadership problem not previously encountered by the coach. Thus, the coach can gain new skills in helping clients address these different problems. Coaches can also acquire new "stories" or exemplars from their clients that can enrich and deepen their understanding of leadership. Finally, as coaches work with clients across different work or industry sectors, they gain knowledge and insights that can be useful in other coaching engagements from that sector.

A comprehensive coaching evaluation from the perspective of coaches could then include not only a focus on the quality of a specific coach-client relationship and the client's learning progress, but also on growth in their professional capital and business portfolio. Such a focus is, of course, much broader than the typical coaching evaluation, but no less important to the success and performance of the coach as a stakeholder in the coaching enterprise. An assessment of these professional and business elements of the coach would require different kinds of evaluation data and methods, a point we return to later in this chapter.

Client's Organization

The client's organization also represents a major stakeholder in a coaching engagement, and therefore in the coaching evaluation. Because clients' organizations pay for coaching engagements as a form of leadership development, their interests are primarily focused on evaluating the outcomes from their investment. Specifically, they are likely to be interested in documenting improvements in clients' performance as well as organizational level results such as retention and employee engagement. Figure 12.4 illustrates the various constituencies and issues that the client's organization may derive or be influenced by the client's involvement in coaching. First, the outcomes from clients' coaching interventions should be reflected in the performance and outcomes of their work units. We noted in our discussion of clients as stakeholders that subordinates, peers, and supervisors represent more distal aspects of their stake in coaching. We referred to these constituencies as beneficiaries of leadership learning by the client. Thus, we can evaluate coaching from the client perspective by assessing changes in how subordinates, peers, and supervisors perceive and behave toward the client. However, from the organization's perspective, if coaching has improved leadership skills of the client, then the total work unit should evidence a rise in performance to justify

Figure 12.4. Client's Organization as Coaching Stakeholder

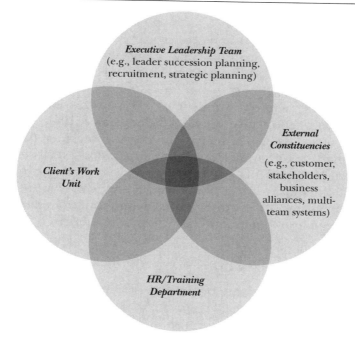

the investment made in coaching—from the perspective of the client's organization as a stakeholder, the unit of analysis rises from the individuals within the unit (including the client) to the work unit as a whole.

Client organizations ideally invest in leadership coaching from a strategic perspective, perhaps as part of leadership and executive succession programs (Grubb & Ting, 2006). In such instances, the executive team becomes a distal constituency in a comprehensive coaching evaluation—the success of a coaching investment may be tabulated in terms of rates of subsequent promotion into executive ranks of participants, increasing recruitment of other rising leaders into coaching-based succession programs, and, even more distally, the success of strategic planning. Also, because coaching programs are typically administered through human resources and training departments, the perceived success of these programs makes such departments important stakeholders in any comprehensive evaluation. Finally, an organization's external customers and clients may also be important distal stakeholders in coaching. For example, in service industries, growth in a client's leadership abilities should translate into better customer service.

These different constituencies represented in the client's organization point to the range of potential outcomes distal to the immediate coaching encounter. As noted, these may include reactions and behavioral outcomes of organizational members systematically connected to the leader-client. Other outcomes may include the performance of units as a whole, including units established to administer coaching programs, executive teams to whom leader-clients are expecting to ascend. Assessing these types of outcomes can provide organizations with comprehensive kinds of evidence that can help determine future levels of funding for similar or expanding leadership development efforts.

Coaching Organization

Two elements in coaching organizations can highlight their interests as stakeholders (see Figure 12.5). First, such entities have a stake in the coaching enterprise in terms of how their coaches and the coaching activities they deliver enhance the organization's client base. Moreover, the overall reputation of the company will rest ultimately on the aggregated range of industry expertise, level of coaching skills and reputation, and professional

Figure 12.5. Coaching Organization as Coaching Stakeholder

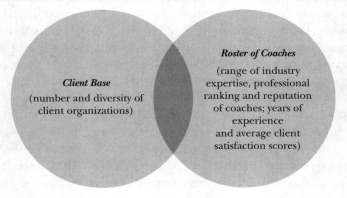

Client Base
(number and diversity of client organizations)

Roster of Coaches
(range of industry expertise, professional ranking and reputation of coaches; years of experience and average client satisfaction scores)

standing embodied in their pool of coaches. Coaching organizations also have an important stake in coaching evaluations to assess and improve the performance of their coaches. Accordingly, they are likely to be interested in evaluating clients' satisfaction and achievements to use as part of marketing efforts to promote their organization and gain additional clients. Additionally, coaching organizations would also be interested in documenting coaches' performance to provide coaches with feedback on their performance and to inform organizational decisions related to coach training and retention. Accordingly, these interests would be part of the drivers of a comprehensive coaching evaluation protocol.

Summary

We have described the various stakeholders and constituencies that may need to be considered in a coaching evaluation, noting that there can be considerable overlap in the kinds of information that would be targets of interest. Thus, as described, although many of these stakeholders are interested in the same outcomes, they may use assessments of these outcomes in different ways and for different reasons. For example, a client's progress toward meeting goals set in coaching would be an indicator of personal growth to the client, while the coach would use such data to help shape the focus of future coaching sessions. The client's organization would also be interested in the client's goal progress, but for the purposes of using the data as evidence of a return on their investment in leadership development. Understanding the stakeholders in an evaluation and their motivations are important for conducting a rigorous evaluation as it helps identify which criteria are critical to the evaluation as well as which data sources would be the most appropriate to include in the evaluation.

As noted in Figure 12.1, the identification of stakeholders to include in a coaching evaluation is a vital precursor to determining assessment criteria. Some evaluations may be limited to documenting client growth, whereas others may include assessment of gains accrued by the client organization. More comprehensive evaluations will include assessments of all four of these

330 ADVANCING EXECUTIVE COACHING

stakeholder groups, with these types of evaluations reflecting considerable inter-stakeholder complexity.

We have also noted that different stakeholders can represent varying degrees of complexity in terms of the constituencies influenced by their participation in a coaching enterprise. A client may work on reducing stress, improving work-life balance, managing conflict at work, developing subordinates, or developing strategic thinking skills. Each of these coaching goals affects different constituencies; accordingly, each affected person or group would need to be incorporated into a coaching evaluation protocol. As intra-stakeholder complexity increases in a coaching enterprise, the more comprehensive will be the necessary set of evaluation criteria.

Thus, we would argue that the initial steps in the construction of a coaching evaluation protocol would entail the following:

1. Determining which and how many stakeholder groups to include in the assessment.
2. Determining which interests of each stakeholder to include in the development of evaluation objectives and criteria.

Identifying Relevant Criteria

After identifying the evaluation stakeholders and determining the range of their interests in coaching evaluation, the next step is to choose the appropriate criteria based on stakeholders' needs. Selecting relevant criteria is a necessary precursor to a successful evaluation of leadership coaching, as the most carefully designed evaluation will "stand or fall on the basis of the adequacy of the criteria chosen" (Goldstein & Ford, 2002, 143). To address the unique aspects of leadership coaching, Ely et al. (in press) suggested that evaluation efforts should adopt a two-pronged approach that includes both formative and summative criteria (see also Beyer, 1995; Bhola, 1990; Brown & Gerhardt, 2002; Patton, 1994). The formative component focuses on process criteria and provides information on how to improve the quality of the coaching intervention (Beyer, 1995; Goldstein & Ford, 2002). Specifically, the formative component of a coaching evaluation examines aspects of the client, coach, client-coach relationship, and coaching process that contribute to the success of the coaching engagement. Formative evaluation data help the coach make adjustments in coaching processes to increase responsiveness to clients' needs in real time (Ely et al., in press).

The summative component of coaching evaluations focuses on assessing the effectiveness of completed interventions and includes more traditionally assessed training criteria. Kirkpatrick's four-level taxonomy (1976, 1994) of reactions, learning, behavior, and results was used to describe these criteria as they apply to coaching evaluations (see also Feldman & Lankau, 2005; Phillips & Phillips, 2007). In the next sections we summarize their discussion of these criteria, and elaborate on how such outcomes should be identified in the context of stakeholder complexity.

Reactions

In coaching evaluations, reaction data reflect clients' degrees of satisfaction and affect regarding their coaching experience (Ely et al., in press; Feldman & Landau, 2005). As such, they are most directly pertinent to the client as a stakeholder. Reactions from others such as the client's coworkers and supervisors that may be influenced by the client's leadership growth would be more indirect markers of client behavior change.

Reactions are typically the primary means by which organizations evaluate their training and development efforts (Sugrue & Rivera, 2005; Twitchell, Holton, & Trott, 2000). Studies that have examined reactions to coaching have generally found that clients experience high levels of satisfaction with coaching (Hall, Otazo, & Hollenbeck, 1999). Such criteria are also one of the easiest coaching outcomes to measure as they can be assessed with simple survey items using a Likert response scale. However, there are limits to the inferences that can be drawn from reactions data and research on training evaluation typically discourages using reactions as the sole evaluation criterion (Dipboye, 1997; Tannenbaum & Yukl, 1992). Specifically, reactions are not a strong predictor of post-training declarative or procedural knowledge (Sitzmann, Brown, Casper, Ely, & Zimmerman, 2008).

Reaction data are perhaps most useful in providing feedback on the coaching engagement. We have noted in our stakeholder analysis that reaction data from clients may have different uses for other stakeholder groups. For example, Ely et al. (in press) defined four dimensions of reactions that are relevant for coaching: the *coaching process, coach-client relationship, coach characteristics,* and *coaching effectiveness* (see Table 12.1). Coaches can use data from assessments of these reactions as part of a formative evaluation to gain valuable feedback on the client's perceptions of the coaching processes. However, to be effective, such assessments need to thoroughly cover the range of these processes. Ting and Hart (2004; see also Ting, 2006) provide a sampling of these processes, including matching coach and client, identifying client needs, developing effective learning goals and plans, challenging and supporting the client, and evaluating progress in meeting set goals. Table 12.1 includes some examples of reaction items to measure coaching progress.

Table 12.1. Dimensions of Reactions Relevant to Coaching Stakeholders

Dimension of Reactions	Sample Items to Assess Reactions
Coaching Process	My coach helped me establish effective learning goals. My coach helped me develop an effective learning plan. My coach helped me evaluate my progress in coaching. I am satisfied with the frequency of the coaching sessions. The assessments used helped me to identify my strengths and weaknesses.
Coach-Client Relationship	I have good rapport with my coach. My coach establishes a climate of trust. My coach motivates me to work on my leadership development. My coach is committed to my growth.

Dimension of Reactions	Sample Items to Assess Reactions
Coach Characteristics	My coach is knowledgeable about my industry.
	My coach has good communication skills.
	My coach has an excellent understanding about leadership and leader development.
	I would recommend my coach to other leaders for coaching.
Coaching Effectiveness	Overall, I am satisfied with my coaching engagement.
	I am enthusiastic about my coaching experience.
	I would recommend leadership coaching for other individuals in my company.
	Coaching has provided me with knowledge, skills, and insights that will help as I advance in my career.
	I intend to continue my leadership coaching.

One example of a scale that could be adapted for a formative evaluation is a scale of coaching effectiveness developed by Smither et al. (2003). The scale examines clients' perceptions of different coaching behaviors such as the degree to which the coach has helped the client to interpret feedback results; linked feedback to client's business plans; offered suggestions, advice, and insight for setting developmental goals; and identified ways to solicit ideas for improvement from others. When administered early in the coaching engagement, the coach can use the information as feedback to inform future coaching behaviors.

Client reaction data can also have considerable importance to client organizations as a means of attracting and motivating other rising leaders to participate in coaching. Likewise, coaches and coaching organizations can often use such data as performance evaluations and for marketing purposes. Accordingly, items in a coaching reaction survey should be carefully worded to offer insight on the characteristics of the coach, and the client's perceptions regarding the value of the program for leader development. Coaching organizations can use responses about coach characteristics to evaluate the breadth of skills and knowledge in their coaching pool, and to market the overall quality of their coaches. Client organizations can use client perceptions about coaching effectiveness to motivate other potential candidates for coaching. Table 12.1 shows sample items of particular interest to these stakeholder groups.

Learning

When evaluating learning outcomes from leadership coaching, it is important to adopt a multidimensional conceptualization that accounts for both cognitive and affective learning outcomes (Kraiger, Ford, & Salas, 1993). Cognitive learning includes changes in knowledge structures and cognitive strategies, while affective learning is defined as changes in attitudes and motivation (Kraiger et al., 1993). Ely et al. (in press) noted that, within the context of leadership coaching, cognitive flexibility and self-awareness represent two critical client cognitive outcomes, whereas two key affective outcomes are self-efficacy and job attitudes (Diedrich, 1996; International Coach Federation, 1998; Schlosser, Steinbrenner, Kumata, & Hunt, 2006; Wasylyshyn, 2003).

Self-Awareness

Self-awareness refers to individuals' ability to reflect on, and accurately assess, their own knowledge, skills, and behaviors (Church, 1997). The assessment phase of the coaching relationship is designed to directly improve a client's self-awareness—leading to changed attitudes regarding self, work, and family (Dingman, 2004; Ely et al., in press; Van Velsor, Moxley, & Bunker, 2004). Indeed, self-awareness is one of the first outcomes that coaching seeks to improve (Dingman, 2004; Feldman & Lankau, 2005; Hall et al., 1999; Wasylyshyn, 2003).

Many coaching engagements begin with some form of 360-degree assessment (Ting & Hart, 2004), which is one of the best approaches to developing a client's self-awareness of strengths and weaknesses (Craig & Hannum, 2007; Feldman & Lankau, 2005). As clients' self-awareness grows, they increase their understanding of their strengths, weaknesses, needs, and internal drivers (Ting & Hart, 2004). Without an accurate perception of their current skill set and how they are perceived by others, clients might not see the need to engage in coaching to learn new skills or improve their leadership performance (Dingman, 2004). This suggests that self-awareness should be assessed throughout coaching as part of the formative component of the evaluation—early on to help establish client readiness for coaching and throughout coaching to assess changes in self-awareness.

Despite the theoretical importance of self-awareness to the coaching process, very few studies are measuring self-awareness in a way that reflects a rigorous approach to evaluation (for an exception see Luthans & Peterson, 2003). Specifically, most studies that examine self-awareness post-coaching tend to ask clients to rate their self-awareness or the degree to which their self-awareness increased (see Seamons, 2004). A more rigorous approach to evaluating self-awareness would involve comparing changes in a client's perception of his or her strengths and weaknesses with the perceptions of knowledgeable others such as supervisors, peers, and subordinates (Craig & Hannum, 2007). These ratings of self-other agreement are important to leadership development and have been linked to leader effectiveness (Atwater & Yammarino, 1992). We note that this approach is often used at the beginning of coaching to help clients understand their strengths and weaknesses (Feldman & Lankau, 2005), however a few studies have documented the level of agreement between clients' perceptions and the perceptions of others later in coaching or post-coaching as a coaching outcome (see Luthans & Peterson, 2003).

Cognitive Flexibility

Coaching has been promoted as a development technique to grow leaders' ability to adapt to changing circumstances (Diedrich, 1996; Jones, Rafferty, & Griffin, 2006). Part of this ability includes cognitive flexibility, or an ability to explore a variety of different approaches and cognitive frames of reference with respect to organizational problems (Griffin & Hesketh, 2003; Raudsepp, 1990).

Two examples of scales that have been used to assess cognitive flexibility in coaching were offered by Jones et al. (2006) and Finn, Mason, and Bradley (2007). Jones and colleagues developed a ten-item flexibility scale designed to assess leaders' proactivity (planning ahead rather than reacting to a situation), adaptability (changing your personal approach for the situation at hand), and resilience (maintaining productivity in challenging circumstances). Similarly, Finn and colleagues developed a four-item scale designed to measure the degree that leaders examine their current strategies and consider alternative strategies ("I step back and consider different approaches to running my team").

Jones et al. (2006) found that clients' flexibility significantly increased pre- to post-coaching using the ten-item scale and a repeated measures design. Finn et al. (2007) found that leaders who received coaching had significantly higher levels of flexibility toward new behaviors than leaders who had not received coaching. Taken together, these findings provide support for the effect of coaching on cognitive flexibility and suggest that assessing changes in cognitive flexibility throughout coaching can provide evidence of coaching effectiveness.

Self-Efficacy

Self-efficacy in this context refers to the confidence clients have that they can use newly acquired leadership skills (Kraiger et al., 1993). Researchers have posited that coaches can strengthen the client's self-efficacy by providing them with a safe environment to practice new skills and receive feedback (Berthal, Cook, & Smith, 2001). Throughout the coaching engagement, the coach provides the client with positive communication and feedback—expressing confidence in the client's ability to succeed which in turn build's the client's self-efficacy (Hall et al., 1999; Kampa-Kokesch & Anderson, 2001).

Research on coaching has highlighted the use of self-efficacy measures in evaluations. For example, in a series of qualitative interviews conducted with twenty-four executive directors who had undergone training, many of the clients noted that participating in coaching had increased their confidence in exercising leadership as well as their confidence in leading the organization toward fulfilling its vision (CompassPoint, 2003). Similarly, Kombarakaran, Yang, Baker, and Fernandes (2008) surveyed 114 executives in a large multinational corporation who had received coaching over a six-month period and found that 72 percent reported that coaching had increased their confidence. In a recent empirical study, Finn, Mason, and Bradley (2007) found that managers who received coaching had significantly higher self-efficacy levels than managers who had not received coaching. Taken together, this suggests that self-efficacy is a key outcome of leadership coaching and its assessment should have a prominent role in evaluating coaching programs.

Job Attitudes

Job attitudes refer to how positively or negatively employees respond to aspects of their employment, including their job satisfaction and organizational commitment (Hulin & Judge, 2003). Depending on the goals of leadership coaching efforts, assessing changes in clients' job attitudes may be an important indicator of coaching effectiveness. For example, when coaching is framed as an investment in clients' development, clients likely perceive that their organizations value them—influencing their attitude toward their job and organization. As such, some of the relevant outcomes from coaching engagements may be changes in organizational commitment and job satisfaction (Dingman, 2004; Luthans & Peterson, 2003).

For example, in a survey of forty-three coaching participants, Anderson (2001) found that 53 percent of participants noted that participating in coaching had a positive effect on job satisfaction. Similarly, Luthans and Peterson (2003) conducted a study of twenty managers from a small manufacturing company who underwent a three-month coaching engagement and found clients' job satisfaction and organizational commitment significantly increased pre- to post-coaching.

Learning Outcomes of Coaches

Thus far, we have emphasized the learning outcomes of clients. However, we noted that coaches as stakeholders in the coaching enterprise may also acquire new skills and knowledge as they help clients confront different and novel kinds of leadership problems. As they work across different business sectors, coaches also increase their industry-specific knowledge. A comprehensive evaluation of a coaching enterprise, especially from the perspective of coaching organizations, could entail assessments of such knowledge gains. Kraiger et al. (1993) discuss the concept of assessing knowledge and knowledge organization in the context of training through changes in trainee mental models. Similar methods can be applied to the assessment of gains in coaches' knowledge and understanding of leadership issues and different work sectors. We note that (a) such assessments ought to occur using a longitudinal perspective after coaches have worked with many clients and (b) such assessment would likely be of most interest to coaching organizations as they seek to showcase the collective knowledge and skills of their coaching pool.

Behavior

The majority of coaching engagements are initiated with the ultimate goal of clients making behavioral changes (Wasylyshyn, 2003). Although the goals of coaching engagements are specific based on the needs of the client, general behavioral coaching goals include initiating personal behavior change, enhancing leader effectiveness, and fostering stronger relationships (Wasylyshyn, 2003). Indeed, measures that focus on clients' engagements in key behaviors are one of the most frequently assessed coaching outcomes (Ely et al., in press). However, many of these studies relied on self-report data from the client.

As the field moves toward more rigorous approaches of coaching evaluation, studies need to supplement self-report client data with assessments from other organizational constituents (such as supervisors, peers, direct reports). Indeed, several researchers have shown evidence of the effectiveness of coaching engagements using multisource ratings. For example, Thach (2002) examined the effects of a coaching intervention on 281 executives and high-potential managers within a telecommunications organization. Behavioral change was assessed with a survey distributed to clients' peers, supervisors, and direct reports that asked them to report the percentage increase in the clients' leadership effectiveness. Across all three sources, raters reported that clients' leadership effectiveness increased between 55 and 63 percent.

Smither and colleagues (2003) collected multisource data on clients' behaviors pre- and post-coaching from their peers, supervisors, and direct reports. In designing the rating form, some of the items were assessed by all three types of raters (for example, "Respectfully confronts problematic behavior"), while some items were only appropriate for certain raters (such as direct reports, "Provides clear goals, written performance appraisals, and follow-up discussions annually"; or supervisors ("Takes calculated risks needed to achieve results"). Smither et al. found that, compared with other managers, clients who worked with a coach exhibited significantly larger improvements in their behavioral ratings from direct reports and supervisors, although the improvement in behavioral ratings from peers was not significant.

Results

Results refer to the degree to which the coaching program meets the organization's objectives (Kirkpatrick, 1976). The challenge in using results data as part of a rigorous coaching evaluation is identifying metrics that are likely to be influenced by leadership coaching. As leadership involves influencing others (Kaiser, Hogan, & Craig, 2008), assessing results from leadership coaching requires a systems-level perspective that accounts for influences on the entire organization (Ely et al., in press; Grove et al., 2006). Our earlier analysis of the client organization as a stakeholder suggests that important results measures might include employee (that is, the client) retention, subordinate job satisfaction and performance, work unit performance, and customer satisfaction. When coaching is part of a leader succession strategy, then longer-term data to be considered in a comprehensive coaching evaluation would include client promotion to executive ranks, and the effectiveness of former coaching participants in those ranks.

The individualized nature of coaching makes this form of leadership development a more expensive approach than more traditional development approaches. Indeed, researchers have noted the need to justify the expense of coaching by demonstrating the financial value to the organization (Waslyshyn, 2003). Accordingly, several researchers and practitioners have tried calculating its return on investment (ROI) (see, for example, Anderson, 2001; Fisher, 2001; McGovern et al., 2001; Parker-Wilkins, 2006; Phillips, 2007). Indeed, most of the concerns of client organizations as stakeholders in coaching enterprises center on evaluating and establishing ROI.

A traditional ROI calculation involves comparing the monetary benefits received from coaching to the cost of coaching expressed as a percentage (Wise & Voss, 2002). Using this formula, Parker-Wilkins (2006) calculated an average ROI of 689 percent. Specifically, Parker-Wilkins asked clients to place a monetary value on the benefits derived from coaching in eight business impact areas—improved teamwork, team member satisfaction, increased retention, increased productivity, increased quality of consulting, accelerated promotions, increased client satisfaction, and increased diversity—and compared the total monetary benefits across the eight business impact areas ($3,268,325) with the cost of coaching ($414,310). Others have used a similar approach and calculated coaching ROIs, finding percentages of 221 percent (Phillips, 2007), 416 percent (Fisher, 2001), 529 percent (Anderson, 2001), and 570 percent (McGovern et al., 2001).

In interpreting these numbers, it is important to note that many of these studies collect the data directly from the clients and are based on the clients' estimates of the business impact of coaching (Fillery-Travis & Lane, 2006). Some have criticized this approach because the complexity of leaders' operating environments makes it challenging to identify direct impacts of coaching engagements on business outcomes (Levenson, 2009). Additionally, not all of the benefits of coaching can have quantifiable financial benefits. For example, Anderson (2001) found that clients could not quantify financial benefits for employee satisfaction, customer satisfaction, and work quality. Schlosser and colleagues (2006) have also cautioned against overgeneralizing from ROI calculations. Specifically, they note that some clients are in positions to have a more significant impact on areas that are of high financial importance to their organization. This is consistent with findings from Anderson (2001), who found that clients with customer or people responsibilities produced proportionally higher financial returns. As such, ROI calculations based on these individuals' coaching experiences may overestimate the ROI for clients in other organizational positions.

Instead of placing monetary values on outcomes, some researchers have focused on asking clients to make comparative judgments of the value of coaching compared to the costs. For example, Seamons (2004) found that 88 percent of participants said they found coaching to be of value when compared to the cost. Similarly, Kombarakaran et al. (2008) found that 73 percent of clients in one organization believed that the "time spent on coaching was a good return on investment" (81). Although these are not traditional ROI calculations—and should not be interpreted as evidence of traditional ROI—they do provide a starting point for investigations examining the value of coaching.

Selecting Appropriate Methodologies

The next step in a coaching evaluation protocol is to select appropriate methodologies for information and data gathering. This includes *identifying data sources, collecting data across organizational levels,* and *incorporating qualitative methods.* Each of these is described in greater detail in the following sections.

Identifying Data Sources

When conducting formative and summative coaching evaluations, many different sources can be used to garner evaluation data. Choosing the right data sources depends on the goals and needs of evaluation for different stakeholder groups. Moreover, each stakeholder group can provide different types of data for an evaluation. The following sections outline three potential data sources—clients, coaches, and constituents from clients' organizations—and the types of evaluation criteria that each source can provide.

Clients

As we have noted, the majority of coaching evaluation research relies on self-report data from the clients (Ely et al., in press). This is not surprising, as coaching engagements are tailored to the needs of the client—making the client well suited to provide key evaluation data related to reactions and learning outcomes. However, past research suggests that for some criteria, relying solely on self-report may not be appropriate (Kruger & Dunning, 1999; Sitzmann, Ely, Brown, & Bauer, in press). Specifically, leaders' self-ratings of their own behaviors tend to be higher than others' ratings of their behaviors (Atwater & Yammarino, 1992; Fleenor, McCauley, & Brutus, 1996). For these types of criteria, evaluation efforts should focus as well on data from other relevant sources, such as organizational constituents.

Coaches

Several coaching evaluation studies have incorporated data from coaches (Kombarakaran et al., 2008; Levenson, 2009). For example, Bowles, Cunningham, De La Rosa, and Picano (2007) used data from coaches to assess clients' engagement in coaching—rating clients' involvement in coaching activities, initiative in contacting the coach, attendance at scheduled coaching meetings, and openness to receiving and acting on coach-related feedback. Other studies have used coaches to provide behavior-level data. Specifically, Kombarakaran et al. (2008) surveyed forty-two coaches after they had completed a six-month coaching engagement—working with 114 executives in a large, multinational corporation. Results of their evaluation indicated that the coaches perceived positive change in their clients' behaviors. However, just as clients may be biased in self-reporting changes in their own performance, coaches may also be biased in reporting on changes in their clients' performance (Levenson, 2009). Specifically, if the coach and client establish a strong relationship, the coach may have difficulty in being objective about the client's performance. Thus, data sources ought to include others outside of the coach-client relationship.

Organizational Constituents

Organizational constituents are other members of clients' organizations that can provide insight or data related to the impact of coaching. This can include clients' subordinates, peers, and supervisors, as well as human resources departments who maintain organizational records (McDermott, Levenson, & Newton, 2007). For evaluating behavioral outcomes, accurate assessment requires choosing organizational constituents who have regular interactions with the client and can speak to changes in behavior relevant to the coaching objectives. Also, using data from multiple organizational constituents can enhance the validity of evaluations by allowing for triangulation across sources (Tesluk, 2008). For example, having five direct reports indicate that the client has increased his transformational leadership behaviors over the past six months provides more compelling evidence of the effectiveness of coaching than having the same data from one direct report. Similarly, if two people provide conflicting data, having additional data points can help to clarify how the majority of people would rate the client's behavior. However, we note that some data sources can have necessarily different interactions with the client that create different perspectives of his or her behaviors (such as supervisors versus direct reports). In such situations, one may not expect the data sources to necessarily agree on the client's behavior; but rather, when the data sources are viewed together they provide a more complete picture of the client's behavior in the organization.

Collecting Data Across Organizational Levels

Evaluating leadership coaching requires the adoption of a systems-level perspective—attending not only to the influence on the leader's performance, but also to the influence of coaching on the organization as a whole (Ely et al., in press; Grove et al., 2006). Indeed, when organizations invest in leadership development, they are expecting improvements in leadership effectiveness that will then influence other important organizational variables (Levenson, 2009). As such, rigorous evaluations of coaching need to attend to a range of multilevel leadership criteria, including subordinate-level outcomes such as work motivation, job satisfaction, and satisfaction with the leader, as well as assessments of changes in work group productivity or quality of outputs (Kaiser et al., 2008). For example, Parker-Wilkins (2006) found that 54 percent of leaders cited subordinate satisfaction as being affected by changes in leader behaviors that resulted from coaching; however, subordinate satisfaction was not directly assessed in the study. In order to conduct more rigorous evaluations, future efforts need to adopt a multilevel perspective of outcomes from leadership coaching that includes trickle-down effects of changes in clients' leadership behaviors on important subordinate outcomes such as job attitudes, performance, and retention.

Incorporating Qualitative Methods

Much of the training evaluation literature focuses on quantitative outcomes. However, because coaching is an individual experience, with different clients having different targeted learning goals, it is also well suited to the use of qualitative methods that can focus more deeply on the coaching process of a limited sample of participants. Indeed, many coaching studies have incorporated qualitative methods such as case studies and interviewing when evaluating coaching.

As noted by Steinbrenner, Kumata, and Schlosser (2007), the value of coaching is not something that can be fully described by any one methodological approach. Indeed, qualitative and quantitative methods can complement each other to provide a more complete evaluation of leadership coaching (Tesluk, 2008). Qualitative interviews can be used to gather stories and probe deeper into coaching engagements to understand some of the factors that lead to more, or less, successful coaching engagements (Steinbrenner et al., 2007). Qualitative data can be used to augment traditional quantitative data by providing a richer source of data about the coaching relationship and the factors that individual clients perceive that hinder or facilitate achievement of their coaching goals.

Summary and Conclusion

As coaching continues to mature as an approach to leadership development, coaching evaluations must also mature—with researchers and practitioners conducting more rigorous evaluations. This chapter elaborated on three essential components of an integrated coaching evaluation—identifying evaluation stakeholders, choosing formative and summative criteria, and selecting appropriate methodologies. Together these three components form the foundation of a rigorous coaching evaluation.

Identifying evaluation stakeholders is a critical first step as it drives the selection of evaluation criteria and provides insight as to the motivations and biases that might influence the evaluation. Based on the needs of the stakeholders, the next step is to select the relevant formative and summative criteria. Formative criteria allow for the identification of areas for improving the coaching process, while summative criteria facilitate evaluations of the effectiveness of the coaching engagement. The final step is to select the appropriate methodologies to collect the relevant data that is of interest to the stakeholders. This includes identifying appropriate data sources, such as clients, coaches, and organizational constituents, adopting a multilevel perspective, and considering the benefits of incorporating qualitative methods. In laying out this multistep protocol for coaching evaluations, we hope that more researchers and practitioners will conduct systematic and rigorous assessments to help further the research and practice of leadership coaching.

References

Anderson, M. C. (2001). Executive briefing: Case study on the return on investment of executive coaching. Retrieved March 12, 2008, from www.coachfederation.org/NR/ rdonlyres/16C73602–871A–43B8–9703–2C4D4D79BDAB/7720/053metrixglobal_coaching_roi_briefing.pdf.

Atwater, L., & Yammarino, F. (1992). Does self-other agreement on leadership perceptions moderate the validity of leadership and performance predictions? *Personnel Psychology, 45*, 141–164.

Berthal, P., Cook, K., & Smith, A. (2001). Needs and outcomes in an executive development program, a matter of perspective. *Journal of Applied Behavioral Science, 37*, 488–512.

Beyer, B. K. (1995). *How to conduct a formative evaluation.* Alexandria, VA: Association for Supervision and Curriculum Development.

Bhola, H. S. (1990). *Evaluating "literacy for development" projects, programs and campaigns: Evaluation planning, design and implementation, and utilization of evaluation results.* Hamburg, Germany: UNESCO Institute for Education.

Bowles, S., Cunningham, C.J.L., De La Rosa, G. M., & Picano, J. (2007). Coaching leaders in middle and executive management: goals, performance, and buy-in. *Leadership & Organization Development Journal, 28*, 388–408.

Brown, K. G., & Gerhardt, M. W. (2002). Formative evaluation: An integrative practice model and case study. *Personnel Psychology, 55*, 951–983.

Church, A. H. (1997). Managerial self-awareness in high-performing individuals in organizations. *Journal of Applied Psychology, 82*, 281–292.

CompassPoint. (2003). *Executive coaching project: Evaluation of findings.* Retrieved March 12, 2008, from www.compasspoint.org/assets/ 2_cpcoachingexecsumm.pdf.

Craig, S. B., & Hannum, K. M. (2007). Experimental and quasi-experimental evaluations. In K. M. Hannum, *The handbook of leadership development evaluation.* Hoboken, NJ: Wiley.

Diedrich, R. C. (1996). An interactive approach to executive coaching. *Consulting Psychology Journal: Practice and Research, 48,* 61–66.

Dingman, M. E. (2004). The effects of executive coaching on job-related attitudes. Unpublished doctoral dissertation. Regent University, Virginia Beach, VA.

Dipboye, R. (1997). Organizational barriers to implementing a rational model of training. In M. Quiñones & A. Ehrenstein (Eds.), *Training for a rapidly changing workforce* (119–148). Washington, DC: American Psychological Association.

Drath, W. H., & Van Velsor, E. (2006). Constructive-developmental coaching. In S. Ting, & P. Scisco (Eds.), *The CCL handbook of coaching: A guide for the leader coach.* San Francisco: Jossey-Bass.

Ely, K., Boyce, L. A., Nelson, J. K., Zaccaro, S. J., Hernez-Broome, G., & Whyman, W. (2010). Evaluating leadership coaching: A review and integrated framework. *Leadership Quarterly, 21*(4), 585–599.

Feldman, D. C., & Lankau, M. J. (2005). Executive coaching: A review and agenda for future research. *Journal of Management, 31,* 829–848.

Fillery-Travis, A., & Lane, D. (2006). Does coaching work or are we asking the wrong question? *International Coaching Psychology Review, 1,* 23–36.

Finn, F. A., Mason, C. M., & Bradley, L. M. (2007, August). Doing well with executive coaching: Psychological and behavioral impacts. Presented at the Academy of Management Conference, Philadelphia, PA.

Fisher, A. (2001). Executive coaching—With returns a CFO could love. *Fortune 143*(4), 250.

Fleenor, J. W., McCauley, C. D., & Brutus, S. (1996). Self-other rating agreement and leader effectiveness. *Leadership Quarterly, 7,* 487–506.

Goldstein, I. L., & Ford, J. K. (2002). *Training in organizations: Needs assessment, development, and evaluation.* Belmont, CA: Wadsworth.

Griffin, B., & Hesketh, B. (2003). Adaptable behaviours for successful work and career adjustment. *Australian Journal of Psychology, 55,* 65–73.

Grove, J. T., Kibel, B. M., & Haas, T. (2006). EvaluLEAD: An open-systems perspective on evaluating leadership development.

In K. M. Hannum, J. W. Martineau, C. Reinelt, & L. C. Leviton (Eds.), *The handbook of leadership development evaluation* (pp. 71–110). San Francisco: Jossey-Bass.

Grubb, T., & Ting, S. (2006). Coaching senior leaders. In S. Ting & P. Scisco (Eds.). *The CCL handbook of coaching: A guide for the leader coach* (pp. 149–176). San Francisco: Jossey-Bass.

Hall, D. T., Otazo, K. L., & Hollenbeck, G. P. (1999). Behind closed doors: What really happens in executive coaching. *Organizational Dynamics, 27*(3), 39–53.

Hulin, C. L., & Judge, T. A. (2003). Job attitudes. In W. C. Borman, D. R. Ilgen, & R. J. Klimoski (Eds.), *Handbook of psychology: Industrial and organizational psychology* (pp. 255–276). Hoboken, NJ: Wiley.

International Coach Federation. (1998). Client survey results and press release: Analysis of the 1998 survey of coaching clients by the International Coach Federation. Retrieved March 12, 2008. From www.coachfederation.org.

Jones, R. A., Rafferty, A. E., & Griffin, M. A. (2006). The executive coaching trend: Towards more flexible executives. *Leadership and Organizational Development Journal, 27*, 584–596.

Kaiser, R. B., Hogan, R., & Craig, S. B. (2008). Leadership and the fate of organizations. *American Psychologist, 63*(2), 96–110.

Kampa-Kokesch, S., & Anderson, M. Z. (2001). Executive coaching: A comprehensive review of the literature. *Consulting Psychology Journal: Practice and Research, 53*, 205–228.

Kirkpatrick, D. L. (1976). Evaluation of training. In R. L. Craig (Ed.), *Training and development handbook: A guide to human resource development* (2nd ed., pp. 1–27). New York: McGraw-Hill.

Kirkpatrick, D. L. (1994). *Evaluating training programs: The four levels.* San Francisco: Berrett-Koehler.

Kombarakaran, F. A., Yang, J. A., Baker, M. N., & Fernandes, P. B. (2008). Executive coaching: It works! *Consulting Psychology Journal: Practice and Research, 60*, 78–90.

Kraiger, K., Ford, J. K., & Salas, E. (1993). Application of cognitive, skill-based, and affective theories of learning outcomes to new methods of training evaluation. *Journal of Applied Psychology, 78*, 311–328.

Kruger, J., & Dunning, D. (1999). Unskilled and unaware of it: How difficulties in recognizing one's own incompetence lead to inflated self-assessments. *Journal of Personality and Social Psychology, 77*, 1121–1134.

Levenson, A. (2009). Measuring and maximizing the business impact of executive coaching. *Consulting Psychology Journal: Practice and Research, 61*, 103–121.

Luthans, F., & Peterson, S. J. (2003). 360 degree feedback with systematic coaching: Empirical analysis suggests a winning combination. *Human Resource Management, 42*, 243–256.

Markus, H., & Nurius, P. (1986). Possible selves. *American Psychologist, 41*, 954–969.

McDermott, M., Levenson, A., & Newton, S. (2007). What coaching can and cannot do for your organization. *Human Resource Planning, 30*, 30–37.

McGovern, J., Lindemann, M., Vergara, M., Murphy, S., Barker, L., & Warrenfeltz, R. (2001). Maximizing the impact of executive coaching: Behavioral change, organizational outcomes, and return on investment. *The Manchester Review, 6*, 1–9.

Murphy, S. E. (2002). Leader self-regulation: The role of self-efficacy and multiple intelligences. In R. E. Riggio, S. E. Murphy, & F. J. Pirozzolo (Eds.), *Multiple intelligences and leadership* (pp. 162–186). Mahwah, NJ: Lawrence Erlbaum.

Parker-Wilkins, V. (2006). Business impact of executive coaching: Demonstrating monetary value. *Industrial and Commercial Training, 38*(3), 122–127.

Patton, M. (1994). Developmental evaluation. *Evaluation Practice, 15*, 347–358.

Phillips, J. J. (2007). Measuring the ROI of a coaching intervention, Part 2. *Performance Improvement, 46*(10), 10–23.

Phillips, J. J., & Phillips, P. P. (2007). Show me the money: The use of ROI in performance improvement, Part 1. *Performance Improvement, 46*(9), 8–22.

Raudsepp, E. (1990). Are you flexible enough to succeed? *Manage, 42*(2), 6–10.

Ruderman, M. N. (2004). Leader development across gender. In McCauley, C. D., & Velsor, E. V. (Eds.), *Handbook of Leadership Development* (2nd ed., pp. 271–303). San Francisco: Jossey-Bass.

Schlosser, B., Steinbrenner, D., Kumata, E., & Hunt, J. (2006). The coaching impact study: Measuring the value of executive coaching. *International Journal of Coaching in Organizations, 4*(3), 8–26.

Seamons, B. L. (2004). The most effective factors in executive coaching engagements according to the coach, the client, and the client's boss. Unpublished doctoral dissertation, Saybrook Graduate School and Research Center, San Francisco, CA.

Sitzmann, T., Brown, K. G., Casper, W. J., Ely, K., & Zimmerman, R. D. (2008). A review and meta-analysis of the nomological network of trainee reactions. *Journal of Applied Psychology, 93*, 280–295.

Sitzmann, T., Ely, K., Brown, K. G., & Bauer, K. N. (in press). Self-assessment of knowledge: A cognitive learning or affective measure? *Academy of Management Learning and Education*.

Smither, J. W., London, M., Flautt, R., Vargas, Y., & Kucine, I. (2003). Can working with an executive coach improve multisource feedback ratings over time? A quasi-experimental study. *Personnel Psychology, 56*, 23–44.

Steinbrenner, D., Kumata, E., & Schlosser, B. (2007). Commentary on the coaching impact study: Measuring the value of executive coaching. *International Journal of Coaching in Organizations, 5*(1), 158–161.

Sugrue B., & Rivera R. J. (2005). *State of the industry: ASTD's annual review of trends in workplace learning and performance.* Alexandria, VA: American Society for Training and Development.

Tannenbaum, S. I., & Yukl, G. (1992). Training and development in work organizations. *Annual Review of Psychology, 43*, 399–441.

Tesluk, P. (2008, October). Meeting the call for rigorous and useful coaching evaluation: Unique challenges and optimal approaches to executive coaching evaluation. Presented at the 2008 SIOP Leading Edge Consortium, Executive coaching for effective performance: Leading edge practice and research. Cincinnati, OH.

Thach, E. (2002). The impact of executive coaching and 360 feedback on leadership effectiveness. *Leadership and Organization Development Journal, 23*(3 and 4), 205–214.

Ting, S. (2006). Our view of coaching for leader development. In S. Ting & P. Scisco (Eds.), *The CCL handbook of coaching: A guide for the leader coach* (pp. 15–33). San Francisco: Jossey-Bass.

Ting, S., & Hart, E. W. (2004). Formal coaching. In C. D. McCauley & E. Van Velsor (Eds.), *The Center for Creative Leadership handbook of leadership development* (pp. 116–150). San Francisco: Jossey-Bass.

Twitchell, K., Holton, E., & Trott, J. W., (2000). Technical training evaluation practices in the United States. *Performance Improvement Quarterly, 13*, 84–109.

Van Velsor, E., & McCauley, C. (2004). Our view of leadership development. In E. Van Velsor & McCauley, C. (Eds.), *The Center for Creative Leadership handbook of leadership development* (pp. 1–22). San Francisco: Jossey-Bass.

Van Velsor, E., Moxley, R. S., & Bunker, K. A. (2004). The leader development process. In E. Van Velsor & McCauley, C. (Eds.), *The Center for Creative Leadership handbook of leadership development* (pp. 204–233). San Francisco: Jossey-Bass.

Wasylyshyn, K. M. (2003). Executive coaching: An outcome study. *Consulting Psychology Journal: Practice and Research, 55*, 94–106.

Wise, P., & Voss, L. (2002). The case for executive coaching, a research report from the Lore Research Institute.

Chapter Thirteen

EVALUATING THE ROI OF COACHING

Telling a Story, Not Just Producing a Number

Merrill C. Anderson

Taking a Coaching Approach to ROI

ROI—return on investment—has recently taken on a negative connotation for many practitioners in the field of learning and coaching. Evaluating ROI for coaching initiatives is viewed as time-consuming, expensive, and difficult to do, akin to setting up a big science experiment in an organization with variables, statistics, equations and working with dreaded spreadsheets. Now though it's true that some in the field of evaluation do approach ROI in this way, it does not have to be this way. In fact, taking a *coaching approach* to ROI evaluation not only offers an alternative approach to the "science experiment," it is a more powerful approach that has proven to be faster, cheaper, and easier to do.

What does taking a coaching approach mean? It means asking the right questions and constructing a story of value creation. We look at value creation as the impact of coaching in terms of both tangible and intangible benefits. Evaluation methodology then becomes a structured process of reflection for telling the value story through conversations. In part, people think that ROI evaluation is difficult because they do not know the right questions to ask. People who have been coached generally love to tell their stories. Taking a coaching approach means asking questions of those who have been coached and giving them a platform to tell their stories. The following example illustrates the point.

Evaluating the ROI of Coaching in a Government Agency

Michelle had been very pleased about how well the coaching initiative had been received in her department. The first eighteen section managers had mostly completed their initial eight months of coaching, and though there had been a few hiccups at first, most everyone felt that they gained value from their coaching relationships. Being a government agency, there was some initial hesitation from her boss, Barry, the department head, about how well coaching would translate to the public sector. Specifically, most of the section heads seemed "set in their ways" and not very open to new ideas or approaches.

In fact, Michelle felt so positive about the coaching that she was going to recommend to Barry to expand the initiative to other managers and even supervisors in the department. The unsolicited feedback she got from the participants was almost uniformly positive and she was sure that others would gain value as well. So imagine her surprise when she met with Barry, sharing her idea to expand coaching, and her proposal was met with a cool reception and skepticism. First of all, Michelle assumed that Barry was also hearing about the positive feedback, which turned out not to be the case. People felt more comfortable coming to Michelle, who after all was the project manager and was the right person to receive the feedback. Second, Michelle was not prepared to fully answer three key questions that Barry posed to her:

1. What did people really learn from their coaching experience?

2. What are people doing differently as a result of what they learned?

3. What impact did these actions have on the organization?

Budgets, of course, were tight and proposals for investment and resources were being met with added scrutiny throughout the government. Barry suggested to Michelle that she build a stronger business case for expanding the coaching initiative and come back to him again. Michelle was not quite sure how best to proceed to answer Barry's three questions and build the business case. She turned to her agency's organization effectiveness (OE) group to sort out what she needed to do. As luck would have it, Sana, one of the OE consultants, did have experience in evaluation and change.

Designing and Piloting the ROI Evaluation

Michelle shared her predicament with Sana and asked her for some ideas about how best to proceed. Sana suggested that Michelle arrange a time to meet with each manager who was coached, something that Michelle had been planning to do anyway but kept putting off. Building from the questions that Barry had posed earlier, Sana suggested the following questions be incorporated into Michelle's conversations with the managers who were coached:

1. What were your key learnings?
2. How did you apply what you learned?
3. What impact did these actions have?
4. How much of this impact would you attribute directly to the coaching you received?
5. How confident are you in this estimate?

Michelle reviewed these questions and had some questions herself. First, she asked Sana about the "impact" question, specifically: "What kind of impact are we looking for?" Sana replied that, typically, the answer to this question comes from the objectives for the coaching initiative or from the expectations of sponsors and stakeholders. Sana then asked Michelle what these objectives and expectations were. Michelle paused before she answered and rather meekly admitted that these had not been well articulated before the coaching initiative was launched. Sana put her at ease by suggesting that the two of them brainstorm some potential impact areas that then be included in the conversations.

Sana asked Michelle to reflect upon conversations she had with Barry regarding his expectations for leadership development in general and coaching in particular. Michelle indicated that improved decision making, collaboration, and communications were at the top of the list. Sana suggested that these areas be explored during the conversations with the managers. Michelle had also heard some anecdotal comments from the managers about their being coached in conflict reduction. In addition,although not limited to leadership development and coaching, Barry had been pushing for increased productivity and improved quality of the services the agency provides. Michelle agreed to explore all of these areas in the managers' conversations.

Michelle's next question revolved around how this impact could be attributed to the coaching and not other potential contributing factors. Sana replied that the intention of the last two questions was, in effect, to isolate the effects on coaching to produce the organizational impact. In fact, these questions make the estimated impact more conservative and more credible. Of course, no estimate is perfect, which is why question 5 is so important—it accounts for the error of the estimate given in question 4. The responses to both questions 4 and 5 are given in terms of percentages. Monetary benefits that are identified are multiplied—or discounted—by these two percentages. This results in monetary benefits that are conservative and credible.

At this point Michelle felt she had a positive and promising course of action; however, she was still a bit hesitant about using these questions in a conversation with the section managers. Upon further digging, Sana realized that Michelle did not feel self-confident in conducting this kind of conversation. They agreed to do some role plays, which helped Michelle immensely, and for Michelle to do one conversation as a pilot and then debrief with Sana. After finalizing the conversation protocol, Michelle was ready. Her first conversation was with Carol, a section manager in the agency, and here is what Michelle learned:

- Carol had worked in the agency for sixteen years, the last two in her current role of a section manager.
- Carol decided to work for the government out of her strong sense of service to others.
- Her strong sense of service was being challenged by budget cuts and reduced resources. For example, of the twelve positions that reported to her, she had two open positions that would not be filled and two other positions that were filled with temporary contractors.
- She was initially reluctant to enter into the coaching relationship because she had so little time and didn't see how talking would get her out of the mess she was in.
- Her coach first settled her down to create more focus in her life. E-mails were dealt with more effectively and meeting time used more efficiently.
- Working with her coach, Carol pared down her priorities and those of her group and focused on only those that were strongly aligned with the goals of the agency and the department. This action opened up new possibilities. Current work was reprioritized and, most important, Carol now felt she could say "no" to requests for her section, whereas before she had felt that saying no was a repudiation of her sense of service. The coach enabled her to realize that she was trying to serve everyone, which resulted in her not serving anyone very well. Carol was now also delegating more.
- Many benefits were realized. Team engagement and morale had increased, teamwork and communications had improved, and the quality of their work was noticeably improved.
- Productivity had also increased; according to Carol she had gained at least an extra four hours a week, as a result of her greater focus. Her team's productivity increased too, as a result of less bickering, shorter meetings and, most important, by recalibrating work priorities, which freed up time by reducing work on lower-value projects. Carol had eight full-time team members (not including open positions and positions temporarily filled with contractors).

- Diligently completing the conversation protocol, Carol directly attributed at least 80 percent of this productivity gain to the coaching (for herself and the team) and was 75 percent confident in the estimate for herself, and somewhat less confident for her team (50 percent confident).

Armed with the data from Carol, Michelle paid another visit to Sana to sort out the analysis. Specifically of interest was how to

Personal Productivity of Carol

4 hours per week × $80 (fully loaded cost per hour for Carol to work) = $320

$320 × 48 weeks (to annualize the benefit, taking out time away from work) = $15,360

$15,360 × 80% (attribution) × 75% (confidence) = $9,216

Therefore Carol's productivity benefits were $9,000 (rounded down)

Productivity of Carol's Team

4 hours per week × $60 (fully loaded average cost per hour for Carol's team members) = $240

$240 × 8 (the number of Carol's team members) = $1,920

$1,920 × 48 weeks (to annualize the benefit, taking out time away from work) = $92,160

$92,160 80% (attribution) × 50% (confidence) = $36,864

Therefore the benefits from Carol's team productivity increase were $36,000 (rounded down).

Note that in both examples, the monetary benefits were annualized by multiplying the benefits by 48 weeks. This value is used, as opposed to 52 weeks, to account for time away from work due to vacations or other reasons. It's reasonable to ask why only one year's worth of benefits are used in the analysis. Certainly, Carol's increased productivity and that of her team will continue beyond one year. Though this is true, we only use one year's worth of benefits in order to be extra conservative and lend additional credibility to the ROI analysis.

convert the productivity benefits to monetary values. The following summarizes their analysis.

Completing the Data Collection

Encouraged by the outcome of this initial conversation with Carol and her debriefing with Sana, Michelle scheduled conversations with the remaining managers. Over the next couple of weeks, Michelle took the opportunity to have conversations, using the format she followed with Carol, with eleven other managers who had been coached. This brought the total number of respondents to twelve, or 67 percent of the total number of participants (eighteen), which Michelle felt was a reasonable response rate. The remaining six managers were unavailable due to travel and vacation schedules.

Determining the ROI

After all of the conversations were completed, Michelle tallied the monetary benefit areas. These areas included the manager's productivity, the productivity of their teams, and the improvement in work quality. These results are presented in Figure 13.1. As can be seen from this figure, a total of $510,000 in monetary benefits was reported by the respondents. Most of these benefits

Figure 13.1. The Monetary Benefits Reported by the Managers Being Coached

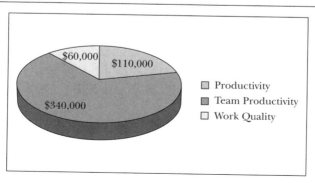

came from team productivity, with the managers' productivity next and quality-related benefits last.

Michelle determined that the total cost of the coaching initiative was $290,000, which included the vendor fees, materials, facilities, other charges, and opportunity costs, for example, the time the managers spent in their respective coaching relationships.

The return on investment was calculated as follows:

$$\text{ROI} = ((\$510{,}000 - \$290{,}000)/\$290{,}000) \times 100 = 75\%$$

Key Learnings from Michelle's Story

Before we move to the next section we will briefly reflect upon some key learnings from Michelle's story.

1. *Taking a coaching approach to evaluation means asking the right questions.* The five questions that Sana suggested to Michelle enabled Carol to reflect upon her experiences and draw greater meaning from what she learned. The deeper issues that Carol revealed were placed in the context of the values that Carol had and how her interpretation of these values no longer served her well. In fact, the coaching enabled Carol to adopt a new worldview, which empowered her, and later her team, to be more effective and efficient.

2. *The power of the data came from the stories that the coaching participants shared.* Michelle did not create the data; she merely asked Carol questions, listened to her answers, collected the data, and organized the data into a master narrative. Evaluation methodology provided a structured process by which Carol was able to organize her thoughts and share her story. The credibility of the data comes in large measure from the credibility of the managers providing the data and the veracity of the stories that they share. The story that Carol told was very powerful and easy to understand. The linkage from the learnings to the actions she took, and then to the impact these actions had in the organization, were transparent and believable.

3. *Conducting an ROI analysis of a coaching initiative does not have to be onerous or time-consuming.* True, conducting twelve

conversations does take time; however, Michelle had planned to do this anyway. The ROI methodology involved only provided structure to these conversations and enabled the storytelling to emerge more readily, and perhaps more naturally than it would have occurred without the ROI methodology.

4. *Taking a coaching approach does finesse some of the challenges to evaluating a coaching initiative.* These challenges include the fact that coaching is a continuous process, not a discrete training event. Not everyone receives the same learning experience: different coaching objectives are set for each person, coaching styles may differ, and even the delivery of coaching will vary in the number of hours delivered and how it was delivered (for example, in person or over the telephone). However, by taking a coaching approach, each coaching relationship is explored on an individual basis and on its own terms. The variation in coaching experiences and time frames is not an impediment; indeed, this variation adds richness and texture to the stories collected.

Metrixglobal® Impact Compass: A Model for Telling the ROI Story

Description of the Model

In telling the ROI story, the critical turning point is converting the benefits into monetary value. The MetrixGlobal® Impact Compass, presented in Figure 13.2, provides a logic for converting benefits to monetary value. It is, in effect, the subtext for the value narrative. There are three elements to the compass: outcomes, conversion, and benefits.

- *Outcomes.* There are four overall types of tangible organizational outcomes for any action taken as a result of coaching (or any other learning experience for that matter): output, quality, cost, or time. Examples of output include productivity (as in the case study) and increased revenue. An example of a quality outcome could be reduced number of reports with errors or reduced product defects. A cost outcome could be reduced cost of operations and a time

Figure 13.2. The MetrixGlobal® Impact Compass

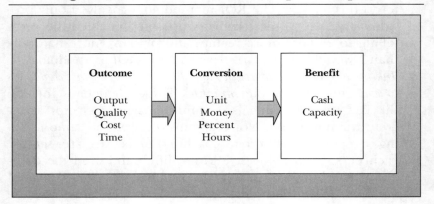

outcome could be reduced product development cycle time. Any tangible organizational outcome will fit one (or more) of each category.

- *Conversion.* There are four major units that are used to convert to monetary benefits: units, money, percent, and hours. A unit could be a report that's written, a loan that's processed, or a product defect. Each of these units would have a monetary value associated with it. For example, in a manufacturing setting an average product defect may have been researched and determined to be $350. Counting units (defects) and multiplying this number by $350 gives you the monetary benefit. The benefit may be converted directly into a monetary benefit—for example, operating cost for a department was cut by $100,000 a year. Percent and hours may also be used to convert monetary benefits. Take productivity for example. Estimating a 10 percent improvement in productivity or gaining four hours a week can be a stepping stone to converting the benefits to monetary value, as we saw Michelle do in the case study (with hours gained).

- *Benefits.* There are two basic types of monetary benefits: capacity and cash. Capacity benefits refer to increasing the time available to accomplish value-added activities. In Carol's case, this was four hours per week. Cash benefits, on the other hand, are benefits that show up on a department's budget or, in the private sector, on financial statements with impact on the bottom line. It is important to note that reductions in capital costs and other one-time cost reductions are not included in the ROI analysis, only recurring (annual) cost reductions. When, for example, Carol took actions that increased the productivity of her team, these productivity improvements were sustainable in coming years.

For Michelle, converting Carol's productivity benefits to monetary value was relatively straightforward. Carol's actions taken as a result of coaching clearly gained her some time. This time benefit was converted to dollars based on the standard values of "dollars per hour," which represented the fully loaded value of Carol's time.

Let's say that in addition to converting productivity benefits to monetary value, Michelle wanted to convert Carol's improvements in *quality* to monetary value as she did with other manager conversations. For this to happen we will need to establish logic that connects outcomes to monetary benefits with a conversion unit. Let's see how the MetrixGlobal Impact Compass can help.

Applying the MetrixGlobal Impact Compass to the Quality Outcome

Converting the quality benefit to monetary value requires Michelle to dig a little deeper into Carol's story by asking some additional questions. Here is a possible scenario for how Michelle could have done this:

Michelle: I would like to explore how you feel work quality was improved by the actions that you took. Could you give me a specific example?

Carol: Sure. We review compliance documents for accuracy, completion, and proof of satisfaction of regulatory requirements. Basically, we want to make sure that everyone is abiding by the law. Of course, there are a lot of other things we do, but compliance review is at the top of the list of priorities for us.

(Continued)

Applying the MetrixGlobal Impact Compass to the Quality Outcome (*Continued*)

Michelle: So earlier you said that you retooled your priorities and this enabled you to reduce work of lesser value. Is this an example of setting priorities?

Carol: Yes, very much so. We retained the work on compliance and reduced some other, lesser value work. This meant that we had more time available for compliance.

Michelle: So how did these actions improve quality of compliance?

Carol: About 10 percent of the compliance reviews we do are reviewed by a board. Since we implemented these actions, our error rate has dropped by 80 percent.

Michelle: Wow, 80 percent sounds impressive to me. About how many reports per week would that translate to?

Carol: Well, let me put it this way. There are at least two or three or maybe up to five more reports that are error free now and don't require us to rework and review them. And at about $500 per reworked report, the money adds up pretty quickly.

Michelle: Yes, I can see that. Doing quick math, that's at least $1,000 per week, if we take the lowest value of two reports per week. Of this $1,000, how much would you directly attribute to the actions you took as a result of your coaching?

Carol: Most all of it, let's say 75 percent.

Michelle: How confident are you in the estimate?

Carol: I'll say 80 percent.

At this point, Michelle has all of the data she needs to convert the quality benefit to monetary value. After the conversation, and with Carol's permission, Michelle did validate the quality improvement by examining the department's performance records, which were reported monthly.

$1,000 per week $\times$ 48 weeks = $48,000 (which annualized the benefit)

$48,000 $\times$ 75% (attribution) $\times$ 80% (confidence) = $28,000

To sum up, let's review how Michelle made this conversion using the MetrixGlobal Impact Compass. Quality (outcome) was explored further and the improvement was expressed in terms of defective reports (units), which was then converted to monetary benefits (cash) using the department-supplied value of $1,000 per unit.

Putting the Pieces Together: Building a Business Case for Coaching

The last time that Michelle talked with her boss, Barry, he wanted her to answer three key questions before he considered expanding the coaching initiative:

1. What did people really learn from their coaching experience?
2. What are people doing differently as a result of what they learned?
3. What impact did these actions have on the organization?

Michelle is now prepared to answer these questions based on her evaluation of the coaching initiative and present a stronger business case to Barry. We'll address each of these questions using the data that Michelle collected through her conversations with coaching participants.

1. What Did People Really Learn from Their Coaching Experience?

In her conversation with Carol, Michelle uncovered that Carol's key learning was that Carol's strong sense of service was leading her to do work that neither she or her team had the capacity to effectively do. She learned that she needed to create more focus in her work and her team needed a clearer set of priorities. These learnings were very similar to what Michelle heard from the other participants, including learning how to better delegate work, gaining insights into how to better manage e-mail messages, and understanding how to better lead meetings.

2. What Are People Doing Differently as a Result of What They Learned?

In Carol's case, she translated her learnings into meaningful actions. Specifically, she worked with her team to pare down their priorities and develop strategies for appropriately turning down work requests. Her coach helped her find ways to delegate more effectively. These actions were in line with actions that other coaching participants reported taking, such as better managing conflict, improving how decisions were made, and solving problems in a more inclusive way.

3. What Impact Did These Actions Have on the Organization?

For Carol, these actions had both intangible and tangible impact. In terms of intangibles, team engagement and morale had increased, teamwork and communications had improved, and the quality of her team members' work was noticeably better. Other coaching participants reported similar intangible benefits, as well as benefits including improved decision making and problem solving, improved "cross-silo" collaboration, and improved performance management.

Tangible benefits were explored as well. In particular, there were three areas that were converted to monetary value following the approach that was illustrated with Carol. These areas included the managers' productivity, the productivity of their teams, and the improvement in work quality. In total, $510,000 in monetary benefits was reported by the respondents. Most of these benefits came from team productivity, with the managers' productivity next, followed by quality-related benefits (Figure 13.1). Given the actions that the managers said they took as a result of coaching, it is easy to see how these actions translated to higher team productivity. The teams' work was reprioritized, which reduced their workload of lower value work; saying "no" to requests for lower value work increased the available capacity of the teams to do higher value work. These benefits are examples of "capacity" benefits (see Figure 13.2), which increase the capacity of the teams to do more work in the same amount of time, and can be distinguished from "cash" benefits, which would show up in the department's budget (or a company's bottom line).

The Business Case as Narrative

A business case is a narrative, a way of succinctly telling a story about the potential of value creation based on experiences, estimates, and assumptions. A business case does not have to be a lengthy document, in fact, less is definitely more. When Michelle assembled her business case, she did estimate the investment in expanding the coaching initiative; however, she also talked about the potential return on this investment based on the experience with the pilot. Her narrative ran as follows:

> Our experience with the pilot shows a clear line-of-sight relationship along what was learned from coaching, how these learnings were translated into meaningful actions, and how these actions unleashed potential and created both intangible and tangible benefits for the agency. Managers found new ways to better align their team's work to agency goals. New priorities were set, which enabled and empowered people to reduce non-value-added work. Time was freed up and the collective capacity of the team to focus more on higher value work was increased. Teamwork, communications, collaboration, engagement all increased. When the benefits from productivity and quality improvements were tallied and compared to the fully loaded cost for the coaching pilot, an ROI of 75 percent was realized. It's clear that the initiative more than paid for itself, and we expect similar results with the expansion of the coaching initiative.

Epilogue

Michelle arranged to meet with Barry again regarding moving forward with the expansion of the coaching initiative. She sent Barry a copy of the business case she developed, organized around the three questions that he had asked her in their last meeting on this subject. After a few pleasantries were exchanged, their conversation proceeded as follows:

Barry: I read your business case, and I can see that you have been busy!

Michelle: Yes, Sana was a big help. I would have been lost without her.

Barry: I see that you interviewed a dozen of the managers who participated in the coaching—what were these conversations like?

(Continued)

Epilogue (*Continued*)

Michelle: For the most part, people appreciated being able to reflect upon their experiences and make some connections between what they learned and the impact that their actions had in the organization.

Barry: Yes, that impact was most impressive. How sustainable do you think that impact is—is it a flash-in-the-pan or will these benefits be with us for a while?

Michelle: Oh, they will be with us for a while. The productivity gains are real and the actions taken will ensure that these gains will be with us next year and the year after that. The changes made in sourcing work, dispositioning work, and following up on work requests are hardwired into our business processes and unlikely to change anytime soon. The same with quality. People have clearly gotten the message about the shift in spending more time on higher value-added work. It's become a new work habit.

Barry: That's good to hear. But let's say we do move forward with expanding the coaching initiative, how are we going to know if we're successful? We did not really know what to expect with the pilot, and while the results have been really good, our expectations are heightened as to what expanding coaching can bring. In particular, I was intrigued by the improvements in quality; however, only three managers of the twelve you talked to noted quality improvements.

Michelle: Yes, that's a good point. There are definitely lessons learned about quality that other managers can leverage in their respective units. In the pilot, we treated each coaching relationship as a stand-alone and did not really intermix any of the learning. I'll give this some thought. One idea is that in the next round of coaching to treat the group of managers as a cohort. Perhaps midway through the engagement we can bring the managers together to talk about their experiences and what has changed for them. Also, we could organize an after-action review (AAR) when the coaching engagement has concluded.

Barry: I like these ideas. In fact we could still organize an AAR for the pilot group. This might be a way to better leverage their learnings, especially around the quality improvements.

Michelle: I agree. I'll get on it, as well as think about some other ideas to share and leverage the learnings.

Barry: Great, I'll look forward to hearing about these, and in the meantime lay out what the next coaching initiative will look like for the next group of twenty-six managers. We're looking at an investment of about $420,000, based on what we spent in the pilot, so any ideas you have about how to do the next initiative for less money will be well received.

Michelle: Will do, and thanks for your support in moving forward.

Reflection

- The value conversations that Michelle had with the coaching participants provided a structured process for these participants to organize their thoughts and tell their stories. Learning led to meaningful actions, which lead to unleashing potential for the managers and their teams. Evaluation methodology is a reflective process that enables people to deepen their learnings from coaching as well as to gain insights into how to create value from what they learned.

- Determining the ROI was important, and at 75 percent was very well received by Barry; however, ROI was only one piece of the story. Many intangible benefits were also gained that were at least as important as the tangible, monetary benefits. With ROI, the key message was that the coaching initiative more than paid for itself, with the exact value of the ROI being less meaningful. Value, like beauty, is in the eye of the beholder. Barry was not looking for coaching to be a profit generator; he was looking for coaching to add strategic value and deliver on its objectives. The ROI was the icing on the cake. Not only did the coaching deliver value, it paid for itself in the bargain.

- What was more meaningful for Michelle was gaining insights into how to make future coaching initiatives even more impactful and valuable. Her initial ideas about how to better manage coaching as a strategic initiative promise to better share and leverage what is gained from the coaching.

- Michelle has likely increased her stature with Barry. She is now being perceived more as a business-focused person who is a stronger steward of the agency's resources. Barry's trust in her increased, and their partnership in advancing development and change in the agency deepened.

Chapter Fourteen

THE COACHING IMPACT STUDY™

A Case Study in Successful Evaluation

Derek Steinbrenner and Barry Schlosser

Introduction

The field of executive coaching has grown considerably in the last several years. By one estimate, the number of practitioners in the marketplace has risen to over 40,000 globally (Frank Bresser Consulting, 2009), and the membership rolls of the International Coach Federation (ICF), a highly recognized professional association of coaches, swelled from just under 8,000 in 2004 to nearly 16,000 in 2009 (International Coach Federation, 2010).

When the authors embarked on the Coaching Impact Study in 2004 as a joint research and practice initiative intended to explore how this burgeoning yet inadequately understood discipline could be measured and evaluated, little research had been done or was being reported beyond the anecdotal. In 2009, as we retire the study and write this chapter, that landscape is changing. There are now a growing number of professional journals publishing coaching research—including many subject to peer review—and an expanding community of academic, behavioral sciences investigators with research programs focused on this area. With SIOP now hosting conferences that highlight coaching (for example, Society for Industrial & Organizational Psychology, 2008) and sponsoring working groups on the subject, a new era of rigor and data-driven knowledge appears to be on the horizon.

The rapid growth and maturation that have occurred in the coaching profession in the intervening years since we began the study offers us an opportunity to reflect on our research from the "early years" and share our experiences and lessons learned with other researchers and practitioners, supporting their efforts to expand our understanding of the field. In this chapter, we describe how a partnership of coaches, organizations, a consulting firm, and an academic conceived a thorough yet straightforward methodology for evaluating the effectiveness, impact, and value of executive coaching engagements as they were taking place in organizations—an approach that was successfully integrated into several organizational coaching initiatives. The chapter tells the story of our study's origins, objectives, design, and implementation within participant organizations. Along the way, we share our process, challenges, and lessons learned (⌶) from this effort with the hope that researchers and practitioners alike will discover new ideas and insights in these pages that will inform, challenge, and encourage them to continue the critical work of linking coaching to outcomes, impact, and value for individuals and organizations.

Origins of the Study

The rapid growth in the popularity of executive coaching over the last decade is remarkable, and is largely due to personal experience and anecdotal evidence of its benefits to the individual being coached and, more recently, to the organization. In that time, organizations increasingly began to shift beyond the use of coaching for executives at risk of derailing and increasingly toward its use to support high-performing executives and high-potential leaders, realizing that these latter two groups, if their development as leaders could be accelerated, could return substantial additional value to their organizations.

But with no concerted, centralized plan to manage and align coaching efforts, apply consistent best-practice principles to coaching processes, and systematically capture, evaluate, and communicate results, its impact was diminished, diffuse, and poorly documented. That was how leadership coaching was largely done—as ad hoc, one-on-one relationships whose focus and outcomes rarely emerged from behind the closed door of the confidential coaching session. It was the exception rather than the rule for the HR generalist, boss, or other key stakeholder to be aware that a coaching engagement had even occurred, let alone be clear about what it had produced.

The Organization

To counter that trend, Wachovia Corporation (which has since become part of Wells Fargo & Company) began to take a different approach to executive coaching across the enterprise. Instead of ad hoc coaching activity, it would implement a strategic coaching practice, with a practice leader tasked with ensuring that all coaching had a purpose aligned with the business's needs, was delivered by a professional coach vetted to meet strict qualification standards, was accountable for delivering key coaching milestones and reporting requirements, and was managed to a visible budget.

Wachovia was thus an early adopter of the core tenets of a "modern" strategic coaching practice, which include coordinating and managing coaching activity, prioritizing its objectives, and aligning its efforts in directions that support the organization's business and talent strategies. The raison d'être of a strategic coaching practice is to focus the organization's investment in coaching to achieve optimal business impact, but business impact can also be its vulnerability as visible, significant, and aggregated expenditures on anything, as "soft" as executive coaching may invite hard-nosed scrutiny. Wachovia's coaching practice leader at the time recognized this risk inherent in a strategic coaching practice. Even though the company's senior executives were committed to—and had experienced—the direct impact of executive coaching themselves, and assured her of their support of the new coaching strategy, she recognized the importance of documenting the success and impact of the practice to its long-term sustainability.

The Coaching and Researcher Team

Looking for a way to both evaluate individual coaching engagements and document the value of executives' achievements through coaching, the practice leader turned to Cambria—the consulting and coaching firm of one of this chapter's authors (Steinbrenner)—which had been working with her on the design and implementation of the bank's strategic coaching practice as well as providing and managing some of the bank's external coaches.

The firm had already begun to consider sponsoring a research program, in partnership with coaching researcher James Hunt of Babson University, to explore coaching efficacy and impact in organizations. Cambria's coaching professionals had established the firm's strategic coaching approach (Kumata, 2002) and were becoming interested in the state of research in the coaching field from the organization's perspective—and aware that there was precious little available. Similarly, Dr. Hunt had been conducting research into the value of coaching behaviors at the individual level within organizations (Hunt & Weintraub, 2002) and was beginning to shift his focus to the value of coaching to the organization as a whole.

Coincidentally, on a parallel course, this chapter's other author (Schlosser)—an executive coach and consultant with extensive experience in assessment services and methodology who happened to be coaching at Wachovia—had also been developing a research design and survey material to explore coaching outcomes and return on investment (ROI).

These contributors joined forces as a research team to collaborate on a unified measurement program that would aim to achieve each party's objectives under a single research design. For participation to be practical for Wachovia—and, we hoped, for other organizations—the study's surveys would have to not only reach our team's research and practice goals, but they would need to be concise, efficient, and simple enough to maximize the chance of their being completed by busy, over-surveyed corporate executives.

Other Organizations

As we were designing the Coaching Impact Study, two other organizations—Credit Suisse and Deloitte—agreed to participate.

Coaching in Credit Suisse's North American division was, like Wachovia's, in the process of shifting to a strategic practice model, where coaching across the division would be managed centrally and follow specific guidelines. The bank's coaching practice leader was planning a significant strategic coaching pilot initiative, providing coaching to a cohort of the bank's directors who were candidates for "election" (promotion) to managing director—an annual talent review event that would result in a challenging new role for those who would be elected that year, and disappointment for those who would not. The goals of the Credit Suisse initiative were threefold: (1) prepare directors' development leading up to the "MD Election" process, (2) support the transition of elected MDs into their new roles and accelerate their time-to-productivity, and (3) work with directors not promoted to identify and focus on their development priorities and increase their chances of success the next time around. Related to the third goal was the bank's hope that coaching support would improve its retention of directors not promoted but who were nonetheless a body of talent that was tremendously valuable to the organization and that had historically seen significant turnover following election decisions. And, beyond measuring retention for this single initiative, the practice leader needed a way to delve beneath the coaching experience to better understand the value it produced for Credit Suisse and its executives. This strategic initiative provided an opportunity to introduce such a measurement effort into the coaching process.

Deloitte's strategic coaching practice was several years older and more established than those of Wachovia and Credit Suisse at the time we developed the Coaching Impact Study. According to Syd Snyder, talent director of Deloitte's Partner Services organization, his firm became involved in the Coaching Impact Study for two reasons:

> At Deloitte, we have known for some time that executive coaching can be effective. We knew this by collecting feedback from the leader who worked with a coach and his/her leader. On a case by case, engagement by engagement basis, we knew the costs of executive coaching were completely justified. What we DIDN'T know is how Deloitte as an organization was impacted or not impacted by executive coaching. The Impact Study provided

us a picture of the organizational shifts as a result of numerous executive coaching engagements with our senior leaders. The good news is the shifts were all in the direction Deloitte as an organization wanted to see.

Secondly, and of equal importance, the Impact Study provided us the opportunity to codify the goals of executive coaching in order for us to learn where we might consider other developmental interventions to supplement, if you will, the one-on-one coaching. By understanding what our leaders as a group believed that they were lacking in leadership capability, we were able to significantly better leverage our development dollars with other development programs. (S. Snyder, personal communication, October 11, 2009)

Ultimately, these first three participating companies, and those that would follow, each had real business needs driving their interest in being involved in the Coaching Impact Study. They did not sign up for the study—with its rigorous surveys of their senior-most leaders (and their managers!) probing for details about a potentially sensitive subject—purely out of an altruistic motivation to contribute research and knowledge to the profession of coaching (though that was part of it). Though needs and interests varied across the group, among them were:

- To develop a foundation of quantitative and qualitative evidence establishing the impact and value of their organization's strategic coaching practice
- To gather data on organizational trends, such as key areas of coaching focus across coaching engagements
- To identify common pitfalls or obstacles to coaching success
- To raise "red flags" that might indicate priorities for the coaching practice, including internal messaging needs (for example, raising awareness of coaching with a key stakeholder group) or coaching process elements (for example, incorporating a check-in with the manager at the end of the coaching process)
- To better align and blend executive coaching with other talent development efforts of the organization
- For a couple of participant organizations, to evaluate the effectiveness and fit of the coaches doing the coaching work

These business needs shaped our study's objectives, and each had an impact on its design and implementation. The study's objectives, design, and implementation are the subjects of the next three segments of this chapter.

Objectives

In large measure, we pursued the Coaching Impact Study to apply quantitative and qualitative research methodology to understanding the focus, process, impact, and value of what is accomplished through executive coaching. At its outset, there was a paucity of studies of actual coaching engagements, and so we took it upon ourselves to research and map out what a contemporary and practical study of executive coaching might consist of at the individual and organizational levels.

Though we agreed that powerful lessons can be drawn from anecdotes and stories, our general sense was that the executive coaching field would benefit from a more empirical, quantitative examination. We were thus determined to design a study that would extend beyond the qualitative to also allow for robust statistical analyses.

We settled on the following key objectives integral to the study's success:

1. **Develop a practical design.** Achieving sufficient response rates was a major concern as we embarked on our study. We were highly aware that the surveys were in some respects an imposition upon the respondents—busy professionals, many of whom have little time or inclination for being surveyed and may already be over-surveyed. Thus, the practicality of our design became a study objective of its own. We labored to strike a balance among comprehensiveness of content, item design, and survey length. We used a straightforward design for the Web-based surveys. We wanted each survey to fit within one scrolling Web page of reasonable length—rather than a series of pages—so that respondents could quickly see the full length of the survey they were being asked to respond to and would therefore be more likely to complete the entire survey.

2. Examine coaching from multiple perspectives. There are three primary stakeholders in most coaching engagements: the executive or "coachee," the coach, and the coachee's manager. We refer to these stakeholders collectively as the "coaching triad." Our participant organizations each expected some level of involvement in the coaching process from the coachee's manager (or, in those more matrixed organizations, a more senior "sponsor" for the coaching effort). Though in some cases the manager's role was primarily to approve funding, most managers were expected to provide input into coaching priorities, confirm action plans, track progress, and provide ongoing feedback. We and our participant organizations were interested in comparing the perspectives of these "managers/sponsors" to those of the other members of the coaching triad.

3. Compare expectations to outcomes. Whereas traditional program evaluation efforts typically focus on measuring reactions, perceptions, and effects following the completion of the program, we were also curious to find out how assessments of impact and value from coaching after the fact compared to expectations going into the engagement. Would overly high expectations at the outset tend to produce disappointment in the end? Would initial skepticism tend to be disabused or confirmed? Or perhaps more important, would levels of initial skepticism persist in influencing perceptions regardless of actual accomplishments? These and similar questions led us to build into our study's design a Time 1—Time 2 methodology.

4. Identify the focus of coaching engagements. The overarching objectives of most developmental coaching are essentially behavioral and attitudinal changes in a particular direction—not increased knowledge of a subject or improvement of a technical skill, which might be better addressed by training or other educational means. Thus, an important aspect of understanding the value that coaching produces for the individual and, by extension, for the organization is to understand the specific kinds of capabilities and behaviors targeted for improvement within a coaching engagement. In formulating our study, we needed to identify a method to help survey respondents zero in on these capabilities and behaviors before appraising their value. This would also allow us to identify trends or themes in areas that receive the most attention in coaching and to compare what was envisioned for improvement at the start of coaching to what actually was addressed.

5. Identify the impact of coaching engagements. To arrive at a reasonable estimate of the value produced by a coaching effort, it is critical to determine what organizational or business-oriented outcomes are achieved. Such insights could provide valuable support for an organization's investment in coaching.

6. Measure perceptions of the value of coaching engagements and factors important to them. Coaching may be perceived to add value to an organization in many ways. Coachees may become more effective by improving their capabilities; a manager/sponsor may have a more connected team member; the organization may find value because desired business metrics have been achieved. These perceptions of value are tied to changes in behavior or capability that lead to business-relevant outcomes that hold merit for the organization. Our objective was not to treat these perceptions as equivalent to econometric notions of ROI, nor were we particularly interested in pursuing the notion of a financial return on the coaching expense as other investigators had (for example, Anderson, 2003). The financial estimates of value we intended to measure would serve more as a proxy for stakeholder *perceptions* of the value that a coaching effort produced for the organization.

7. Produce useful reports for organizations. For our participant organizations, a main goal was to gain access to organizational-level survey data that would allow them to influence the use and direction of coaching at their own organization, as well as to share information with their own leaders. A major benefit to these organizations was the opportunity to compare data from their own surveys to benchmark data from other participants.

8. Share our findings with coaching researchers and practitioners. From the outset of the Coaching Impact Study, we intended to explore unanswered questions in the coaching field and to convey our insights and findings to the broader coaching community—and to encourage dialogue, questioning, and further study. Throughout the life of the study, therefore, various combinations of our investigator team and participant organizations have endeavored to broadcast the aim of the study and our findings to a variety of audiences, including professional associations, research groups, practitioner groups, and stakeholder communities internal to our participant organizations.

Design

The preceding eight objectives drove the ultimate design of the Coaching Impact Study, which we detail here along with several key findings and lessons learned along the way.

Study Methodology

The Coaching Impact Study methodology consisted of identical online surveys sent to multiple stakeholders of a coaching engagement at two points in the coaching process: near the outset and at the conclusion. These fundamental design elements—Identical Surveys Across Stakeholders and Time 1—Time 2 Surveys—have been described previously (Schlosser, Steinbrenner, Kumata, & Hunt, 2006), but bear further discussion here before we examine the details of survey construction.

Identical Surveys Across Stakeholders

Because we wanted to be able to compare responses on survey items not just within but across stakeholder groups, we created a standardized survey whose primary focus of evaluation was the engagement itself, with each item identical across the coaching triad. This gave us the opportunity, for example, to collect what was essentially a self-assessment rating of the commitment of the manager/sponsor to the coaching engagement.

We ultimately found that the stakeholder group with the highest response rate was the coach group. In our view, this was largely because coaching program managers hold the purse strings and therefore have significant influence over their coaches. The second highest responders were the coachees: most of our participant organizations asked their coaches to encourage their coachees to respond to the surveys. Lowest of the response rates was that of managers/sponsors, and the organizations most successful in getting their responses were those who explicitly defined a role for that individual in the coaching process itself and clearly communicated that surveys were an important element of the process. ⒧*With all groups, personal follow-up on uncompleted surveys by coaching practice staff produced the highest success rate in obtaining responses to the surveys.*

Time 1—Time 2 Surveys

To meet our objective of comparing expectations to outcomes, we created two versions of the survey: the first—Time 1 (T1)—to be distributed near the outset of the coaching engagement, and the second—Time 2 (T2)—to be distributed at or soon after the conclusion of the coaching engagement. The T1 and T2 surveys were nearly identical, with most items differing only in verb tense (that is, forward-looking at T1 and primarily backward-looking at T2). Our initial intent was to use the T1 survey to establish a baseline of initial expectations of what would be achieved by the coaching engagement and then to compare those expectations to T2 evaluations after coaching had occurred.

What actually happened was that most of our participant organizations began by administering the T2 survey for coaching engagements that had recently ended (without having administered the T1 survey for those engagements) and then proceeded with both T1 and T2 surveys as new coaching engagements began and ended over time. We therefore collected considerably more T2 data over the life of the study than T1 data. Furthermore, due both to inconsistent response rates from individual stakeholders at both T1 and T2, and to occasional changes in manager/ sponsor over the course of an engagement, we ultimately had relatively few responses to both surveys from the same individual manager/sponsor. ⒧*Although we were able to pool a very modest amount of data **across** organizations to link some individual responses from T1 to T2 and begin to explore differences in those responses, organizations were unable to link their own results across the two points in time for reliable insights into such differences.*

However, the T1—T2 design proved quite valuable in other ways. As our participant organizations began to administer the T1 surveys in new coaching engagements, an interesting phenomenon emerged. The surveys, by their very introduction into the coaching process, began to influence the behavior of those involved. Coaches, after being briefed on the surveys by the coaching program manager, began discussing them with their coachees at the outset of the engagement. The language of the T1 survey, such as its lists of behaviors and outcomes, and the survey items probing organizational impact and value, began to filter into initial coaching discussions themselves (the actual survey items are shown later in this chapter). Coaches and coachees, and even managers, began to link the coaching objectives they were including in their action plans to business results and impact. And they were quantifying them—what will the value be to the organization if we achieve this objective? ⌐*We discovered that a survey we had introduced to **measure** a dynamic system had **influenced** that system—*not in every case, surely, but enough to cause lively discussion of the phenomenon among the coaches and program managers of most of our participant organizations. This result seems to us a highly desirable by-product of a coaching evaluation process. Encouraging the explicit linking of coaching outcomes to business impact and value in the context of a coaching engagement must increase the likelihood that the stakeholders of the coaching engagement will recognize and acknowledge the business value when there is coaching success. For a coaching program manager attempting to build visibility and recognition for the value coaching delivers to the organization, facilitating that recognition is a worthwhile goal.

⌐*Another way in which the T1—T2 design proved valuable was in looking at different group aggregates.* For coaching cohort groups (coaching engagements starting at the same time and proceeding together as part of a common initiative), the aggregate data provided (at T1) insight into the group's initial expectations of what coaching would achieve, as well as (at T2) an overall picture of what the program ultimately achieved. At the organizational level, aggregate data revealed trends across the organization's executive population, such as the most common areas of development, as well as both statistics and qualitative anecdotes describing the impact and value that coaching was delivering to the organization (including, as we will discuss, enough information to calculate a type of ROI).

Survey Construction

Construction of effective yet practical surveys was no small challenge. For the remainder of this segment of the chapter, we provide a brief walk-through of the surveys themselves, section by section, showing the T2 (Follow-Up Survey) version while describing the differences in phrasing of the T1 (Initial Survey). A reproduction of the study's Follow-Up Survey is provided for reference in Figure 14.1, at the end of the chapter.

Section 1: Capabilities/Behaviors

The survey began by focusing on what we called "Capabilities/ Behaviors," which comprised a pick-list of competencies and behaviors that we compiled through an iterative design-and-feedback process involving the study's authors, our initial participant organizations, and a handful of executive coaches. The first item asked respondents to select all Capabilities/Behaviors from the list that applied to this coaching engagement (see Figure 14.1 Section 1[1]).

Our objective with this list was to provide the respondents with an opportunity to expand their thinking about what could be (T1), or had been (T2), accomplished through coaching. The list was not intended to be orthogonal—indeed many of the options overlap conceptually—nor did our need for a practical design allow us to define each term in detail. Rather, we wanted to present as complete a list as possible to maximize the likelihood that the accomplishments of most any coaching engagement could be identified. Subsequent analyses would allow us to connect and group related items to identify patterns of coaching focus and achievement. To provide additional flexibility, we included options for "None (no change in any area)" and "Other"—the latter of which included a text box to allow a brief description of the meaning of that response.

Item 1 of the survey included a second component, where we asked respondents to select up to three of the Capabilities/ Behaviors they had chosen from the full list and describe them in greater detail by responding to three additional questions for each Capability/Behavior they selected. The rating scale and scale anchors for these survey fields are shown in Table 14.1.

Table 14.1. Rating Scale and Scale Anchors for Drop-Down Response Fields

	Scale Anchors		
Scale	Dollar Value	Importance	Confidence
1	$0	Very Little	Very Little
2	$1 to $5,000		
3	$5,001 to $10,000		
4	$10,001 to $25,000		
5	$25,001 to $50,000		
6	$50,001 to $100,000		
7	$100,001 to $250,000		
8	$250,001 to $500,000		
9	$500,001 to $1,000,000		
10	over $1,000,000	Very Much	Very Much

Our biggest concern with this item, and the whole survey itself, was whether respondents would ultimately be willing to provide an estimate of the financial value of what was attained in a coaching engagement. We worried that stakeholders would not be able to quantify coaching's impact in any meaningful way, and thus not respond. ⌐*We ultimately found that this particular design—starting with a broad pick-list of possible behavior changes, then asking respondents to select a few of the most important ones, describe them in their own words, and assess their importance to the organization, before asking for a financial value of that impact—provided a sufficiently robust **chain of logic** for the respondents, and that most did actually think through the process, follow it to its end, and provide a response to the financial value question.* This being the first of several questions asking for financial value ratings, it also brought respondents further down the pathway toward the ultimate goal: an estimated overall financial value rating for the coaching engagement as a whole.

This item ("Capabilities/Behaviors") ultimately produced some important results for our participant organizations. ⌐*The item revealed the areas coachees were focusing on for development, which showed their organizations how coaching was being used by executives across the enterprise and revealed trends in the development needs of the organization's leaders.* Findings such as respondents' most frequent selections, which have been reported elsewhere (Schlosser, Steinbrenner, Kumata, & Hunt, 2006, 17), helped coaching practice leaders better market their practices to organizational leaders based on the needs they served and highlighted potential development priorities for their executive and high-potential populations as a whole. The item provided quantitative and qualitative documentation of the kinds of behavioral changes being focused on and achieved through coaching as well as the perceived value of those changes to the stakeholder groups surveyed.

Section 2: Outcomes/Metrics

The next section of our survey, numbered as Item 2, exactly mirrored the format of the first section, but focused on the business-related by-products of behavioral change, which we called "Outcomes/Metrics" (see Figure 14.1 Section 2[2]). Again, we employed the same process as for our list of "Capabilities/ Behaviors" to develop a master list for this item. Our rationale for this item was twofold: (1) to build a greater understanding of the concrete ways coaching was being seen as producing real impact and value for organizations, and (2) to lead our respondents *further down the chain of logic* to arrive at an assessment of the financial value of that coaching engagement overall.

This item also produced valuable findings for our participant organizations. Their practice leaders were able to draw from its responses and develop a body of quantitative and qualitative data demonstrating how the organization's coaching investment was producing outcomes of real business value.

Section 3: Impact Narrative

We followed the first two narrowly defined, largely quantitative survey items with a qualitative item asking respondents for a description, in their own words, of what the coaching would or did produce (see Figure 14.1 Section 3[3]). This narrative response item allowed respondents to describe their experiences, observations, and expectations regarding the impact and success of the coaching engagement outside of the structure of a selection box or rating scale. *Narrative responses gave our participant organizations access to a wealth of insights into the experiences of those involved in their coaching engagements and valuable anecdotes they could use in reports and presentations on their coaching programs.*

Section 4: Scale Response Items

The next ten survey items (items numbered 4 to 13; see Figure 14.1 Section 4[4]) were designed for responding using a simple 10-point scale. These items captured a variety of assessments of the value of the coaching, as well as evaluations of several factors that we and our initial participant organizations believed might mediate respondent perceptions of that value. Challenges with this section included keeping items sufficiently brief and uncomplicated.

We deliberately chose to exclude evaluations of coach methods and styles because doing so would have exceeded the practical limits we placed on our survey design. Coaching methodologies and their efficacy were beyond our study's focus and, thankfully, have become the subject of increasing examination (for example, McKenna & Davis, 2009; Stober & Grant, 2006;). For the purposes of our study, it was enough to know that a coaching engagement was roughly defined as a six-to-twelve-month one-to-one development process facilitated by a vetted professional executive coach, and that executive coaching engagements were implemented and managed with some consistency within a given participant organization.

This section provided a wealth of insight into stakeholder perceptions of the value of coaching engagements and their assessments of factors affecting that value. For example, we found that ratings provided by managers/sponsors were significantly lower than those of coachees and coaches, which were similar to each other. These lower ratings from managers/sponsors sparked a fair amount of concerned speculation among the study's research team and our participant organizations and prompted extensive discussion and some further writing (Steinbrenner, Kumata, & Schlosser, 2007). ⊩*The key imperative we took away from this finding was this: get the manager more involved from the outset and throughout the coaching process.* This makes managers more aware of the focus of the coaching engagement and better positioned to observe and appropriately value the changes that occur. We return to this discussion again in the next segment of this chapter.

It is interesting to note that manager/sponsor ratings weren't lower across the board; one item bucked the trend. The item with the highest average rating from managers/sponsors, consistently higher than the ratings it received from the other respondent groups, was Item 6, which assessed their own commitment to the coaching process.

Section 5: Overall Impact Assessments

Items 14 and 15 of the Follow-Up Survey (see Figure 14.1 Section 5[5]—the Initial Survey did not include an item corresponding to 15) were designed to gather summative assessments of the overall impact and value of the coaching engagement.

A Surprising Finding

The result that most captured our—and our participant organizations'—attention were data plots, by respondent group, of the financial values estimated for the coachee's change in overall effectiveness. Data from the Initial Survey showed strong agreement across rater groups, with most ratings of expected financial value from coaching on the high end of the scale (over 90 percent of respondents in each group expecting the value to be above $50,000, and 39 to 49 percent expecting the value to be above $1,000,000). Data from the Follow-Up Survey revealed a striking difference: whereas the coach and coachee data followed a similar pattern (albeit a bit more spread out), the manager/sponsor group was dramatically split. Although most managers/sponsors continued to perceive significant value from the coaching, over 15 percent of them estimated the financial value of the impact of the coaching engagement at $0!

This result generated numerous questions among the study's authors and our participant organizations. What were these managers thinking about the coaching investment that they and their company were making in their direct report? Were they not noticing any behavior change and, if not, was there really no impact, or were they just not connected enough to the coachee or his or her development to fully recognize and appreciate change? Or were they actually noticing change, but not seeing it as valuable to the organization? We were not able to go back to individual respondents to probe further into these responses, but we did arrive at two important conclusions and related suggestions from this finding—both rather intuitive, yet subtle:

- *Get the manager more involved.* Involve the coachee's manager early in the coaching engagement to foster insight into the coachee's development priorities and buy-in on the coaching action plan. Then, continue to keep the manager in the loop as the coaching engagement unfolds. Check in with the manager at milestone points during the engagement to gather feedback on the coachee's progress (and facilitate recognition of that progress). The less input managers have into the coaching plan, and the less they are primed and encouraged to observe change and development, the less likely they are ultimately to recognize achievements made through coaching.
- *Link coaching and development plans to business outcomes and anticipated organizational value.* Creating an action-oriented coaching plan with specific, clear objectives for the coaching engagement, usually with documented success metrics, has been a long-standing hallmark of good coaching practice. But the results articulated for such well-conceived goals are often limited to descriptions of the behavior change being targeted. Rarely do they include successful business outcomes resulting from that change. Even more rarely do they put an estimated financial value on successful achievement of the goal—it's hard to do. Yet, for the coach, coachee, and manager to agree at the end of the coaching engagement that the investment of time and money in coaching was worthwhile, it seems to us that those bridges must somehow be crossed. Encourage that discussion by incorporating it into formal coaching processes, development plan templates, and other elements of the coaching program's architecture.

In the next segment of this chapter we will come back to some of these findings and conclusions and discuss how they influenced, and were influenced by, the implementation of the Coaching Impact Study within our participant organizations.

A Note to Empirical Survey Designers

We realize our surveys were not without flaw. We relied on single items to measure some phenomena, used a variety of response scales, and included no reverse-scored items. Our lists of behaviors and outcomes were derived from a committee process and are not orthogonal (that is, they are not all independent of one another). And while we led respondents through a conceptual chain of logic, encouraging them to work from high-level concepts down to concrete metrics, we left it to them to take some logical leaps, such as asking them to derive financial value figures from descriptions of their coaching progress.

Implementation

Once our study methodology and surveys were in place, the next steps were to implement them within the established, active coaching practices of participant organizations, accumulate survey responses, and analyze and report on the results.

Start-Up

Although the formal design of the study included both the Initial and Follow-Up Surveys for each coaching engagement, our implementation was flexible enough to allow individual respondents and participant organizations to participate in either or both surveys independently. The data for each survey could easily stand alone, and in fact most of our survey reporting and analyses examined the T1 and T2 surveys separately. We incorporated that flexibility by choice. We realized early on that we could not expect high survey completion rates within any stakeholder group at both points in time, from frequently over-surveyed individuals, given the separation of many months from T1 to T2 and under circumstances where job roles may shift during the process.

◳*A major benefit of this flexible approach was that it allowed an organization to launch the study in one major introduction.* In addition to "rolling into" the study by administering the Initial Survey as new coaching engagements began, organizations were also able to send the Follow-Up Survey to large batches of coaching engagements that had recently completed. These engagements may have closed anytime in the prior few months and would not have previously received the Initial Survey. By starting participation in this way, organizations were quickly able to obtain meaningful results from a large number of coaching engagements.

Change Management

Our participant organizations all realized that embarking on the study was an exercise in change management within their coaching programs. This change management effort required planning ways to communicate about the study and its relevance to coaching stakeholders and to encourage responses to the surveys.

The communication effort was twofold: first, organizations had to embed the study into their formal coaching programs, introducing it to the coaching triad (as stakeholders) from the beginning of new coaching engagements, explaining the rationale for it and its importance, and informing stakeholders that they would receive the study's two surveys over the course of the coaching program. Second, they had to present the study to the stakeholders of coaching engagements that were already in progress, or that had recently ended, where the surveys would not have been initially expected by the stakeholders.

For most organizations, this communication process began with their communities of coaches. These were primarily professional executive coaches hired by the organization to provide coaching services to executives. Among each organization's first objectives were educating its coach community about the study, ensuring that all coaches understood the process and highlighting the importance to the organization of their participation. Coaches were then encouraged to reinforce that message with coachees and their coachees' managers/sponsors.

Most, but not all, coaches reacted positively to this message. ◳*Coaches who reacted with initial opposition to the study fell into two categories: those who believed the surveys to be an intrusion into the confidentiality of their coaching relationship, and those who believed that the business-related impact of coaching, and the financial value of that impact, was either inappropriate or impossible to measure in this way.*

Most of the resistant coaches perceived the surveys to be an intrusion into the sanctity of their confidential relationship with their coachee. In their opinion, any request for information of the kind in our study, such as the behavioral changes and business outcomes pursued through coaching, compromised that confidentiality. These objections primarily surfaced among coaches in organizations whose coaching programs were less structured and were managed with a lighter touch. Coaches in such programs tended to have a higher degree of latitude in how they delivered coaching and relatively little accountability to the program manager for following a defined coaching process. They had not been asked by their program managers to report much, if anything, about what they were doing in their coaching engagements, and in that context the surveys were a startling change in procedure. Organizations whose programs were more structured and included other process and reporting expectations, such as shared action plans and progress reports, did not encounter much of this kind of resistance.

Program managers who did encounter this resistance successfully dealt with it through open dialogue, both one-on-one with resistant coaches and in group settings with their coach community. These program managers explained to their coaches that the information provided by the surveys was highly important to the coaching practice and to the organization, that no confidential details from coaching sessions would be collected, and that survey data would only be reported in aggregate.

The second reason for resistance among coaches was a refutation of the notion that the outcomes of coaching could be measured or quantified in any meaningful way through the use of a survey. In their view, the only valid approach to understanding the value of coaching was through the same anecdotal evidence that represented the bulk of research into coaching efficacy at the time we designed our study. Coaches in this group believed that although the individual coachee gains personal value from an executive coaching engagement, the organization does not, or more accurately should not, expect to realize any meaningful, quantifiable value from it. In their minds, it was not appropriate for the organization to measure the business impact of coaching.

This view is, of course, antithetical to ours and to that of our participant organizations. Companies that pay for executive coaching do so not out of pure altruism, or simply as an element of an executive's compensation package. They do so largely because they believe it will provide enough value to the organization to justify its expense; in other words, they expect some form of ROI. They may not expect to be able to attribute a direct financial return on a coaching investment, but their decision to pay for coaches is certainly based on a business case for coaching that includes not just individual benefit but positive organizational outcomes as well.

We were surprised at first that our study met this kind of resistance and skepticism from some professional executive coaches. Perhaps, when we launched the study in 2004, the field was still young enough, in some corners of the practitioner population, to react defensively against inquiry into its inner workings, to fear exposure of its (or a given coach's) processes to scientific scrutiny. It could be that these coaches simply disagreed with the specific design of our study, but our interactions with these coaches led us to believe that most or all of them would have objected to any study having the general intent of our own. Happily, this kind of resistance among the coach community appears to be on the decline. Increasingly, coaches realize that their work does, and should, produce discernible value for organizations. Perhaps the coaching community is also becoming more confident in the soundness of its processes and approaches. Certainly evidence is mounting to support that confidence.

Organizational Reports

In return for their participation in our study, organizations received comprehensive aggregate reports of the data collected from each survey. For many of the survey items (the quantitative items in particular), these reports showed the organization's results alongside the aggregated results of the other participant organizations (rolled into one). ⌐*This benchmarking capability was a key benefit of a standardized survey design implemented across multiple organizations.*

⌐*Most organizations chose to publicize some of the findings from their surveys to their coaching communities in some way, revealing highlights and surprising findings to their coaches as a way of demonstrating the value of the survey effort, and also to spawn discussion and reflection on the meaning of certain results.* In a few cases, the organization invited us to present the findings from the organization's surveys to scheduled gatherings of their coaches. These interactive presentations and ensuing discussions were well received by the coaches who attended. Many of these coaches developed a better appreciation for the purpose and value of the measurement effort, and discussions among coaches and program managers often produced insights about how to increase response rates and improve perceptions of the value of coaching.

In fact, it was from one of these participant-sponsored coach meetings where a discussion first surfaced about the effect the survey process was having on the coaching process itself. A coach attending the meeting mentioned that, anticipating the Initial Survey shortly after the start of a coaching engagement, he had begun to incorporate into initial conversations with his coachees some discussions of the business outcomes that they might expect from coaching success, and even the value of those outcomes to the organization. One of this chapter's authors (Schlosser) had already observed a similar change in his own coaching process.

Further, the common finding that the manager/sponsor group had both the lowest response rate and the greatest proportion of respondents attributing little impact and value to coaching prompted extensive dialogue among the coaching communities of several participant organizations. In response, coaches and program managers began to discuss ways to better engage managers in the coaching process, to make them more aware of the focus and goals of the coaching, and to get their buy-in into its efficacy. Again, a number of coaches described making changes to their own coaching processes that they found increased involvement and responses from the managers/sponsors of their coachees.

└─*Clearly, the act of measurement was, itself, having an effect on the phenomenon being measured.*

Publication

Although providing timely and valuable reporting on survey results to our participant organizations was critical to guaranteeing and growing our participant base, another important objective was to communicate our study design, experience, and findings to the broader coaching community through presentation and publication opportunities. Throughout the years of our study, this included presentations to multiple industry and academic audiences (for example, Kumata, Schlosser, Hunt, Gentry, & Steinbrenner, 2005; Steinbrenner, Schlosser, & Snyder, 2008; Steinbrenner & Schlosser, 2008; Steinbrenner & Schlosser, 2009)—some that included representatives of our participant organizations—and articles in a few industry and research publications (for example, Kumata, 2007; Schlosser, Steinbrenner, Kumata, & Hunt, 2006; Steinbrenner, Kumata, & Schlosser, 2007). For each, we examined and reported on different aspects of our study's data and, since data collection was a continuous process that occurred over several years, we updated findings with new data at later dates. And as our dataset grew, we were able to expand our analyses into new areas and identify new findings.

Moving Forward

The Lifespan of the Study

Work on the Coaching Impact Study began in mid-2004, and in the intervening years we worked with six formal participant organizations—Wachovia, Deloitte, Credit Suisse, Booz Allen Hamilton, Citi, and Assurant—gathering and feeding back data on over three hundred coaching engagements. By mid-2009, after five years in total, we announced the study's retirement and began to wind down data collection with remaining participant organizations. We closed the study feeling that we had accomplished our primary mission of examining some of the workings of the coaching process from start to finish and making a useful contribution to the field of coaching and the growing foundation of research underlying it.

⌐*One key learning was just how challenging it is to run a complex longitudinal study staffed by volunteers who were not full-time researchers (for whom such an effort is a familiar drill).* Perhaps our biggest unanticipated challenge was the sheer number of hours the project would consume to bring it to life and sustain it—seeking participants, developing and delivering reports for participant organizations, running analyses of the data collected, organizing our findings, and publishing and presenting our work to various audiences. We often relied on the generosity and kindness of colleagues who helped with such tasks as survey and report programming, graphic design, statistical analysis, and general editorial support. Participant organizations contributed modest funding to help defray expenses, which was of great help in offsetting some of the programming and travel costs. The majority of funding, however, came from the principle investigators ourselves.

All told, the study was worth the effort. We are grateful to have found the enthusiasm and commitment of several world-class coaching practices to help launch the study and it was gratifying to see the data begin to accumulate in sufficient quantities to permit meaningful analyses. And, ultimately, it was rewarding to find such receptive, encouraging audiences for our findings.

It is conceivable that we could launch a "Round 2" of the study. Should the Coaching Impact Study continue in a future iteration, we envision engagement-level reports that would be used by the coaching triad to see, for instance, how aligned the parties are at the beginning and conclusion of coaching. Such a report from the Initial Survey, for example, might prompt conversations among the coaching triad regarding focus and priorities that could help to put the coaching engagement on a more refined path to success from all perspectives.

Adaptations of the Study

Many organizations do not wish to, or may not be able to, gear up for a full-scale assessment of their coaching initiatives. Common reasons include not having a dedicated coaching staff or strategically oriented coaching program, lack of time, insufficient funding, or having an approach to coaching based mostly on responding to the occasional "one-off" coaching need. Even though our study was engineered to be readily adopted, it did require a certain scale and scope of coaching program. It was also standardized, and not equipped to include items customized to evaluate specific aspects of a particular coaching initiative. For smaller programs and those with unique evaluation needs, we have also explored with success a modified impact study approach using short forms or portions of the surveys supplemented by custom items. This is another avenue by which we hope the Coaching Impact Study might live on in some form, contributing to future coaching evaluation and research efforts. ⌐*A key takeaway from our experience is that "simpler is better" and, even then, it is likely to be mainly the coach and coachee who will be the most willing survey respondents.*

Recommendations for Coaching Practice Leaders

Whether you are responsible for a handful of coaching engagements or a substantial practice, it is valuable to have a window into understanding what is specifically being addressed in your organization's coaching engagements in order to build strategic alignment between business needs and individuals' behavior changes. As a practice leader, part of your responsibility is to help ensure that the organization meets its aims by providing employee development resources, such as executive coaching, so that leaders, managers, and teams can function at their best. Your understanding of the metrics of impact helps you align your efforts and optimally invest your limited resources, and having a way to assess the value of this impact to the organization provides you with a tool to differentiate among such investments and a unique window into the perceptions of key stakeholders of your practice.

Other recommendations for coaching practice leaders, based on our experiences throughout the study, include:

1. Using data as a foundation, convey the success stories of your coaching engagements to others in your organization to help

build up your coaching culture. Encourage leaders to share their own coaching success stories. This will increase the overall credibility of the coaching initiatives.

2. Share what you learn about patterns of impact and value, in the aggregate, with your coaches. Include the main themes about what is being worked on, what the business and other desirable outcomes are, and how these are valued. If you find that coaching efforts are directed toward pursuits that are off-course from the organization's strategic priorities, use what outcome and valuation data you may have as a resource for redirection.

3. Consider banding together with other like-minded organizations and coaches to form a coalition in which you can disseminate best practices about coaching evaluation approaches. Survey items used in common with other organizations can also provide useful benchmarks for comparison.

4. Once enough data are available to begin reporting in the aggregate, do so. Build interest among key organizational communities in the accomplishments and trends of coaching in your organization.

Recommendations for Coaching Researchers and Evaluation Consultants

With hindsight from our experience with the study, we also offer a few suggestions to fellow researchers and consultants embarking on the evaluation of coaching initiatives:

1. Keep the survey material brief and digestible.
2. Ensure that the language used in the surveys is not laden with professional coaching or research jargon, but instead is couched in language meaningful to business executives.
3. If possible, use a pre-post design and link expectations to outcomes.
4. Include the "coaching triad" (that is, coachee, coach, and manager/sponsor). The views of each stakeholder group are different, and each is valuable. Develop a practical strategy to maximize participation of managers/sponsors. Institutionalize

clear accountability from the outset and encourage personal follow-up from program managers, coaches, and coachees.

5. Don't reinvent the wheel unless your road has very unique requirements. Leverage existing survey items, such as those from our study, and compare your results from them to other findings where available.

6. Plan periodic data-sharing events with your participant organizations and interested stakeholder groups, such as coach communities.

Challenge to Coaches

Coaching professionals know that an interview-based 360 process can serve not only to gather critical contextual information for a coaching engagement, but also as a communications medium to the coachee's broader workplace social environment. Broadcasting in this medium sends a message that the coachee is pursuing desirable change toward one or more end states. Likewise, a formal assessment of impact and value among the coaching triad before and after coaching provides a similar benefit.

Our challenge for coaches is to *energetically* communicate to their coaching engagement stakeholders important aspects of what will be addressed in coaching at the front end of each engagement, and what was specifically accomplished, and its value, at the conclusion. This can be done through persistent and collaborative follow-up with those in key relationships with the coachee, and it can be sought by both the coach and coachee (and, for that matter, anyone else positioned to broadcast the message of success). A conceptual framework for describing what will be and has been addressed through coaching and its impact on the organization, such as that provided by our study, can help meet this challenge.

Figure 14.1. Coaching Impact Follow-Up Survey

CAMBRIA CONSULTING

Coaching Impact: Follow-up Survey

Thank you for providing feedback regarding the ABC Corporation coaching engagement identified below. Your feedback is being sought in an ongoing effort to measure the effectiveness and value of this organization's coaching initiative, and to identify opportunities for improvement. This survey will take approximately 30 minutes of your time.

If you have any questions, please contact: Donna Star (dstar@abc.com) or Betty Henderson (bhenderson@abc.com).

ⓘ **Please respond to this survey in reference to the following coaching engagement:**

Person Being Coached: Jack Connolly, ABC Corporation
Your relationship to him/her: Executive Sponsor

Is the above information correct? ◯ Yes ◯ No
If not, please explain:

1. From the list below, select the **capabilites/behaviors** that you think Jack Connolly has improved as a result of this coaching engagement:

☐ Big-picture/Detail Balance ☐ Diversity Considerations/Sensitivity ☐ Meeting Facilitation
☐ Building Enthusiasm ☐ Executive Presence ☐ Negotiation Skills
☐ Building Relationships ☐ External Visibility/Image ☐ Partnering across Boundaries/Silos
☐ Building Team Morale ☐ Field Presence/Field Experience ☐ Personal Energy/Optimism
☐ Business Acumen/Knowledge ☐ Following Others ☐ Productivity/Time Management
☐ Business Results/Execution ☐ Fostering Innovation ☐ Project Management
☐ Career Advancement ☐ Global/International Perspective ☐ Quality of Work Product
☐ Communication Skills ☐ Goal Setting ☐ Self-Awareness/Self-Reflection
☐ Collaboration/Teamwork ☐ Influence ☐ Self-Confidence
☐ Conflict Management/Resolution ☐ Internal Visibility/Image ☐ Sense of Urgency/Responsiveness
☐ Client Focus/Service ☐ Interpersonal Skills ☐ Setting Direction and Vision
☐ Decision Making and Judgment ☐ Job Satisfaction and Enjoyment ☐ Strategic Thinking
☐ Delegation/Empowering Others ☐ Leading/Driving Change ☐ Stress Management
☐ Developing/Coaching Employees ☐ Listening Skills ☐ Technical Skills Mastery
☐ Developing Self ☐ Managing Performance Issues ☐ Work/Life Balance
☐ None (no change in any area)

☐ Other (If other, enter here.)

Based on your selection(s) above, select and describe up to 3 of the most important **capabilities/behaviors** that you think Jack Connolly has improved as a result of this coaching engagement:

Capabilities/Behaviors	Describe what progress in this area has looked like	Importance to the results of the business	Estimated dollar value* of coaching success in this area
Please select - >		Please select - >	Please select - >
Please select - >		Please select - >	Please select - >
Please select - >		Please select - >	Please select - >

Please give your best guess - we're just looking for your general perceptions.*

(continued on p.398)

Survey Sections

Figure 14.1. (Continued)

2. From the list below, select the **outcomes/metrics** that you think Jack Connolly has improved as a result of this coaching engagement:

☐ Alignment with Business Priorities	☐ Employee/Team Retention	☐ Product/Service Launch
☐ Avoidance of Termination/Separation	☐ External Client Sat./Relationships	☐ Productivity
☐ Base of Committed Followers	☐ Increased Sales/Revenue	☐ Profitability
☐ Client Retention/Growth	☐ Internal Client Sat./Relationships	☐ Promotability/Career Progression
☐ Efficiency/Cost Reduction	☐ Intention to Remain with Organization	☐ Quality Management
☐ Employee Alignment	☐ Merger Integration	☐ Reduce Loss/Business Decline
☐ Employee Engagement	☐ Process Improvement	☐ Risk/Liability Reduction
☐ Employee Satisfaction	☐ Product/Service Development	☐ Turnaround/Business Recovery
☐ None (no change in any area)		
☐ Other (If other, enter here.) [_____]		

Based on your selection(s) above, select and describe up to 3 of the most important **outcomes/metrics** that indicate the success level of this coaching engagement:

Outcomes/Metrics	Describe what progress in this area has looked like	Importance to the results of the business	Estimated dollar value* of coaching success in this area
Please select - >		Please select - >	Please select - >
Please select - >		Please select - >	Please select - >
Please select - >		Please select - >	Please select - >

Please give your best guess - we're just looking for your general perceptions.*

3. In concrete terms, what has the coaching experience produced for Jack Connolly and ABC Corporation in the last six (6) months?

[   ]

For questions 4–13 please select "?" if you have no basis for making an assessment.

Please select a response to each question.	Very Little 1	2	3	4	5	6	7	8	9	Very Much 10	?
4. To what extent has coaching positively impacted Jack Connolly's overall effectiveness in his/her role?	○	○	○	○	○	○	○	○	○	○	○
5. To what extent was the coaching worth Jack Connolly's investment of time?	○	○	○	○	○	○	○	○	○	○	○
6. To what extent was the coaching worth ABC Corporation's dollar investment?	○	○	○	○	○	○	○	○	○	○	○
7. How important was coaching success, in this instance, to the part(s) of ABC Corporation for which Jack Connolly works?	○	○	○	○	○	○	○	○	○	○	○
8. To what extent was Jack Connolly personally committed to the coaching process?	○	○	○	○	○	○	○	○	○	○	○
9. To what extent was Jack Connolly's manager(s) personally committed to the coaching process?	○	○	○	○	○	○	○	○	○	○	○
10. To what extent did ABC Corporation set clear expectations about coaching deliverables?	○	○	○	○	○	○	○	○	○	○	○
11. To what degree was coaching useful in facilitating understanding of ABC Corporation strategic goals?	○	○	○	○	○	○	○	○	○	○	○
12. At present, how satisfied are you with the value of coaching for Jack Connolly?	○	○	○	○	○	○	○	○	○	○	○
13. At present, how satisfied are you with the value of coaching initiatives across ABC Corporation?	○	○	○	○	○	○	○	○	○	○	○

14. Recognizing that there are numerous factors involved, please estimate the dollar value to ABC Corporation of Jack Connolly's change in overall effectiveness **over the next 18 months** as a direct result of coaching: [Please select - >]

   - How much confidence do you have in your dollar value estimate above? [Please select - >]

15. How much has Jack Connolly's performance improved since starting his/her coaching engagement? [   ] %

   - What percentage of this improvement do you attribute directly to coaching? [   ] %

Footnotes

1. The corresponding item in the Initial Survey varied as follows (varying text <u>underlined</u>): "From the list below, select the **capabilities/ behaviors** that you think Jack Connolly <u>must improve in order for the</u> coaching engagement <u>to be a success</u>:"; "Based on your selection(s) above, select and describe up to 3 of the most important **capabilities/behaviors** <u>to focus on in this</u> coaching engagement:"; and "Describe what progress in this area <u>would look</u> like"

2. The corresponding item in the Initial Survey varied as follows (varying text <u>underlined</u>): "From the list below, select the **outcomes/ metrics** that you think Jack Connolly <u>must improve in order for the</u> coaching engagement <u>to be a success</u>:"; "Based on your selection(s) above, select and describe up to 3 of the most important **outcomes/ metrics** that <u>would</u> indicate the success level of this coaching engagement:" and "Describe what progress in this area <u>would look</u> like"

3. The corresponding item in the Initial Survey varied as follows (varying text <u>underlined</u>): "In concrete terms, what <u>outcomes would a successful</u> coaching experience <u>produce</u> for Jack Connolly and ABC Corporation in six (6) months?"

4. The corresponding items in the Initial Survey varied as follows (varying text <u>underlined</u>): "To what extent <u>will</u> coaching positively <u>impact</u> Jack Connolly's overall effectiveness in his/her role?"; To what extent <u>will</u> the outcomes of coaching be worth Jack Connolly's investment of time?"; To what extent <u>will</u> the outcomes of coaching <u>be</u> worth ABC Corporation's dollar investment?"; How important <u>is</u> coaching success, in this instance, to the part(s) of ABC Corporation for which Jack Connolly works?"; "To what extent <u>is</u> Jack Connolly personally committed to the coaching process?"; "To what extent <u>is</u> Jack Connolly's manager personally committed to the coaching process?"; "To what extent <u>has</u> ABC Corporation set clear expectations about coaching deliverables?"; and "To what degree <u>will</u> coaching <u>be</u> useful in facilitating understanding of ABC Corporation strategic goals?"

5. The corresponding item in the Initial Survey varied as follows (varying text <u>underlined</u>): "Recognizing that there are numerous factors involved, please estimate the dollar value to ABC Corporation of Jack Connolly's change in overall effectiveness over the next <u>24</u> months as a direct result of coaching:"

References

Anderson, M. (2003). *Bottom-line organizational development: Implementing and evaluating strategic change for lasting value*. Burlington, MA: Elsevier.

Frank Bresser Consulting. (2009). *The state of coaching across the globe: The results of the Global Coaching Survey 2008/2009.* www.frank-bresser-consulting.com/globalconsultingsurvey.html.

Hunt, J., & Weintraub, J. (2002). *The coaching manager: Developing top talent in business.* Thousand Oaks, CA: Sage.

International Coach Federation. (2010). *Background information & membership facts—February 2010.* http://coachfederation.org.

Kumata, E. (2002). Aligning executive coaching with strategic business goals. *Performance Improvement, 41*(9), 16–19.

Kumata, E. (2007). Establishing the value of executive coaching: ROI insights for coaches and their stakeholders. *CoachLeader Update, 1*(3), 2–4.

Kumata, E., Schlosser, B., Hunt, J., Gentry, C., & Steinbrenner, D. (2005). Coaching impact: Identifying individual and organizational outcomes of coaching. Presented to the Society for Industrial and Organizational Psychology's 20th Annual Conference, Los Angeles.

McKenna, D., & Davis, S. (2009). Hidden in plain sight: The active ingredients of executive coaching. *Industrial & Organizational Psychology, 2*(3), 244–260.

Schlosser, B., Steinbrenner, D., Kumata, E., & Hunt, J. (2006). The Coaching impact study: Measuring the value of executive coaching. *The International Journal of Coaching in Organizations, 4*(3), 8–26.

Society for Industrial and Organizational Psychology. (2008). *Executive coaching for effective performance: Leading edge practice and research.* 4th Annual SIOP Fall Consortium 2008, October 17–18, Cincinnati, OH.

Steinbrenner, D., Kumata, E., & Schlosser, B. (2007). Commentary on the coaching impact study: Measuring the value of executive coaching. *The International Journal of Coaching in Organizations, 5*(1), 158–161.

Steinbrenner, D., & Schlosser, B. (2008). *The coaching impact study: Understanding the value of executive coaching.* 4th Annual SIOP Fall Consortium 2008: Executive Coaching for Effective Performance: Leading Edge Practice and Research, October 17–18, Cincinnati, OH.

Steinbrenner, D., Schlosser, B., & Snyder, S. (2008). *Measuring the impact and value of executive coaching.* 23rd Annual Conference of the Society for Industrial & Organizational Psychology, April 9, San Francisco, CA.

Steinbrenner, D., & Schlosser, B. (2009). The coaching relationship: How clients view coaches and their impact. In L. Boyce, & G. Hernez-Broome (Eds.), *The client-coach relationship: Examining a critical component of successful coaching.* 24th Annual Conference of the Society for Industrial & Organizational Psychology, April 2, New Orleans, Louisiana.

Stober, D., & Grant, A. (2006). *Evidence-based coaching handbook.* Hoboken, NJ: Wiley.

Chapter Fifteen

WHAT CLIENTS WANT

Coaching in Organizational Context

Douglas Riddle and Natalie Pothier

How can a client or practitioner make sense of the increasingly complex array of coaching services, definitions, and approaches available in the marketplace? The pressing need is for a simple, pragmatic model of what clients want based on the characteristics of their organizations. As the coaching field matures, the need for organizing schemas that permit knowledge sharing becomes more important. The model presented in this chapter will help readers make predictions about client requests and design solutions that address client needs in the organizational context.

In our experience of working with hundreds of companies on six continents through many thousands of coaching engagements, we have found that there are important patterns to the coaching services that organizations and leaders want. Coaching services in organizational life can be described in terms of five levels or patterns of coaching use. We will describe the five levels and spell out how each shapes the needs of clients as they contemplate the use of coaching services and suggest how coaching professionals can meet those needs.

Organization Life Cycles

Like individuals, organizations develop across trajectories that can be seen as life cycles (Lippett & Schmidt, 1967; Miller & Friesen, 1984; Smith, Mitchell, & Summer, 1985; Torbert, 1974). Every organization is shaped by its history, culture or cultures, business growth or decline, and its role in its markets. Similarly, organizations grow in the maturity or sophistication of talent management and leadership development over time if they are to manage the increased complexity that accompanies growth. This level of maturity affects the ways that the organization manages coaching. In particular, organizations tend to use coaching in more collective or systemic ways as they mature.

This movement from coaching as an individual intervention to coaching as a fully integrated element of comprehensive business strategy affects the kinds of coaching services organizations seek. Based on our daily interactions with global clients, we have seen that coaching demands correspond to the culture and climate of the organization: more collective cultures with systemic approaches use coaching in a wider variety of ways. This can range from the typical one-on-one executive coaching by external professionals to multidimensional coaching programs with training and certification for internal staff, coaching skills for all managers, and team coaching for the board.

Organization Characteristics

The kinds of requests that clients make for coaching services depend directly on the situation of the organization and how coaching fits into its leadership strategy. In this case, the situation refers to characteristics of the organization as well as its place in its market. Characteristics of the organization include the degree to which control is centralized or distributed across locations and business units. An organization with strong central control or one small enough that there is line-of-sight from the senior leadership to the rest of the enterprise may not have the same challenges in implementing coaching systems as will a highly distributed organization with multiple centers of decision making.

A second characteristic is the degree to which human resources, learning and development, and organizational effectiveness processes are mature and fully implemented. In organizations in which attention to leadership development and talent management systems are haphazard or in early stages of formation, the coaching systems will typically reflect that immaturity. Conversely, organizations that have developed processes and leadership over significant periods of time will often have a more comprehensive and strategic use of coaching to support those processes.

Of course, one organization can display a range of styles because of mergers or geographic expansion. One of our global clients, a financial services firm, is highly advanced in its use of organizational development resources, employs mature and efficient human resources practices, and has effective talent management processes in place. The mother company is located outside Europe and opened a regional subsidiary office in southern Europe six months ago. The subsidiary is struggling to find its footing from both business and management viewpoints. It lacks any history of using coaching, so when the regional head approached the Center for Creative Leadership (CCL) for help with coaching services, the challenge included how to introduce something quite foreign to the experience of the regional office. Although the head of the region said that his team and the regional office "badly need(ed)" coaching, even the words "coaching" or "leadership coaching" were new to the staff. Thus, the situation of the organization may reflect several of the levels simultaneously. It is important to be clear about both the circumstances and experience of the whole organization and the part with which one is working.

Organizational Culture

So what are the key elements of the organization's situation that will shape coaching requests? The most significant is how it thinks about leadership (see Figure 15.1). It ranges from organizations whose leadership culture and processes are focused on individual improvement, through those who also think of leadership in collective terms, all the way to those enterprises who add a systemic

Figure 15.1. Organizational Culture

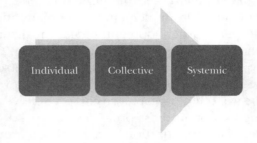

view. An example of individual leadership culture is a company focused only on the improvement of those in designated leadership roles or who are believed to have high potential. In these organizations coaching may be either a remedy for derailment or a benefit for a few key leaders, but it will probably be provided as straightforward one-on-one executive coaching by external professional coaches. The competencies in the organization's leadership model would focus on what a leader should be doing to increase the effectiveness of the organization.

Collective models of leadership focus more attention on the creation and leadership of teams and the development of others in addition to the competencies of the individual leader. In organizations with a collective frame, coaching may be used in a variety of ways. There may be greater use of internal professionals, and team coaching may also be used. Coaching skills may be seen as essential in the toolbox of practicing managers and training for managers to use coaching may be a common element in internal leadership development programs.

Systemic leadership models take seriously the importance of the contribution of both designated leaders and the whole organization to the leadership culture. They assume that leadership can come from the recognized leaders and from members of teams and groups when the right climate of initiation, innovation, and collaboration is operating. In organizations with systemic views, coaching may be a key component in efforts to change the culture through cascading of coaching systems throughout the organization. In some cases, the organization will build coaching into its plan for executing business strategy as well. We will provide examples of each of these as the organizational levels are discussed in the next section.

Organizational Levels of Coaching

Although the five levels are arrayed along an axis from simpler to more complex and from a focus on the individual to a focus on the whole organization, our evidence that any given organization will work through the different levels in the order they are presented (see Figure 15.2) is anecdotal. Each level makes certain demands on the organization, so a client will always be balancing resource needs with the organizational advancement goals. It is helpful to understand the particular pattern of a given level (Table 15.1), because this can help those responsible for managing coaching make wise choices about realistic targets and appropriate allocation of resources. Such information can also guide an external professional in proposing the right kinds of solutions based on an understanding of the organizational context in one of the five levels.

Figure 15.2. Organizational Levels of Coaching

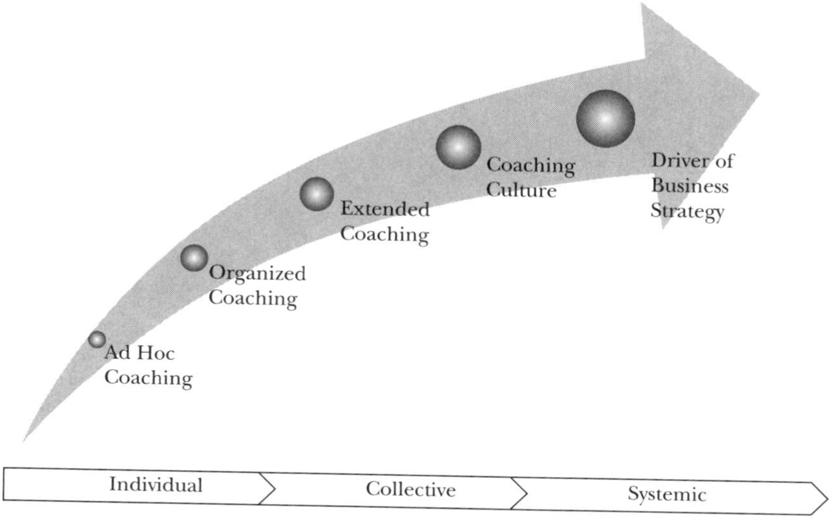

Table 15.1. Five Levels of Organizational Use of Coaching

Level of Coaching Organization	Organizational Need	Purpose of Coaching	Organizational Involvement
Ad Hoc Coaching	Rudimentary leadership development systems leave gaps	Remediation, accelerated individual growth, retention of top talent	Fragmented and dispersed to units or individuals
Organized Coaching	Bring coaching under management of organization	Greater focus on accelerating development	Create policies and standards for coaches and coaching use
Extended Coaching	Leadership development a shared responsibility	Management skill, team development, accelerated performance, change management	Coaching skills part of leadership metrics and tied to rewards; Internal and external resources supported
Coaching Culture	Innovation and rapid adaptation to changes	Attitudes and skills are embedded in all organizational processes	Consistent comprehensive training in coaching cascades through organization
Coaching Drives Business Strategy	Conscientious utilization of all resources; improved execution of organization business strategy	Everyone throughout the organization uses coaching approaches to develop others, strengthen client relationships, and increase group performance	Coaching elements built into business strategy; primary focus on coaching as execution expediter

Level 1: Ad Hoc Coaching

When an organization is at the Ad Hoc level, they may be using a large number of coaches or only a few, but there is little or no enterprise-level involvement in the process. Coaches are engaged by individuals or by a human resources business partner, but it is an individual engagement and not part of a larger program. From a management point of view, Ad Hoc coaching is very informal and neither coordinated nor managed on an enterprise basis. We have repeatedly had the same conversation with different clients in which the client says, "We have a lot of coaching taking place in our company, but we don't know who's getting it, how it's being paid for, or how coaches are selected."

In many cases the funding comes directly from the group or unit budget and because it is not incorporated into the strategic planning for development it may show up in a variety of accounts with different designations. The amount of money spent by the organization on coaching can often be startling because it is largely hidden from consistent review. In several companies we have found that individual coaches were billing more than $500,000 per year while working with several leaders. These costs were buried in the budgets of multiple groups until our process of discovery uncovered this unmanaged expense.

In this level, coaches may start with one leader and gradually add coachees based on their involvement with that first leader. Sometimes, coaches are introduced to the company because they come with a leader who used them previously in another firm. Coaches have seldom been assessed against any standards because the organization has not developed any such metrics. It is highly unusual at this level to find that anyone is evaluating the value provided by coaching.

This is not to say that coaches are not providing good value. We might expect that those they coach are very happy with the coaching process, but there might be no oversight by a leader's manager or anyone else. As a result, the purposes for coaching and the objectives of the particular engagements are largely unknown to the organization. Because of the unregulated nature of Ad Hoc Coaching, the organization has no way to determine whether it is getting any significant benefit from these expenditures. In some cases, the ability of the coach to inspire dependent relationships appears to be more important than any value to the business purposes of the organization. This level is often found in organizations that have experienced tectonic shifts in their market or gone through a merger, and it is not necessarily the case that the organization is newly formed. Some long-standing firms with a history of good human resource development have still not tackled the unmanaged state of their coaching use.

Finally, Ad Hoc coaching is disconnected from other human resource initiatives when they exist. The choice of coach, goals for the coaching, fees paid, and length of the engagement are all in the hands of the individual coachee or the HR leader who has recommended coaching. Take for example the newly appointed learning and development professional responsible for coaching at a global food and beverage company had developed a variety of ideas for her new position. She wanted to incorporate coaching into the talent management and leadership development that was being renewed for the company. She began to shop her ideas around, only to discover that long-timers could each tell her of multiple coaching engagements taking place across the company. When she tried to get an accurate picture of what coaching was taking place, she discovered that it was nearly impossible. Business unit HR partners were, in some cases, reluctant to disclose what coaching was taking place and were anxious about losing what little control they had. She had to enlist the support of the executive vice president of human resources before she began to get a more complete picture of what coaching was taking place and who the coaches were.

This kind of unregulated coaching involvement is what drives HR professionals to push their organizations toward the next level. No modern competitive company can afford to have such a large source of unmanaged costs or such a haphazard approach to the development of leadership. Organizations at the Ad Hoc level must take steps to move toward more Organized Coaching if leaders are to be responsible stewards of organizational resources.

Level 2: Organized Coaching

Organizations move to Organized Coaching because they wish to manage costs, demonstrate the value of coaching, ensure quality coaches, and increase accountability within the coaching work.

These benefits require increased organization around several elements, particularly coaching philosophy, standards, policies, and management systems. In some organizations, these efforts are part of larger initiatives to bring greater maturity to HR learning and development processes. In any case, it requires a commitment by senior HR staff in order to allow the time and resources necessary to bring order to the organization's coaching.

For example, we have seen the demand for better organized coaching expand dramatically in Russia. Over the last several years, more organizations have been making use of leadership coaching services and there has been a remarkable explosion of coaching schools to respond to the demand. As in much of the rest of the world, there are no agreed-on standards or even definitions for coaching. In many regions, this Western import carries a cachet that every up-and-coming executive must have a coach. Having a leadership coach is a symbol of importance, talent, and potential—and represents a badge of the elite. As one can imagine, this pressure cannot be helpful in the long run for coaching or leadership because it does not encourage the kind of deep commitment to change needed for organizational impact.

A Russian technology firm wanted executive coaching for a group of high-potential managers, but they expected a few sessions interspersed between leadership courses would ready them for taking on much more strategic responsibilities. This expectation betrays that the organization is still at the Ad Hoc Coaching level heading toward Organized Coaching, even though they may be asking for team coaching or action learning coaching more appropriate at a higher level of organizational maturity.

As noted in the Russian example, the kinds of coaching services employed by the organization may begin to expand at this stage (coaching skills training, greater use of internal coaching professionals, some kinds of team coaching interventions, for example), but the focus is still largely on managing the use of external professional coaches. The need to "grandfather in" existing coaching relationships may postpone the hard work of setting standards or getting agreement on a coaching philosophy. At some point those responsible will need to tackle the formation of a point of view and set of standards and practices for coaching. They will also need to address the political challenges of gaining acceptance across regions, groups, and divisions.

Though every organization may approach the development of a coaching philosophy and standards somewhat differently, there are some common patterns. For example, the philosophy of coaching often is developed in reaction to problems that have emerged. It is not uncommon to find an organization that is ineffective at managing poor performance turning naively to coaching as a way of "fixing" problem leaders who should have been dealt with by managers. To avoid this, coaching policies may preclude the use of coaching for inappropriate aims and frame a philosophy that encourages the use of coaching to improve the performance of successful leaders and to prepare leaders for increased responsibility. In a recent research study conducted with over three hundred executive coaches working across all industry sectors on the realities of executive coaching, the number one reason for hiring external coaches was developing capabilities of high-potential managers (Coutu & Kauffman, 2009). One global pharmaceutical company for whom we provide executive coaching limits the amount of coaching to rescue or restore derailing leaders to less than 5 percent of the coaching engagements.

Organizations moving into Organized Coaching draw heavily on published models of coaching practice and management or enlist consultants to help them develop the approach that will be most effective for them. The key questions managers of coaching initiatives ask are "How will we recruit and select the right coaches?" "How will we match coaches with eligible coachees?" "What will the eligibility standards be for coachees?" and "How will we keep track of all the coaching taking place across our enterprise, manage the expenses associated with it, and assess the value to the organization?" These questions represent the client needs that shape their relationship with providers and researchers.

Level 3: Extended Coaching

The third level is characterized by the integration of coaching into the overall HR strategy and execution for both leadership development and talent management. Coaching becomes recognized as an essential leadership skill, perhaps even the differentiating leadership success factor for retention of employees and increased productivity. Also, professional coaching begins to be integrated with other development and talent management processes. At this level, coaching becomes more visible to the business and line staff as a key skill for leaders. In some cases, companies incorporate coaching competence in performance management and leadership competency matrixes. The key aspect that differentiates this level from the prior one is that coaching services and skills begin to be used for a wider variety of purposes and in a larger set of contexts.

At this level, the rubrics for the use of external coaches and the involvement of internal coaching staff are consistent and widely known throughout the organization. Process improvements in the selection of coaches, the kinds of situations or opportunities that merit the investment for an executive coach, and the matching and measuring of coaches are often fully implemented. Typically, internal professional coaches are used for most professional coaching engagements except for executives at higher levels in the organization. Fewer coaching engagements are intended to address some deficit, and more are aimed at effective transitions into new, more demanding roles or support during significant times of challenge. Also, whether the coach is an internal professional or external, there are well-established processes for managing coaching and measuring the results. The continued use of coaching is clearly linked to the performance and development objectives of the organization.

It can be seen that the biggest differences between Extended Coaching (level three) and Organized Coaching (level two) are in the overall framework and integration of coaching services, rather than in the specific activities themselves. One may still find that there is considerable executive coaching taking place and that managers are being trained to make better use of coaching skills, but these activities are part of larger initiatives. They are not seen as isolated programs, but are part of the talent management or leadership development systems of the organization. As a result, even the use of external executive coaches is shaped to be part of the overall development plans for those leaders.

Leaders may get access to a coach to help apply what they have learned as part of an executive education program or when they have moved into an executive position.

Coaching is "programmatic" in the sense that it supports comprehensive programs of development and may be incorporated into succession planning or other talent management systems. Programmatic coaching can take different forms: part of a leadership development program that surrounds the classroom portion to deepen the learning experience; follow-up to such a program to ensure transfer of lessons to the worksite or accomplishment of action goals; facilitation of peer support groups to increase collaborative solutions; or development of coaching skills programs to spawn the greater of use of coaching behaviors with peers and direct reports.

A large European client in the chemical sector approached us to design and deliver a coaching program over a period of twelve months for their top twenty global executives, those reporting directly to the CEO. Although the individual coaching sessions were free to address any issues of importance to the executive, the purpose of the program was to create a shared and parallel experience for the whole group. As a result, the design incorporated clear milestones for progress, full assessment including interviews with stakeholders, individual debriefing and goal setting with the coach, developmental planning, and a clear emphasis on alignment with organizational goals. The design included strong evaluation of the coaching, the advancement of the executive's performance, and organizational and leadership trends unearthed in the process. There are many such examples of level three organizations that are marked by high organizational investment in external coaching for a specific top leadership group as part of the leadership development and talent management strategy of the companies. Companies at this level of maturity are able to combine these functions while maintaining the confidentiality of the coaching relationships and building on the knowledge gained from year to year.

Building Internal Coaching Capability

A key portion of level three coaching use is the systematic improvement of internal coaching capability. This manifests in the development of internal coaching professionals whose training and competence in coaching is the equal of most external executive coaches. It also shows up in the creation of systematic training of practicing managers and executives in the use of appropriate coaching skills. Though these organizations have greater capacity for professional level one-to-one coaching, they also have come to realize the larger impact on the functioning of the organization if they invest in encouraging managers to use these skills in their everyday management tasks. Part of the reason is the simple reality that the typical cost for an executive coaching engagement could cover a substantial training workshop for twenty or more leaders (Richard Kilburg, private communication). There are good arguments for both services, but the more experience that organizations have with coaching the more likely they are to want the skill set to be widely held and practiced. Additionally, the investment in long-term executive coaching with external professionals does little to improve the environment beyond those touched by the few leaders. Thus, even small improvements in the competence of a broad range of managers can have a salutary impact on the work climate.

Leaders as Competent Coaches

Organizations within level three often differentiate the skill levels and applications of coaching competence expected of managers at different levels. For example, a first-time team leader may need to learn the basics of coaching as a performance improvement and correction tool. Managers with more experience may benefit from clearly understanding the difference between performance coaching and developmental coaching.

Both are valuable, but developmental coaching has an impact on staff retention and morale for those who want to advance in the organization. It is also a concrete contribution to the leadership pipeline for leaders at all levels. Developmental coaching skills include how to provide feedback, how to listen well, and how to elicit solutions from others rather than struggling to impose one's own. The key insight missing for many managers is that coaching is not another task on their to-do list, but a management style and approach to people that will increase their effectiveness.

In entrepreneurial companies accustomed to a fast pace and rapid growth (technology or telecommunications, for instance), the value of taking time to address motivational and engagement issues may not be obvious. When senior leadership model these behaviors, it can be seen that coaching can actually reduce the managerial demands necessary to persuade, beguile, order, direct, or impose motivation from outside the person. At higher levels, coaching skills training might include how to balance directive and elicitive approaches. The most effective managers refuse to get stuck in one pattern of relating to their fellows. When needed, they can be quite directive, but often are able to engage others in thinking things through for themselves. Clearly, when a direct report is able to formulate solutions to her own challenges, she will be much more committed to implementing the changes than if she feels decisions are forced on her by her manager. In addition, tools such as personality factors and/or situational assessment can enhance the managerial use of coaching.

Level three organizations often are moving toward framing coaching as a contributing element of organizational culture. We will see that those elements receive full attention in what we have called level four organizations. The value of seeing coaching as a way of being rather than a set of behaviors is already emerging in many organizations who have made major investments in coaching.

Internal Professional Coaches

Internal coaches can be a subset of HR representatives selected based on previous coaching experience, accreditations, knowledge, interest, and talent. However, many companies also develop a cadre of internal coaches who are managers and who are made available alongside the HR peers. The development of this cadre can include specialized external coaching accreditation programs, customized versions developed by an external supplier, or can be run internally developed by an HR professional who has extensive coaching experience and can customize a tailored program.

When an organization adds internal coaching champions to the managerial ranks, their formal coaching work is almost always with individuals outside their normal chain of responsibility. Role confusion brought on by coaching within one's own span of control would be substantial. The consequence is that a leader being coached by someone in his chain of command is unlikely to feel confident that there would be no impact on his performance evaluation. Coaches need to be nonjudgmental and receptive to the full range of thoughts and feelings of the coachee as they are explored. That cannot be easily combined with the need for clear-eyed judgment about the performance of a direct report.

We are seeing fewer companies embarking on the development of internal quasi-professional coaches because the business case is not compelling. Most leaders have delivery requirements that are more obviously pressing for the company. Also, using coaching champions has not tended to yield the organizational impact that some had hoped and there's a greater movement toward more sophisticated approaches to creating coaching culture. We will explore this theme more when we review level four organizations, but we must take a brief excursion into discussion of mentoring as a part of coaching programs.

Mentoring Programs

The Wall Street Journal estimated that 70 percent of companies have some formal mentoring programs (Gutner, 2009). These can be quite formal, more casual, or targeted to just a specific group, such as new employees or transitioning leaders. A common question is the difference between coaching and mentoring. The critical difference is that the mentor is expected to have experience in the organization and the knowledge drawn from that experience that can guide and protect the person being mentored. A coach may not have specific managerial experience in that role, department, or the company itself, so would not be expected to play the same expert role.

Though a mentor needs to have coaching skills, a good coach may not have been in the role himself or herself. The role of a mentor in organizations is to guide and advise a less experienced employee by drawing from past experience within the organization. This employee could be a new staff member who needs to learn how to navigate the political and organizational system, and a more experienced manager can help accomplish that. It may be that a high-potential employee is being groomed

to move into a more senior role through an accelerated process and requires the help of a mentor. A mentor therefore has
a specific role to play and within that role can use a coaching
approach or provide direct guidance and advice to support the
progress of the other person. In formal mentoring programs, it
is highly unusual for the mentor to be the direct manager of the
person being mentored. More often, a mentor is two or more
levels above the mentee or drawn from another line or function
within the organization. In informal mentoring relationships
(initiated by the mentee or mutual connection), the mentor may
be an especially gifted boss who is able to delineate the various
roles without significant conflict.

It is not unusual to find both coaching and mentoring programs in the same organization. Because they target different
kinds of development, they can work well together and reinforce
the power of the whole program. A coaching program can target
development that can be beneficial in a broad range of circumstances because it focuses on improving learning ability across
situations. Mentoring may be superior when the challenges of
politically complex environments are full of hidden dangers
(multiple uncooperative constituencies, for instance). Sadly, in
a number of companies with whom we have worked, the coaching and mentoring programs are not linked and the managers
responsible for them may not even stand in the same group. It
seems likely that a comprehensive extended coaching plan would
best incorporate both kinds of programs.

Level 4: Coaching Culture

The fourth level in organizational maturity is seen when the enterprise seeks to make coaching a foundational element of everyday
behavior and attitudes within the organization. Culture encompasses all the habits, processes, systems, and relationships of the
organization, but it goes beyond structures and is embedded
in the unwritten rules of the organization. In practical terms, it
means that any sampling of behavior, any observation of a meeting
or work group, is going to be characterized by a common way of
thinking, behaving, and relating. Level four organizations seek to
make the values and practices of coaching a core element of the
culture.

Companies who reach this stage of coaching evolution are embracing the notion that coaching is not merely a tool for improving individual performance but a scalable means to increase team and organizational performance, too. These companies will make use of coaching in a wide variety of ways, combining coaching training for managers, executive coaching for leaders, performance metrics that incorporate coaching skills and many other elements (Bloom, Castagna, Moir, & Warren, 2005). The motivation for moving in this direction often comes from the results of climate and engagement surveys that have shown higher performance, higher retention, and increased involvement in those parts of the business where leaders are known to do more coaching of their teams on an everyday basis.

The organizations with which we have worked whose aim is fostering high-performance cultures with leadership excellence have embraced level four in different ways. Some started by identifying a body of coaching role models among their own top leaders, hoping to make those leaders ambassadors for change in the coaching environment. Role models are often drawn deliberately from multiple levels of managerial leadership, from the executive suite to first-line supervisors. Other organizations have launched major initiatives to get everybody on board. A large global banking sector organization based in the United Kingdom made the education of coaching leadership skills at entry, middle, and advanced levels a mandatory part of their talent and succession development programs. The result was that the selected managers were talent ambassadors encouraging new managers and aspiring managers to sharpen their coaching skills. For this financial services company, coaching has become a "must-have" competence for success. Some organizations have used more of a "stealth" approach and begun increasing commitment to coaching in a more organic way. One of our clients has adopted a top-down approach with the CEO, his team, and the next level, making use of regular team coaching and involvement in coaching skills training. As can be imagined, this has generated considerable interest throughout the leadership ranks of the organization.

Success Factors

The most effective and satisfied companies aiming at a coaching culture tend to have several success factors in common. The first factor is an understanding of coaching as more than a set of behaviors or techniques. Organizations that are serious about embedding a coaching culture expect that the core values of coaching will be necessary for their advancement in their marketplaces or as leaders in their mission field. Those core values are a belief that people who can think things through for themselves will come up with better ideas than their manager might have proposed; that people who are encouraged to dig deeper and reflect more fully and who are given the tools and support to do so will have more adequate and longer-lasting solutions to their challenges; and that people will always be more committed to the ideas they personally surfaced than to those of others. Companies that are in highly competitive, fast-changing markets or environments that are rapidly increasing in complexity need the dispersion of brainpower and heart commitment. These things cannot be mandated but must be elicited by leaders who listen, probe, believe in the capability of others, and who will remove obstacles to innovation. When senior leadership prizes these values, then the chances for culture change are improved.

The second success factor is the engagement of the chief executive and the senior leadership in being coached themselves and willingness to openly model and advocate for coaching approaches. The expansion of coaching culture in an organization to level four appears to be almost entirely linked to its beginning with or adoption by the top leaders. From there coaching can cascade throughout the organization with real investment by all levels. The commitment of resources is always important for coaching interventions to be successful, but for a coaching culture, the investment of time and commitment to consistent exhibition of coaching behaviors in all meetings and relationships appears to be critical.

The third success factor is a long-term commitment. Coaching culture never appears by fiat or simply because of the increase in the amount of coaching services or resources available. The multiplication of training opportunities, the investment in coaching metrics in performance standards, the open use of professional coaches, and the explicit commitment to coaching are necessary. In our experience the challenge is in taking the long-term view when short-term business results are easier to measure. It is much more challenging to identify the leaders who employ coaching well and ensure that reward systems recognize them. Patience and persistence are both required for credible change to take place in the enterprise, when the objective is a true desire to shift the culture. Internal systems (such as reward, performance, and appraisal systems), technology, and other HR and support infrastructure, as well as the hearts and minds of the leadership must be altered before coaching becomes part of the organizational DNA.

A fourth success factor is making the case for the substantial investment required for true culture change, which can require many elements. Surveys, anecdotes of success, personal testimonies, and exemplary coaching leaders can be collected and promoted, but they may not be enough to persuade many business leaders who might be willing to settle for compliance instead of commitment. A recent study of over three hundred top leaders from various industry sectors on coaching culture (Anderson, Frankovelgia, & Hernez-Broome, 2009) showed that there are specific organizational culture barriers that make it difficult to fully implement a coaching culture and must be addressed for organizations to smoothly move to level four in the coaching evolution. These barriers include such issues as senior leaders who "don't walk the talk" and the lack of financial metrics of impact. Developing the right metrics to make the business case for coaching culture is the next wave of coaching research.

Classic coaching metrics tend to be dominated by Kirkpatrick's level one measures (1994) that ask the opinions of the person being coached and rely on reaction and subjective measure of value. Some measures are not persuasive for those beyond the person being coached and cannot drive the level of commitment required of an organization to tackle the culture issue. Meaningful financial measures, such as return on investment (ROI), might more powerfully demonstrate the benefits, but they are difficult to calculate because of many intervening variables (Anderson & Anderson, 2005).

A fifth success factor is culture change that happens in a systematic or consistent way. A European subsidiary was faced with large differences from one regional office to another based on national differences in how coaching was seen. Although a major part of the company was on board and much excitement was being generated, others found the concepts associated with coaching to be a singular challenge. Intentional culture change across national borders often raises concerns about "cultural imperialism" or excessive central control. Companies need to address these issues explicitly and be patient for attitudes to change over time. A region may have to go through its own developmental process in its own time if a global culture change initiative is to be successful.

Finally, at level four, the perception that managers and employees have of top leaders' modeling coaching behaviors is a critical success factor. They are observing to see whether leaders ask open questions or tell, whether they guide or direct, and whether they demonstrate positive responses to increasing employee self-confidence. Leaders who show a commitment to empowering others through their conversations, listening, and responses can hasten the adoption of coaching as an organizational imperative. Our level four clients frequently ask for coaching for the senior executive team, both as individuals and as a team because of the difficulty creating truly collaborative and generative environments. Change process leadership requires a level of transparency, vulnerability, and willingness to both teach and learn and represents real growth to most leaders. Leaders who are aware of their limitations in these areas find it extremely valuable to make use of a coach as they navigate these major changes.

Take, for example, a leading petrochemical company with whom we are working. This client asked for help to support a major culture transformation program in which coaching was both a means and the end itself. The senior leadership team (a group of seven leaders at the top of the organization) started the program with a team coaching process rolled out over twelve months, tailored to their expressed development goals. The goals were:

1. To become leadership role models for the organization and key drivers of the culture change program.
2. To increase their ability to coach others, to provide and be open to regular feedback and become coach role models in the organization.

WHAT CLIENTS WANT 421

3. To increase trust, cohesiveness, and accountability within their team.
4. To act as change agents shifting the culture away from a risk adverse mind-set towards a more collaborative, innovative mind-set though the creation of a coaching culture.

Each of the senior leadership team members also received individual executive coaching to address individual coaching and development needs. One of the critical outcomes sought was that all members learn how to role model and use coaching behaviors with their teams and peers in their everyday interactions and meetings. Thus, the focus of the coaching intervention at the senior leadership level was to address both group and individual transformation.

Once this was achieved, the same program with slightly different pre-assessment tools was cascaded to the next-level managers and direct reports of the senior team and the succeeding level as well, totaling more than one-hundred leaders and managers. In this program, external coaches facilitated the individual coaching sessions, but all other team coaching sessions were facilitated by the senior manager with his or her team. This way the cascading of the coaching behavior is owned and pushed down from the top.

This example illustrates that level four organizations will use a wide variety of coaching services and methods, incorporating external and internal coaches, individual and team coaching, and coaching training at multiple levels, in order to deeply engrain coaching throughout the organization. More important, it shows that effective implementation of coaching at this level requires top leader involvement, a long-term commitment to the cascading elements, and an awareness that coaching is most powerful when it becomes part of who leaders are and how they behave as leaders, the identity of the organization, and its leadership culture.

Level 5: Coaching as a Driver of Business Strategy

Although we have very few examples of this final level, our experience suggests that some organizations that have realized the power of coaching are moving toward incorporating it as a major element of strategy development and execution. How does an organization effectively use coaching as a driver of business strategy? An organization may build coaching into its strategic planning process to increase involvement and engagement of a major part of the workforce. Coaching conversations can provide a real platform for creative thinking, solution exploration and exchange, eliciting more useful information about the real experiences of clients and the actual processes used to meet customer needs. Rather than the typical decision-based strategy development, level five organizations expect leaders to have coaching conversations that can open up novel solutions and nurture creative exploration at all levels of the organization.

Although we have seen some companies incorporate a coaching process into their strategic review as a way of getting deeper and more thoughtful discovery, more are seeing coaching methodology as a boon for execution. For example, one North American retail powerhouse recognized that the skills of coaching were at the core of the most successful sales relationships. They also were aware that well-coached teams demonstrate increased cohesion and higher performance. When it came time to look at capability development around new sales models and the creation of a more customer-aware store management, they implemented a coaching process cascaded through the enterprise. The theme that governed the program was that customers, sales people, managers, and executives all benefit from coaching relationships. The incorporation of coaching as a sales approach made this a level five initiative.

Some organizations have moved beyond seeing coaching skills and services as something "nice to have" toward incorporating them as key drivers of market differentiation and improved performance. In those organizations, we see top executive teams including the CEO fully endorse coaching as part of their leadership behavior. They expect coaching thinking to drive positive interactions among peers and direct reports as well as helping to shape their conversations with vendors and customers. Coaching has become part of the company's DNA and the language people use, the metrics for performance, the focus on mutual development, and the way of doing business all reflect that.

Another major U.S. retailer (automotive products and services) studied the practices of their regional managers to see what might be influencing the differences in revenue, customer loyalty, and team performance in their stores. They were able to identify a number of factors and decided that coaching would be the key to change. Each regional manager was provided with a coach who would work closely with that manager, traveling with her or him to the stores. The objectives were to increase the coaching behavior of the regional managers with their store managers and cross-fertilize best practices of the top performers. The program was measured in terms of consistency of interactions between the regional manager and the store managers and, ultimately, same-store revenue growth. The key here is that the coaching program itself embedded the company's strategic driver of Focused Management Attention in the business practices of the company. To no one's surprise, the coaching program had a significantly positive effect on revenue growth consistent with expectations that persistence of management involvement tends to predict improved retail performance.

The likelihood for coaching to consistently contribute in a direct way to the accomplishment of business objectives is increased by a substantial history of use of coaching in its many forms and across the organization. When an organization has been building a coaching culture over a significant time period, the workforce can come to trust in the commitment of senior leadership to the process and objectives. When that long-term commitment is missing, much of the workforce will see it as just another program among many.

The likelihood of organizations (particularly in the business community) operating at a level five is affected by the experience of companies with coaching. To engage a large percentage of senior staff, the consistent delivery of benefits from coaching initiatives is critical. Becoming a believer in the power of coaching methods often requires seeing the work of professional coaches, using coaching in one's own leadership roles, and observing the improvement in management performance when managers are adequately trained to incorporate coaching methods.

That sounds very much like moving through the levels leading up to the fifth and we suspect that is why we have observed so few organizations that get the full benefit from coaching. Clearly, the full engagement of the chief executive and the heads of any operational units is required, but that is only part of the story. In the few companies that exemplify level five, the learning and development, leadership development, and talent management professionals of the company are fully involved on the business side of the house. They are not sequestered in their own developmental corner, but are seen as full partners in the accomplishment of the business's mission. We know of only a handful of such organizations.

Progressing Through Levels

Most organizations will find themselves moving through the levels described here in a messy but recognizable order. If an organization has not learned to bring a measure of order and management to its coaching (moving from level one to level two), it is unlikely that it will find extensions of coaching broadly valuable (level three). Without experience managing the components of comprehensive coaching use, it can be daunting to aim at actual climate and culture change around the values of coaching (level four). Each level increases the organizational impact of the use of coaching and makes the identification of its value clearer. Also, each level demands a greater investment in corporate resources than the previous in order to achieve the benefits.

As an example, levels one through three are crucial in ensuring that certain fundamentals are built to allow coaching to "blossom" in a productive way in the organization and for the business. Integration of coaching with the business strategy of the organization requires a number of foundational elements: (1) a clear HR strategy and process in place with coaching embedded, (2) growing consciousness of the value coaching brings to the whole enterprise, and (3) broad support of critical internal stakeholders. A higher level of coaching use in an organization is not only more systematic and more widely deployed coaching, it is a difference in the scope and purposes to which coaching is put.

Implications for Action

In partnership with our clients and coaches, we have developed models for working with clients for each of the five levels and in assisting client movement to higher impact and greater benefit from their coaching initiatives (Frankovelgia & Riddle, 2010). We believe that using the five level this schema has helped us create greater value for our clients because we are less likely to propose solutions that lack the appropriate internal support or for which the organization is unready. The truth is that coaches and coaching providers can add value for clients at every level, but the value proposition varies depending on the needs of the organization.

At the first level, it is clear that any competent coach will be able to provide executive leadership coaching, but will not be able to rely on the organization's leaders for guidelines about managing the relationship with the company. At this level, the coach may need to propose metrics for evaluation and may not find that the company is interested in consistent measurement of value. If they welcome such an effort, it may very well be that it will only be used by the particular coach or coaching vendor. Though a client may want coaching skills training, the impact will be limited by the degree of support for change in the working context.

At each of the subsequent levels, the internal professional staff is going to be an important partner, and the coaching provider will do well to understand expectations and the role that external coaching providers can play within the maturing systems. Coaching providers who develop a wider repertoire of solutions (team coaching, coaching skills training workshops, expertise in mentoring systems) will be more useful to clients. At these levels, less money may be spent on external executive coaches, but the overall impact of coaching methods and practices is larger because many more people are involved in coaching work.

Internal professionals and those who manage coaching initiatives for their organizations can use this schema to make intelligent decisions about where to put energy. If one's organization is at level one, the greatest benefit to the organization will be created by getting the support of senior management to bring order and organization to the use of coaching. Establishing policies about the use of coaching and making decisions about how coaches will be selected or approved, how they will be matched with coachees, and how the coaching will be evaluated set the level for a more comprehensive approach to this powerful methodology.

Clients (frequently the HR staff or learning and development) have to demonstrate high value for coaching initiatives, and to do that they need to have proven coaches and measurable demonstrated value for coaching. Unfortunately, the absence of meaningful coaching credentials and of consistent, dependable measures of coaching impact makes this a treacherous course. We are in the curious condition common to many professional practices that there is an emerging consensus on coaching practice, but an absence of studies to support it empirically (Zan & Riddle, 2010). In fact, it is nearly impossible to find studies of coaching impact that are not contaminated by placebo effects or similar design problems. This is an area where controlled studies could contribute an immediate and significant benefit to the field.

It is essential that coaching providers do adequate discovery to move beyond demographic or other factors that may be unrelated to the effectiveness of a given coach. In the best case, the coaching provider has direct experience with coaches and continuously measures the impact of their coaching work with clients. It is the provider's obligation to help clients think beyond untested assumptions about coaches and coaching and to think more deeply about the individual and organizational outcomes needed. One of our clients in the services sector, based in the Netherlands, asked us to do exactly this: develop a criteria framework to allow preselecting a pool of external executive coaches. Those coaches were vetted against company-specific values and objectives. In this way they were able to ensure that the coaching process and policy created by the company enabled consistency across the enterprise. The coaching provider should also have appropriate measurements of past performance by coaches with enough specificity to suggest propriety for a given industry, organizational level, and culture.

Conclusion: What Clients Need and Want

Earlier we described the ways that coaching use is expanding in organizations as their understanding becomes more sophisticated and the systems needed to support it are developed. We believe that we will see many more organizations moving up the levels as described. At this point, the great majority of companies globally may be found at level one: ad hoc coaching. This is already changing in the case of large companies with substantial coaching programs because HR leadership is continuously challenged to demonstrate value. We believe that this trend will only accelerate. Advancing from lower to higher levels of coaching requires a considerable investment in coaching as a major component of culture change or (in level five) a high degree of commitment by senior leadership to culture as a driver of business performance. It appears likely that organizations that have made such a bet will be watched to see how well it pays off in the marketplace before others will take the leap.

Until very recently, coaching was spreading across the globe in a more or less systematic way. Modern leadership coaching as a recognized practice appears to have begun appearing first in the English-speaking West, primarily the United States, the United Kingdom, and Australia. The next movements were to regions where the English language has been in use, such as South Africa, Singapore, and India. It then began moving away from those roots and, as it did, the level of complexity and sophistication of coaching could be measured in relationship to its distance from western culture and English as the dominant business language. Table 15.2 spells out what we had observed until recently in the dispersal of leadership coaching as far as the role of the coach, the main purposes to which coaching was put, and the penetration of coaching use.

However, this straightforward schematic is quickly becoming outdated as new trends and players enter the picture. We can use India as an example of how situations are changing. As recently as 2006, many companies in India were intrigued by coaching and the number of coaches had exploded. However, there were very few coaches with significant credentials and fewer clients who could figure out how they wanted to advance the use

Table 15.2. The Spread of Leadership Coaching

	English-Speaking Regions	Western Culture Dominant	Eastern Europe, Asia, Middle East
Role of Coach	Stimulus to reflection, growth, change	Collaborator for a more "whole" life and improved performance	Teacher or expert; fewer differences between mentor and coach
Dominant Purpose of Coaching	Acceleration of development; increased performance	Problem solving, but increasing developmental uses	Correction of gaps; teaching of better or the "right" ways
Penetration of Coaching Use	High, no stigma; seen as perquisite for high performers	Medium, some stigma; valuable collaborator for executives	Low; still mostly global firms with roots in West

of coaching. In the last couple of years, we are seeing a broad expansion of leadership coaching with the addition of large investments in coaching as a management skill, the addition of team coaching, and a greater willingness to encourage coaching for very senior leaders. In some cases, organizations have made explicit commitments to increase their progress toward a coaching culture.

Similarly, in western Africa we are seeing companies in technology, telecommunications, and financial services beginning to invest in coaching to address the leadership deficit as their commercial sectors grow rapidly. New leaders are promoted so quickly that they do not have the time and opportunity to learn basic leadership skills, and companies are responding by training senior leaders in coaching and mentoring skills. The economic situation has made the use of external professional coaches so expensive that only a very small number of the elite use them, and most trusted coaches are European or other expatriates.

We have seen this phenomenon in former Soviet-bloc countries like Estonia, where coaching training for leaders in the banking sector has been embraced with enthusiasm. And it is not only in the developing world that this move to training is growing. In the U.S. educational sector, more voices are being raised to criticize the expenditure of large amounts of money on executive coaches when the same money could provide significant training for a larger group of managers or department heads.

In addition to this movement toward more organized and complex uses for coaching methods, we expect that there will continue to be increasing differentiation within the coaching services used. We are finding that top clients are looking for more differentiated use of coaching. This means something besides more coaches and better training for internal staff. Beyond these uses, we are finding that some advanced organizations are applying coaching to talent management challenges such as executive integration. Coaching skills are particularly valuable for encouraging emerging leaders to think through career paths with an organization or within a field. We suspect that the great growth in coaching will come as more coaches become experts in a particular industry or organizational level. The coaching generalist, who is expert in coaching methodology but not in the engagement between specific leadership challenges and that methodology, may be of less and less interest to clients. Most clients now have many more coaches from which to choose, and their ability to select coaches with specific experience (often with the particular company) and demonstrated results with certain kinds of leaders or leadership issues will shape the coaching landscape.

Finally, let us consider a word about coaching and coaches. Although the media has focused on a few coaching "stars" and the training and certification provided by the International Coach Federation, the actual coaching world has been maturing at a rapid rate. Recent research located over four hundred coach training organizations (Kuzmycz & Riddle, 2010). The incorporation of coaching programs in graduate programs in business and interdisciplinary programs for professional preparation is providing a rapid increase in the talent available and the shaping of a true global standard of practice in coaching. Far from a fringe activity, the research reported in this book and the constantly increasing demand suggest that coaching will continue to be a significant development tool. We are seeing strong pressure coming to bear on the need for controlled research, the development of evaluation tools, and a commitment to measurement. These movements will shape the client landscape in ways that are beginning to emerge, but still are yet to be formed. The most interesting phase in coaching development is still to appear.

References

Anderson, D., & Anderson, M. (2005). *Coaching that counts*, Philadelphia: Elsevier Brutterworth-Heinemann.

Anderson, M., Frankovelgia, C. C., & Hernez-Broome, G. (2009). *Creating coaching cultures: What business leaders expect and strategies to get there.* Research white paper. Greensboro, NC: Center for Creative Leadership.

Bloom, G., Castagna, C., Moir, E., & Warren, B. (2005). *Blended coaching: Skills & strategies to support principal development.* Thousand Oaks, CA: Corwin Press.

Coutu, D., & Kauffman, C. (2009). *The realities of executive coaching.* Cambridge, MA: Harvard Business Research Report.

Frankovelgia, C. C., & Riddle, D. D. (2010). Leadership coaching. In C. McCauley, E. Van Velsor, & M. N. Ruderman (Eds.), *Handbook of leadership development* (pp. 125–146). Greensboro, NC: Center for Creative Leadership.

Gutner, T. (2009). Finding anchors in the storm: Mentoring. *The Wall Street Journal,* January 27, 2009, D4.

Kirkpatrick, D. L. (1994). *Evaluating training programs: The four levels.* San Francisco: Berrett-Koehler.

Kuzmycz, D., & Riddle, D. D. (2010). *Coach credentialing: State of the field.* Research report. San Diego, CA: The Center for Creative Leadership.

Lippitt, G. L., & Schmidt, W. H. (1967). Crises in a developing organization. *Harvard Business Review, 45*(6), 102–112.

Miller, D., & Friesen P. H. (1984): A longitudinal study of the corporate life-cycle. *Management Science, 30*(10), 1161–1183.

Smith, K. G., Mitchell, T. R., & Summer, C. E. (1985). Top level management priorities in different stages of the organization life-cycle. *Academy of Management Journal, 28*(4), 799–820.

Torbert, W. R. (1974). Pre-bureaucratic and post-bureaucratic stages of organization development. *Interpersonal Development, 5*(1), 1–25.

Zan, L., & Riddle, D. D. (2010). *Global coaching standards.* Unpublished research report. San Diego, CA: Center for Creative Leadership.

Chapter Sixteen

NEW DIRECTIONS

Perspective on Current and Future Leadership Coaching Issues

Paul Tesluk and Jeffrey Kudisch

It was not long ago that an assessment of the state of the field of executive coaching conjured to mind a "Wild West" image of a frontier that "is chaotic, largely unexplored, fraught with risk, yet immensely promising" (Sherman & Freas, 2004, 83). As the contributions in this book demonstrate, leadership coaching has emerged out of the Wild West into a defined discipline and with more promise than ever before, as witnessed by the increasing investments that organizations are making in leadership coaching and the large numbers flocking to careers in executive coaching.

Here are some clear indicators of the maturation of the field that go beyond just the increasing utilization of leadership coaching by organizations and executives (see the Introduction to this book for a helpful description of the growth of the field of leadership coaching). First, there has been a flurry of interest and attention to the topic of executive and leadership coaching as seen in the number of books, articles, chapters, and reports on the topic. For instance, a good indication of whether a field is maturing is whether there are handbooks or major edited volumes (like this one), as this shows an accumulating body of knowledge. Within the just the past three years alone there have been more than a half dozen handbooks and dozens of books, chapters, and articles published on executive coaching (Peterson, 2009). Second, executive coaching is receiving increasing attention at major academic and practitioner conferences as witnessed, for instance, from a level of virtually no presence in the annual Society for Industrial and Organizational Psychology (SIOP) conference just five years ago to a consistently increasing number of papers at poster sessions and in symposia, panel discussions, and the like, on the topic of executive coaching. Finally, as another "leading indicator" of the increasing academic and research interest in the field on executive coaching, we are seeing a significant increase in the number of dissertations on executive coaching, and the trend is continuing at an accelerating rate. Until 1999 there were only four dissertations on executive coaching, whereas between 2000 and 2009 there were at least seventy-seven identified dissertations (Peterson, 2009). These are all indicators of a discipline that is maturing and attracting significant interest within the leadership development practitioner and academic communities.

At the same time, the promise that executive coaching holds as an established discipline based on well-developed theory, a clear and agreed-on set of professional standards and guidelines for practices, and a robust set of research findings and validated practices that can point to an agreed-on body of evidence-based coaching practices is yet to be realized. Polite but heated debates are taking place on the potential contributions of different theoretical and disciplinary approaches to executive coaching, such as those based on counseling or psychoanalytic perspectives compared to more behavioral or industrial/organizational psychology–based perspectives (see, for example, the exchanges between McKenna & Davis, 2009, in their focal article on executive coaching and related commentaries). These differing points of view require an emergent consensus and, ideally, an integration among different theoretical perspectives to create a clearly defined identity for executive coaching that is more than the sum of its various disciplinary parts. Further, though various coaching standards and competencies have been offered (such as the

Executive Coaching Forum, 2008; Worldwide Association of Business Coaches, 2007), these models vary widely and reflect the lack of consensus on underlying theoretical orientations and perspectives and present a barrier to effective training, development, and credentialing of executive coaches (Griffiths & Campbell, 2008). Another obstacle to leadership coaching fulfilling its promise is the dearth of established empirical findings that can be used to support evidence-based coaching practices. Although research on executive coaching is rapidly accumulating, very little work has begun to appear in the top journals, and there are very few focused research questions that have been systematically studied to the point where findings have accumulated sufficiently to draw clear conclusions of evidence-based findings. These are just a few of the challenges that the emerging discipline of leadership coaching needs to overcome in order to fulfill its promise as serving a central role in leadership development.

The perspectives in this book articulate many of the advancements in leadership coaching that mark its emergence from the "Wild West" frontier to an emerging and established discipline. They also point to how much more we need to learn in advancing the practice and science of leadership coaching. Our role in this concluding chapter is to help to summarize the contributions from this book's authors, provide some synthesis and integration that attempts to capture the current state of leadership coaching from a global (that is, holistic) perspective, and suggest future directions from the field as inspired by this volume's contributors.

The Boyce and Hernez-Broome introduction (summarized in Figure I.1) provides a useful organizing framework beginning with the "input" factors that contribute to the leadership coaching process and how fit between coach and client and the supporting role of the organization help to shape the nature of the resulting coaching process and lead to coaching outcomes that are a function of the various mechanisms or modes by which coaching can occur. We use their framework to draw connections between the coach, client, and organizational participants—that is, the parties that together are at the heart of leadership coaching and serve to define and shape the coaching process. We also point to what we see as important areas in need of further development in understanding the role of these important input factors. We then go on to focus on the resulting coaching process in terms of coaching relationships, ethical considerations, tools and techniques, and coaching modes such as e-coaching. From there we speak to contributions on evaluating the outcomes and coaching process overall. We conclude with our final thoughts—informed and inspired by the themes covered throughout this volume—for advancing the future of the science and practice of leadership coaching.

Coach, Client, and Organizational Issues

As the Boyce and Hernez-Broome framework suggests, the coach, client, and organization come together to shape the resulting coaching dynamic that results in learning, behavioral change, and productive and psychologically meaningful outcomes. Collectively, the authors in the first section of the book (Chapters One through Six) covering coach, client, and organizational issues contribute to a picture of leadership coaching as a multilevel phenomenon, spanning individual, dyadic, group, and organizational levels. Beginning at the individual level, the coach, of course, plays a significant role in the nature of the coach-client relationship, the coaching methods and techniques that are used, the content of the interactions and discussions between the coach, client, and other relevant parties (such as the client's peers and superiors), and how the coaching engagement is evaluated in terms of progress and defining success.

As Davis and McKenna highlight (Chapter One), given that coaching is ultimately about enabling individual change in developing leaders, coaches' theories about individual change are important for coaches to have positive influences on their clients' abilities to successfully change how they think, act, and perform. Building from established findings in the psychotherapy literature that identify the "active ingredients" of executive coaching which include the clients (their readiness to change, ability to learn, coping styles, skill needs, personality, and developmental goals), the coach-client relationship (establishing and maintaining rapport, building and maintaining trust), positive expectancies, and theory and techniques, they point out how various psychological theories such as cognitive, behavioral, psychodynamic, adult-learning and person-centered theories provide different, but also potentially complementary, contributions to triggering these active ingredients for coaching success.

From their work some intriguing questions can be posed, for example: What psychological theories are most helpful to trigger client factors, such as readiness to change, that are associated with more successful coaching outcomes like increased self-awareness, behavioral change, and performance? Are coaches who utilize a broad repertoire of psychological approaches more successful than those who are perhaps more experienced in a more limited range of approaches? and What enables successful coaches to shift approaches when needed? Building from these questions, it would be very helpful to extend Davis and McKenna's discussion of the different unique advantages of alternative psychological theories to develop a working taxonomy of psychological theories with active ingredients of coaching that can both guide future research on leadership coaching techniques and give direction to coaches on strategies to consider when working with clients in different situations. Likewise, we need research to better understand how highly effective coaches build and master skills that enable them to apply various techniques to their full potential and how to flexibly adapt during the course of a coaching engagement and across clients (see Peterson, Chapter Four; McKenna & Davis, 2009).

Expanding to the relationship level, Davis and McKenna also point to the importance of alignment between the coach and client on the psychological approach(es) that serve as the basis of the coaching relationship. As such, building a strong relationship with the client, asking probing questions to identify a client's underlying "theory in use," and carefully calibrating one's approach as coach with the client's expectations and evolving thinking to form a strong coach-client alliance points to a potentially important meta-coaching skill. This, consistent with Boyce and Hernez-Broome's framework, suggests that not only is coach-client fit important for facilitating how coach factors such as coaching technique influence coaching processes and outcomes, but that coaches play an active and important role in shaping fit with their clients.

Another element of the Boyce and Hernez-Broome framework that has implications for coach-client fit deals with the way in which organizational support factors—in this case, sourcing and matching systems used by organizations—come together to shape the coach-client fit. Underhill (Chapter Two) focuses squarely on this topic by articulating how organizations with significant coaching efforts go about sourcing and screening for coaches, describing how coach-client matching and fit is also significantly shaped by organizational processes such as sourcing and screening methods and discussing the underlying decision rules on questions such as whether to rely on external, internal, or some combination for coaches. For instance, a carefully developed and intensive coaching recruiting and selection process that takes into account coaches' knowledge of the organizational context and fit with the level, function, experience, and personality of the executive is likely to facilitate fit between an individual client's leadership coaching needs and the coach's capabilities. Understanding this dynamic between organizational practices on coach sourcing and selection and the quality of the resulting coaching dynamic on dimensions such as coach-client fit is important for advancing both the practice and science of coaching itself as well as building organizational coaching capabilities. This is a topic that we return to at the conclusion of this chapter with specific recommendations.

In addition to sourcing and selection, the training and development of leadership coaches has unique requirements compared to other forms of coaching. As Lee and Frisch point out in Chapter Three, coaching leaders is different from other forms of coaching that, for instance, emphasize the coach's providing advice or guidance based on his or her business content expertise or experience. Leadership coaching involves helping executives build self-awareness, understanding, and sets of skills and competencies in areas that are inherently difficult to master. Thus, effective leadership coaches must not only understand leadership theories and how adults learn and develop, but they also have to understand and incorporate knowledge about the organizational context in which executives function and the unique challenges and issues they face. With this in mind, Lee and Frisch propose what they see as two essential elements in training coaches to develop leaders through one-on-one coaching engagements. The first is the personal model of coaching, which captures how the coach thinks about his or her own personal characteristics that he or she brings to the coaching situation (such as education, experiences, strengths), the coach's understanding and beliefs about leadership and organizational dynamics, and the coach's preferences and beliefs about various coaching approaches and practices. Coaches' personal models shape how they approach their coaching practice, how they actually deliver their coaching through engagements with clients, and how they manage their own professional development as coaches. The second important component to training effective coaches, argue Lee and Frisch, is case experience with structured supervision following an apprenticeship, a learning-by-doing model. Lee and Frisch's components and set of topics that compose the heart of a leadership coaching training program provide an effective framework and summarize much of what is known in the practice community about developing leadership coaches.

Moving from being a good to a great leadership coach is tremendously difficult, argues Peterson (Chapter Four). Great coaches have developed a high level of expertise about the nature of human learning and are able to successfully coach developing leaders even in situations that are quite complex, urgent, or unfavorable, such as working with clients who are perhaps inaccurately labeled as being "uncoachable." Drawing from the expertise literature (for example, Colvin, 2008; Ericsson, 2006), Peterson articulates the challenges that leadership coaches face as they attempt to move from being good to becoming great. These include engaging in required deliberative practice and sustained, focused effort, sorting through the complexity of coaching engagements to understand relationships between coaching actions and client outcomes, mastering a broad knowledge base and diverse set of skills, and persevering through the tedious and frustrating aspects of the difficult areas of executive coaching (such as helping clients translate insights into action). Again, drawing from expertise research, Peterson's recommendations to leadership coaches on how to overcome these challenges include specific methods of engaging in deliberative practice, adopting specific learning goals, seeking client feedback, and practicing active self-awareness and self-reflection. These recommendations can offer the structure of a development plan, if you will, for leadership coaches to improve their own coaching competencies (and personal model of coaching, to use Lee and Frisch's terminology) and have implications for leadership coaching training, continuous development, and certification.

Great leadership coaching, however, also necessitates careful consideration of the client/coachee. As Valerio and Deal (Chapter Five) articulate, leadership coaching requires carefully observing and understanding characteristics of the client and knowing how to take coachee/client characteristics into account in the coaching engagement. Specifically, they stress the need for leadership coaches to pay close attention to two important sets of considerations when it comes to understanding clients in ways that can enable more effective leadership coaching. First, coaches need to systematically assess clients in terms of "categorizations that matter" such as life stage and goals, level in the organization, and the client's culture of origin; Valerio and Deal provide suggestions on the types of questions to ask to develop an understanding of these factors and how they may play out during the coaching engagement. Second, they highlight key transitions that clients often experience, such as transitioning to a new organization, moving into a global responsibility, or taking on an expatriate assignment, and the unique coaching approaches that are required once a leadership coach understands the challenges these transitions present to their client. Consistent with the Hernez-Broome and Boyce framework, this points to the importance of understanding the unique situation of the coachee/client in facilitating coach-client fit.

Valerio and Deal's contribution also highlights an important feature of the increasingly global environment that leaders experience and how it relates to leadership coaching. First, as cultural and racial diversity increases and use of leadership coaching expands internationally (see Riddle and Pothier, Chapter Fifteen), increasingly coaches will find that they will be working with clients from different cultural backgrounds. At a minimum, leadership coaches need to be aware of these differences and seek to understand how cultural values (their client's and their own) may affect the coaching engagement. Given that recent research has shown the significance of cultural differences in views of leadership (see House, Hanges, Javidan, Drofman, & Gupta, 2004), research taking cross-cultural concepts and applying them to the study of leadership coaching will be very helpful. Second, as many leadership coaches will work with clients taking on international assignments, helping their clients prepare for and learn from these developmental experiences will be greatly aided by understanding the cultural adjustment challenges faced by expatriates and how to help their clients manage and learn from those challenges.

The ingredients to successful coaching extend beyond the individual level of the coach and client and the dyadic level of fit and the coaching relationship. The role of the organizational system supporting coaching and, in particular, the resulting partnerships between coaches and the sponsoring organization, are critical as well. Although coaching is often considered in isolation as a stand-alone leadership development practice (see the Introduction), leadership coaching almost always occurs in a context defined by the coachee's role and position as well as the larger organizational context and its integration within a larger leadership development system.

As Desrosiers and Oliver point out (Chapter Six), the effectiveness of leadership coaching is often contingent on the extent to which coaching is connected within a larger leadership development system and how well coaches and the coaching engagement process are integrated within that system (see also the Boyce and Hernez-Broome framework). They go on to offer a useful framework for how organizations can enhance coaching by developing strong partnerships between the organization and coach. This begins with alignment at the engagement and organization levels on the purpose, goals, and philosophy of coaching, then shift to ensuring ongoing support for coaches working in the organization, and then move to further reinforcing strong coach-organization partnerships through evaluation at the engagement and system levels. Practices such as (1) the two-day Executive Coach Certification Program at PepsiCo that facilitates alignment through coach selection, education regarding the organizational culture and its approach to coaching, and development and clarifying issues of confidentiality and boundaries; (2) Microsoft's

Coaching Forum that provides coaches with valuable support in the form of development opportunities and sharing of coaching trends between coaches and the organization; and (3) Lockheed Martin's pairing of external coaches with internal coaches who provide ongoing support and assist in evaluating engagements of external coaches all provide best practice examples of how organizations can create strong partnerships between coaches and organizations through systematic alignment, support, and evaluation.

In summary, for leadership coaching to realize its promise, we have to begin by carefully considering how the traveling companions—the coach, client, and organization—come together to shape the coaching dynamic. By considering leadership coaching in both its individual parts (coaches, clients, the organization) *and* how these important players can work in unison as part of a multilevel system at the individual, dyadic, group, organizational, and environmental (or cultural) levels, we can better understand the coaching process and outcomes.

Processes and Practices of Leadership Coaching

The processes and practices involved in leadership coaching—the "journey," if you will, of coaching—consists of the coaching relationship, practices, content, tools and techniques, and coaching modes (Chapters Seven through Eleven). Together, these features define what takes places in leadership coaching and how the coaching occurs.

Although clear empirically based evidence is still lacking, there is emerging consensus within the field that specific coaching techniques, methods, or following certain models may be less important in determining coaching outcomes than the ability of the coach to develop a strong working relationship with the client and foster client motivation and willingness to engage (Feldman & Lankau, 2005; McKenna & Davis, 2009). With this in mind, Kemp (Chapter Seven) orients attention to the coaching process on the relationship that coaches establish with their clients. He begins by bringing into focus what is a very likely phenomenon in many, maybe even most, leadership coaching engagements: that clients often do not have well-informed and clearly articulated goals for coaching at the start of the process. In addition, in trying to understand their clients' needs and fulfill the helping relationship, coaches are subject—just as we all are—to a host of perceptual, attribution, and decision-making biases that make it challenging to really understand their clients, their needs, and coaching goals.

Kemp offers the "The Coaching Alliance Lens" as a reflective process-based set of guidelines that coaches can use for developing a strong alliance with their clients that is characterized by high levels of shared meaning, purpose, and commitment to the coaching process and high levels of shared trust, respect, and empathy in the coach-client relationship. The strategies he offers for the alliance-building process (for example, introspection and surfacing for awareness, reflecting for meaning) lead to potentially testable questions such as: Do coaches who follow an alliance-building process at the onset of the coaching engagement develop stronger working relationships characterized by higher levels of mutual trust, respect, rapport, and shared commitment to the coaching process that form the basis for achieving greater progress in the coaching engagement? Does the order of these processes matter in terms of the strength of the resulting coach-client alliance? Are coaches who systematically engage in a comprehensive alliance-building process less susceptible to perceptual and attribution errors and biases when assessing their clients?

Keeping the multilevel lens again in perspective, Stomski, Ward, and Battista (Chapter Eight) shift attention on the coaching process from the perspective of the individual coaching engagement based on the dyadic relationship to viewing coaching as a comprehensive, enterprise-wide initiative. For organizations with extensive coaching in place, they argue, leadership coaching should be part of a larger comprehensive set of related practices for developing leadership talent in ways that directly further the organization's strategic objectives. Creating a coaching culture, one where developmental feedback and continuous improvement are emphasized, is facilitated by an interrelated set of practices. These include initiating coaching at the top of the organization, actively promoting coaching and encouraging transparency, aligning coaching efforts with achieving strategic business needs, making developmental feedback a leadership responsibility, and embedding coaching in a variety of development activities that go beyond one-on-one engagements such as action learning projects, succession planning, and executive onboarding. By emphasizing attention to leadership coaching practices in terms of strategically designed, enterprise-wide programs versus a set of independent coaching engagements, Stomski, Ward, and Battista provide a way of viewing leadership coaching in terms of the strategic management of human capital that can potentially lead to organizational transformation and performance (see Becker & Huselid, 2006).

Moving from practices to content, Passmore and Mortimer (Chapter Nine) draw attention to ethics in coaching. As they point out, there has not been much explicit attention to ethics in the burgeoning coaching literature, there are a wide variety of ethical standards across professional bodies, and based on limited research on coaching practices on the treatment of ethical issues, many coaches appear to not have a well-developed approach for how they address ethical issues with their clients. This appears to be the case, especially in some international settings where leadership coaching has emerged more recently. In short, the image of the "Wild West" of executive coaching still remains when it comes to treatment of ethics. Although there may be value in developing ethical coaching guidelines in drawing from other fields (such as counseling and clinical psychology, nursing, and so on), there are many ethical considerations that are unique in coaching (for example, weighting executive coachee and organizational client interests and priorities when coaching in an organization-sponsored coaching program). Passmore and Mortimer argue that guidelines are of limited practical value in actually ensuring ethical behaviors by coaches, and so they emphasize the need to educate clients on ethical concerns and offer a model that leadership coaches can use to guide their own decision making and examine ethical considerations that arise during coaching.

Though Passmore and Mortimer's treatment of ethics in coaching is intended to give guidance directly to coaches, it is important to note that the systemic perspective advanced by

Desrosiers and Oliver (Chapter Six) on alignment, support, and evaluation for forming strong partnerships between organizations and the coaches who support their leadership development activities also notes that organizations can and should actively lead on creative, clear, ethical guidelines that clarify boundaries and ethical considerations that coaches may encounter in coaching engagements. Therefore, responsibility for ensuring ethical conduct in coaching resides not just at the coach level; it is also an important aspect of the coaching content that organizations can proactively manage through alignment, support, and evaluation activities.

Another critical element of leadership coaching are the tools and techniques used at different phases of the coaching process. Recent reviews of executive coaches and their practices have shown that there is considerable variance in which tools and techniques are used and how they are used (see Bono, Purvanova, Towler, & Peterson, 2009). Herd and Russell provide a comprehensive review (Chapter Ten) of various tools and techniques that leadership coaches can use at different stages of the coaching process—ranging from contracting and establishing the coaching relationship, to gathering feedback and assessment data, to action planning, and finally to evaluating progress and transitioning the coaching relationship. The authors also include important criteria for assessing the usefulness of different tools and techniques, thus providing a useful resource and an avenue for establishing potential best practices when it comes to coaching content. At the same time, when combined with the perspectives provided in the first section of the book that pointed out differences in coaches' underlying theoretical orientations and preferences for different approaches (Davis and McKenna, Chapter One), the Herd and Russell chapter raises important questions that go beyond the tools themselves and speak to the fit between coaching models and the types and uses of various coaching tools.

The manner by which coaching relationships, practices, content, and tools and techniques are actually translated into engagements with clients that result in coaching outcomes is a function of the various modes in which coaching can occur (see Figure I.1). In a rapidly evolving world marked by increasing reliance on technology to bridge and mediate interactions and exchanges, it is not surprising to learn that, as Boyce and Clutterbuck (Chapter Eleven) report, the large majority of executive coaches do at least some of their coaching in virtual media that rely on some form of technology, in place of face-to-face interaction. E-coaching offers leadership coaches the ability to successfully engage with their clients in meaningful coaching exchanges in ways that offer greater flexibility, accessibility, and availability to accommodate clients' hectic schedules and allows coaching to occur in an often more efficient and economical fashion. Moreover, Boyce and Clutterbuck employ media richness theory (MRT) (Daft, Lengel, & Trevino, 1987) to demonstrate that different technologies and face-to-face interactions are more appropriate for different coaching needs and situations. For instance, face-to-face interactions offer the highest levels of synchronous (real-time) exchange and interpersonal intimacy, which are both important for developing trust and handling difficult discussions that require uncensored self-disclosure. However, e-mail can offer important advantages in situations that benefit from asynchronous interactions that can provide coach and client opportunities for reflective thinking or instances when maintaining written records is helpful (such as when a client is making a specific improvement goal). Their analysis of features of different types of technologies that coaches may consider utilizing as part of their coaching practice to best fit the coaching medium with coaching objectives highlights the need to develop a comprehensive taxonomy to elucidate such choices for coaches and to guide research on the role of various forms of coaching media and how they shape the relations of coaching processes to outcomes (see Maruping & Agarwal, 2004, for an example on virtual team collaboration). Additionally, it will be important to understand if greater use of e-coaching increases the extent to which leadership coaches find themselves working with international clients, making it all the more important for us to learn more about cross-cultural issues and the practice of leadership coaching as the field takes on a more global flavor.

In summary, the leadership coaching processes and practices covered in this book range from approaches that are aimed at strengthening the coach-client relationship to those that consider coaching as an enterprise-wide set of related practices that build a coaching culture for the organization. As the field advances we suspect that it will increasingly be viewed at multiple levels of analysis and there will be greater attention to understanding how coaching at the relationship, group, and organization levels can influence and support one another. The content of coaching is advancing too in the form of greater attention to ethical issues and the use of various tools and techniques that are available to coaches at different stages in the coaching process and for different leadership coaching needs. Finally, the perspectives in this book promote our understanding of the variety of means by which coaching can occur, such as through various forms of e-coaching in an increasingly networked, global, and virtually connected world.

Evaluating the Effectiveness of Leadership Coaching

Last, but certainly not least in terms of importance, is evaluation. Evaluation is significant because it (1) serves as a critical source of feedback for coaches, clients, and the sponsoring organization, (2) is the method to ensure efficient use of resources, which is particularly important given that leadership coaching is among the most resource-intensive developmental activities, (3) ensures accountability to various stakeholders in the coaching process, and (4) is the primary means of learning and improvement for the coaching process itself. Evaluation is critical for the advancement of both the science and the practice of leadership coaching. The advancement of coaching as a science requires clearly developed and defined constructs, measurement methods that ensure construct validity and reliability, and analytical approaches that lead to defendable conclusions. Rigorous and thorough evaluation is essential for practice and requires the same considerations. As more and more organizations approach evaluation not just as a mechanistic endeavor to validate use of past resources and provide a business case for future investments, they perceive evaluation as a critical means of improving the organization's leadership development system. As the field of leadership coaching continues to mature, there will be an increasing need for more robust, rigorous, and multilevel research. Evaluation is no longer the "Rodney Dangerfield" of leadership coaching, lacking respect; it is the primary means by which the field will advance as both a legitimate science and a valued practice.

In this vein, as leadership coaching continues to advance as a discipline, a more systematic approach will be needed to evaluate coaching efforts. Ely and Zaccaro's integrated framework (Chapter Twelve) is a very helpful way to consider the options available for conducting rigorous evaluation. Consistent with the viewpoints expressed earlier regarding the importance of evaluation to multiple parties that are part of the coaching process, Ely and Zaccaro begin with identifying evaluation stakeholders because various stakeholders have different interests among various criteria, which, in turn have implications for the most appropriate methodologies to employ. For instance, consider a leadership coaching engagement with a coach who is working to improve his coaching expertise and advance from a "good to great" coach (see Peterson, Chapter Four) and is working with the CEO of a small start-up. Evaluation data identifying changes in behavior and performance is critical to the client who understands that the company's very existence rests squarely on her leadership and who is also highly anxious about spending precious start-up resources on developmental activities. Similarly, for the coach who is highly focused on developing her expertise, she looks to evaluation data to not only build her reputation as a successful coach (that is, summative criteria), but also to help provide feedback that will enable her to understand the complexity inherent in applying alternative coaching techniques and resulting responses from the client and providing data that will allow her to successfully reflect and learn (that is, formative criteria). Contrast this with a scenario of an organization with a highly developed and systemic approach where coaching is integrated within a larger set of leadership development activities and intended to drive business results (see Stomski, Ward, and Battista, Chapter Eight). Here, in addition to client and coach, the client organization is a key stakeholder interested in the relationships between coaching practices and business results at the organizational level. In both cases, evaluation is clearly critical for advancing the goals of the key stakeholders in the coaching process, however, it is also clear the most appropriate evaluation measures, methods, and analyses will be quite different. The Ely and Zaccaro framework will be quite helpful in giving guidance to practitioners and researchers with their coaching evaluation efforts (see also, Smith, Borneman, Brummel, & Connelly, 2009).

Given the resource intensity of leadership coaching, it is not surprising that coaches, coaching organizations, and organizations sponsoring coaching as part of their leadership development activities have a vested interest in understanding return on investment (ROI). Unfortunately, as Anderson (Chapter Thirteen) points out, evaluating ROI for coaching is time-consuming, expensive, and difficult. Perhaps an even more significant limitation to traditional approaches to ROI is that managers have been shown to be highly skeptical of ROI/utility calculations conducted by HR professionals (Latham & Whyte, 1994; Whyte & Latham, 1997). This makes Anderson's "coaching approach" to ROI, which blends traditional quantitative and monetary estimations with rich narrative descriptions that essentially involve following a set of probing questions designed to uncover the return to coachees and the organization, an intriguing alternative. Consistent with Ely and Zaccaro's framework (Chapter Twelve), this shifts the ROI process beyond standard summative financial return estimates into formative measurement by capturing rich descriptive details on what coaching-related benefits accrue based on learning and changes in attitudes and behaviors. It would be very informative to see if the approach for generating coaching ROI by Anderson overcomes some of the limitations that have hampered traditional ROI/utility analysis methods that lead to managerial skepticism.

With the diversity of stakeholders with different interests involved in leadership coaching, it is not surprising that forming partnerships between coaches, organizations, consulting firms, and academics to design and carry out long-term, systematic coaching evaluations is rare. Steinbrenner and Schlosser (Chapter Fourteen) provide one such example that demonstrates many of the features from Ely and Zaccaro's framework, including the systematic assessment of the evaluation needs of different stakeholders, the use of both formative and summative criteria that span reactions, learning, behavior, and results, and combine multiple sources, levels of analysis, and qualitative and quantitative methods. The level of depth of the systematic analysis helps identify some surprising findings that demonstrate the importance of the connections that leadership coaching efforts have with coachees' managers and development plans that could lead to very specific and actionable improvements.

As Riddle and Pothier (Chapter Fifteen) argue, it is for these very reasons, and a desire to understand how to improve leadership coaching efforts through greater integration of coaching as part of a systematic leadership development process, that this type of comprehensive, multilevel, multimethod, ongoing evaluation will be increasingly sought after by organizations. Riddle and Pothier offer an organizing framework of levels of coaching organization. These range from individually focused coaching efforts where coaching is conducted in primarily an ad hoc fashion, to more collective models where coaching occurs in a variety of ways, including individual and team coaching, and coaching skills are included in leadership models for developing managers, to systematic efforts where coaching is utilized at all levels of the organizations and is cascaded downward and viewed as a comprehensive approach to facilitate culture change. This framework helps identify what clients are seeking from their coaching efforts and how to best conduct evaluations. For instance, the Riddle and Pothier framework helps clarify some of the sources of resistance that Steinbrenner and Schlosser document that they encountered in their systematic evaluation effort. For many of the coaches who were quite likely viewing their coaching as individual, ad hoc exercises, the value of the systematic, multimethod, and comprehensive evaluation was likely to be questionable. However, it was certainly appreciated by the organizational sponsors who were viewing the coaching process as a more enterprise-wide activity designed to take a strategic approach to leadership development. The Riddle and Pothier framework is also helpful in making sense of how leadership coaching is expanding globally. What originated as marked differences in the purpose of leadership coaching, the coach's role, and in the use of coaching across the United States, in English-speaking countries, Western Europe, Eastern Europe, Asia, and the Middle East is rapidly changing as experience with and accelerating needs for leadership coaching and leadership development more generally are pushing organizations to adopt more systemic approaches. If Riddle and Pothier's predictions continue, it is further evidence of a shift away from a highly fragmented and differentiated approach to coaching (the "Wild West" image) to a more consistent philosophy and methodology on a global scale that could accelerate spread of best practices and integration.

Again, as with the previous two sections of the book, the contributions in this section on evaluation point to a maturing in the field of leadership coaching that increasingly recognizes the importance of rigorous evaluation and a movement to organized, systematic approaches that take into account the evaluation needs of various stakeholders, the importance of evaluating coaching using both formative as well as summative criteria, and using methodologies that include multiple sources, qualitative and quantitative approaches, and multiple levels.

Concluding Comments

In closing, we would like to share some final observations, themes, and directions for future research that emerge from the perspectives shared in this book. These are themes that cut across the sections on coach, client, and organizational issues, leadership coaching processes and practices, and evaluation.

Training and Development of Leadership Coaches

One conclusion that is clear from viewing the contributions in this book in total is that the discipline of leadership coaching is rapidly advancing and this has important implications for the training, development, and professional certification of leadership coaches and those who lead coaching efforts. Although various competency models have been developed, there is a great deal of variation in terms of the knowledge and skills that are listed when comparing across models (see Peterson, Chapter Four), which is undoubtedly driven by the interdisciplinary nature of leadership coaching and the nascent state of the field. Nonetheless, if the practice of leadership is to advance, the quality of the training and development of leadership coaches needs to improve as well. Focused attention on developing and validating leadership coaching competency models will help as will defined approaches to building leadership coach training and development programs around those competency models (see Lee and Frisch, Chapter Three). Here, Peterson's distinction between what differentiates good coaches from great coaches is important because it helps to specify potential levels of development of coaching expertise (basic or core competencies versus more advanced competencies such as how to motivate resistant executives or those who lack basic self-awareness).

Integration of Leadership Coaching Within a Leadership Development System

Several authors in this book point to an emerging approach whereby leadership coaching is integrated into an organizational systematic and strategically driven leadership development system (for example, Boyce and Hernez-Broome; Desrosiers and Oliver, Chapter Six; Stomski, Ward, and Battista, Chapter Eight; Riddle and Pothier, Chapter Fifteen). The effectiveness of leadership coaching is often contingent on how well coaching is integrated within a larger leadership development system that includes leadership identification and selection, performance management, development and feedback, and succession planning. We fully agree with the position of Stomski, Ward, and Battista that organizations will realize the greatest value from their coaching investments when they are part of a systematic approach to leadership development that creates a coaching culture by interweaving leadership coaching in different leadership development activities. Unfortunately, as the authors note, during economic downturns, when organizations need to actually invest more in leadership development to address the underlying causes of poor performance and to stimulate innovation, they actually reduce these investments and consequently move away from developing these types of systematic, comprehensive, multifaceted, and integrated leadership coaching practices. Research attempting to relate the impact of systematic approaches of leadership coaching to multifaceted leadership development efforts and, ultimately, indicators of leadership or human capital effectiveness (such as effectiveness of succession planning) and organization outcomes will be critical for developing an understanding of the strategic value of leadership coaching.

If we had to recommend one place to start that might help begin reversing this state of affairs it would be by pursuing an aggressive integration of leadership coaching with developmental experiences. For instance, McCall (2010) recently advocated for a recasting of leadership development around developmental job and workplace experiences. He provided a thoughtful discussion of all the ways in which on-the-job assignments and other work-related experiences are instrumental for promoting development of leadership knowledge, skills, and abilities, and he noted the contingencies that need to be addressed in order for developing leaders to effectively learn from their experiences. What was missing from this, however, aside from a couple short and indirect references, was the role of leadership coaching. Indeed, leadership coaches, with their understanding and ability to help executives learn, actually could be the key catalysts for making developmental experiences be a more effective leadership development approach. In addition, leadership coaching and developmental experiences should be explored in conjunction with concepts such as developmental readiness (for example, Avolio & Hannah, 2009) and learning goal orientation (for example, Dragoni, Tesluk, Russell, & Oh, 2009) to understand how client motivational factors shape learning through developmental experiences and how coaches can influence these client motivational factors. Further, at an aggregate level, we suspect that when integrated with other important leadership development practices, such as leadership identification and selection, performance management, development and feedback, and succession planning, leadership coaching can work in an interactive manner to strengthen relationships among various leadership development activities that can make for a more robust leadership development system.

Advance the Practice and Science of Executive Coaching by Connecting the Two

A final observation that we feel reflects the contributions from this book, written by an eclectic combination of experienced coaches and those who lead coaching practices, academics, and practitioners, is that the discipline of leadership coaching will advance more rapidly if the field explicitly pursues a strategy that links the practice and the science of leadership coaching together and creates mechanisms of exchange that will jointly benefit practice and science. Potential mechanisms might include creating consortia linking professional coaching organizations (such as the International Coach Federation), private and public sector organizations that are committed to executive coaching and have established coaching practices and programs, leadership coaches, and researchers to developed focused agendas on different leadership coaching questions (such as those identified in this book), and pursue projects and initiatives that have explicit goals of advancing the practice and science of leadership coaching.

We end with reiterating the observation that we made at the beginning of this chapter, that this book represents how far the discipline of leadership coaching has come in a very short period of time. More important, however, the contributions in this book show that the promise of leadership coaching is greater than initially known. It's now time to build on these contributions and help advance the science and practice of leadership coaching even more aggressively.

References

Avolio, B. J., & Hannah, S. T. (2009). Leadership developmental readiness. *Industrial and Organizational Psychology, 2,* 284–287.

Becker, B. E., & Huselid, M. A. (2006). Strategic human resources management: Where do we go from here? *Journal of Management, 32,* 898–925.

Bono, J. E., Purvanova, R. K., Towler, A. J., & Peterson, D. B. (2009). A survey of executive coaching practices. *Personnel Psychology, 62,* 361–404.

Colvin, G. (2008). *Talent is overrated: What really separates world-class performers from everybody else.* New York: Portfolio.

Daft, R., & Lengel, R. (1986). Organizational information requirements, media richness and structural design. *Management Science, 32,* 554–571.

Daft, R., Lengel, R., & Trevino, L. (1987). Message equivocality: Media selection and manager performance implications for information systems. *MIS Quarterly, 11*(3), 355–366.

Dragoni. L., Tesluk, P. E., Russell, J. E. A., & Oh, I. S. (2009). Understanding managerial development: Integrating developmental assignments, learning orientation and access to developmental opportunities in predicting managerial competencies. *Academy of Management Journal, 52*, 731–743.

Ericsson, K. A. (2006). The influence of experience and deliberate practice on the development of superior expert performance. In K. A. Ericsson, N. Charness, R. R., Hoffman, & P. J. Feltovich (Eds.), *The Cambridge handbook of expertise and expert performance* (pp. 683–703). New York: Cambridge University.

Executive Coaching Forum. (2008). *The executive coaching handbook: Principles and guidelines for a successful coaching partnership* (4th ed.). Available at www.executivecoachingforum.com.

Feldman, D. C., & Lankau, M. J. (2005). Executive coaching: A review and agenda for future research. *Journal of Management, 31*, 829–848.

Griffiths, K., & Campbell, M. (2008). Regulating the regulators: Paving the way for international, evidence-based coaching standards. *International Journal of Evidence Based Coaching & Mentoring, 6*(1), 19–31.

House, R. J., Hanges, P. J., Javidan, M., Drofman, P., & Gupta, V. (2004). *Culture, leadership, and organizations: The GLOBE study of 62 societies.* Thousand Oaks, CA: Sage.

Latham G. P., & Whyte G. (1994). The futility of utility analysis. *Personnel Psychology, 47*, 31–46.

Maruping, L. A., & Agarwal, R. (2004). Managing team interpersonal processes through technology: A task-technology fit perspective. *Journal of Applied Psychology, 89*, 975–990.

McCall, M. M. (2010). Recasting leadership development. *Industrial and Organizational Psychology, 3*, 3–19.

McKenna, D. D., & Davis, S.L. (2009). Hidden in plain sight: The active ingredients of executive coaching. *Industrial and Organizational Psychology, 2*, 244–260.

Peterson, D. B. (2009). "Essential" readings in professional coaching. Unpublished bibliography.

Sherman, S., & Freas, A. (2004). The wild west of executive coaching. *Harvard Business Review, 82*(11), 82–90.

Smith, I. M., Borneman, M. J., Brummel, B. J., & Connelly, B. S. (2009). The criterion problem in executive coaching. *Industrial and Organizational Psychology, 2*, 288–292.

Whyte G., & Latham G. P. (1997). The futility of utility analysis revisited: When even an expert fails. *Personnel Psychology, 50*, 601–610.

Worldwide Association of Business Coaches. (2007). *Business coaching definition and competencies.* Available from: www.wabccoaches .com/includes/popups/defi.

Name Index

Subject Index

Page references followed by *fig* indicate an illustrated figure; followed by *t* indicate a table.

A

ABCDE model of coaching, 248
ACT model of coaching, 248
ACTION ethical decision-making model, 222–224 *fig*, 225
Action ideas, 74–75
Action learning coaches: action learning challenges faced by, 188; coaching role of, 185–186; forming, norming, and storming practices by, 186–187; global issues to watch out for, 188–189; individual versus project-based approaches by, 189–190; providing feedback modeling by, 187–188
Action learning coaching: action learning projects used in, 184–185; aligning organization's talent strategy to, 189; challenges in, 188; description of, 183–184; global issues in, 188–189; individual versus project-based approaches to, 189–190; providing feedback during, 186, 187–188; role of action learning coach in, 185–187
Action learning conversations, 252
Action-observer-reflection model, 239, 248
Active coaching, 96
Ad Hoc Coaching level, 407–408

Adult behavior change/growth: as coaching evaluation criteria, 338–339; cognitive behavioral approach to, 12–13, 18*t*, 249; as evaluation criteria, 338–339; theory lenses about, 62–63; transtheoretical model of behavior change, 250
Adult learning theory, 13, 19*t*
Advanced beginner coaches, 85
Age differences: of current client populations, 106; stereotypes related to, 111–112
ALIFE model of coaching, 248
Alignment of coaching: alignment at the engagement level, 134–137; to business strategy, 180–181; as coaching technique, 252; educating coaches to achieve, 129–132; importance of, 125–126; matching coaches with executives for, 135–136; model for coaching in organizations and, 125 *fig*; at the organizational level, 126–134; to organization's talent strategy, 189; rapid alignment model of, 198–202; selecting the right coaches to achieve, 128–129; setting boundaries to achieve, 132–134; with stakeholders, 136–137. *See also* Coaching; Leadership coaching

American Management Association
(AMA), 41
American Psychological
Association, 133
APA (American Psychological
Association) ethical principles, 209*t*
Applied ethics, 207
Appreciative inquiry model, 234,
238, 248
Assessment tools: career interest
inventories, 262; conflict
management measures, 272–273;
critical thinking and reasoning
measures, 266; cultural styles
and adaptability, 267; emotional
intelligence, 274–275; executive
derailers, 266; general leadership,
270–271; general performance
measures or multisource ratings,
268–269; measures of learning
and innovation, 263; measures of
strengths, 269–270; personality
inventories, 263–265; self-awareness
and life values, 260–261; stress
management measures, 271–272;
team orientation and decision
making, 273–274; work values and/
or motivation, 261
Association for Coaching (AC),
205, 218
Assurant, 392
Attribution bias, 154

B

Baby Boomers, 111, 112
Bank of New York, 181
Bank of New York Mellon, 181–183
Bar-On Emotional Quotient
Inventory EQ-i, 274
Behavior change. *See* Adult behavior
change/growth
Behaviorism, 12, 18*t*
Belbin Team Role Inventory, 273
Benchmarks: executive derailers
assessment using, 266; general

performance measures/
multisource ratings using, 268
Blink (Gladwell), 85
Body work/somatics, 256
Booz Allen Hamilton, 392
Boundaries: alignment and role of
setting, 132–134; ethical issues
related to, 221
Brief solution-focused coaching, 239
British Association for Counseling
(BACP), 211
British Association for Counseling
and Psychotherapy (BACP), 211
British Psychological Society (BPS),
210*t*, 211
Building alliances to leverage
organizational arrangements
exercise, 252
Bureau of Labor Statistics, 105, 106
Buros Mental Measurements Yearbook, 234
Business acumen, 92
Business ethics: framework for
understanding, 214 *fig*; overview
of, 213–215

C

California Personality Inventory (CPI)
Assessments, 263
Cards (coaching technique), 253
Career interest inventories: Career
Anchors, 262; Strong Interest
Inventory, 262; The Work
Expectations Profile, 262
Center for Creative Leadership
(CCL), 235, 237, 300, 403
Certification issue, 37, 40
Challenging deeply held assumptions
exercise, 252
Change. *See* Adult behavior
change/growth
Chunking coaching content, 60
Citi, 392
Client population: case example of
challenges facing, 116–120;
challenge of coaching issues for,

Coaches (*continued*)
leaders and, 79; challenges of being a great, 90–94; client screening of, 37–42; as coaching stakeholder, 324–326; competent, 85–86, 92–93; confidentiality ethics for, 132–134; danger of stereotyping clients by, 109–112; developing expertise, 94–99; dimensions of reactions relevant to characteristics of, 333*t*; Dreyfus and Dreyfus's five-stage model of, 85; e-coaching challenges for the, 296–299; as evaluation data source, 342; executive on-boarding role of, 196–198; experts, 85–86; external, 36–37, 43, 140–141, 145; feedback from client to, 97; good, 84–90; internal, 36–37, 140–141, 145, 412–413, 414–415; leaders as competent, 413–414; leadership coaching issues for, 434–440; learning outcomes of, 337–338; matching executives with, 135–136; need for flexibility by, 16; orientation sessions for, 131–132; origins and success rates of, 47–48; personal model of coaching, 51–55, 76–79; screening of organizations by, 42–43; use of self by, 71–72; self-calibration process by, 158–172; sourcing, 32–45; supervision of, 55–56, 160–161, 220; three key questions when appointing a, 220*e*; training and development of leadership, 449–450; walking the talk, 55, 78. *See also* Coaching competencies; Executives
Coaching: active, 96; active ingredients of psychotherapy applied to, 5 *fig*–24; Ad Hoc, 407–408; alignment of, 125 *fig*–137; closure of engagement, 75–76, 241–242; connecting practice and science of, 451–452; contributions of psychologists to, 3–5; developing expertise in, 94–99; as driver

of business strategy, 421–424; e-coaching, 285–309; ethics in, 205–225; evaluation of, 125 *fig*, 143–146; executive on-boarding, 195–202; historical perspective of clients and, 105–108; model for coaching in organizations, 124–147; organizational context of, 401–430; organizational levels of, 405 *fig*–426; pedagogy of teaching leadership, 51–59; principles of effective leadership, 79–80; ROI (return on investment) of, 339–341, 351–368, 447; streams and banks of, 60–62; success factors of, 417–421; succession planning, 190–195; support of, 125 *fig*, 137–143; topics and processes of, 59–76, 241–242; transpersonal, 256; as whole-person activity, 55, 56. *See also* Alignment of coaching; Coaching frameworks; Leadership coaching
Coaching Alliance Lens (CAL): description of, 164, 441; emergence of the coaching alliance using, 170; illustrated diagram of, 165 *fig*; inquiring for insight, 169; introspection and surfacing for awareness using, 164–166; reflecting for meaning using the, 166–167; self-management process using, 167–168; sharing for authenticity, 168–169
Coaching alliances: CAL (Coaching Alliance Lens) template for, 164–170, 441; challenges to building, 153–158; client outcomes of effective, 170–172; discourse and research on building, 152–153; exercise on leveraging organizational arrangements through, 252; HFL (human factors lens) framework for building, 158 *fig*–161; organizational dynamic of, 163 *fig*; psychodynamic factors impacting, 155–158; relationship

DISC Profile, 264
Dreyfus and Dreyfus's five-stage model of coaches, 85

E

E-coaching: advantages of, 291*t*–292*t*; definitions of, 286–287; state of, 290, 293; technologies of, 287–290, 303–305
E-coaching logistics: confidentiality, 303; contracting, 302; scheduling, 302–303
E-coaching practice: building the future of, 299; client challenges of, 294–296; coach challenges of, 296–299; organization challenges of, 293–294
E-coaching process: building and maintaining relationships, 305–307; evaluation and transition, 307–308; logistics of, 301–303; matching client-coach fit as part of, 300–301; supporting the, 299–308; technology used during, 287–290, 303–305
eCF Personal Work Values, 261
Emotional Competence Inventory (ECI), 275
Emotional intelligence assessment: Bar-On Emotional Quotient Inventory EQ-i, 274; Emotional Competence Inventory (ECI), 275; Mayer-Salovey-Caruso Emotional Intelligence Test (MSCEIT), 275
Energy management and balance activities, 253
Ethical codes: APA ethical principles for, 209*t*; BPS ethical principles for, 210*t*; compared across sectors, 216*t*–217*t*; in practice of coaching, 218–220
Ethical decision-making models: for business, 214 *fig*; coaching ACTION model, 222–224 *fig*, 225; four stages of ethical decision, 215

Ethics: in business, 213–215; classification of approaches to, 208*t*; in coaching, 220–222; in counseling profession, 211–212; definitions and types of, 206–207; history of, 206; in nursing profession, 212–213
European Mentoring and Coaching Council (EMCC), 205, 218, 297
Evaluation. *See* Coaching evaluation
Executive Coaching Forum, 92, 433
Executive Coaching for Results: The Definitive Guide to Developing Organizational Leaders (Underhill, McAnally, & Koriath), 33, 34 *fig*
Executive derailers assessment: benchmarks used for, 266; Hogan Development Survey (HDS), 266
Executive Dimensions tool, 268
Executive on-boarding coaching: coach's role in, 196–198; illustrated diagram of model, 196 *fig*; making the business case for, 195; rapid alignment model of, 198–202
Executives: case example of challenges facing, 116–120; coaching for on-boarding, 195–202; coaching tools for assessment of, 260–275; culture of origins and, 114–115, 119; effort issue, 44; gender issues faced by, 117–118; Individual Development Plan (IDP) for, 237–239, 281–283; job attitudes of, 337; level in organization, 113, 118–119; life stage of, 112–113; matching coaches with, 135–136; stereotypes of, 110–112; succession planning coaching for, 190–195; work-life integration issue faced by, 108. *See also* Clients; Coaches; Leadership coaching; Talent
Expectancy, hope, and placebo effects: a client story for exploring the, 24–25; description of, 8; percentage of outcome